新世纪大学应用英语

综合教程

教师用书 **3**

INTEGRATED COURSE

主 编／傅　玉
编 者／傅　玉　　朱玉山　　李茨婷
　　　　徐　永　　刘　芹

上海外语教育出版社
SHANGHAI FOREIGN LANGUAGE EDUCATION PRESS
www.sflep.com

图书在版编目(CIP)数据

综合教程3教师用书/傅玉主编. —上海：上海外语教育出版社，2019
新世纪大学应用英语
ISBN 978-7-5446-5643-6

I. ①综⋯ II. ①傅⋯ III. ①英语—高等学校—教学参考资料 IV. ①H319.39

中国版本图书馆CIP数据核字(2019)第014351号

出版发行：**上海外语教育出版社**
（上海外国语大学内）　邮编：200083
电　　话：021-65425300（总机）
电子邮箱：bookinfo@sflep.com.cn
网　　址：http://www.sflep.com
责任编辑：张传根

印　　刷：常熟高专印刷有限公司
开　　本：850×1168　1/16　印张 15.75　字数 452千字
版　　次：2019年5月第1版　2019年5月第1次印刷
印　　数：3 100 册

书　　号：ISBN 978-7-5446-5643-6 / H
定　　价：56.00 元

本版图书如有印装质量问题，可向本社调换
质量服务热线：4008-213-263　电子邮箱：editorial@sflep.com

前 言

根据《大学英语教学指南》（以下简称《指南》），"大学英语的教学目标是培养学生的英语应用能力，增强跨文化交际意识和交际能力，同时发展自主学习能力，提高综合文化素养，使他们在学习、生活、社会交往和未来工作中能够有效地使用英语，满足国家、社会、学校和个人发展的需要。""大学英语教学以英语的实际使用为导向，以培养学生的英语应用能力为重点。英语应用能力是指用英语在学习、生活和未来工作中进行沟通、交流的能力。"

本着《指南》的精神，本套教材针对应用型高校学生的特点和需求，重在帮助学生进一步打好英语基础，提高英语应用能力，为将来就业做好准备。同时，教材充分贯彻落实立德树人根本任务，注重学生综合素质的培养，帮助他们成长为新时代所需的有用人才。

《综合教程》：

一、编写总则

1. 以《指南》为依据，以国内外先进的外语教学理论为指导，注意运用灵活多样的教学方法和手段。
2. 提倡以学生为中心的教学理念，充分调动学生的积极性，增强学生的自信心，培养学习兴趣。
3. 在教学过程中做到"四个结合"：语言知识与语言技能相结合，单项技能与综合应用能力相结合，语言教学与文化传授相结合，课堂教学与自主学习相结合。
4. 注重培养学生的语言应用能力、学习策略和综合文化素养。
5. 读写为主，听说为辅；以有效交际为最终目标，重视应用能力的培养。

二、选材

内容具有时代性、人文性、基础性和实用性，体现应用特色。选文内涵丰富，主题贴近时代和学生的学习与生活。

三、练习特点

1. 形式多样，有新意，注重情景化。
2. 鼓励课堂师生互动和生生互动。

3. 融合语言能力的训练和语言知识的强化。

四、教程架构

本教材共三册，每册包含学生用书、教师用书。

五、单元框架

	学生用书		教师用书
READING	Text A: 　　Before Reading 　　Reading 　　After Reading 　　Oral Work		Background Information Text Analysis New Words and Expressions Language Study Reference Answers Translation of Text A
	Text B: 　　Before Reading 　　Reading 　　After Reading 　　Oral Work		Background Information New Words and Expressions Language Study Reference Answers Translation of Text B
INTEGRATED EXERCISES	Public Speech Training Dictation Vocabulary Study Grammar Focus Translation Classroom Interaction		Reference Answers
WRITING	Explanation Assignment		Reference Answers

六、教师用书指南

（一）课文学习部分：

1. 补充背景知识（Background Information）。这部分主要根据单元主题，提供相关信息和知识，以帮助教师在课堂教学中拓宽学生的知识面。背景知识较简单的课文则不再提供。

2. 针对Text A提供课文分析（Text Analysis）。此部分由四块内容组成：课文小结（Text Summary）、课文结构（Text Organization）、

写作特色（Text Features）和重难点句讲解（Key Sentences）。课文小结板块以凝练的语言道出课文的主题思想和核心内容，帮助教师高屋建瓴地把握文章的框架；课文结构板块勾勒出课文的行文脉络，并给出各个篇章段落的主要内容；写作特色板块主要讲解课文的修辞手段，包括句法和词汇特色。重难点句讲解板块以点带面，从剖析重点句、难句的语法特征着手，引出相关语法点的讲解和例证。

课文分析部分采取由上至下的文本解剖模式，引导教师更全面、深入地讲解课文，是教师用书的核心板块。

3. 语言学习（Language Study）部分主要讲解部分生词的扩展意义，以扩大学生的词汇量。比如，litter在词表中意为rubbish（垃圾）。在Language Study中我们介绍了litter的扩展释义，比如：

1) an untidy collection of things lying about 乱七八糟

　　e.g. a litter of sleeping bags on the floor

　　　　He was surprised to see his room in such a litter.

2) a number of young animals born to an animal at one time 一窝（仔畜）

　　e.g. a litter of five kittens　　　five young at a litter

4. 课文处理采用"三段式"教学模式：读前（Before Reading），读中（Reading）和读后（After Reading）。Before Reading旨在通过小组活动的形式，激活学生的相关经历和知识，提高学生对单元主题的兴趣。Reading旨在培养学生的阅读技巧，提高阅读理解能力。After Reading部分包括不同类型的阅读练习，用于检查学生的阅读理解效率。Before Reading，Reading和After Reading三个部分组成一个阅读教学有机体，循序渐进地培养学生的阅读能力。

《综合教程》在每篇课文后设计了一个口语活动（Oral Work）。该部分是一个扩展性教学活动：即教师围绕课文内容，在课堂上组织学生开展各种口语活动（小组讨论、角色扮演、课堂讲演等），以巩固和运用已学内容和技能。

（二）综合练习（Integrated Exercises）：综合练习包括听力、口语、语法、词汇、翻译等方面。口语训练主要体现在Public Speech Training和Classroom Interaction。Public Speech Training是贯穿本系列教材的一项练习，它采用循序渐进的方式培养学生的口语基本功、表达能力等。第一册侧重单词、词组和句子的朗读（语音、语调、句子重音/重读等）；第二册着重训练学生的短文朗读技巧（语音、语调、句子重音/重读、节奏等）；第三册简单介绍公共演讲的基本技巧以及跨文化交际技能。

Classroom Interaction是一个集口语、听力为一体的综合性练习，突出语言的实用性和应用性。

Grammar Focus注重语法知识的运用。第一册主要培养学生对英语句子的正确认识和运用能力。第二、三册则侧重段落和篇章层面上语法知识的运用。

Translation练习的难度采取螺旋式上升方式，从易到难。第一册和第二册的汉译英均为句子翻译，第三册为段落翻译。

（三）写作：第一册以讲解句子为主，第二册侧重段落和应用文写作，第三册主要教授各种类型短文的写作技巧。学生用书的写作部分讲解和练习并重，教师用书包括附加解释。

《综合教程》的编者具备深厚的理论语言学、二语习得及外语教学理论功底，同时长期在英语教学一线工作，有着丰富的教学经验。愿本教材能以其时代性、人文性、基础性、实用性以及应用特色，为推动我国大学英语教学改革助一臂之力。

编　者

Contents

Unit 1   **FAMILY LOVE** ___ *1*
         TEXT A What Dads Are Made Of ___ *1*
         TEXT B Brotherly Love ___ *15*
         INTEGRATED EXERCISES ___ *24*
         WRITING ___ *29*

Unit 2   **JOBS** ___ *32*
         TEXT A The First Job of Some Celebrities ___ *32*
         TEXT B Success of a Clothing Website ___ *44*
         INTEGRATED EXERCISES ___ *52*
         WRITING ___ *57*

Unit 3   **MOTIVATION AND PASSION** ___ *59*
         TEXT A Why Passion Matters ___ *59*
         TEXT B Motivation ___ *71*
         INTEGRATED EXERCISES ___ *79*
         WRITING ___ *85*

Unit 4   **KNOWLEDGE AND DEVELOPMENT** ___ *86*
         TEXT A The Earth's Learning Curve ___ *86*
         TEXT B Thinking Patterns ___ *97*
         INTEGRATED EXERCISES ___ *107*
         WRITING ___ *113*

Unit 5   BUSINESS COMMUNICATION ___ 115

         TEXT A   Nonverbal Business Conventions in Face-to-Face Encounters ___ 115

         TEXT B   Dumb Things We Do ___ 127

         INTEGRATED EXERCISES ___ 136

         WRITING ___ 143

Unit 6   MASS MEDIA ___ 145

         TEXT A   Who Killed the Newspaper? ___ 145

         TEXT B   Web Journalism ___ 158

         INTEGRATED EXERCISES ___ 167

         WRITING ___ 175

Unit 7   LEARNING ___ 177

         TEXT A   Two Kinds ___ 177

         TEXT B   Learning Styles ___ 190

         INTEGRATED EXERCISES ___ 201

         WRITING ___ 208

Unit 8   EDUCATION ___ 210

         TEXT A   Do Colleges Have a Future? ___ 210

         TEXT B   Turning Study Skills into Life Skills ___ 223

         INTEGRATED EXERCISES ___ 236

         WRITING ___ 242

FAMILY LOVE

TEXT A   What Dads Are Made Of

Before Reading

The purpose of this section is to arouse the students' interest in the theme of the unit, reactivate their relevant background knowledge or elicit their opinions on the related topics, so as to better prepare them for the succeeding tasks.

Before Reading activities can be organized as group work so that the students share with each other their knowledge about families in the United States and other countries.

Background Information

1 American Families

Belonging to a family is one bond almost everyone in the world shares, but family patterns vary. Some families consist of several generations while others are just composed of parents and children, which is also called "core family".

The United States has many different types of families, but the traditional structure of the American family — mother, father and children — continues to prevail for the most part. Yet, over the past several decades, US society has witnessed an evolution in family structure and daily life in many respects. Single parenthood, adoptive households, step-parenting, stay-at-home fathers, grandparents raising children are but a few of the newer tiles in the mosaic.

2 Father and Son

Today a quiet but thoroughly monumental revolution is taking place in the American family. The number of fathers solely responsible for the care of their children is growing at a rate almost twice that of single mothers. Fully one-fifth of single parents today are single fathers — more than two million of them.

This is up from 1970, when single mother households comprised approximately 90 percent of the single family population. Among minorities, the rate of increase is as high, or higher: between 1970 and 1995, the rate of African-American single dads increased 329%; for Hispanic single fathers, 450%. And though the media almost always focus on mothers when portraying working single parents, nearly 30 percent of working single parents are now men.

3 Differences Between American and Chinese Families

Families in America and China are quite different from each other. The following are some major differences.

1) Many American children do not call their parents Father or Mother, but just name their names. Chinese children usually call their parents Father or Mother.
2) Most American parents pay more attention to their children's ability and independence, while many Chinese parents pay close attention to their children's school performance.
3) American parents give more freedom to their children than Chinese parents do.
4) American families often have more than one child, while most Chinese families have one or two.
5) Chinese parents like to make decisions for their children, while American parents emphasize individualism.

Reading

Text Analysis

- **Text Summary**

This article first depicts a vivid picture of Dad's role in a family. By taking the McAlpine, Pike, Otterman families as examples, the author displays the three main roles of a dad: being a source of stimulation, being an explorer and expert, and being a unique teacher. With these advantages, the author argues, dads should be encouraged to take more responsibility for childcare.

- **Text Organization**

Paragraphs 1-4: introduction	In McAlpine and Pike families, Dad plays an important role in the nurture of kids. Dad's mischief annoys Mom, but it is beneficial to kids in how they play, communicate with the world, and learn. There are three advantages in dads helping with the nurture of their kids.
Paragraphs 5-13: main body	First, dads' roughness while playing with kids helps build cognitive skills and acquire social and emotional experiences. Second, dads' interest in exploring helps build curiosity and problem-solving skills. Third, daddy-style reading helps set up verbal skills, fluency, word recognition and knowledge base of the kids.
Paragraphs 14-18: conclusion	With all the distinctive features mentioned above, dads are encouraged to take part in the nurture of their kids. Different styles of mom and dad care complement perfectly to the advantage of children.

- **Text Features**

The style of the text is characterized by a mixture of both formal words (e.g. *interaction, significantly, unpredictable*) and colloquial words and phrases (e.g. *squirb, get-go, boost me up, pick their battles*), and by a flexible use of simple, compound, and complex sentences. Riming of words is also frequently used to make the article more pleasant to read (e.g. *mess-maker, rule-breaker, risk-taker; social, physical, intellectual; affection, not aggression; choose nonfiction over fiction*).

In this argumentative essay, the author provides vivid examples to support his viewpoint, and uses a lot of factual statements and direct speeches. To make his points more convincing, contrast between Mom's role and Dad's role is adopted as well (e.g. *Dad is a mess-maker, rule-breaker, risk-taker. In general, he's the opposite of Mom, the master nurturer, creator of law and order. Babies as young as eight weeks old notice the difference between a mom's protectiveness and a dad's stimulation.*)

This article moves between the past and the present tenses with clarity, in which the past is mainly used to reflect personal experience whilst the present is adopted to display facts, current events and viewpoints. The relatively smaller part of the past tense is used to add a touch of diversity to the style of the text. The passage also features a variety of sentence patterns, such as parenthetical statement(插入语，see Item 1 in Key Sentences below), adverbial clause(状语从句，see Item 2 in Key Sentences), nominal clause(名词性从句，see Item 3 in Key Sentences), and attributive clause(定语从句，see Item 4 in Key Sentences). Besides, combination of sentence patterns is used to make the passage more varied, such as a combination of objective clause, attributive clause and infinitive as appositive(宾语从句、定语从句、用作同位语的不定式并用，see Item 5 in Key Sentences), and one of nominal clause, attributive clause, participle and infinitive(名词性从句、定语从句、分词、不定式并用，see Item 6 in Key Sentences).

• Key Sentences

1. Will McAlpine, two and a half years old, likes to "help" his dad, Eric, in their suburban backyard in Glen Ellyn, Illinois. (Para. 1)

This sentence uses two parenthetical statements *two and a half years old* and *Eric* to make it more concise and compact. Parenthetical statements can be separated by a couple of commas(逗号) or dashes(破折号). Other examples of parenthetical statements in this passage are:

A: The intellectual gains are measurable as early as the first year of life, and they continue to show up through high school, especially when dads, *together with moms*, are actively involved in school and learning. (Para. 4)

B: According to the experts, fathers create this intelligence advantage, *as well as many others*, in three important ways: in how they play, interact in everyday situations, and teach. (Para. 4)

C: When pediatric researcher Michael W. Yogman videotaped two-month-olds, *for example*, the little ones showed special signs of excitement when their fathers approached. (Para. 6)

D: Kids value the information and novelty, and their conversations about real things — *what educators call "science process talk"* — create the curiosity and problem-solving skills needed for science and math. (Para. 9)

2. As father and son toss grass, leaves and rocks into a wheelbarrow, Eric points out different colours and shapes. (Para. 1)

This sentence uses adverbial clause(状语从句) *as father and son toss grass, leaves and rocks into a wheelbarrow* to indicate time. There are mainly eight types of adverbial clauses, i.e. adverbial clause of time(时间状语从句), adverbial clause of place(地点状语从句), adverbial clause of manner(方式状语从句), adverbial clause of cause(原因状语从句), adverbial clause of result(结果状语从句), adverbial clause of purpose(目的状语从句), adverbial clause of condition(条件状语从句) and adverbial clause of concession(让

步状语从句). In this passage, there are many sentences embodying adverbial clause of time, such as:

When fathers teach how to build with blocks or throw a ball, they're constructing large- and small-motor skills, sensory pathways and body awareness.

Adverbial clause of condition is also used in the passage:

Children do well when they know that their father cares — for example, *if he supplements visits with telephone calls, letters or e-mails.*

Other examples of adverbial clause are:
- A: She was born in the same hospital *where her mother was born.* (adverbial clause of place)
- B: You must do the exercises *as the teacher told.* (adverbial clause of manner)
- C: *As it began to rain,* we hurried back home. (adverbial clause of cause)
- D: He had overslept, *so that he was late for school.* (adverbial clause of result)
- E: We climbed to the top of the hill *in order that we could get a better view of the village.* (adverbial clause of purpose)
- F: *Young as he is,* Michael is not healthy at all. (adverbial clause of concession)

3. What they don't pay attention to is the mess of mud on their shoes… (Para. 1)

This sentence uses a nominal clause *what they don't pay attention to* as the subject. Nominal clause is usually used as a noun or noun phrase, functioning as subject(主语), object(宾语), appositive(同位语), subjective complement(主语补足语), prepositional complement(介词补足语) etc., headed by *that*, by linking pronouns(连接代词) such as *who, whom, whose, what, which, whoever, whatever* and *whichever*, or by linking adverbs(连接副词) such as *where, when, how* and *why*. For example:
- A: *Who lit the fire* is still a mystery. (as subject)
- B: We never doubt *that honesty is virtue.* (as object)
- C: Have you got any idea *why he did it at all*? (as appositive)
- D: The fact is *that he realized it too late.* (as subjective complement)
- E: Before the public speech, he prepared himself very carefully for *what he must say.* (as prepositional complement)

4. The same daddy-like interactions that sometimes annoy moms will significantly contribute to children's social skills and success in school. (Para. 3)

This sentence uses an attributive clause, also referred to as relative clause(关系分句), *that sometimes annoy moms* to modify the noun *interactions*. Attributive clauses can be restrictive(限制性的), which has a close connection with its antecedent(先行词), and non-restrictive(非限制性的), which has a loose connection with its antecedent, headed by a comma(逗号). For example:
- A: The man who did the robbery has never been caught. (restrictive attributive clause)
- B: My elder brother, who is a surgeon, has saved many lives. (non-restrictive attributive clause)

5. Research shows that this kind of daddy-style play builds cognitive skills, and helps children acquire social and emotional experiences that prepare them for school — how to take turns, how to negotiate, regulate and understand feelings, and how to be a leader. (Para. 7)

This sentence has got four layers of meanings. The first layer is reflected by the subject-predicate structure(主谓结构) *Research shows that...* In the second layer, which is an objective clause, headed by the antecedent *that*, the subject is *this kind of daddy-style play*, predicates(谓语) are *builds cognitive skills* and *helps children acquire social and emotional experiences*. The third layer is embedded in the second layer, i.e. *that prepare them for school*. The fourth layer *how to take turns, how to negotiate, regulate and understand feelings, and how to be a leader* is the appositive of the preceding noun *experiences*.

6. **The shortage of male teachers in preschools and grammar schools means that most kids miss out on the experience and competence that men can share — making it even more important for dads to play an active role at home. (Para. 10)**

    In this sentence, the nominal phrase *The shortage of male teachers in preschools and grammar schools* is the subject and the remaining part after *means* is the object, which is the first layer of the meaning. In the second layer, *most kids* is the subject and *miss out on the experience and competence that men can share* is the predicate, in which the attributive clause *that men can share* is the third layer. The part *making it even more important for dads to play an active role at home* is present participle embedded with an infinitive, serving as a complement(补足语) of the entire sentence.

New Words and Expressions

parent /ˈpeərənt/ *v.* to be or act as a mother or father 做……的父母
e.g. He hardly knows how to parent his first child.

suburban /səˈbɜːbən/ *a.* of or characteristic of a residential area away from the center of a town or city 郊区的
e.g. urban and suburban schools
   a suburban lifestyle

wheelbarrow /ˈhwiːlˌbærəʊ/ *n.* a small cart with a single wheel at the front and two supporting legs and two handles at the rear, used typically for carrying loads in building work or gardening 手推车；独轮车

chore /tʃɔː/ *n.* a household routine task 家务
e.g. After a day's hard work, she didn't want to do any chores.

overhead /ˌəʊvəˈhed/ *ad.* above the level of the head; in the sky 头顶上；在天空
e.g. A helicopter buzzed overhead.

trail /treɪl/ *n.* a trace 痕迹；踪迹
e.g. wagon trails
   The carriage left a trail of dust.

wake /weɪk/ *n.* a track made by a person or thing 路线；行踪
e.g. the wake of a storm
   The car left a wake of dust.

in sb.'s or sth.'s wake behind or after sb. or sth. 在…之后，在…身后

e.g. The car left clouds of dust in its wake.

relish /ˈrelɪʃ/ *v.* to enjoy greatly 喜爱，从……得到乐趣
e.g. relish the challenge of competition
   He was relishing his moment of glory.

settle down make sb. quiet and calm 使安静下来
e.g. She settled herself down in a chair with a book and a cup of tea.

giggle /ˈɡɪɡl/ *n.* a light laugh in a nervous, affected or silly manner 咯咯的笑
e.g. The young girls burst into giggles.

fest /fest/ *n.* a gathering of a specified kind 集会
e.g. a media-fest

erupt /ɪˈrʌpt/ *v.* to break out suddenly and dramatically 突然爆发
e.g. Fierce fighting erupted between the two armies.
   Noise erupted from the classroom.

plead /pliːd/ *v.* to make an emotional appeal 请求；恳求
e.g. plead for forgiveness
   She pleaded with them not to hit her boy.

belly /ˈbelɪ/ *n.* the front part of the human trunk below the ribs 肚子
e.g. a full belly
   He had an awful ache in the belly.

wide /waɪd/ *ad.* to the full extent 完全地；充

分地

e.g. He always opened the window wide in summer.
He eyes opened wide.

awake /ə'weɪk/ *a.* not asleep 醒着的
e.g. The noise kept me awake all night.
She was still wide awake despite the lateness of the hour.

nurturer /'nɜːtʃərə/ *n.* a person who brings up sb. 抚养者
e.g. She is the nurturer of three kids.

mischief /'mɪstʃɪf/ *n.* playful misbehaviour 胡闹；捣蛋
e.g. get into mischief
She will make sure that her son does not get into mischief.

interaction /ˌɪntər'ækʃən/ *n.* reciprocal action or influence 相互作用
e.g. interaction between the two languages
interaction of the heart and lungs

annoy /ə'nɔɪ/ *v.* to make sb. a little angry; irritate 使烦恼；打搅
e.g. She was annoyed at the boy for being so careless.
He was annoyed at being woken up so early.
A mosquito keeps annoying me.

significantly /sɪg'nɪfɪkəntlɪ/ *ad.* sufficiently 相当；显著地
e.g. He works significantly harder than his colleagues.

contribute /kən'trɪbjuːt/ *v.* to help to cause or bring about 导致；起作用
e.g. The government imposed a tax on fuels which contributed to global warming.
His action contributed to further dispute.

intellectual /ˌɪntə'lektjʊəl/ *a.* relating to the ability to understand things and think clearly 智力的
e.g. intellectual curiosity
intellectual powers
Children need intellectual stimulation.

benefit from to gain advantage from 获益；收益
e.g. Who is most likely to benefit from the victim's death?
The small businesses have benefited greatly from the fall in interest rates.

involvement /ɪn'vɒlvmənt/ *n.* participation in sth. 参与
e.g. have no direct involvement in politics

psychiatry /psaɪ'kaɪətrɪ/ *n.* the study and treatment of mental illness 精神病学

measurable /'meʒərəbl/ *a.* large enough to be measured; noticeable 重要的；值得注意的
e.g. a measurable improvement

intelligence /ɪn'telɪdʒəns/ *n.* the ability to acquire and apply knowledge and skills 智力
e.g. a man of average intelligence
He writes with intelligence and wit.

tumble /'tʌmbl/ *v.* to move or rush in an uncontrolled way 跌跌撞撞；仓促行动
e.g. Dogs tumbled from the vehicle.
We tumbled downstairs.

rough-and-tumble /'rʌfən'tʌmbl/ *a.* without rules or organization 杂乱的；不守规则的
e.g. She was shocked at the rough-and-tumble atmosphere of the room.

arousing /ə'raʊzɪŋ/ *a.* evoking; exciting 激发的；唤起的
e.g. The arousing noise woke me.
The phone call was so arousing that he rushed back home.

unpredictable /ˌʌnprɪ'dɪktəbl/ *a.* not able to be predicted; changeable 不可预测的；易变的
e.g. unpredictable risks
British weather is unpredictable.

get-go /'getgəʊ/ *n.* the very beginning 开端，开始
e.g. From the get-go, I knew these tapes were special.

rock /rɒk/ *v.* to move gently to and fro 摇晃
e.g. rock a cradle
The waves rocked the boat.
She rocked the baby in her arms.

infant /'ɪnfənt/ *n.* a very young child or baby 婴儿
e.g. This is their second infant.

roll around to move about, rotate 四处滚动
e.g. Due to stomachache, she rolled around on her bed.

stimulation /ˌstɪmjʊ'leɪʃən/ *n.* encouragement 刺激
e.g. His new idea is a stimulation to us.
Illusions may be produced by stimulation of the temporal cortex.

pediatric /ˌpiː'diːætrɪk/ *a.* (of a branch of medicine) dealing with children 儿科的

scrunch /skrʌntʃ/ *v.* to become crushed or squeezed into a compact mass 缩紧
e.g. The cat scrunched itself up in the sofa.

preference /ˈprefərəns/ *n.* a greater liking for one alternative over another 喜好，偏好
e.g. He has a preference for fruit over vegetables.
Which is your preference, coffee or tea?

affection /əˈfekʃən/ *n.* a gentle feeling of liking 喜爱
e.g. She felt affection for the wise old man.
My daughter has a great affection for the new teacher.

aggression /əˈgreʃən/ *n.* the action of attacking 侵犯
e.g. an aggression upon his rights
an aggression against personal liberty
He called for an end to foreign aggression against his country.

cognitive /ˈkɒgnɪtɪv/ *a.* relating to the mental action or process of acquiring knowledge and understanding 认知能力的
e.g. the cognitive elements of perception

emotional /ɪˈməʊʃənəl/ *a.* relating to a person's feelings 感情上的
e.g. gain emotional support
in a state of emotional stress

regulate /ˈregjʊleɪt/ *v.* to control or maintain the rate or speed of sth. so that it operates properly 调节
e.g. a well-regulated clock
Please regulate the heat in this room.

distinguished /dɪˈstɪŋgwɪʃt/ *a.* very successful, authoritative 卓越的，杰出的
e.g. a distinguished professor
a distinguished performance

boost up to lift ... up highly 高高举起
e.g. Her father likes to boost her up.

spellbinding /ˈspelˈbaɪndɪŋ/ *a.* attractive; fascinating 迷人的
e.g. I found his description of life in ancient Rome absolutely spellbinding.

swap /swɒp/ *v.* to substitute one thing for another 换上，替代
e.g. She swapped her long skirts for jeans and T-shirts.

botany /ˈbɒtəni/ *n.* the scientific study of plants 植物学
e.g. His brother majored in botany.

value /ˈvæljuː/ *v.* to consider sth. important 重视；珍视
e.g. value him for what he achieves
value sincerity beyond all things

novelty /ˈnɒvəlti/ *n.* the quality of being new, originality 新鲜感
e.g. The novelty of being married soon wore off.
After the novelty of being a waitress wore off, she did not want to stay in that restaurant.

curiosity /ˌkjʊərɪˈɒsəti/ *n.* a strong desire to know or learn sth. 好奇心
e.g. Out of curiosity, he walked into the house.
Does that act stir your curiosity?

shortage /ˈʃɔːtɪdʒ/ *n.* a state in which sth. needed cannot be obtained in sufficient amounts 短缺
e.g. a shortage of hard cash
food shortage
land shortage in the countryside

miss out on to lose a chance for, to fail to achieve 错过机会
e.g. He missed out on promotion.
You really missed out on a lot of fun by not coming to the party.

competence /ˈkɒmpɪtəns/ *n.* the ability to do sth. successfully 能力；胜任
e.g. competence in handling money
competence for a task
The players displayed varying degrees of competence.

nonfiction /nɒnˈfɪkʃən/ *n.* prose writing that is informative or factual rather than fictional 非小说类写实文学
e.g. He likes to read nonfiction in his spare time.

fiction /ˈfɪkʃən/ *n.* literature in the form of prose, especially novels 小说
e.g. a work of fiction
I have read much detective fiction.

varied /ˈveərɪd/ *a.* incorporating a number of different types or elements 各种各样的；丰富的
e.g. a long and varied career
varied opinions

enticing /ɪnˈtaɪsɪŋ/ *a.* attractive 迷人的，有吸引力的
e.g. an enticing advertisement
an enticing opportunity

intonation /ˌɪntəʊˈneɪʃən/ *n.* the rise and fall of the voice in speaking 声调
e.g. a rising/falling intonation

verbal /ˈvɜːbəl/ *a.* relating to words 言辞的；文字的
e.g. verbal abuse
a verbal protest

The root of the problem is visual rather than verbal.
stake /steɪk/ *n.* cost, risk 利害关系，代价
e.g. The investment is dangerous and the stakes are high.
model /ˈmɒdəl/ *v.* to set an example 做榜样
e.g. He modeled himself on his father.
handicap /ˈhændɪkæp/ *v.* to act as an impediment to 妨碍；使……不利
e.g. He was handicapped by his age.
Ignorance can handicap the progress of a city.
Lack of funding has handicapped the development of the research.
recognition /ˌrekəɡˈnɪʃən/ *n.* the action or process of identifying or being identified 识别
e.g. word recognition
My recognition of him was immediate.
She saw him pass by without a sign of recognition.
block /blɒk/ *n.* one of a set of small wooden or plastic pieces used as a building toy 积木
e.g. alphabet blocks
motor /ˈməʊtə/ *a.* relating to muscular movement 肌肉运动的
e.g. a motor nerve
impaired motor function
sensory /ˈsensərɪ/ *a.* relating to sensation 感官的
e.g. sensory input

a sensory organ
pathway /ˈpɑːθweɪ/ *n.* a way that constitutes or serves as a path 途径
intervene /ˌɪntəˈviːn/ *v.* to prevent 干扰；干涉
e.g. intervene in the internal affairs of other countries
He acted outside his authority when he intervened in the dispute.
perspective /pəˈspektɪv/ *n.* a point of view, an opinion 观点，想法
e.g. He tends to view most issues from a religious perspective.
Most guidebooks of history are written from the editor's perspective.
presence /ˈprezəns/ *n.* the state of existing 存在
e.g. She was so quiet that her presence has hardly been noticed.
supplement /ˈsʌplɪmənt/ *v.* to add an extra element or amount to 补充
e.g. do odd jobs to supplement his income
She took the job to supplement her husband's income.
distinctive /dɪˈstɪŋktɪv/ *a.* characteristic of one person or thing 特别的，有特色的
e.g. the distinctive scent of roses
a distinctive habit
complement /ˈkɒmplɪmənt/ *v.* to contribute extra features to 补充，补足
e.g. The TV networks and newspapers complement each other.

Language Study

suburb *n.* an outlying district of a city 郊区
    e.g. A lot of original suburbs of cities have been combined into the inner area.
        We have bought a new apartment in the suburb.

urban *a.* characteristic of a town or city 市区的
    e.g. The urban population of that city has reached 17 million already.
        Compared to suburban area, I prefer to stay in the urban area.

wide
    a.
    1. of great or more than average width 宽的
        e.g. This is a wide road.
            There is a wide gap between the two generations.
    2. including a great variety of people or things 广泛的
        e.g. He has got a wide circle of friends.
            My daughter has a wide scope of interest.
    3. at a considerable distance from an intended point or target 远离目标的
        e.g. His shot was just wide of the goal.
            We are wide from our goal.

ad. far from a particular or intended point or target 远离目标地

    e.g. His final touchline conversion drifted wide.

    The first shot went wide, the second hit the engine room.

contribute *v.*

1. to give, provide 贡献

    e.g. Ancient China contributed four inventions to world civilization.

    Taxpayers had contributed more than 200 million US dollars towards the cost of local services.

2. to supply (an article) for publication in a newspaper 投稿；撰稿

    e.g. She only contributes articles to a local evening paper.

3. to give one's opinions in a discussion 提供建议

    e.g. He did not contribute to the meetings.

    She never contributes to the discussion.

two-thirds

Expression of fractions 分数的表达方法：

1. Numerators appear as cardinal numbers while denominators appear as ordinal numbers. 分子是基数词，分母是序数词。

2. When the numerator is only one, both the numerator and the denominator are singular. 当分子为1时，分子和分母都是单数形式。

    e.g. 1/5 — one-fifth; 1/3 — one-third

3. When the numerator is more than one, the denominator is plural. 当分子大于1时，分母是复数形式。

    e.g. 2/3 — two-thirds; 3/7 — three-sevenths

fatherhood

Usage of the suffix *-hood* 后缀-hood的用法：

1. denoting a condition or quality 表示状况

    e.g. fatherhood; falsehood; likelihood; manhood; womanhood

2. denoting a collection or group 表示团体

    e.g. brotherhood; knighthood

3. denoting a period of time 表示时期

    e.g. childhood; widowhood

4. denoting a special characteristic 表示特征

    e.g. hardihood; sainthood

prefer *v.*

1. to submit (a charge or a piece of information) for consideration 提出；举报

    e.g. The police will prefer charges.

    He refused to prefer his claim as legal heir.

2. to promote or advance (sb.) 提升；提拔

    e.g. He was preferred to general manager.

value

    n.

1. [U] quality of being useful or worthwhile or important 价值

    e.g. Your support is of great value.

2. price 价格

    e.g. current value

    Market values rose sharply.

3. benefit 益处

    e.g. This book will be of great value to you.

    The value of a college education is limitless.

4. equitable reward 等值；相当的回报

    e.g. It was poor value for money.

    I take his wages because I give good value for them.

5. evaluation 评估

   e.g. set the value of something

   He placed a high value on this painting at the auction.

v.

1. to evaluate the price of 估价；评价

   e.g. value the old relics

   He valued this house at 2 million US dollars.

2. to praise oneself 夸耀

   e.g. She valued herself on her conversational powers.

verbal *a.*

1. oral 口头的

   e.g. a verbal protest

   They arrived at a verbal agreement.

2. of every word 一字不差的

   e.g. verbal translation

   This is a verbal copy of the original work.

3. of a verb 源自动词的

   e.g. verbal inflexions

   Do you know the verbal forms of these words?

ex-husband

Usage of the prefix *ex-* 前缀ex-的用法：

1. (plus a noun) previous 附在名词前，表示"以前的"，"前任"

   e.g. ex-husband; ex-wife; ex-president

2. (forming a verb) coming from 构成动词，表示"出自"，"向外"，"超出"

   e.g. express; exclave; extol; excess

3. (forming a verb) complete 构成动词，表示"完全"，"彻底"

   e.g. exterminate

After Reading

READING COMPREHENSION TASKS

1. Complete the following table based on the information in TEXT A.

Fatherly Love	Motherly Love
Dad is a __mess-maker__, __rule-breaker__, and __risk-taker__.	Mom is the __master nurturer__, creator of __law__ and __order__.
While holding babies, dads let them face __the world__, giving __stimulation__.	While holding babies, moms let them face __themselves__, giving __protectiveness__.
Dads tend to read __nonfiction__ to kids.	Moms tend to read __fiction__ to kids.
When playing with the kids, dads are __enthusiastic__ with love.	When playing with the kids, moms have concerns about __sleep__, __safety__ or __cleanliness__.

2. Answer the following questions.

1) Why does Will McAlpine like to help his dad in yard work?

   Because he can learn different colours and shapes as well as observing planes and clouds overhead.

2) What are the favourite stories of David Pike's daughters?
   Goodnight Moon and *Green Eggs and Ham*.

3) What is "a giggle fest" in David Pike's home?
   After the kids get into bed, they plead David to make funny sounds on their bellies as a game.

4) How can dads create the intelligence advantage of their kids?
   By playing with kids, interacting in everyday situations and teaching kids in a unique way.

5) In Michael W. Yogman's research, how did two-month-olds behave when their fathers approached?
   They scrunched up their shoulders, breathed more rapidly and opened their eyes wide.

6) How does daddy-style play build cognitive skills of kids?
   It helps kids learn how to take turns, how to negotiate, regulate and understand feelings, and how to be a leader.

7) What are the fundamental elements of "science process talk"?
   Curiosity and problem-solving skills needed for science and math.

8) How can dads help kids by reading together with them?
   The books dads select and the way they read and talk about them strongly influence kids' language development, reading skills and general knowledge.

9) How will dads engage more with their kids?
   By considering themselves partners in parenting and not merely helpers.

10) What does the saying "There are ex-husbands but no ex-fathers" imply?
    It means that even when a couple gets divorced and the father doesn't live with the children, his presence in their lives is still vital.

3. Write down the effect of fathers' actions on kids.

1) Dads play with kids without obeying many family rules.
   Kids gain social skills and success in school.

2) Dads wrestle with kids.
   Kids learn their capabilities and limitations.

3) Dads take kids to work in the open.
   Kids begin to know a world beyond their own neighbourhood.

4) Dads ask kids to help with yard work.
   Kids begin to get interested in biology and botany.

5) Dads read books to kids.
   Girls show much higher verbal skills, while boys develop fluency, word recognition and knowledge base.

6) Dads teach kids how to build with blocks or throw a ball.
   Kids develop large- and small-motor skills, sensory pathways and body awareness.

7) Ex-husbands visit, telephone, or write to kids.
   Kids do well because they know that their father cares.

4. Explain the underlined parts in your own words.

1) But for all his mischief, Dad is doing something quite right. (Para. 3)
   Although he might have done a lot of wrong things

2) The same daddy-like interactions that sometimes annoy moms will <u>significantly contribute to</u> children's social skills and success in school. (Para. 3)
   help…a lot

3) …how to <u>take turns</u>… (Para. 7)
   do something one after another

4) When a father doesn't model reading, a son may decide that it's not an activity <u>meant for males</u>. (Para. 12)
   suitable for men

5) <u>She also talks up Daddy to Will</u>… (Para. 16)
   She also praises Daddy in front of Will

6) …if <u>he supplements visits with telephone calls, letters or e-mails</u>. (Para. 17)
   he goes to see them in addition to making telephone calls and writing letters or e-mails

ORAL WORK

Work in groups and make a TV talk show on fathers' care for children. All your group members should participate in this show, acting different roles mentioned in TEXT A.

The teacher can ask the students to form groups to prepare for the different roles mentioned in TEXT A. The students can either work within groups or individually at this stage of preparation. Once they feel ready, the teacher can ask them to present the show first within the group, and then to the whole class. The following table is a summary of the different people that appear in TEXT A.

Kids	Parents	Researchers
Will	Eric and Caroline McAlpine	Kyle Pruett
Aidan, Herron	David and Katie Pike	Michael W. Yogman
Chad, Andrew	Tim Otterman	Alison Clarke-Stewart
the author as a young child	the author's father Ralph	Ross Parke

TRANSLATION OF TEXT A

何为父亲

贾德森·卡尔布雷斯

父亲的风格

1 　两岁半的威尔·麦克阿宾喜欢"帮助"他的父亲埃里克在他们位于伊利诺斯州格兰艾林郊区的住宅后院里劳作。父子二人一边把杂草、树叶和石块扔进手推车，埃里克一边教儿子识别不同的颜色和形状。有时候他们会停下手上的活，看看头顶的飞机和云彩。他们可不关心鞋上沾的泥巴，进屋时身后还拖着一条泥土的痕迹。

2 　北卡罗来纳州夏洛特市的大卫·派克非常喜欢给三个小女儿读睡前故事。他读她们听不厌的《月亮晚安》和《绿鸡蛋与火腿》。每次母亲凯蒂以为大卫把孩子们哄睡了时，"咯咯笑活动开始了，"她说。五岁的艾敦开始请求大卫给她"挠痒痒"（这是家庭自创词，意思是在孩子们的肚子上弄出滑稽的声音）。三岁的海洛在旁边大叫"挠挠我，也挠挠我。"这下每个人都毫无睡意了。

3 　父亲是捣蛋鬼、违规者和冒险家。通常来说，他与母亲截然相反。母亲是养育大师，创建家里的法律和秩序。虽然父亲会添乱，但他做的事情是对的。有父亲特征的互动活动有时会惹恼母亲，但这类活动非常有利于培养孩子在学校的社交能力，帮助他们成功。

12

4 耶鲁大学儿童精神病学教授凯尔·普鲁特博士说："孩子的社交能力、身体和智力发展很大程度上得益于父亲的参与。"智力上的收效早在孩子一岁时就颇为明显了，而且可以一直持续到高中。若父母一起积极关心孩子的学业，这种影响会更大。据专家称，父亲在三方面创造了这种智力上的优势，及许多其他优势：如何同孩子玩耍、如何与孩子进行日常交流和如何教导孩子。

粗率莽撞的父亲

5 与母亲相比，父亲从与孩子相处的一开始就更能激发他们的能力，方式也更多变。他们摇晃婴儿的次数比母亲多，也会在地板上和孩子一起滚来滚去。八周大的婴儿就能区分母亲的保护性和父亲的刺激性。

6 比如儿科研究专家迈克尔·W·约曼在给两个月大的婴儿录像时发现，当父亲靠近时孩子们会有特别的兴奋表现。他们耸起肩膀，呼吸加快，睁大眼睛。加利福尼亚大学尔湾分校的心理学教授埃里森·克拉克·斯图尔特在研究两岁半儿童喜好时发现，孩子有三分之二以上的时间选择父亲而非母亲一起玩耍或运动。新泽西州莫里斯镇的蒂姆·奥特曼和两个儿子(九岁的查德和八岁的安德鲁)练摔跤，他说："这么玩表达的是喜爱，而非侵犯。他们也通过这个游戏知道了自己的能力和不足。"

7 研究发现这种与父亲一起的玩耍能培养认知技能，并帮助孩子获得社交和情感经验，例如如何轮流做事，如何与人协商，如何控制自己的感情并理解别人的情感，如何成为领导者等，将来上学就更顺利。加利福尼亚大学河滨分校著名心理学教授，《父亲的责任》一书作者罗斯·帕克说："从父亲那儿学会这些早期社交技能的孩子更能与同龄人和睦相处。"

作为探险家和专家的父亲

8 我至今记得我父亲拉尔夫第一次带我去工作的时刻。那一年我才四岁，我们太阳一升起就起床了。父亲举起我放到他的油罐车里，我们驶向着北卡罗来纳州东部的农场出发了。成片成片的庄稼、大牲畜和农机具都非常迷人。我当时想：他是怎么找到这些地方的？他怎么知道如何与人交谈？我虽是个小孩子，却理解了那次经历的独特性：父亲把我带出了身边的小天地，带进了一个新世界。

9 从生命早期，父亲就帮助我们面对世界。大多数母亲喜欢面对面抱婴儿，孩子们觉得这样安全而舒适。父亲以更大的视野替换了这种安全感，他们让孩子感觉到周边的景物和声音。例如，父亲让孩子帮忙在院子里干活的时候，就打开了一扇生物学和植物学的非正式教学之门。孩子很看重这种信息和新鲜感，而他们关于实物的对话——教育学家把它称为"科学进展对话"——培养起了研究科学和数学所需的好奇心和解决问题的技能。

作为独特教师的父亲

10 在我国，大多数孩子在中学以前接触不到男性班主任教师。学前班和小学男性教师的短缺意味着大多数孩子没有机会认识男人特有的经验和能力，而这也使父亲在家里担任积极角色显得更为重要。

11 要做到这一点，一种方法是和孩子一起阅读。父亲挑选的书籍以及他们朗读和评论的方式都将极大地影响孩子的语言发展、阅读技能和常识。相比小说，父亲更乐于挑选纪实作品。他可能会选择一本有关飞机的书籍，教给孩子丰富的词汇，让他们听他吸引人的男声朗诵。

12 很多专家认为父亲式阅读对孩子的学业确实有重要作用。根据密歇根州的一项研究，听父亲朗读的女孩有更强的言语表达能力。对男孩而言，这种利害关系或许更明显。如果父亲不给儿子提供阅读的榜样，儿子会觉得阅读与男人无关。而如果男孩不会从阅读中寻找乐趣，将阻碍其流利表达、认知词汇和知识基础的发展。

13 父亲与孩子相处的其他好处还有：当父亲教会孩子搭积木或投球时，也培养了孩子的大肌肉和小肌肉运动技能、感官通路和身体意识。

鼓励与父亲共处

14　母亲有时会因为担心睡觉时间、安全问题或家里整洁而扫了孩子们玩闹的兴头。帕克建议母亲选择在一边待着。母亲凯蒂·派克同意这一点。她说:"大卫非常爱我们的几个女儿,我根本不想干涉他们。事实上,每当听到他们在楼上耍闹的声音,我都会感觉很温暖。"

15　帕克教授说:"当父亲在照顾孩子这件事上被当成伙伴而不仅仅是帮手时",他们更乐于付出精力。"让父亲自己选择一项与孩子一起的活动,他会热情得多。"

16　卡洛琳·麦克阿宾说:"我非常欢迎埃里克的新颖观点和对威尔的具体注意力。当埃里克走进房门的时候,威尔会爬到他身上。"为了增进这种父子交流,卡洛琳在白天给丈夫打电话,告诉他威尔说了他些什么话,或告诉他儿子非常想看到他。她也和威尔说父亲的好话,以增进他们两人的关系。这是母亲擅长的角色。

17　即使男人不和妻儿同住,他们在孩子生活中的存在依然重要。帕克教授说:"我们有句老话,叫做'只有前夫,没有前父'。关于离婚的研究非常清楚地表明了这一点。当孩子们得知父亲仍关心他们,例如不仅来看看孩子,还打打电话,写写信,发发邮件什么的,他们会表现得很好。"

18　母亲和父亲确实不同,帕克总结道。"但他们各自独特的照顾方式完美互补,对孩子有利。"

TEXT B Brotherly Love

Before Reading

The purpose of this section is to arouse the students' interest in the theme of the unit, reactivate their relevant background knowledge or elicit their opinions on the related topics, so as to better prepare them for the succeeding tasks.

Before Reading activities can be organized as group work so that the students share with each other their knowledge about poor families and child adoption in the United States.

Background Information

1 Child Custody in the US

Child custody is a court's determination of which parent, relative or other adult should have physical and/or legal control and responsibility for a minor (child) under 18. Child custody can be decided by a local court in a divorce or if a child, relative, close friend or state agency questions whether one or both parents are unfit, absent, dead, in prison or dangerous to the child's well-being. In such cases custody can be awarded to a grandparent or other relative, a foster parent, an orphanage or other organization.

2 Guardianship

A guardian is a person who has been appointed by a judge to take care of a minor child or incompetent adult (both called "ward") personally and/or manage that person's affairs. To become a guardian of a child either the party intending to be the guardian or another family member, a close friend or a local official responsible for a minor's welfare will petition the court to appoint the guardian. In the case of a minor, the guardianship remains under court supervision until the child reaches maturity at 18.

3 Child Adoption

In actual practice, adoption encompasses two different types of arrangements. It occurs through both formal and informal processes. Formal adoption occurs when a legal recognition of a parental relationship is made. Informal adoption occurs when the birth mother allows another person (or persons), usually another family member, to take parental responsibility for her child without obtaining legal approval or recognition of that arrangement.

Reading

New Words and Expressions

> **devastation** /ˌdevəˈsteɪʃən/ *n.* damage, ruin 破坏；毁坏
> e.g. The huge earthquake was a devastation to the town people.
> The country is still feeling the devastation of the war.

detour /ˈdiːˌtʊə/ *n.* a long or roundabout route 绕路；迂回
e.g. He has made a detour to a restaurant.
　　The plan took a number of detours before it was approved.

tip /tɪp/ *v.* to strike or touch lightly 轻触，轻碰
e.g. I tipped his hoof with the handle of a knife.
　　The sword tipped his shoulder.

layer /ˈleɪə/ *n.* a sheet of sth. 层
e.g. a layer of paint
　　a fine layer of snow

bedspread /ˈbedspred/ *n.* a decorative cloth used to cover a bed when it is not in use 床罩

pull away to drive away from the side of the road or another moving vehicle 驶离(离开路边或另一辆车)
e.g. He jumped onto the bus just as it was pulling away.
　　The thieves steadily pulled away from the police car.

curb /kɜːb/ *n.* the side part of a road 路缘
e.g. He parked his car close to the curb.

bleak /bliːk/ *a.* charmless and inhospitable; dreary 单调的
e.g. a bleak desert
　　He looked round the bleak little room in despair.

major /ˈmeɪdʒə/ *n.* a student's principal subject or course 主修科目
e.g. His major is chemistry.

minor /ˈmaɪnə/ *n.* a student's subsidiary subject or course 辅修科目
e.g. She has obtained a minor in American Indian studies.

glance /ɡlɑːns/ *v.* to give a quick short look 匆匆看一眼
e.g. He glanced at his watch.
　　She glanced down the list of names.

inspiration /ˌɪnspəˈreɪʃən/ *n.* a person or thing that makes sb. feel encouraged to be as good, successful etc. as possible 鼓舞人心的人或物
e.g. My mother has been a constant inspiration to me.
　　His glorious life will always be an inspiration to us.

tighten /ˈtaɪtən/ *v.* to make or become stiff 变紧；绷紧
e.g. His lips tightened into a thin line.
　　He felt his muscles tighten with fatigue.

HIV *abbr.* abbreviation for *human immunodeficiency virus*, a retrovirus which causes AIDS 人体免疫缺损病毒，艾滋病病毒

grip /ɡrɪp/ *v.* to take and keep a firm hold of; to grasp tightly 握紧，抓牢
e.g. Fear gripped his heart.
　　His knuckles were white as he gripped the steering wheel.

admit /ədˈmɪt/ *v.* to receive a patient into a hospital for treatment 为……办理入院手续
e.g. He was admitted to hospital suffering from burns.

ward /wɔːd/ *n.* a child or young person under the care and control of a guardian appointed by their parents or a court 受监护的人
e.g. The court made me a ward of my aunt and she brought me up.

supervision /ˌsjuːpəˈvɪʒən/ *n.* management and control 监督；管理
e.g. take personal supervision of
　　exercise effective supervision over a large fund

custody /ˈkʌstədɪ/ *n.* the protective care or guardianship of sb. or sth. 监护
e.g. The property was placed in the custody of a trustee.
　　In the divorce settlement the mother was given custody of the children.

talk over to speak about thoroughly and seriously (彻底而严肃地)商议
e.g. talk sth. over with sb.
　　If you are worried about this change of career, why don't you talk it over with your family?

guts /ɡʌts/ *n.* (pl.) personal courage and determination [复]勇气；胆量
e.g. The job requires a bit of guts.
　　He didn't have the guts to tell the truth.

sibling /ˈsɪblɪŋ/ *n.* a brother or sister 兄弟(或姊妹)；同胞

postpone /ˌpəʊstˈpəʊn/ *v.* to arrange for sth. to take place at a time later than that first scheduled 延迟
e.g. We are postponing our trip until the weather grows warmer.
　　The visit had to be postponed for some time.

split up to separate 分裂
e.g. The ancient Roman Empire split up.

No one wants the family to split up.

pray /preɪ/ *v.* to wish or hope strongly for a particular outcome or situation 祈求

e.g. After several days of rain, we were praying for the sun.
I'm praying for Mother to get better.
He prayed for her forgiveness.

attorney /əˈtɜːnɪ/ *n.* a lawyer 律师

bluntly /ˈblʌntlɪ/ *ad.* frankly 坦率地

e.g. He criticized me bluntly.

hearing /ˈhɪərɪŋ/ *n.* an act of listening to evidence in a court of law or before an official 审讯；听讯

e.g. condemn sb. without a hearing

instill /ɪnˈstɪl/ *v.* to cause sb. gradually to acquire (a particular desirable quality) 逐渐使某人获得（某种可取的品质）；逐渐灌输

e.g. instill a sense of responsibility in our students

turn around to change completely 扭转；使……突然好转

e.g. turn around the public opinion
They hope the new boss can turn around their company in a few months.

lousy /ˈlaʊzɪ/ *a.* very poor or bad 蹩脚的；劣等的

e.g. a lousy idea
The service is really lousy.
He gave me a lousy "D+" for this paper.

sneaky /ˈsniːkɪ/ *a.* furtive, sly 鬼鬼祟祟的

e.g. a sneaky trick
sneaky tactics

dilapidated /dɪˈlæpɪdeɪtɪd/ *a.* in a state of disrepair or ruin as a result of age or neglect 损坏的；破烂的

e.g. a dilapidated house
a dilapidated alley

pace /peɪs/ *v.* to walk at a steady speed 踱步

e.g. He paced his new office.
She paced the room angrily.

tape /teɪp/ *v.* to attach with adhesive tape; to stick 用胶布固定

e.g. tape a note to the door
He taped the reproduction of a famous painting to the wall.

moan /məʊn/ *v.* to complain; to grumble 悲叹；抱怨

e.g. Don't moan; it doesn't help solve your problem.
Passengers moaned about overcrowded coaches.

hustle /ˈhʌsl/ *v.* to move hurriedly 赶忙

e.g. hustle across a street
We need to hustle or we will be late.

impose /ɪmˈpəʊz/ *v.* to put (a restriction) in place 把……强制性地加于

e.g. Economic sanctions were imposed on the country.
He imposed on me his own ideas about the novel.

curfew /ˈkɜːfjuː/ *n.* a regulation requiring people to remain indoors between specified hours, typically at night 宵禁

e.g. impose a curfew on a city
a dusk-to-dawn curfew
the night curfew on juveniles

fall in with to mix socially with 与……交往

e.g. His son fell in with a bad crowd.

choir /ˈkwaɪə/ *n.* an organized group of singers 合唱团

counselor /ˈkaʊnsələ/ *n.* a person who gives advice on a specified subject 顾问

e.g. a debt counselor
a counselor to the President

yawn /jɔːn/ *v.* to involuntarily open one's mouth wide and inhale deeply due to tiredness or boredom 打哈欠

e.g. He sat up and stretched and yawned.
The audience began yawning after the speaker talked more than an hour.

rub /rʌb/ *v.* to move back and forth against a surface 揉擦；按摩

e.g. He rubbed a finger round the rim of his mug.

doable /ˈduːəbl/ *a.* within one's powers; feasible 可做的；切实可行的

e.g. He likes to get something done that is not considered doable.
None of the jobs were fun, but they were doable.

Language Study

tip

n.
1. the pointed or rounded end or extremity of sth. slender or tapering 尖端；尖儿
   e.g. the northern tip of Scotland
   George pressed the tips of his fingers together.
2. a sum of money given to sb. as a reward for a service 小费
   e.g. We normally give waiters or waitresses 15% tip at restaurants.
   Chinese people do not have the habit of giving others tips.
3. a small but useful piece of practical advice 有用的小提示或建议
   e.g. Barry had a hot tip.
   We are waiting for your tip on our proposal.

v.
1. to give sb. a sum of money as a reward for a service 给小费
   e.g. I tipped the waiter five dollars.
   You don't need to tip at Chinese restaurants.
2. to predict as likely to win or achieve sth. 事先指出获胜者
   e.g. Linda was widely tipped to get the job.
   We all tip him to win the match.

That's where this journey of his had begun…

Usage of nominal clauses 名词性从句的用法：
Nominal clauses are linked to the main clauses by connectives such as *if, whether, that* and interrogatives, functioning as nouns. 名词性从句是由if，whether，that和各种疑问词引导的从句，与名词具有同样的用途。

1. as a subject: It is placed before the predicate of the main clause to serve as the subject. It is sometimes placed at the end of the main clause while *it* is used at the subject part. 作为主语：放在主句谓语动词之前，或由形式主语it代替，本身放在主句的末尾。
   e.g. How the students of this school study English so successfully is of great interest to us English teachers.
   It is not known yet when we shall hold a discussion of the plan.
2. as an object: It is placed after the predicate (transitive verb) of the main clause or a preposition. 作为宾语：放在主句谓语动词（及物动词）或介词之后。
   e.g. Do you know what he is doing?
   I was surprised at what he said.
3. as a predicative: It is placed after the predicate (linking verb) of the main clause. 作为表语：放在主句谓语动词（连系动词）之后。
   e.g. The question is whether we can finish our work by tomorrow evening.
   My suggestion is that we go by bus instead of by train.
4. as an appositive: It is placed after some abstract nouns to state the concrete content of that noun. 作为同位语：放在某些抽象名词之后，用来说明该名词的具体内容。
   e.g. Here comes the news that some foreigners will visit our school.
   We all know the truth that practice makes perfect.

major

a. important, serious, or significant （较）重要的；（较）大的
   e.g. The use of drugs is a major problem.
   Making economic development is the major task of Chinese people.

v. to specialize in a particular subject at college or university 主修（大专院校的）科目
   e.g. I was trying to decide if I should major in drama or fiction.
   He majors in physics according to his parents' suggestions.

minor

a. lesser in importance, seriousness, or significance 次要的；程度较轻的
   e.g. She requested a number of minor alterations.
   The article is well written except for some minor mistakes.

  v. to study or qualify in a subsidiary subject at college or university 副修(大专院校的)科目
    e.g. Which would you like to minor in, accounting or management?
      I don't want to minor in any subject, because I have already spent too much time and energy on my major.

sense
 n.
 1. one of the faculties of sight, smell, hearing, taste and touch 感官；官能
  e.g. The bear has a keen sense of smell which enables it to hunt at dusk.
    Intuition is often considered as women's sixth sense.
 2. a feeling that sth. is the case 感觉
  e.g. She had the sense of being a political outsider.
    You can improve your general health and sense of well-being.
 3. a meaning 意义；含意
  e.g. It is not clear which sense of the word "character" is intended in this passage.
    Can you make the sense of your sentences clear?
 v. to perceive by a sense or senses 感觉到；意识到
  e.g. With the first frost, they could sense a change in the days.
    He could sense that she didn't like him.

cold-hearted
 Antonyms 反义词:
 warm-blooded; warm-hearted
 Another word with *cold* as a prefix:
 cold-blooded *a.*
 1. having a body temperature that changes according to the temperature of the surroundings 冷血的
  e.g. cold-blooded animal
    Snakes are cold-blooded.
 2. showing complete lack of feeling; cruel 无情的；残酷的
  e.g. a cold-blooded murderer
    How can you be so cold-blooded to your family?

pace
 n.
 1. a single step taken when walking or running 一步
  e.g. He walks with quiet pace.
 2. speed in walking, running, or moving 步速，走(跑)的速度
  e.g. He is an aggressive player with plenty of pace.
    The ring road allows traffic to flow at a remarkably fast pace.
 v. to move or develop at a particular rate or speed 以某种速度做某事；掌握速度
  e.g. Sam stood up and paced the floor, deep in thought.
    Urban people are leading fast-paced daily lives.

And he demanded each of them find a passion …
Verbs with subjunctive mood 采用虚拟语气的动词:
Verbs expressing suggestion or request such as *advise, ask, command, demand, desire, insist, move, order, prefer, propose, recommend, request, require, suggest* and *urge* are often followed by that-clauses in subjunctive mood. The verb in such a that-clause is in the original form or led by "should". 表示建议或请求的动词后的that从句用虚拟语气，从句中的动词要用原形或"should+原形"。
  e.g. I advise that he go at once.
    They demanded that every adult have the right to vote.
    She requires that they should work overnight.
    The king ordered that the man be released.

nonprofit
 Usage of the prefix *non-* 前缀non-的用法:
 1. not, other than, reverse of, absence of, lacking the usual especially positive characteristics of the thing 表示"非"，"不"，"不具备某种特征的"

e.g. nontoxic; nonlinear; nonnegotiable

2. of little or no consequence, unimportant, worthless 表示"不重要的"

e.g. nonissue; nonsense; nonsystem; nonconformity

After Reading

READING COMPREHENSION TASKS

1. Complete the following table based on the information in TEXT B.

	In the Past	At Present
Shronda	Her grades were __lousy__ because no one pushed her to __do better__.	Her grades went from __C's and D's__ to __A's__.
Keyera	She __worried too much__ and didn't __believe in__ herself.	She joined __the dance team__ at church.
Torrian	He liked to be __sneaky__ and never feared __being caught__.	He liked __singing__ and joined the school __choir__.
Corrian	He was a __follower__ who __got in trouble__ because his friends __manipulated__ him.	He played on the __football team__.

2. Answer the following questions.

1) What was Antonio's family background?
   He was from a very poor family with only mother and many kids. They lived in a bleak neighbourhood where drug dealing always happened.

2) What were Antonio's dreams for himself?
   He wanted to earn a good living after graduation from college.

3) What were the possible effects of Antonio's mother's death?
   The family would split up. Antonio's younger brothers and sisters would be sent to foster homes.

4) Why didn't Antonio's relatives want to bring up his siblings?
   They were poor themselves and they did not want to bear the burden.

5) Who helped Antonio prepare for court?
   A legal aid attorney.

6) What was Antonio's siblings' reaction toward his attempt to request legal custody of them?
   They were eager to live with him.

7) How did Antonio manage the family?
   He asked each of his siblings to take some chores. He set up goals for each of them and helped them finish homework on time.

8) What were Antonio's dreams for his siblings?
   He wanted them to study hard and go to college.

9) What changes did his siblings make after he took care of them?
   They made much progress at school and each of them found a hobby.

10) How did Antonio think of his current life?
    He thought it hard but still manageable. And it was hopeful.

3. Fill in the following table of Antonio's schedule based on the information in TEXT B.

Time	Task
5:30 am	Get up, make breakfast, drive siblings to school, go to work
12:00	Lunch break, grab grocery for dinner
5:00 pm	Stop work, pick up siblings from school, prepare dinner
7:00 pm	Check siblings' homework

4. Explain the underlined parts in your own words.
    1) … tipped the photograph back and forth in his hands. (Para. 1)
       from side to side
    2) … but only if he left behind his sisters … (Para. 10)
       on condition that
    3) … before turning her attention to his siblings. (Para. 19)
       noticing his brothers and sisters
    4) Keyera worried too much and didn't believe in herself. (Para. 23)
       didn't have confidence in herself
    5) But he was just warming up. (Para. 26)
       setting small requirements to let them ready for stricter ones

ORAL WORK

Imagine it is ten years later and the four siblings of Antonio come to his house to celebrate his birthday. They also report to him their respective achievements. Make a short play on this family get-together.

The teacher can ask the students to form groups to prepare for the five different roles. The students can either work within groups or individually at this stage of preparation. Once they feel ready, the teacher can ask them to present the show first within the group, and then to the whole class.

TRANSLATION OF TEXT B

兄长情

小汤姆·霍尔曼

晴天霹雳和漫漫长路

1 安东尼奥·西耶坐在床边，手上来来回回摆弄着一张相片。那是几年前他在北方读大学时拍的照片。他摸了摸照片上的自己，拂去上面的灰尘。

2　忘了过去吧，他告诉自己，松了手，照片掉落在蓝色的床罩上。他闭上眼睛，仿佛听到了母亲的声音。那天，母亲让他开车送她去商店。四年前去商店之路成了他现在人生的起点。

3　2002年一个炎热的8月下午，安东尼奥摇下车窗驶离路缘。他几乎没有注意空荡荡的街区，那是他和四个弟妹与母亲居住的地方。他觉得自己已经生活在未来了。

4　他是家中第一个考上大学的孩子，十个月之后他将从新泽西州的圣彼得大学毕业，主修工商管理，辅修刑事司法。

5　他看了一眼坐在前座安静地看着窗外的母亲。母亲始终给他鼓舞，她是这个没有父亲的家庭的中坚力量。她从未抱怨过。她所有的愿望就是孩子们能聪明一点，避免她犯过的错误。

6　"亲爱的，"她轻轻地说道："我有事要告诉你。"

7　安东尼奥的心抽了一下。他知道当母亲这样说话时，必定有严重的事情。

8　母亲接着说："我知道我应该早点告诉你这件事，但我开不了口。"她顿了一下，想找到合适的词。"我想告诉你，我们娘俩不瞒着了，我得了艾滋病。"安东尼奥沉默着。他的双手紧紧握住方向盘。

9　"亲爱的，"母亲说："我就快死了。"但儿子五月份从大学毕业回家时她还在。两个月后，她住进了医院。

10　她的去世将使这个家四分五裂。安东尼奥可以逃避，前提是他弃两个妹妹——15岁的史蓉妲和13岁的凯耶拉——以及14岁的双胞胎弟弟陶利安和考利安于不顾。

11　叔叔阿姨们就住在附近，其他州也有亲人，但他们都不愿意抚养孩子。孩子们将作为法定被监护人，按照佛罗里达州儿童与家庭部的安排寄养给别人。

12　这时他有了这个疯狂的念头。可不可以由他来做法定监护人？他以前从没听说过这种做法，但试一试又何妨？他和一些朋友商量了一下。有人欣赏他的勇气，也有人说如果他尚有理智的话，就应该离开这个家，再也不要回头。他清楚他的弟弟妹妹是负担。如果他这样做，必须把任何对美好生活的憧憬推迟八年，直到他最小的妹妹长到21岁。也许这奔东西对大家都有好处。他们都能开始崭新的生活。选项很清楚——抛弃弟妹或放弃梦想。他祈祷能做出正确的选择。

13　法律援助律师帮助他准备开庭的资料。她提了些问题，填了些表格。安东尼奥在2003年8月的一天来到她的办公室办手续，正好是母亲告诉他坏消息的一周年。

14　几小时后他在家里的起居室召集了弟弟妹妹，坦率地和他们谈论未来。他含着泪说："我们一定要坚强。妈妈去世了，但这不是世界末日。我们还是一家人，仍然要生活下去，无论发生什么事。为了彼此，我们必须待在一起。"

15　在法庭听证会上，法官让安东尼奥和弟妹们站起来。她问安东尼奥："你看上去很年轻，多大了？"

16　他回答说："23岁。"

17　法官说："这是很大的责任。大多数男人可能都不愿意照顾自己的孩子，可是你来这儿争取弟弟妹妹的法定监护权。"

18　法官认真研究了法律援助律师提供的书面资料。

19　"我很敬佩你。"法官说，然后问他的弟妹们："你们想和他住在一起吗？"

20　"是的。"他们齐声回答。

21　五分钟后听证会结束。安东尼奥签署了文件，开车载着家人回家，开始新生活。

灌注激情

22　一天晚上，他关上房门，对弟弟妹妹做了个评估，就像他是个冷血老板，受命让一家快要倒闭的公司扭亏为盈。

23　史蓉妲的学习成绩惨不忍睹，因为没有人督促她。考利安整天跟着别人，他的朋友们操纵他，使他惹尽麻烦。他的双胞胎哥哥陶利安喜欢鬼鬼祟祟地捣乱，而且从不害怕被逮住。凯耶拉则老是忧心忡忡，对自己缺乏自信。

24　那天夜里，安东尼奥召开了家庭会议。大家在亲戚给的破烂沙发上找地方坐下。安东尼奥在弟妹们面前踱着步，以确保他们听清他的每一句话。他说道："我们是彼此在这个世界上拥有的全部。我们要走成功之路，让妈妈高兴。"

25　他开始在四张纸片上写字，走到厨房把它们贴到冰箱上，然后大叫一声："家务，你们的家务。"弟妹们嘟哝着赶紧跑进厨房。洗碗。打扫浴室和厨房。倒垃圾。打扫起居室。每个人都分配了工作，周六大家一起干活。

26　他们抱怨着说他太严格了。但那只不过是热身而已。他禁止弟妹们晚上出门。作业必须按时完成。他检查他们所有的作业，帮他们解答每一道从前母亲无法解答的数学题。

27　他还要求他们每个人找到一项热爱的事，一个爱好，或一种运动，任何能让他们超越周边环境，看到广阔世界的东西。他们的未来不能在大街上度过，或与毒贩交往。他们得上大学，就像他一样。

28　最终，史蓉姐的成绩从C和D上升到A。她和双胞胎一起上了成绩优异者光荣榜。考利安加入了橄榄球队。陶利安发现自己喜欢唱歌，加入了学校合唱团。凯耶拉和姐姐参加了教堂的舞蹈队。一天，妹妹们带回来两张贴在汽车保险杠上的小标语，上面写着"我是优秀学生自豪的家长。"他们把标语贴在前门上，让邻里都知道谁住在这所房子里。

29　2003年12月，安东尼奥在一家非营利部门找了一份青少年问题咨询师的工作，每年挣31,000美元。这份工作有固定的工作时间，让他每天能按时回家给孩子们做晚餐。他去参加他们的橄榄球赛、教堂演出和家长会。每个月他都在每个人的账户里存上一小笔钱。

30　今天晚上，2006年迈阿密又一个炎热的夜晚，这家的男主人打了个哈欠，用手搓了搓脸。每天他必须五点半起床，叫醒弟妹们，做好大家的早餐，送他们上学。然后他去办公室上班。中午休息时他要赶紧买好晚上的菜。时间很紧，但可以做到。他坐在床边，怀揣梦想的孩子的照片还在那儿。一切都好。

INTEGRATED EXERCISES

1 PUBLIC SPEECH TRAINING

Public speaking is an act of communication, that is, it is speaking with a purpose. People speak to inform, to persuade, to entertain, to inspire, etc. Now listen to a speech that tells a story, and then practice after the recording.

(The speech will be read twice. For the first time, the students just listen and try to understand the meaning. When it is read for the second time, there are pauses in the recording. Ask the students to practice after the speaker during these pauses and pay attention to the speaker's intonation, voice [e.g. loudness, pitch, tempo] etc.)

Script

There I stood, wearing a surgical mask / in the middle of a large, brightly lit room. / In the centre of the room were five figures huddled over a table. / I found it difficult to see, / since everything was draped in blue sheets, / yet I didn't dare to take a step toward that table. / Then one of the figures called to me, / "Angela, get over here and take a closer look." / My knees buckled as I walked through the sterile environment. / But eventually, I was there, / standing over an unconscious body in the operating room.

2 DICTATION

Listen to the following passage and write it down. The passage will be read four times. During the first reading, which will be done at normal speed, listen and try to understand the meaning. For the second and third readings, the passage will be read sentence by sentence, or phrase by phrase, with intervals of 15 seconds. Write down what you hear. The last reading will be done at normal speed again and during this time you should check your work.

Script

All families have their stories, their dramas, / their private jokes, nicknames and phrases. / They're the place where our personalities were made. / How often have you heard someone with young children complain / "Oh no, I think I'm turning into my parents"? / The other day I found myself turning into one of my grandparents. / I was trying to get my baby daughter to eat her dinner / and I said "That'll make your hair curl." / Now, I don't think that green vegetables give you curly hair, / or even that curly hair is a great thing to have. / It's just a phrase I heard from my Granddad a hundred times when I was small. / It had stayed in my mind, half-forgotten, / until the time I could use it myself. / I wonder if he heard it from his own grandparents. / How many other old-fashioned phrases like this stay inside families, / when the rest of the world has forgotten them?

3 VOCABULARY STUDY

Task One
Put the proper form of the words in the corresponding blanks.

1) Out of __curiosity__, he walked into the house. (curious)
2) In this disguise, you can escape __recognition__. (recognize)
3) Juniper berries give gin its __distinctive__ flavour. (distinct)
4) They fought for social __justice__ all their lives. (just)
5) Hearing the bad news, she __tightened__ her lips for a long time. (tight)
6) He likes to get something done that is not considered __doable__. (do)
7) He began to take over the __management__ of his mother's estate after she died. (manage)
8) He has led a __varied__ life after graduation from college. (vary)
9) She is, among her many __competences__, an excellent cook. (competent)
10) There is a world __shortage__ of fuel. (short)

Task Two
Replace the underlined words with the correct form of the words in the box. You may need to make other changes.

1) He __prefers__ bananas rather than apples.
2) Under my parents' __supervision__, I finished the task quickly.
3) She has made __significant__ achievements these years.
4) The walls were topped by a __layer__ of concrete.
5) He was in prison for his __involvement__ in a plot to overthrow the government.
6) It was his __responsibility__ to find witnesses.
7) He is a man of formidable __intellectual__ capacity.
8) After retirement, he led a relaxing __suburban__ life.
9) She __awoke__ late the following morning.
10) The volcano __erupted__ even last year.

Task Three
Choose the best answers from the options given.

1) The flow of the river has been _____ with floodgates.
   A. removed   **B. regulated**   C. reproduced   D. reacted
2) Had the war not _____, they might have married.
   A. intervened   B. interviewed   C. interacted   D. interchanged
3) Mary has a very _____ voice, extremely clear and ringing.
   A. instinctive   B. common   **C. distinctive**   D. distorted
4) Subway and bus service _____ each other in this city.
   A. supplement   B. contrast   C. compliment   **D. complement**
5) This piece of good news is a _____ to her, which made her achieve her best in the competition.
   A. provocation   B. simulation   **C. stimulation**   D. provision
6) The teacher has been a constant _____ to his students.
   A. inspiration   B. inspection   C. inclusion   D. installation

7) The terrorists have claimed _____ for a string of murders.
   A. response   **B. responsibility**   C. reaction   D. recovery
8) The great singer always sings with _____.
   A. fashion   B. heat   **C. passion**   D. fascination
9) He _____ his new office happily as soon as he moved in.
   A. moved   B. walked   C. wandered   **D. paced**
10) She joined the school _____ and had frequent performances.
    A. chore   **B. choir**   C. chock   D. choice

Task Four
Fill in the following blanks with appropriate words from the box.

If we were to believe the 1) _commercials_ on television, we'd think that a child simply can't be happy without the 2) _latest_ toys and expensive video games. Actually, the gift kids love 3) _most_ is your undivided 4) _attention_, which is free. And though toys and games are 5) _fun_ to have, they need not cost a 6) _fortune_ to be enjoyable. Time spent 7) _together_ as a family can be a treat for all and doesn't have to break the 8) _budget_. It may require a stretch of the 9) _imagination_ on occasion. Once in a while — not just on a 10) _significant_ occasion, such as a birthday — set your table as if company were coming and treat your children like 11) _honoured_ guests. Serve their milk in 12) _special_ glasses, light 13) _candles_, have music playing in the 14) _background_, and encourage the family to dress up. That doesn't have to mean putting on uncomfortable 15) _fancy_ clothing: Everyone might wear 16) _dress-up_ clothes, pajamas and bathrobes, or Halloween 17) _costumes_ for fun. The whole occasion won't cost you a cent more than a 18) _regular_ meal. Impromptu picnic meals, out of doors or in, can make a simple meal much more fun and save you money in the 19) _bargain_. Your kids will 20) _enjoy_ it, too.

4 GRAMMAR FOCUS

Read the following passage, underline the one mistake in each line and write the correction after the bracketed number.

British researcher Ned Herrmann <u>tests</u> more than 7000 people to   1) tested
find out <u>what</u> side of the brain they favoured. He found a strong   2) which
relationship <u>of</u> hemisphere dominance and the way   3) between
subjects <u>made living</u>: left-brain-oriented subjects were   4) made a living
<u>often</u> lawyers, writers, bookkeepers, doctors, tax experts, etc.   5) more often
— jobs dealing <u>about</u> logical, language-related information.   6) with
Those who favoured the right hemisphere <u>turned</u> to be poets,   7) turned out
politicians, musicians, <u>architectures</u>, entrepreneurs, dancers and top   8) architects
executives. Herrmann's studies <u>show</u> that the most successful   9) showed
people in <u>the</u> occupation are those who use both the left and the   10) any
right brains. One test <u>of</u> hemisphere dominance is to observe how   11) for
you turn your head and eyes when pondering questions <u>asks</u> by   12) asked
someone in front of <u>us</u>. Research suggests that if you generally turn   13) you
to the left, you have a <u>left-brain</u> tendency; if you turn to the right,   14) right-brain
chances are you prefer work that <u>involve</u> use of logic or language.   15) involves

1) 时态错误：整个事件发生在过去，应该用过去时。
2) 连接代词错误：表示哪一边大脑，应该用which。
3) 介词搭配错误：relationship between A and B。
4) 动词词组错误："谋生"应该是make a living。
5) 前后照应错误：前文说到使用大脑半球的倾向与谋生方式之间的关系，应突出左脑使用者和右脑使用者之间的比较，因此加上more。
6) 动词词组错误："与……相关"应该是deal with。
7) 动词词组错误："结果是……"应该是turn out to be。
8) 名词错误：该句表达倾向于使用右脑的人士会成为什么样的人物，应该用表示人的architects。
9) 时态错误：研究发生在过去，应该用过去时。
10) 冠词错误：该部分表示任何职业，而且occupation一词第一次出现，不能用定冠词。
11) 介词错误：此处介词词组意思是"为检验大脑半球使用情况"，介词应该用表示目的的for，而非表示内容的of。
12) 语态错误：根据句意和后面的by可知应该用被动语态。
13) 前后照应错误：前面的人称代词一直用you，这里应该统一。
14) 前后照应错误：根据下文，如果头和眼睛朝右边转，说明喜欢使用逻辑或语言。再看前文，这种人倾向于使用左脑。所以该句中提到的头和眼睛朝左边转的人应该倾向于使用右脑。
15) 时态错误：该动词的主语是work，动词应为单数第三人称形式。

5 TRANSLATION

Task One

Translate the following paragraph from English into Chinese.

根据《兰登书屋韦氏词典》，"家庭"这个词的字面意思是"父母亲和孩子组成的一群人"。它指拥有同一身份，在一起的一群人。由于具有团结所有成员的强大力量，家庭经常能超越社会等级制度。这意味着家庭不仅仅是各位成员的简单总和。"家庭"一词包含很多内容。家庭成员来源于同一祖先，拥有共同的血缘。俗话说"血浓于水"，血缘关系在家庭出现危机时能使成员显示出超凡力量。血缘感使人们拥有全世界最特别、最独一无二的家庭身份。"家"是"家庭"的另一种称呼。虽然家庭成员不一定都住在一起，但是他们心里始终觉得家是每个成员唯一的，也是最佳的住所。家庭是最高级的教育场所，这所学校几乎什么都教，包括爱。爱是家庭能够教导的最佳美德。缺失爱的家庭不再是家庭，它也意味着世界末日的到来。

Task Two

Translate the following paragraph from Chinese into English.

When talking about "single-parent family", many people consider it as a family after divorce according to their instinct. However, with the diversity of families and social structure, single-parent families may be caused by various factors, such as divorce, death of a spouse, different working or living places of spouses, and even premarital pregnancy. Because of different reasons of single-parent families as well as inner and outer resources of children themselves, feelings in and ways of adapting themselves to this situation are different. Psychologists argue that parents need to pay more attention to the mental health of their children. They need to seek suitable means of education according to their children's personal characteristics. Both "simple rudeness" and "excessive spoiling" should be avoided. Parents need to discover problems at an early stage and try to solve them by seeking professional help. Otherwise, those unsolved mental problems will severely affect their children's life, study and lifelong happiness.

6 CLASSROOM INTERACTION

Activity A Listening

1) Kids who eat with their family do better in school and are less likely to smoke, drink, do drugs or get into fights than those who don't.
2) An associate professor of pediatrics at Harvard Medical School and author of *Ending the Food Fight*.
3) Even if the meal is served in front of the television, kids eat healthier than those who don't dine with loved ones.
4) Information about the kids' lives.

Script

Finding time to eat dinner as a family has a host of benefits that go far beyond nutrition. Kids who eat with their family do better in school and are less likely to smoke, drink, do drugs or get into fights than those who are left to their own devices(让……自行其是) at dinnertime. But with two-career households and demanding schedules, who has the time? You do, if you remember some key rules.

In addition to all its other benefits, "having dinner together is probably the single most important way to promote good health and nutrition," says David Ludwig, an associate professor of pediatrics at Harvard Medical School and author of *Ending the Food Fight*. But experts agree that the family meal doesn't have to mean Mom, Dad and all the kids sitting in the dining room at six o'clock five nights a week, eating a made-from-scratch meal. Surprising new research from the University of Minnesota's School of Public Health shows that even if the meal is served in front of the television, kids eat healthier than those who don't dine with loved ones.

Share a meal with your children and they'll share information about their lives. That's what happened with the Macchi family of Hastings-on-Hudson, New York. No matter how busy they are, Susan and Kevin try to eat dinner with their sons, ages 11 and 14, most nights, even if the food comes from a restaurant and even if just one parent can get there. "Without a lot of prodding, things just spill out," Susan says. "I've learned so much more than when we didn't have dinner together regularly."

Activity B Debate

The teacher can let the students fill in the following table of opinions before asking them to carry out the debate.

Pro Side	Con Side

Activity C Mini-speech

The teacher can give the students ten minutes to prepare and then choose a few students to give mini-speeches to the whole class.

WRITING

Writing Skills: Essay Basics

The writing part in Book III teaches essay writing, which means that the students will learn to produce writings of richer content and more independent thoughts. However, considering the course objectives and the students' competence, the essays intended for this book are still simple, mainly comprising three paragraphs. Longer essays made up of more than five paragraphs may be discussed later.

This unit introduces the students to the basic knowledge of essay structure. As they have already learned paragraph writing, it may be more efficient to learn essay structure by comparing an essay with a paragraph. The Student's Book provides the students with an essay (abridged from a longer one) and a paragraph (further abridged from the essay). After studying them, the students may be able to discover the similarities and differences in their structure.

The Student's Book provides a brief discussion of the two pieces. To facilitate the comparison task, the teacher may tell the students to divide the paragraph and the essay into different sections, and underline some important sentences, as shown below.

Paragraph

Although British English and American English are almost exactly the same, <u>there are some minor differences between them.</u> / <u>To begin with, they are different in vocabulary.</u> For example, "an apartment" in America will be called "a flat" in Britain, and "I will call you up" in America will become "I will ring you up" in Britain. / <u>Besides, the pronunciation is also different.</u> For the word "can't", an American will read /kænt/, but a Briton may read /kɑːnt/. / <u>The third difference worth mentioning is spelling.</u> For example, the word spelled as C-E-N-T-R-E in Britain will be spelled as C-E-N-T-E-R in America. / Therefore, <u>vocabulary, pronunciation and spelling constitute some of the differences between these two varieties of English.</u>

Essay

British English and American English are almost exactly the same. <u>But there are minor differences between them in three areas.</u>

<u>The first difference is vocabulary, especially idioms.</u> A small number of words … / <u>The second difference between British and American English is pronunciation.</u> The main difference in pronunciation concerns … / <u>The third difference is in spelling.</u> A few kinds of words are spelled differently …

<u>Generally speaking, we can say that three small areas of difference between British English and American English are found in vocabulary, pronunciation and spelling.</u> Knowing these differences can help us when meeting English speakers from these two countries.

	Paragraph		Essay	
Topic sentence	Although … there are some minor differences between them.	Sentence of central idea	But there are minor differences between them in three areas.
Supporting ideas	1. They are different in vocabulary. 2. The pronunciation is also different. 3. The third difference worth mentioning is spelling.	Evidence to develop the main idea	1. The first difference is vocabulary, especially idioms. 2. The second difference is pronunciation. 3. The third difference is in spelling.
Concluding sentence	Therefore … the differences between these two varieties of English.	Sentence of conclusion	Generally speaking … in vocabulary, pronunciation and spelling.

The teacher may also show the following graph to the students in illustrating the similarities and differences between a paragraph and an essay, though the essay in the graph is more complex than we aim at in this book.

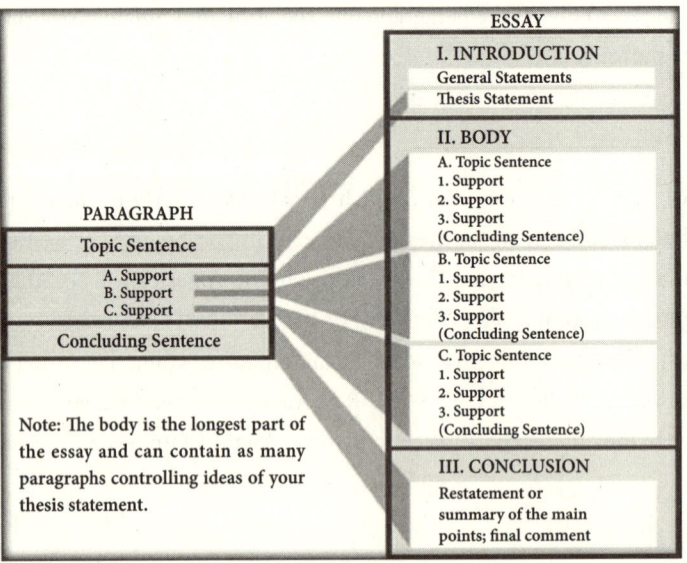

Writing Assignment

1. The following graph shows the relationship between a paragraph and an essay. Fill in the missing information.

Paragraph

Topic Sentence
A. Support 1 B. Support 2 C. Support 3
Concluding sentence

Essay

I. Introduction General statements Thesis statement

II. Body
   A. Supporting point 1
      Supporting evidence
   B. Supporting point 2
      Supporting evidence
   C. Supporting point 3
      Supporting evidence

III. Conclusion

2. Study the following essay; underline the thesis statement, the main supporting points and the conclusion sentence. Then write an outline for it.

The Most Important Personal Quality of a University Student for Future Success

As society develops…but <u>the most important personal quality for a university student, in my opinion, is adaptability</u>.

<u>Adaptability helps university students keep in pace with the knowledge development.</u> Knowledge about human society…<u>Besides, adaptability helps university students better follow the social changes.</u> In this era of globalization… <u>Most importantly, adaptability can help us deal with failures.</u> In this society of intense competition…

<u>To sum up, adaptability is the most important personal quality for contemporary university students because it can help us to follow development in knowledge and society and to deal with possible failures.</u> Only when we students can satisfy these requirements …

Possible outline
I. Thesis statement

   The most important personal quality for a university student is adaptability.
II. Body

   A. Adaptability helps university students keep in pace with the knowledge development.

   B. Adaptability helps university students better follow the social changes.

   C. Adaptability can help us deal with failures.
III. Conclusion

   Adaptability is the most important personal quality for contemporary university students because it can help us to follow development in knowledge and society and to deal with possible failures.

3. Write an essay on one of the following topics. Pay attention to its structure.

Answers may vary.

2 JOBS

TEXT A The First Job of Some Celebrities

Before Reading

The purpose of this section is to arouse the students' interest in the theme of the unit, reactivate their relevant background knowledge or elicit their opinions on the related topics, so as to better prepare them for the succeeding tasks.

Before Reading activities can be organized as group work so that the students share with each other their knowledge about the educational system in the United States.

Background Information

1 American Education System

Education in the United States is mainly provided by the public sector, with control and funding coming from three levels: federal, state, and local. Child education is compulsory.

Public education is universally available. In most public and private schools, education is divided into three levels: elementary school, middle school (sometimes called junior high school), and high school (sometimes referred to as secondary education). Post-secondary education, better known as "college" in the United States, is generally governed separately from the elementary and high school system.

2 Types of Colleges and Universities in the U.S.

Liberal arts colleges

Liberal arts colleges offer a broad base of courses in the humanities, social sciences, and sciences. Most are private and focus mainly on undergraduate students. Classes tend to be small and personal attention is available.

Universities

Generally, a university is bigger than a college and offers more majors and research facilities. Class size often reflects institutional size and some classes may be taught by graduate students.

Community or junior colleges

Community colleges offer a degree after the completion of two years of full-time study. They frequently offer technical programs that prepare the students for immediate entry into the job market.

3 Ivy League

It is the name generally applied to eight US universities (Brown, Columbia, Cornell, Dartmouth, Harvard, Pennsylvania, Princeton, and Yale) that over the years have had common interests in scholarship as well as in athletics. Stanley Woodward, *New York Herald Tribune* sports writer, coined the phrase in the 1930s.

The name represents an educational philosophy inherent to the nation's oldest schools. Ivy League schools are often viewed as some of the most prestigious and are ranked among the best universities in the United States and worldwide.

4 Degrees

Degree Type	Explanation
Certificate	A document issued to evidence completion of a course, seminar, or an academic program. An academic program awarding a certificate is usually shorter in length than a program resulting in a diploma.
Diploma	A document issued to evidence successful completion of an academic program. A diploma is awarded for programs varying in length from only a few months to those lasting several years and awarding degrees.
Associate Degree	The academic credential granted upon successful completion of an educational program of at least two but less than four academic years of college work.
Bachelor Degree	The academic credential granted upon successful completion of an educational program of at least four academic years of college work.
Master's Degree	An academic degree granted to individuals who have undergone study demonstrating a mastery or high-order overview of a specific field of study or area of professional practice.
Doctor of Philosophy (PhD)	An advanced academic degree awarded by universities. In most English-speaking countries, the PhD is the highest degree one can earn. The PhD or equivalent has become a requirement for a career as a university professor or researcher in most fields.

Reading

Text Analysis

- ### Text Summary

This narrative tells the first job experiences of three American celebrities and how those experiences later helped in their career development. Clint Black gained perseverance from soliciting newspaper subscriptions as a teenager and became a famous country singer when he grew up. Louis Caldera learned discipline, a strong work ethic and the importance of balancing life's competing interests from getting up very early in the morning to clean the parking lot as a boy. He later became the 17th United States Secretary of the Army. Suze Orman gained confidence and opportunities from being a waitress in her early 20s and became a bestselling financial author.

• Text Organization

Paragraphs 1-6: Narration 1	Clint Black's first job was soliciting newspaper subscriptions door-to-door. He was frequently refused and got doors slammed on his face. Through this job, he gained perseverance, which helped him tremendously in his career as a singer.
Paragraphs 7-13: Narration 2	Louis Caldera grew up in a very poor immigrant family. He helped his parents clean the parking lot on early morning three times a week when he was only ten. He learned discipline and a strong work ethic from this experience and later became the 17th United States Secretary of the Army.
Paragraphs 14-25: Narration 3	Suze Orman worked as a waitress when she was 22. She gained confidence from her hard work and acquired respect from her customers, who helped her in starting her own career. She succeeded in brokerage and also became a bestselling financial author.

• Text Features

This text combines three narrations of American celebrities. The author mainly uses the first person and past tense. To achieve coherence, a lot of chronological linking words are adopted (e.g. *when, even though, one time, soon, around this time, before long, early in my music career* in the first narration; *when, during my senior year of high school, later* in the second narration; and *when, the next day, the first time, after, eventually, five years later* in the third narration).

Factual statements and direct speeches are used in the narratives. To make it rhetorically various, however, the author uses a combination of simple sentences, compound sentences and complex sentences, such as present participial phrase as subject(现在分词短语用作主语, see Item 1 in Key Sentences), adverbial clause of concession(让步状语从句, see Item 2 in Key Sentences), non-restrictive attributive clause(非限制性定语从句, see Item 3 in Key Sentences), adverbial clause of time embedded with present participle transition(时间状语从句嵌套现在分词结构, see Item 4 in Key Sentences), objective clause embedded with adverbial clause of condition(宾语从句嵌套条件状语从句, see Item 5 in Key Sentences), adverbial clause of place embedded with present participle(地点状语从句嵌套现在分词结构, see Item 6 in Key Sentences).

• Key Sentences

1. Having all those doors slammed in my face as a kid gave me the strength to stand up to this intimidating figure. (Para. 5)

The present participial phrase *Having all those doors slammed in my face as a kid* serves as the subject of this sentence. A present participial phrase can be led by a subject, a linking word, or none. For example:

A: He denied having studied here. (without subject or linking word)
B: When sleeping, he never remembers anything. (with linking word)
C: Do you mind my making a suggestion first? (with subject)

A present participial phrase can be used as prepositional complement(介词补足语), subject(主语), object(宾语), predicative(表语), adverbial(状语), or independent structure(独立结构), which can sometimes be led by the preposition *with*. For example:

A: I'm worried about Henry's telling lies again. (used as prepositional complement)

B: His winning the champion of the competition is the climax of the novel. (used as subject)

C: Please pardon my disturbing you. (used as object)

D: Our duty is serving the people wholeheartedly. (used as predicative)

E: Climbing to the top of the hill, we saw the whole picture of the village. (used as adverbial)

F: The news having been read, a heated discussion began. (used as independent structure)

G: The teacher stepped into the classroom with his hands holding a pile of exercise books. (used as independent structure, led by the preposition *with*)

2. Even though we struggled to make ends meet, my parents stressed to me and my four brothers and sisters how fortunate we were to live in a great country with limitless opportunities. (Para. 8)

In this sentence *Even though we struggled to make ends meet* is an adverbial clause of concession. This kind of adverbial clause is often headed by *although*, *though*, *even though*, *even if*, etc. For example:

A: Although he had been sick for a month, he managed to pass the final exam.

B: Though she was small, she defeated many competitors in the wrestling competition.

C: You shouldn't have fired him even if he had made serious mistakes.

3. The owner of the shopping center gave Dad a discount on his rent for cleaning the parking lot three nights a week, which meant getting up at 3 a.m. (Para. 10)

In this sentence, *which meant getting up at 3 a.m.* is a non-restrictive attributive clause. A non-restrictive attributive clause can be led by *who(m)*, *whose* to indicate a person or *which* to indicate an object. For example:

A: The driver, who drove very fast, had just got his license.

B: This film, which was launched only three days ago, has reached a box-office record of one million US dollars.

4. This really helped during my senior year of high school, when I worked 40 hours a week flipping burgers at a fast-food joint while taking a full load of college-prep courses. (Para. 11)

This sentence has got two layers of meanings. The first meaning is reflected by the subject-predicate structure(主谓结构) *This really helped...* In the second layer, which is an adverbial clause of time(时间状语从句), headed by the antecedent(先行词) *when*, the author uses present participle linked by *while*.

5. The experience taught me that there is dignity in all work and that if people are working to provide for themselves and their families, that is something we should honour. (Para. 12)

This sentence has got three layers of meanings. The first layer is reflected by the subject-predicate structure(主谓结构) *The experience taught me...* In the second layer, there are two objects. The first object is a *that*-clause: *that there is dignity in all work*. The second object, also a *that*-clause, embodies an adverbial clause of condition *if people are working to provide for themselves and their families*, which is the third layer of the whole sentence.

6. We ended up in Berkeley, Calif., where I got a job cutting down eucalyptus trees with a chain saw for $3.50 an hour. (Para. 14)

In this sentence, the adverbial clause of place *where I got a job...* is embedded by a present participle *cutting down eucalyptus trees with a chain saw for $3.50 an hour*, which is used as object complement（宾语补足语）.

New Words and Expressions

solicitor /səˈlɪsɪtə/ *n.* a salesman 推销员
e.g. a magazine solicitor
solicit /səˈlɪsɪt/ *v.* to sell 兜售货物
e.g. Salesmen used to call at the houses of newcomers to a district soliciting for customers.
No soliciting is allowed in this building.
scramble /ˈskræmbl/ *v.* to make one's way quickly or clumsily over rough ground (especially using one's hands to help) 攀爬；艰难地行走
e.g. They scrambled over the boulders.
grateful /ˈɡreɪtfʊl/ *a.* showing appreciation; thankful 感激的
e.g. I'm grateful to you for your help.
She gave him a grateful smile.
challenge /ˈtʃælɪndʒ/ *n.* a task that tests sb.'s abilities 挑战
e.g. The government has to face yet another foreign policy challenge.
He took up the challenge of organizing a sports afternoon.
slam /slæm/ *v.* to shut forcefully and loudly 砰地关上
e.g. slam the window shut
He slammed the door behind him as he left the house.
damn /dæm/ *a.* used for emphasis, especially to express anger or frustration 该死的；讨厌的
e.g. Turn that damn thing off!
end up to be in a particular situation, state, or place after a series of events 结束，告终
e.g. He ended up as head of the firm.
We set off for New York but ended up in Chicago.
subscription /səbˈskrɪpʃən/ *n.* an advance payment in order to receive copies of a newspaper or magazine 订阅
e.g. regular subscription
renew one's subscription to a journal
harmonica /hɑːˈmɒnɪkə/ *n.* mouth organ 口琴
chilli /ˈtʃɪlɪ/ *n.* a very hot-tasting pepper 辣椒

cook-off /ˈkʊkɒf/ *n.* cooking match 烹饪比赛
lose sight of to fail to consider; to forget 忽略
e.g. He didn't lose sight of his dream of going to college.
In the heat of the argument we mustn't lose sight of our main objective.
perseverance /ˌpɜːsɪˈvɪərəns/ *n.* persistence in doing sth. despite difficulty 坚持不懈
e.g. Medicine is a field which requires dedication and perseverance.
By perseverance the crippled boy learned how to swim.
dispute /dɪˈspjuːt/ *n.* a disagreement or argument 争端
e.g. a territorial dispute between the two countries
The Commission is in dispute with the government.
pressure /ˈpreʃə/ *v.* to force 对……施加压力
e.g. pressure sb. for money
The children are not pressured to empty their plates.
back off to stop trying to do sth. 放弃原来的主张；打退堂鼓
e.g. I saw I was upsetting her, so I backed off.
stand up to to refuse to accept unjust treatment by sb. 拒绝接受不公正待遇
e.g. stand up to unfair treatment
Don't let her say things like that about your work — you should stand up to her a bit more.
intimidating /ɪnˈtɪmɪdeɪtɪŋ/ *a.* threatening 恐吓的
e.g. intimidating words
I am not afraid of his intimidating actions.
stress /stres/ *v.* to give particular emphasis or importance to 强调
e.g. They stressed the need for reform.
She was anxious to stress that her daughter's safety was her only concern.
limitless /ˈlɪmɪtlɪs/ *a.* without end, limit, or boundary 无限的
e.g. My patience is not limitless.

Our resources are not limitless.

imbue /ɪmˈbjuː/ *v.* to inspire or fill with (a feeling or quality) 使充满；灌输

e.g. He was imbued with a deep Christian piety.
His work is imbued with the evolutionary spirit.

patriotism /ˈpætrɪətɪzəm/ *n.* love for one's own country 爱国主义

cardboard /ˈkɑːdbɔːd/ *n.* pasteboard or stiff paper 卡纸板

e.g. a cardboard box

retrain /riːˈtreɪn/ *v.* to teach sb. new skills to enable them to do a different job 再(就业)培训

e.g. train and retrain teachers
retrain suitable people in other skills which are still in demand

hairstylist /ˈheəˌstaɪlɪst/ *n.* a person who cuts and styles people's hair professionally 发型师

rent /rent/ *v.* to pay sb. for the use of sth. 租借，租用

e.g. a rented apartment
They rented a house together.

n. a tenant's regular payment to a landlord for the use of property or land 租金

e.g. The flat's monthly rent is very high.
I can't afford to pay the rent.

coiffure /kwɑːˈfjʊə/ *n.* hairstyle 发式

discount /ˈdɪskaʊnt/ *n.* deduction from the usual cost of sth. 折扣

e.g. Students get a discount of 20% on air fares.
They are 1 pound each but if you buy ten, I will give you a 10% discount.

mower /ˈməʊə/ *n.* a machine that cuts grass 割草机

litter /ˈlɪtə/ *n.* rubbish 垃圾

e.g. The children picked up all the litter on the playground.
Remember to clear up after your picnic and do not drop litter.

discipline /ˈdɪsɪplɪn/ *n.* the ability to control one's own behaviour 自制；守纪律

flip /flɪp/ *v.* to turn over quickly 快速翻动

e.g. The plane flipped over and then exploded.
The six-foot wave flipped the boat over.

burger /ˈbɜːgə/ *n.* a flat round cake of minced beef that is fried or grilled 汉堡

pay off to yield good results 得到好结果；获得回报

e.g. Have all of your efforts paid off?

military /ˈmɪlɪtərɪ/ *a.* relating to armed forces 军事的；军用的

e.g. the build-up of military activity
military training

academy /əˈkædəmɪ/ *n.* a place of study or training in a special field 学院

e.g. the US Military Academy at West Point
a police academy

graduate /ˈgrædʒʊət/ *a.* relating to or involved in studies done at a university after completing a first degree 研究生的

e.g. a graduate student
a graduate course

dignity /ˈdɪgnətɪ/ *n.* the quality of being worthy of honour or respect 尊严

e.g. the dignity of labour
A man's dignity depends not upon his wealth or rank but upon his character.

honour /ˈɒnə/ *v.* to regard with great respect 尊敬；尊重

e.g. an honoured guest
honour the principles of peaceful coexistence

pile into (of a group of people) to get into (a vehicle) in a disorganized manner 挤进(车辆)

e.g. pile into a car
Ten children piled into the minibus.

eucalyptus /ˌjuːkəˈlɪptəs/ *n.* a fast-growing evergreen Australasian tree 桉树

saw /sɔː/ *n.* a hand tool for cutting wood or other hard materials 锯子

diner /ˈdaɪnə/ *n.* a small restaurant that serves cheap meals 小餐馆

incredible /ɪnˈkredəbl/ *a.* unbelievable; extremely good 难以置信的；妙极的

e.g. at incredible speeds
incredible news

look up to to respect; to admire 尊敬；敬仰

e.g. We always look up to Mark for his honesty and efficiency.

accomplishment /əˈkʌmplɪʃmənt/ *n.* sth. that has been achieved successfully 成绩；成就

e.g. The reduction of inflation was a remarkable accomplishment.
She is known for her accomplishment in improving the country's hospitals.

grill /grɪl/ *n.* a device on a cooker that radiates heat downwards for cooking food 烤架；烤盘

over easy (of a fried egg) turned over when almost cooked and fried lightly on the other side, so that the yolk remains slightly liquid

双面煎而一面嫩煎的

newfound /ˈnjuːfaʊnd/ *a.* newly discovered or obtained 新发现的；新得到的

regular /ˈreɡjʊlə/ *n.* sb. who often goes to the same bar, restaurant etc. 常客
  e.g. pub regulars
  Regulars can get a 10% discount in this restaurant.

total /ˈtəʊtəl/ *v.* to reach a particular total 总计
  e.g. Trade between the two countries totaled 3 billion US dollars last year.

collateral /kɒˈlætərəl/ *n.* sth. pledged as security for repayment of a loan 担保品
  e.g. a loan without collateral

honesty /ˈɒnɪstɪ/ *n.* the quality of being truthful and sincere 诚实；真诚
  e.g. They spoke with convincing honesty about their fears.

brokerage /ˈbrəʊkərɪdʒ/ *n.* the business of buying and selling stocks and bonds for clients 经纪业

invest /ɪnˈvest/ *v.* to put (money) into financial schemes, shares, property, or a commercial venture with the expectation of achieving a profit 投资
  e.g. The company is to invest 12 million pounds in its new manufacturing site.
  He tried to get his workers to invest in private pension funds.

investment /ɪnˈvestmənt/ *n.* the action or process of investing money for profit 投资
  e.g. They held a debate over private investment in road-building.
  They received a total investment of 50,000 US dollars.

sour /ˈsaʊə/ *v.* to fail 变坏
  e.g. General business sours and car sales dip.
  Their company began to sour because of the war.

stockbroker /ˈstɒkˌbrəʊkə/ *n.* a person who buys and sells securities on a stock exchange on behalf of clients 股票经纪人

deliberation /dɪˌlɪbəˈreɪʃən/ *n.* long and careful consideration 深思熟虑
  e.g. After much deliberation I decided to take this job.
  Try to make up your mind after deliberation.

apply for to request sth. formally 正式申请
  e.g. I will apply for the medical school this year.
  We've applied to the council for a home improvement grant.

broker /ˈbrəʊkə/ *n.* a person who buys and sells goods or assets for others 经纪人

plus /plʌs/ *prep.* with the addition of 加上
  e.g. a room plus bathroom
  He was awarded the full amount plus interest.

imprint /ɪmˈprɪnt/ *v.* to impress; to stamp 铭刻
  e.g. Tyre marks were imprinted in the snow.
  I will imprint on my memory what I have seen and heard.

mount /maʊnt/ *v.* to grow larger or more numerous 增加；增长
  e.g. Production costs are steadily mounting.
  Problems began mounting.

Language Study

have sth. done to get sb. else to do sth. for you 让别人帮你做某事
  e.g. I'm going to have my hair cut.
  She's having her house redecorated.
In informal English, *have* can be replaced by *get*. 非正式英语中，have可以替换为get。
  e.g. We're getting a new telephone system installed.
  I got the bill sent direct to the company.

litter
  n.
  1. an untidy collection of things lying about 乱七八糟
     e.g. a litter of sleeping bags on the floor
     He was surprised to see his room in such a litter.
  2. a number of young animals born to an animal at one time 一窝(仔畜)
     e.g. a litter of five kittens
     five young at a litter

    v. to make (a place or area) untidy with rubbish 乱扔
        e.g. Clothes and newspapers littered the floor.
            The sitting room was littered with books.

discipline
  n.
  1. a system of rules of conduct 纪律；规章制度
      e.g. lack of discipline
          He doesn't have to submit to normal disciplines.
  2. a branch of knowledge, typically one studied in higher education 学科
      e.g. Sociology is a fairly new discipline.
          Students can choose their own disciplines after entering college.
  v. to train (sb.) to obey rules or a code of behaviour, using punishment to correct disobedience 训练；训导
      e.g. discipline the trainees
          Parents must discipline their children.

in my case
  in sb.'s case   according to sb.'s situation 就某人的情况而言
      e.g. In my case, I don't think money can buy happiness.
          In his case, he realized the importance of helping others.
  Some other phrases with *case*   一些带有case的词组：

in case
  1. if 假使
      e.g. In case she comes back, let me know immediately.
          In case you don't feel well, call me at this number.
  2. for fear 以防
      e.g. Take the raincoat in case it rains.
          Shut all the windows in case it gets cold in the evening.

in any case   no matter what 无论如何
    e.g. In any case, book the tickets first.
        In any case, I don't drink wine.

in no case   not do ... no matter what 无论如何不，决不
    e.g. In no case should the temperature of the store room be over 20.
        In no case have I noticed that he left early.

co-worker
  Usage of the prefix *co-*   前缀co-的用法：
  1. (forming nouns) joint; mutual; common 构成名词，表示"共同"，"互相"。
      e.g. co-driver; coauthor
  2. (forming adjectives) jointly; mutually 构成形容词，表示"共同的"，"互相的"。
      e.g. coequal; coextensive
  3. (forming verbs) together with another or others 构成动词，表示"共同"，"联合"。
      e.g. coproduce; coexist

pride
  n.
  1. a person or thing that arouses a feeling of deep pleasure or satisfaction 让人自豪的人或物
      e.g. The pride of the village is the swimming pool.
          She is the pride of the whole school.
  2. consciousness of one's own dignity 自尊心
      e.g. He swallowed his pride and asked for help.
          No one can live in sheer pride.
  v. **pride oneself on**   to be especially proud of (a particular quality or skill) 对……感到自豪
      e.g. He prided himself on his honesty.
          We pride ourselves on our children.

eventually

Eventually and its synonyms　eventually及近义词辨析：
at last: 多指经主观努力，克服各种困难后才终于达到目的。
at length: 强调经历较长时间后终于完成，侧重时间。
eventually: 侧重动作或行为的结果。
finally: 常可与at last换用，都可用于对往事的描述，但finally不带感情色彩，指一系列事情的最后结局。
in the end: 与at last同义，但in the end不仅可指过去，还可表示对未来的预计。
lastly: 指序列的最后，通常用于列举事物。

annual

Frequency of time　时间频率：
daily: once a day 每日
weekly: once a week 每周
biweekly: once two weeks; twice a week 两周一次；一周两次
monthly: once a month 每月
bimonthly: once two months; twice a month 两月一次；一月两次
quarterly: once three months 每季
yearly, annually: once a year 每年
biyearly: once two years; twice a year 两年一次；一年两次

After Reading

READING COMPREHENSION TASKS

1. Complete the following table based on the information in TEXT A.

	First Job	Experience
Clint Black	He sold __subscriptions__ to a paper at the age of __14__. He worked after dark in __bad areas__ searching for __garage apartments__. People there didn't like a stranger __knocking on their door__.	He gained __perseverance__ from knocking on __strangers'__ doors. Besides, having all those doors __slammed in his face__ as a kid gave him the __strength__ to stand up to difficulties.
Louis Caldera	He helped his parents to clean __the parking lot__ three nights a week. He got up at __3 a.m.__, emptied garbage cans, picked up litter __by hand__, and __got sleep__ on the way home.	He acquired __discipline__ and a strong __work ethic__, and learned the importance of __balancing life's competing interests__.
Suze Orman	She worked at __a local diner__ for __seven__ years.	She gained __confidence__ and learned the importance of __taking pride in__ life's __little accomplishments__. With the help of some diner regulars, she started her own business.

2. Choose the best answers based on TEXT A.

1) How did Clint Black react when he was locked in a legal dispute with a former manager?

　A. He was afraid and gave up.　　B. He was forced to give up.
　C. He stood up to the intimidation and won.　　D. He hired a lawyer to help the case.

2) What helped Louis Caldera most when he worked his way through the senior year of high school?

　A. Great interest.　　**B. Balancing work and study.**
　C. Courage.　　D. Hard work.

3) Who gave Suze Orman the loan when she wanted to open her own restaurant?

A. Helen.   B. Her parents.   **C. Her customers.**   D. Merrill Lynch.

3. Write down the three celebrities' life experience.

Clint Black

    newspaper salesman — band player — famous country singer

Louis Caldera

    parking-lot sweeper — fast-food joint waiter — student of U.S. Military Academy — student of Harvard law and business schools — joined a big Los Angeles law firm — member of the California state assembly — the 17th Secretary of the Army

Suze Orman

    eucalyptus trees cutter — diner waitress — stockbroker at Merrill Lynch — opened her own firm — bestselling financial author

4. Explain the underlined parts in your own words.

1) <u>Before long</u> I was playing … (Para. 3)

   soon

2) Even though we struggled to <u>make ends meet</u> … (Para. 8)

   survive on limited income

3) He rented space in a little strip mall and gave his shop <u>the fancy name</u> of … (Para. 9)

   the beautiful name

4) Mom and I emptied garbage cans and picked up litter <u>by hand</u>. (Para. 10)

   without any tools

5) … if people are working to <u>provide for themselves and their families</u> … (Para. 12)

   support themselves and their family members

6) <u>Thanks to</u> the newfound confidence I picked up from Helen … (Para. 19)

   because of

7) But when I called my parents <u>to ask for a loan</u> … (Para. 19)

   to borrow money

8) … I know I can do more if somebody would just <u>have faith in</u> me. (Para. 20)

   believe in

9) …along with a note that I have <u>to this day</u>. (Para. 21)

   until now

ORAL WORK

Work in groups of four and make a TV interview on the life experience of the three celebrities. All your group members should participate in this interview, who can act the roles of a TV anchor, Clint Black, Louis Caldera and Suze Orman.

The teacher can ask the students to do the role play in groups first and then choose a few groups to present their interviews to the whole class.

TRANSLATION OF TEXT A

几位名人的第一份工作

丹尼尔·莱文

报纸推销员

1 我14岁那年得到了一份放学后推销家乡报纸《休斯敦邮报》的工作。我被派到城里最差的几个居民区挨家挨户推销。尽管我常常天黑后还穿行在不安全地域,搜寻车库公寓卖报,我仍很感激这份工作。

2 这是一个挑战,因为人们不喜欢陌生人敲门,尤其是一个小孩想要卖东西给他们。有一次,一个男人砰地把我关在门外,叫道:"我可不要什么他妈的报纸。"我逼着自己又敲了一次门,告诉他这份报纸有多棒。最后我终于卖给他一份。不久我成了销售量最大的推销员之一,并和其他成功的推销员一样,受命培训新人。

3 那时我开始吹口琴,弹吉他。不久我就参加了乐队,在辣椒厨艺比赛等场合演奏。18岁时,我集中精力准备成为职业音乐家。我从未忘记过这个梦想。我坚信我的坚韧不拔来自于敲陌生人房门的经历。

4 那次经历在许多方面对我有用。在我的早期音乐生涯中,我曾与以前的经纪人有过法律纠纷。他强迫我放弃,但我拒绝了。

5 小时候有过那么多扇门在我面前砰地关上,我现在自然有力量拒绝这副恐吓的嘴脸。只是这次有一点不同:我是那个说"不"的人。我赢了。

6 *乡村音乐歌手克林特·布莱克已售出1,600万张专辑。*

停车场清扫员

7 我的父母都来自墨西哥的小镇。我出生在得克萨斯州埃尔帕索市。四岁那年,我们全家搬到洛杉矶东部的一个廉价住宅区。

8 虽然我们好不容易才勉强度日,父母仍一直向我和四个兄弟姐妹强调,我们能生活在一个机遇无穷的伟大国家是何等幸运。他们让我们懂得了家庭、信念和爱国主义的观念。

9 我十岁时得到了第一份工作。我的父亲本杰明在纸板盒工厂干活时背受伤了,只能再培训做一名发型师。他在公路旁的小购物中心租了个店面,起了个很花哨的店名叫做"本先生发型屋"。

10 购物中心的老板给父亲的租金打了折,条件是每周三个晚上打扫停车场。这就意味着我们得凌晨三点起床干活。为了捡拾垃圾,父亲使用一个看上去像割草机的小机器。我和母亲清空垃圾箱,用手捡垃圾。我们需要两至三个小时才能清扫完毕。在坐车回家的路上,我经常会睡着。

11 这个活我只做了两年,学到的东西却受用一生。我学到了纪律性和敬业精神,而且在小小年纪就知道了在生活的各个矛盾之间保持平衡有多重要——就我而言,是保持上学、作业和工作之间的平衡。这一点在我高中毕业那年尤其帮了我的忙,那时我在快餐店翻炸汉堡包,一周工作40小时,还得开足马力准备大学预科课程。

12 辛劳有了回报。我考上了美国军校,毕业后又在哈佛大学攻读了法律和商学两个硕士学位。后来,我在洛杉矶一家大律师行工作,又被选入加利福尼亚州众议院。在做这些工作和其他任何事情的时候,我从未忘记那些在停车场的夜晚。这份经历告诉我任何工作都有尊严,只要是为自己和家人的生存而工作,就值得尊重。

13 *路易斯·卡尔德拉是美国第17任陆军部长。*

餐厅招待

14 1973年我22岁时,和三个朋友挤进了一辆福特小型货车,从家乡芝加哥出发准备周游美国。我们最终到达加利福尼亚州的伯克利。我在那儿找了份用链锯锯桉树的活,每小时挣3.5美元。

15 但我第一份长期工作是在当地一家叫做"毛茛面包房"的餐馆打工。我在那儿工作了七年,学到了很多东西,尤其是从一位女同事身上。

16　她叫海伦，当时六十多岁了，有着一头红发和极强的自尊心，而这正是我所缺少的。我尊敬海伦，因为她从事自己热爱的服务行业，而且无人能及。她让每个人都微笑愉快，顾客和同事都如此。

17　我还明白了对生活中的小成绩感到自豪是多么重要。当我在厨房帮忙时，最让我得意的就是把两枚鸡蛋放在烤盘上煎得很嫩，正是客人想要的熟度。

18　做服务员的经历改变了我的生活。我的一位常客是电子产品推销员弗莱德·海斯布鲁克。他总是吃一种火腿蒙特雷杰克干酪煎蛋卷。当看见他往餐厅走的时候，我就开始准备，等他一坐下我就把蛋卷放到桌上。

19　由于从海伦那儿找到了新的自信，我开始梦想开一家自己的餐馆。但当我给父母打电话向他们借钱时，得到的回答却是："我们没有钱。"

20　第二天，弗莱德看到我，问道："你怎么了，开心果？今天怎么不笑了？"我把自己的梦想告诉了他，说："弗莱德，我知道，只要有人相信我，我还能做更大的事呢。"

21　他走到一些常客那儿说了些什么。第二天，他交给我几张总额五万美元的支票，还有一张我至今保存着的纸条，上面写着："这笔贷款唯一的抵押品是我相信你的诚实。怀抱梦想的好人应该有机会使梦想成真。"

22　我拿着支票来到美林证券给自己投了一笔资，这是我平生第一次走进经纪公司。我仍然在"毛茛面包房"工作，同时筹划着准备开的饭店。然而，我的投资失败，输光了钱。

23　我开始考虑做股票经纪人会怎样。深思熟虑之后我决定申请在美林证券工作。虽然我没有经验，但却被雇用了，后来还成为相当出色的经纪人。我终于还清了弗莱德和其他顾客的五万美元，并加上了14%的年利息。五年以后，我开了自己的公司。

24　我收到弗莱德寄来的感谢信，这封信将永远印在我心中。他当时病了，我的支票帮他还清了高涨的医药费。他在信中说："那笔贷款也许是我最成功的投资之一。能有几个投资者有机会像我一样，对一位人格品质价值百万的餐厅服务员进行投资，并亲眼目睹她成为一名非常成功的事业女性呢？"

25　苏斯·奥曼是理财畅销书作家，代表作有《九步达到财务自由》和《致富之勇气》。

TEXT B Success of a Clothing Website

Before Reading

The purpose of this section is to arouse the students' interest in the theme of the unit, reactivate their relevant background knowledge or elicit their opinions on the related topics, so as to better prepare them for the succeeding tasks.

Before Reading activities can be organized as group work so that the students share with each other their knowledge and experiences about online activities.

Background Information

1 Online Shopping

Online shopping is the process whereby consumers directly buy goods or services from a seller in real time, often without an intermediary service, over the Internet. An online shop, e-shop, e-store, Internet shop, webshop, webstore, online store, or virtual store evokes the physical analogy of buying products or services at a bricks-and-mortar retailer or in a shopping mall. The process is called Business-to-Consumer (B2C) online shopping. When a business buys from another business it is called Business-to-Business (B2B) online shopping. Both B2C and B2B online shopping are forms of e-commerce.

In 1990 Tim Berners-Lee created the first World Wide Web server and browser. It opened for commercial use in 1991. In 1994 other advances took place, such as online banking and the opening of an online pizza shop by Pizza Hut. During that same year, Netscape introduced SSL encryption of data transferred online, which has become essential for secure online shopping. Also in 1994 the German company Intershop introduced its first online shopping system. In 1995 Amazon launched its online shopping site, and in 1996 eBay appeared. More recently Overstock has also become one of the world's largest and reliable online shopping stores.

2 Internet Marketing

Internet marketing, also referred to as i-marketing, web-marketing, online-marketing or e-marketing, is the marketing of products or services over the Internet.

The Internet has brought media to a global audience. The interactive nature of Internet marketing in terms of providing instant responses and eliciting responses are the unique qualities of the medium. Internet marketing is sometimes considered to be broad in scope because it not only refers to marketing on the Internet, but also includes marketing done via e-mail and wireless media. Management of digital customer data and electronic customer relationship management (ECRM) systems are also often grouped together under Internet marketing.

Internet marketing ties together creative and technical aspects of the Internet, including: design, development, advertising, and sales.

Advantages

Internet marketing is relatively inexpensive when we consider the ratio of cost against the reach of the target audience. Companies can reach a wide audience for a small fraction of traditional advertising budgets. The nature of the medium allows consumers to research and purchase products and services at their own convenience. Therefore, businesses have the advantage of appealing to consumers in a medium that can bring results quickly. The strategy and overall effectiveness of marketing campaigns depend on business goals and cost-volume-profit (CVP) analysis.

Internet marketers also have the advantage of measuring statistics easily and inexpensively. Nearly all aspects of an Internet marketing campaign can be traced, measured, and tested. The advertisers can use a variety of methods: pay per impression, pay per click, pay per play, or pay per action. Therefore, marketers can determine which messages or offerings are more appealing to the audience. The results of campaigns can be measured and tracked immediately because online marketing initiatives usually require users to click on an advertisement, visit a website, and perform a targeted action. Such measurement cannot be achieved through billboard advertising, where an individual will at best be interested, then decide to obtain more information at a later time.

Limitations

Internet marketing requires customers to use newer technologies rather than traditional media. Low-speed Internet connections are another barrier. If companies build large or over-complicated websites, individuals connected to the Internet may experience significant delays in content delivery.

From the buyer's perspective, the inability to touch, smell, taste or "try on" tangible goods before making an online purchase can be depressing. However, there is an industry standard for e-commerce vendors to reassure customers by having liberal return policies as well as providing in-store pick-up services.

A survey of 410 marketing executives listed the following barriers to entry for large companies looking to market online: insufficient ability to measure impact, lack of internal capability, and difficulty convincing senior management.

Reading

New Words and Expressions

eternal /ɪˈtɜːnəl/ *a.* lasting or existing forever 永恒的；永存的
e.g. eternal truths
　　the secret of eternal youth
proportion /prəʊˈpɔːʃən/ *n.* a part, share, or number considered in comparative relation to a whole 比例
e.g. the proportion of imports to exports
　　The proportion of greenhouse gases in the atmosphere is rising.
label /ˈleɪbəl/ *n.* the name or trademark of a fashion company 商标；牌子
e.g. She plans to launch her own designer clothes label.
　　She buys clothes more for the label than the style.
frustrated /frʌˈstreɪtɪd/ *a.* feeling annoyed, upset and impatient because of an inability to change or achieve sth. 失望的
e.g. He gets frustrated when his parents can't understand him.
launch /lɔːntʃ/ *v.* to start or set in motion (an activity or enterprise) 使投入；使开始从事
e.g. The government is to launch a 10-million publicity campaign.
　　He launched his son into business.
length /leŋθ/ *n.* the measurement or extent of sth. from end to end 长度
e.g. The fish reaches a length of 10 inches.
　　The delta is twenty kilometers in length.
width /wɪdθ/ *n.* the measurement or extent of sth. from side to side 宽度
e.g. a narrow corridor barely the width of a man
　　The yard was about seven feet in width.
top /tɒp/ *n.* a garment covering the upper part

of the body 上装

glam /glæm/ *n.* (informal) glamour 魅力，迷人

e.g. an actress with glam

trendy /ˈtrendɪ/ *n.* a person who is very fashionable or up to date 时髦的人

e.g. He enjoyed being able to go out and live like a trendy.

attire /əˈtaɪə/ *n.* clothes 服装

e.g. night attire
the usually sober attire of British security service personnel

dress-up /ˈdresʌp/ *n.* elegant dress used for formal occasions 盛装

e.g. a dress-up day
a dress-up dinner

textile /ˈtekstaɪl/ *n.* a type of cloth or woven fabric 纺织品

e.g. a fascinating range of jewelry and textiles
The factory produces woolen textiles.

garment /ˈɡɑːmənt/ *n.* an item of clothing 衣服

e.g. fashion garments
a windproof outer garment

kick-start /ˈkɪkˌstɑːt/ *v.* to provide an impetus to start 启动

e.g. lower interest rates to kick-start the economy
They need to kick-start the website as soon as possible.

leotard /ˈliːəʊtɑːd/ *n.* a close-fitting one-piece garment 紧身连衣裤

lump /lʌmp/ *n.* a compact mass of a substance 块；隆起

e.g. lumps from mosquito bites
There was a lump of ice floating in the milk.

bulge /bʌldʒ/ *n.* a rounded swelling which distorts an otherwise flat surface 膨胀；突起

complete with having particular equipment or features 备有，具有

e.g. The house comes complete with swimming pool and sauna.

patent /ˈpeɪtənt/ *v.* to obtain a special document giving you the right to make or sell a new invention or product 得到专利权

e.g. The company has patented many new inventions.
An invention is not your own until it is patented.

prototype /ˈprəʊtəʊtaɪp/ *n.* a first or preliminary version of sth. from which other forms are developed 原型；样本

e.g. the prototype of a character
The firm is testing a prototype of the weapon.

potential /pəʊˈtenʃəl/ *a.* having or showing the capacity to develop into sth. in the future 潜在的；可能的

e.g. a campaign to woo potential customers
the potential uses of nuclear energy

double-check /ˈdʌblˈtʃek/ *v.* to check for a second time to ensure that it is accurate or safe 复核

e.g. double-check a report
You need to double-check the safety apparatus.

sceptical /ˈskeptɪkəl/ *a.* not easily convinced; having doubts or reservations 怀疑的

e.g. The public were deeply sceptical about some of the proposals.
He listened to me with a sceptical expression.

entrust /ɪnˈtrʌst/ *v.* to put sth. into sb.'s care or protection 委托

e.g. Many parents entrust their children to babysitters.
I entrusted her with the duty of locking up.

established /ɪˈstæblɪʃt/ *a.* generally accepted 确立的；公认的

e.g. He was well established as a painter.
The ceremony was an established event in the annual calendar.

delighted /dɪˈlaɪtɪd/ *a.* feeling or showing great pleasure 高兴的

e.g. a delighted smile
We were delighted to see her.

returns /rɪˈtɜːnz/ *n.* (pl.) goods returned to a shop due to various reasons [复]退货

e.g. The bookstores would not accept returns, even ones in good condition.
She began working on her sales samples, sorting out broken packages and returns.

profitable /ˈprɒfɪtəbl/ *a.* (of a business) yielding profit or financial gain 有赢利的

e.g. a profitable business

It's more profitable to import flour.

personalization /ˌpɜːsənəlaɪˈzeɪʃən/ *n.* the process of meeting sb.'s individual requirements 个人化；个性化
e.g. The main advantage of our store is personalization.

be committed to to promise a certain course of action 承担义务；承诺
e.g. The government has been committed to improving health education.
The director has been asked to state the company's position, but so far he has not been committed to this issue.

correspond to to match or agree most exactly 相符合；成一致
e.g. The numbers correspond to the points on the map.

eclectic /ɪˈklektɪk/ *a.* deriving ideas, style, or taste from a broad and diverse range of sources (兴趣爱好等)不拘一格的；兼收并蓄的
e.g. Universities offer an eclectic mix of courses.
The goods in our antique shop are eclectic.

come clean to be completely honest; to keep nothing hidden 和盘托出；说实话
e.g. We'd better come clean now.
Congressmen in the banking scandal decided to come clean before the electorate.

turn out to happen to be 结果(是)
e.g. It has turned out nice and sunny again.
The party turned out a success.

complicated /ˈkɒmplɪkeɪtɪd/ *a.* consisting of many interconnecting parts or elements 复杂的
e.g. It is a really complicated issue.
Don't make easy things complicated.

salsa /ˈsɑːlsə/ *n.* a dance performed to a type of Latin American music incorporating elements of jazz and rock 萨尔萨舞

mentor /ˈmentɔː/ *v.* to advise or train 指导
e.g. The old professor mentors his graduate students once a week.
It is very lucky to get mentored by this renowned director.

budding /ˈbʌdɪŋ/ *a.* (of a person) beginning and showing signs of promise in a particular sphere 崭露头角的
e.g. budding young actors
a budding diplomat

otherwise /ˈʌðəwaɪz/ *conj.* or else 否则的话
e.g. I'm not motivated by money, otherwise I would have quit.
Go home, otherwise your mother will worry about you.

whip /hwɪp/ *v.* to take out fast or suddenly 突然拿出
e.g. He whipped out his revolver and shot him.

Language Study

eternal *a.* without stop 无休止的
e.g. eternal arguments
When will we have an end to this eternal noise?

launch

v.

1. to set (a boat) in motion by pushing it or allowing it to roll into the water 使(船)下水
e.g. The town's lifeboat was launched to rescue the fishermen.
The ship was launched in 1843 by Prince Albert.

2. to send (a missile, satellite, or spacecraft) on its course 发射
e.g. launch a satellite
They launched two Scud missiles.

n. an act or instance of launching sth. 发射；发起
e.g. the launch of a new campaign against drinking and driving
the launch of a space vehicle

potential *n.*
1. latent qualities or abilities that may be developed and lead to future success or usefulness 潜力
   - e.g. a young broadcaster with great potential
     The potentials of the technology were never wholly controllable.
2. possibility 可能性
   - e.g. She recognized the potential for error in the method being used.
     He has got the potential to get defeated.

demand
n.
1. an insistent and immediate request 要求
   - e.g. a series of demands for far-reaching reforms
     She demands a meeting tonight.
2. pressing requirements 强求；索求
   - e.g. demonstrations in support of the nationalists' demands
     He's got enough demands on his time already.

v. to ask authoritatively or abruptly 要求
   - e.g. An outraged public demanded retribution.
     Too much was being demanded of the top players.

prove *v.* (with *oneself*) to demonstrate 表现
   - e.g. He has proved himself untrustworthy.
     He had to prove himself as a man.

return *n.*
1. an act of coming or going back to a place or person 返回
   - e.g. a return flight
     He celebrated his safe return from the war.
2. a profit from an investment 回报；收益
   - e.g. small profits and quick returns
     Companies seek higher returns by investing in other corporations.

but

Usage of *but* but的用法：
conj.
1. however 用作连词，表示转折。
   - e.g. He is old but he looks very healthy.
     Life is limited, but there is no limit to learning.
2. after negative or interrogative word, meaning "that not" 用作连词，放在否定词或疑问词之后，表示"而不"。
   - e.g. No man is so old but he may learn.
     He is not so sick but he can eat.

prep. apart from; except; other than 用作介词，表示"除……之外"，"不同于"。
   - e.g. You can come any day but Sunday.
     Everyone went to the cinema but me.

ad. only, no more than, only just 用作副词，表示"仅仅"，"只是"。
   - e.g. We can but try for once.
     She has seen him but once.

otherwise *ad.*
1. in circumstances different from those present or considered; or else 否则的话；别样
   - e.g. The collection is a good draw that brings visitors who might not come otherwise.
     I think it will rain this afternoon, but my brother thinks otherwise.
2. in other respects; apart from that 在其他方面
   - e.g. an otherwise totally black cat with a single white whisker
     The cement is slightly cracked but otherwise in good order.

3. in a different way 不然

    e.g. an otherwise blameless career
    He reminded me of what I should otherwise have forgotten.

After Reading

READING COMPREHENSION TASKS

1. Complete the following table based on the information in TEXT B.

Why did Wannier want to set up myshape.com?	In her fashion sketching class, she was learning to draw __exact-proportion__ sketches but from one __standard model__. She suddenly understood why some labels __fit__ and some __don't__. She realized then there was a __business__ in helping women quickly find clothes __for their shape__ and that it needed to __be online__.
How did Wannier set up myshape.com?	Wannier sold one of her earlier __businesses__ to get money to __kick-start__ MyShape. Then she asked potential __investors__ to see models of __various shapes and sizes__ in leotards, complete with lumps, bumps, and bulges. They were impressed with __her vision__ and invested enough money to help her develop __a business plan__ while she designed and __patented the technology__.
How should myshape.com make money?	She got a __percentage__ of the price of the __clothes__. In this economy, women are __spending less__. In order to make money, Wannier and her employees have to attract more customers who will __come back again and again__.
What is the future of myshape.com?	She will provide the technology to __other online stores__. Her dream is that their way of shopping becomes the way __everyone does it__.

2. Answer the following questions.

1) How old is Wannier?
   53.

2) What degrees did Wannier have before entering into the garment industry?
   She had a degree in textile design and an MBA.

3) What was the result of Wannier's online survey?
   Within 24 hours, she got over 700 responses; a third of them signed up.

4) What was Wannier's period of "a bit of madness" like?
   She moved into an office and brought in retail specialists. They helped her persuade sceptical designers to entrust their clothes to her newly launched company.

5) Why is it very hard to realize personalization on the Internet?
   Because people are so different, not just in terms of fashion and lifestyle but also in behaviours and tastes.

6) According to Wannier, what is the hardest part of running a business?
   She thinks it is to get people to speak what they think.

7) What is Wannier's favourite feedback from her customers?
   It is an e-mail from a woman in California: "When I tried on the dress, my husband whipped out the camera. It looked that good!"

3. Complete the process of buying clothes on myshape.com.

1) Go online to enter 11 measurements   <u>from arm length to hip width</u> ;
2) Get one of seven body types   <u>based on their proportions</u> ;
3) Select clothes of the particular shape
   by price: <u>as low as $14.49 for a top, up to $605 for a coat</u> ;
   by profile: <u>modern classic, romantic glam, and artistic trendy</u> ;
   by designer: <u>from August Silk to Tadashi</u> ;
   by lifestyle: <u>from work attire to dress-up</u> .

4. Explain the underlined parts in your own words.

1) There are 5,000 designers, and <u>each one designs to his own model</u>. (Para. 1)
   each one designs clothes according to the shape of his own model
2) … who double-checked the results <u>just to be sure</u>. (Para. 6)
   just to make sure everything was correct
3) It convinced us <u>there really was a demand</u>. (Para. 6)
   there were certain customers who wanted our service
4) … to entrust their clothes to <u>a start-up</u> without an established reputation. (Para. 8)
   a newly established company
5) <u>Asked what the future she holds for MyShape</u>, she says … (Para. 11)
   When asked what she thinks the future of MyShape would be like
6) … not just <u>in terms of</u> fashion and lifestyle … (Para. 12)
   with regard to
7) The hardest part of running a business is to get people <u>to speak their minds</u>. (Para. 14)
   to speak what they think
8) It turned out <u>everyone was in agreement</u> … (Para. 14)
   everyone had the same opinion

ORAL WORK

Work in pairs and make an interview with myshape.com. One of the pair should act the role of Wannier and the other the interviewer.

The teacher can ask the students to do the interview in pairs first and then choose a few pairs to present their interviews to the whole class.

TRANSLATION OF TEXT B

一个服装网站的成功奥秘

玛格丽特·赫弗南

1　露易丝·瓦尼尔在一堂时尚素描课上终于解开了一个长久以来的谜团——为什么有的衣服合身而有的不合身。53岁的瓦尼尔回忆说："我们学习的是根据一位标准模特画精确比例的素描。因为女性的身材和体型各异，我问老师我们什么时候学习画其他身材比例的模特。她回答说：'我们不用学。有5000个设计师，每位设计师只根据他自己的一个模特设计服装。'"

2　瓦尼尔突然明白了为什么有些品牌的服装合身而有些不合身，为什么满世界的试衣室里都是失望沮丧的妇女。"我那时突然意识到有一项产业可以帮助妇女快速找到适合体型的服装，而且这项产业必须上网。"

3　瓦尼尔说："我喜欢拥有自己的免费导购员。"

4　曾成功创办了两家技术公司的瓦尼尔冲回家开始这个新创意。两年之后的2006年10月，她注册了myshape.com（我的形象）网站。顾客在网上填写尺寸（共有臂长、臀围等11项）后会根据比例得到七种体型中的一种。软件随后根据所选价格（最低14.49美元的上装，最高605美元的外套）、形象（现代简约型，浪漫魅力型或艺术时髦型）、设计师（从奥古斯特·斯尔克到塔达希）和生活方式（从职业装到礼服）来确定适合该体型的服装。

5　瓦尼尔拥有纺织品设计文凭和工商管理硕士文凭，但她仍需要学习服装业的很多东西。她出售了一家公司，用这笔钱启动了"我的形象"网站，但仍需要更多的投资商。大多数可能投资的人是男性，但他们不理解她的理念——直到他们亲眼看见穿着紧身衣的不同体型和身材的模特实际上是在身上垫了各种衬垫。他们为瓦尼尔的眼光所打动，纷纷投资，凑齐了3200万美元，帮助她做了企划，她同时完成了技术设计和专利注册。

6　瓦尼尔一旦有了原型，就在网上做民意调查，搜索潜在客户。在24小时内，她得到了700多条反馈，其中三分之一注册成了客户。瓦尼尔复核了结果才敢确认这一信息。她回忆说："我们都惊呆了。这说明确实有市场需求。"

7　瓦尼尔有了一个电子商务网站，但她仍需要在网站上销售的商品。

8　她不能再在家中厨房里上网办公了，她找了间办公室，聘来一些零售专家，让他们说服疑心重重的设计师把他们的服装委托给一家毫无声誉的新公司销售。她把那段日子称为"疯狂期"。

9　今天，网站拥有70万客户和300名设计师，充分证明了它的成功。瓦尼尔说："有几个星期我们的客户满意率是100%。设计师也很高兴，因为他们有了新的销售渠道、客户的完全信赖和低于其他网站10%的退货率。"

10　虽然"我的形象"网站继续注册新客户和设计师，公司却还未赢利。瓦尼尔说："我们可以按服装价格的比例获得回报。在当今经济不景气的情况下，妇女花在服装上的钱越来越少。因此，为了挣到钱，我们必须吸引更多的回头客。"

11　当被问及"我的形象"网站的未来时，瓦尼尔说："明年我们准备向其他网络商店提供这一技术，我的梦想就是让我们的购物方式成为大家都乐于接受的形式。"

12　瓦尼尔的最大挑战是什么？她认为她想推行的是"自我"经济。想在因特网上满足个性化需求非常难，因为个体是千差万别的，不仅时尚理念和生活方式大不一样，在行为举止、品位喜好方面也是如此。她说："我们必须尽力倾听客户的需要，也必须找出为什么有人还不是我们客户的原因。"

13　瓦尼尔的形象和风格是什么样的？七种形象对应"我的形象"网站名称的七个字母。瓦尼尔认为她的形象是字母A，臀部大、肩膀窄。"我兼收并蓄，除了传统什么都喜欢。"瓦尼尔如是说。

14　经营企业最难的是让所有人畅所欲言。有一次她在以前的公司里开发一款软件产品，她知道有些地方不对劲。她听到员工私下里议论这件事，所以把他们都召集起来，坚持让他们当面说清楚。结果是每个人的想法一致：那款产品太复杂，特征太多。他们一周后就做了调整。

15　在业余时间，瓦尼尔喜欢安安静静地进行设计。她喜欢和丈夫（他可是个顶呱呱的厨师！）和21岁至27岁的四个孩子相处。她喜欢摄影，与朋友一起放松休闲，跳萨尔萨舞和民间舞。她也喜欢和崭露头角的创业者碰面，为他们指点迷津。

16　当被问及大多数新兴公司倒闭的原因时，她说："因为机会太多，很难把精力集中在原先的任务上。我在自己的每家公司新创业时都经历过此类挣扎。一开始我都会有个五至十年的全盘计划。后来我发现可能性众多，就想在几年内把它们都完成。但那是不可能的。所以我学会了一定要把注意力集中在让企业赢利上。否则就是在做慈善，不是在做生意。"

17　瓦尼尔一直倾听客户的反馈。她最喜欢的一封电子邮件来自加利福尼亚州的一位妇女，内容如下："我试穿衣服的时候，我的丈夫赶紧拿出了照相机。衣服看起来太美了！"

INTEGRATED EXERCISES

1 PUBLIC SPEECH TRAINING

The following is part of a speech about Yoga. In this part the speaker informs the audience of what she will talk about later. Listen and then practice after the recording.

(The speech will be read twice. For the first time, the students just listen and try to understand the meaning. When it is read for the second time, there are pauses in the recording. Ask the students to practice after the speaker during these pauses and pay attention to the speaker's intonation, voice [e.g. loudness, pitch, tempo] etc.)

Script

What do you think of when I do this? / If you said yoga, you are absolutely correct. / For five thousand years people have been practicing yoga / in order to enhance their mental, physical, and emotional health. / Yoga comes from the Sanskrit word meaning "to unite" or "to join". / And as Stella Weller says in her book, / *Finding Balance and Serenity in Everyday Life*, / "Yoga is the practice of uniting one's mind, body and spirit." / I've been practicing yoga for over eight years / and I'm in the process of getting my certification to become a yoga instructor. / And although there are many dimensions of yoga, / today I'm going to focus on two: / yoga breathing and yoga postures. / And along the way I'm going to share with you some of the health benefits / that come along with these simple yoga practices.

2 DICTATION

Listen to the following passage and write it down. The passage will be read four times. During the first reading, which will be done at normal speed, listen and try to understand the meaning. For the second and third readings, the passage will be read sentence by sentence, or phrase by phrase, with intervals of 15 seconds. Write down what you hear. The last reading will be done at normal speed again and during this time you should check your work.

Script

The phrase "job fair" doesn't exactly describe the events that bring together recruiters and job seekers, / or even your chances of getting a job offer at this venue. / Today, fewer companies send fewer recruiters to these meet-and-greet gatherings, / which are drawing larger numbers of applicants. / Still, if you're looking for an entry-level position, / a mid-level career change, or a job in a specific geographic area, / a job fair may come under the "leave-no-stone-unturned strategy". / The following tips are offered by the general manager of a job fair. / First, preregister online to avoid the lines, / and research the companies you want to approach. / Second, dress as though you're going on a job interview. / You are, actually. / Third, take multiple copies of your résumé. / Fourth, arrive early to get the complete list of jobs that recruiters are offering that day. / And finally, network with everyone, not just recruiters. / Follow these tips and good luck.

3 VOCABULARY STUDY

Task One
Put the proper form of the words in the corresponding blanks.

1) Membership of the club is available at an annual __subscription__ of 1800 yuan a year. (subscribe)
2) She has been a remarkably steadfast, __persevering__, and dutiful woman. (perseverance)
3) We provide a reasonable __discount__ for regular customers. (discount)
4) Upon __graduation__ he took a commission in the Marine Corps. (graduate)
5) She is known for her __accomplishment__ in improving the country's public welfare. (accomplish)
6) As usual, he put on one of his __fashionable__ clothes. (fashion)
7) I spent a __profitable__ afternoon in the museum. (profit)
8) The __mysterious__ smile of Mona Lisa has attracted many visitors. (mystery)
9) Children put their __trust__ in their parents. (entrust)
10) Let's not __personalize__ this argument. (personalization)

Task Two

Replace the underlined words with the correct form of the words in the box. You may need to make other changes.

1) The plot of the book is __incredible__.
2) She has got __limitless__ patience to her students.
3) Campaign workers were busy __soliciting__ votes.
4) I am convinced of your __loyalty__ to the cause.
5) They seemed __proud__ of what they have accomplished.
6) If you have any __proof__ of that aggregation, you'd better make it known.
7) Your haircut to this __length__ will look very nice.
8) The current situation is very __frustrating__ for us.
9) This picture was painted by a famous __artist__ in the 1960's.
10) Last year, she travelled abroad in search of __romance__.

Task Three

Choose the best answers from the options given.

1) The strikers began to _____ hotly with members of management.
   A. dispute   B. discuss   C. disagree   D. disrupt
2) The lady cried loudly after her boyfriend slammed his door _____ her face.
   A. on   B. at   C. to   **D. in**
3) It is very difficult for anyone not to stand _____ this kind of injustice.
   A. to   B. off   **C. up to**   D. for
4) He tried his best in the competition and his efforts finally paid _____.
   A. off   B. of   C. to   D. on
5) They had a wonderful time at the picnic _____ beautiful weather.
   A. because of   **B. thanks to**   C. owing to   D. due to
6) The apartment they are living in is the only _____ they can offer to apply for the loan.
   A. property   **B. collateral**   C. means   D. collection
7) For the Nordic ancestors, hell was the land of _____ cold.
   A. evasive   B. ethnic   C. external   **D. eternal**
8) Within only one month, the newly established website has successfully signed _____ more than 10,000 clients.
   A. in   B. out   **C. up**   D. to

9) In order to collect information, he managed to let his employees _____ at every meeting.
   A. talk
   B. **speak their minds**
   C. reveal their feelings
   D. keep silence

10) We must hurry up. _____ we will miss the beginning of the film.
    A. Otherwise   B. However   C. Moreover   D. Nonetheless

Task Four
Fill in the following blanks with appropriate words from the box.

Lawrence Bossidy, the former chairman and chief 1) __executive__ of Allied Signal, suggests a new way of doing performance appraisals. He wrote that the 2) __typical__ appraisal form is often three pages long and filled with the "vaguest, most 3) __uncommunicative__ language imaginable." "People write and write and write — and say nothing." Appraisals, he says, should be on a form that takes up less than half a page, and 4) __covers__ three topics only: What the boss likes about your 5) __performance__, what you can 6) __improve__ and how you and your boss are going to make sure that improvement 7) __happens__. Mr. Bossidy doesn't think the 8) __descriptions__ that fill up the three categories need a lot of words, but they do require 9) __detailed__ information. For example, under "what the boss likes", a manager might write that you are 10) __ambitious__, a team player, you 11) __volunteer__ to lead 12) __initiatives__. And he would be as brief, but 13) __specific__, in the "what can improve" category. "It might include phrases about you such as: '14) __inconsistent__ communicator; impetuous; often fail to 15) __anticipate__ and vague in appraising performance of others.' " The 16) __crucial__ thing is what you do with your 17) __evaluation__. In the comment section, Mr. Bossidy said he might write something like: "Joe, it's great to have you and your 18) __talents__, but we need to decide how to 19) __progress__ on your development. Let's meet on Tuesday, after you've had a chance to consider an 20) __action__ plan."

4 GRAMMAR FOCUS

Read the following passage, underline the one mistake in each line and write the correction after the bracketed number.

The system of arranging marriage in India was well established	1) arranged
during the Vedic Period and has been closely adhered by the vast	2) adhered to
majority of the population of that period. Marriage is seen as an	3) since
indispensable event in the life of a Hindu and the married person	4) unmarried
is viewed as ineligible at participation in certain social and	5) for
religious activity. The practice of arranged marriage cuts across	6) activities
all caste lines, regional boundaries and language barriers of India.	7) in
Marriage is treated as an alliance between two families and two	8) rather than
individuals. In the common joint family arrangement when several	9) where
generations are living separately, the prospective bride is evaluated	10) together
by her suitability as part of the entire family environment rather than	11) on
only as a wife to her husband. Love is viewed as an important element	12) is not
in mate selection. Or is courtship thought to be necessary for testing	13) Nor
the relationship. So romantic love is regarded as an explosive emotion	14) In fact
which interferes the use of reason and logic in decision making.	15) interferes with

1) 分词错误:"父母安排的婚姻"应该用过去分词表示被动态,下文也出现了该词组,可以参照。
2) 动词词组错误:"遵守"应该是adhere to。
3) 前后照应错误:前文用现在完成时,此处应该用since。
4) 语篇意思错误:前文提到婚姻很重要,下文提到不能参加社会活动,此处应该指未结婚人士。
5) 介词错误:ineligible后面应该用for。
6) 单复数错误:前文提到social和religious两个方面,应该使用复数形式。
7) 介词错误:应该用表示范围的in。
8) 衔接错误:此处表示转折。
9) 衔接错误:此处表示处于某种情况。
10) 语篇意思错误:前文提到大家庭,此处应该是一起生活。
11) 介词错误:应该用表示"就……而言"的on。
12) 语篇意思错误:纵观全文,在印度,婚姻应该遵循父母的安排,与爱情无关。
13) 衔接错误:"也不是"应该用nor。
14) 衔接错误:上文指出爱情并不是选择伴侣的重要因素,与下文不是因果关系。下文用in fact表达递进意思。
15) 动词词组错误:"干扰"应该是interfere with。

5 TRANSLATION

Task One

Translate the following paragraph from English into Chinese.

大公司和小公司有两个基本的差别。在小公司,你通过与个人交往就能工作。在大公司,你必须遵循已有的"政策"、组织"程序"和相当严格的步骤。另外,在小公司,你会在很小的一个领域快速取得成果。只要你稍稍升到底层之上,就能立即看到自己的工作和所做决定的效果。在大公司,即使位于顶层的人也只是大机器的一个齿轮。诚然,他的行为比起小公司里人的行为和决定,其影响的领域要大得多,但他的效果是遥远的,间接的,而且很难第一眼就发现。在小公司,哪怕是中等公司,你可以经历各种事,而且别人希望你在没什么帮助或指导的情况下做很多事。你是否会因为是一家著名大机构的一员而深深满足?抑或认为在你自己的小池塘里成为知名的重要人物更为重要?这两种满足感是根本不同的:一种来源于成为大型、强势和知名机构的一员,另一种来源于成为家庭的一员;一种是没有人情味的辉煌,另一种是人际间的亲密;一种是摩天大楼顶层一间小办公室里的生活,另一种是十字路口加油站的生活。

Task Two

Translate the following paragraph from Chinese into English.

An old Chinese saying goes: "Men are afraid of getting a wrong job and women are afraid of marrying a wrong person." The first job usually determines the profession you will be working in. A person usually finds the first job when he/she is not well-off, which means he/she cannot easily abandon it. You will value this job a lot, put great energy and time into it and therefore gain knowledge and experience. All this weighs in favour of your future change of jobs. So normally you will lead your way further in this profession. Your first job usually determines your course of career. It is very difficult to change a profession in the midway. The difficulty of starting a new profession all over again is just like starting a new life upon senility.

6 CLASSROOM INTERACTION

Activity A   Listening

1) Walking that line between promoting yourself and being untruthful.

2) If you haven't earned a degree, disclose how far you've gotten. For example, "completed 50% of requirements for Bachelor of Science in Business Administration" or "Bachelor of Arts Candidate, anticipate completion in 2019."
3) If you've never held a leadership position, state the activities and achievements that convey leadership skills and experience.
4) You may just leave that detail out. But be prepared to discuss it during an interview if asked.

Script

The art of résumé writing does allow you to push skills to the limit of an imaginary line, says Wendy S. Enelow, an executive career consultant. "It's about merchandising and selling a product. You do want to highlight the benefits and value of that product, but only within the realm of reality."

The hard part, of course, is to avoid crossing that line. Walking that line between promoting yourself and being untruthful can be difficult. Here are some ways to do so.

- If you haven't earned a degree, disclose how far you've gotten. For example, "completed 50% of requirements for Bachelor of Science in Business Administration" or "Bachelor of Arts Candidate, anticipate completion in 2019."
- If you were fired from your last job, leave that detail out. But be prepared to discuss it during an interview if asked.
- If you've never held a leadership position, state the activities and achievements that convey leadership skills and experience.
- If you're looking for a salary boost, don't state salary requirements or inflate your most recent salary.

Also a no-no: stating that you were part of a mass downsizing when you were actually fired. But do leave off the reason for leaving a previous job.

If you're asked or it looks like a job offer is imminent, you have to be honest, since more companies are doing reference and background checks.

You should be upfront and briefly explain why you parted on negative terms with a former employer. Don't blame anyone but yourself, and end your story about your situation with what you have learned.

Activity B   Debate

The teacher can let the students fill in the following table of opinions before asking them to carry out the debate.

Pro Side	Con Side

Activity C   Mini-speech

The teacher can give the students ten minutes to prepare and then choose a few students to give mini-speeches to the whole class.

WRITING

Writing Skills: Essay Quality Criteria

This unit discusses the quality criteria of essays. These criteria aim to help the students learn how to evaluate their writing systematically. Since the teacher usually applies the same set of criteria to both paragraphs and essays, he/she can start with a review of the quality criteria of paragraphs. That is why the Student's Book asks the students to briefly write down the meaning of unity, coherence and cohesion. The following is a reference to the definition exercise.

Unity: <u>The paragraph deals with one, and only one, central idea.</u>
Coherence: <u>Ideas in the paragraph are organized in a logical order.</u>
Cohesion: <u>Proper connective phrases are used to connect different ideas in the paragraph.</u>

Of course, the teacher needs to know that a list of three criteria is far from complete. If possible, the teacher can ask the students to brainstorm for other possible criteria. Suggestions may include information sufficiency, language accuracy, and language fluency.

The essay about hiring cleaners is used for practice. Some comments on the essay are offered in the Student's Book. The teacher can first ask the students to read and discuss the essay in terms of unity, coherence and cohesion. In addition, the teacher can ask the students to underline important sentences and phrases to better understand the essay. Here are some of the important places.

Should University Students Hire Cleaners?

Now it is common to see spoiled children in colleges. They do not know how to buy daily necessities, how to wash their clothes, and some of them even try to hire cleaners to clean their dorms. <u>In my opinion, hiring cleaners is a very unwise decision.</u>

<u>To begin with,</u> <u>hiring cleaners may deprive us possible opportunities to improve our health.</u> Cleaning our dorms is not only a daily chore, but also a kind of physical exercise. It can help us stretch our body, build up strength and energy, which will in turn contribute to our academic study. According to a recent research, 14.7% students are physically weak due to lack of physical exercise. Among many possible ways, cleaning dorms is a very convenient one to keep ourselves healthy.

<u>Moreover,</u> <u>hiring cleaners may increase our parents' financial pressure.</u> As we do not work to earn money, the expense on cleaners may have to come to our parents. Our tuition, which is rather high, has already been a very heavy burden. Many parents have to spend less on themselves in order to cover our tuition and daily expenses, so how can we ask them to save more to pay for something that we should and are able to do by ourselves?

<u>In a word,</u> <u>considering the influence on ourselves and on our parents, we college students should not hire cleaners.</u> By doing the cleaning ourselves, we can enjoy not only better health but also a happier family.

If possible, the teacher can ask the students to go back to Unit One and evaluate the quality of the essays there. This may provide more practice and, as a result, enhance their understanding of the three concepts.

Writing Assignment

1. How can you tell a good essay? Besides the three criteria, what other aspects can you think of?

According to this unit, we have to pay attention to content, structure and connective devices. There should not be irrelevant information, no matter how interesting it may seem. The ideas in the essay should be logically arranged, especially following the three-part requirement. There should also be suitable words and phrases to join ideas so that the article can move smoothly.

Besides these three points, there may be some other aspects that deserve attention. For example, the sufficiency of supporting evidence, and the clarity, accuracy and appropriacy of the language.

2. The following essay is supposed to explain the writer's reasons for coming to study in the US. Study it carefully and evaluate it according to the quality criteria for essays.

The biggest problem in this essay is that it lacks unity. According to the title, the writer should mainly explain the reasons for coming to study in the US rather than staying in China, but he does not provide much information in this aspect. The first reason he gives is to study English, but instead of explaining why he can study English better in the US, he mainly lists the necessity of learning English. He merely provides one reason to support his point of view, which is not only awkward but also far from enough. The third point explains how he responds to homesickness, and is totally unrelated to the topic.

But it seems that the writer has learned something about coherence and cohesion. He has made efforts to divide his work into three parts, and uses connective phrases to indicate the thesis statement, the main supporting points and the conclusion. Unfortunately, these merits in form are not backed up by the content, so the whole essay is still a failure.

3. Write an essay on the following topic. Pay attention to its unity, coherence and cohesion.

Answers may vary.

3 MOTIVATION AND PASSION

TEXT A Why Passion Matters

Before Reading

The purpose of this section is to arouse the students' interest in the theme of the unit, reactivate their relevant background knowledge or elicit their opinions on the related topics, so as to better prepare them for the succeeding tasks.

Before Reading activities can be organized as group work so that the students share with each other their thoughts about happiness, dreams and success.

Background Information

1 Where Do You Shine?

People may have different ideas about happiness and success. Some think money is the key while others think health or sense of achievement in their career is the key. On our way to success, what is the most important thing for us to do? Should we yield to our own limitations or should we dream big dreams instead?

Money is not the key to happiness. More "stuff" is not the key to happiness. Winning the lottery and spending the rest of your life on a tropical island — while intoxicating to the ear — is not the key to happiness. Through his work at the University of Pennsylvania, Dr. Seligman has discovered that happiness is tied tightly to your strengths — the things you're good at. People have been proven to be happiest when applying their unique skills toward a challenging project or goal. You don't need millions of dollars or a personal island to be happy. All that you need is already within you. Discover your strengths, apply them to a challenging goal, and you'll see for yourself.

2 Living Without Limits

The starting point of great success and achievement has always been the same. It is for you to dream big dreams. There is nothing more important, and nothing that works faster than for you to cast off your own limitations, than for you to begin dreaming and fantasizing about the wonderful things that you can become, have, and do. As a wise man once said, "You must dream big dreams, for only big dreams have the power to move the minds of men." When you begin to dream big dreams, your levels of self-esteem and self-confidence will go up immediately. You will feel more powerful about yourself. The reason so many people accomplish so little is that they never allow themselves to lean back and imagine the kind of life that is possible for them.

Whatever you have learned, you can unlearn. Whatever situation you have gotten yourself into, you can probably get yourself out of. If your real goal is to dream big dreams and to live without limits, you can set this as your standard and compare everything that you do against it.

The three keys to living without limits have always been the same. They are clarity, competence, and concentration.

Clarity means that you are absolutely clear about who you are, what you want, and where you're going. Competence means that you begin to become very, very good in the key result areas of your chosen field. Concentration is having the self-discipline to force yourself to concentrate single-mindedly on one thing, the most important thing, and stay with it until it's complete.

Reading

Text Analysis

- ### Text Summary

Through a series of examples and experiences in her real life, the author tells the readers that passion matters and enthusiasm can lead everywhere. As a parent, she tried to steer her five children (Rob, Dan, Marty, Francie and Mia) towards their strengths with encouragement rather than squelch their passions and aptitudes, just as her own mother encouraged her Plan A from the get-go. Grab Plan A — that's the advice she offers to the readers.

- ### Text Organization

Paragraphs 1-10: introduction	The author encourages her children to pursue their dreams instead of asking them to study "safe" things that barely hold their interest.
Paragraphs 11-22: main body	The author makes the claim that "fear leads nowhere; enthusiasm can lead everywhere". She further claims that wise parents are honest and maintain a supportive relationship with their children. Even though she doesn't know if her children will suffer more for dreaming big, she'd rather they plunge in than hang back. By sharing her own experiences, she makes the opinion very convincing.
Paragraph 23: conclusion	She advises the readers to always grab Plan A.

- ### Text Features

This text is in the first person. However, this is not strictly a narrative because there is not a clear storyline. It is more of a piece of free writing targeted at the general public. The author uses simple, vivid language in anecdotes and dialogues, while for analysis and comment she uses complex sentences that involve emphatic structures (强调句型) and parallel construction (并列结构). In the anecdotes, the author alternatively uses past tense, past perfect tense (see Item 5 in Key Sentences) and present tense, depending on the time the event takes place.

- **Key Sentences**

1. Not long ago, someone asked the dad of a young pop star what his son would have done if he hadn't become a singer-songwriter. (Para. 5)

This sentence uses subjunctive mood *what his son would have done if he hadn't become a singer-songwriter* to indicate a situation that is not real. Subjunctive mood is a verb mood typically used in subordinate clauses to express various states of irreality such as wish, emotion, possibility, judgment, opinion, necessity, or action that has not yet occurred. A verb is in the subjunctive mood when it expresses a condition which is doubtful or not factual. It is often found in a clause beginning with the word *if*. It is also found in clauses following a verb that expresses doubt, wish, regret, request, demand, or proposal. These are verbs typically followed by clauses that take the subjunctive: *ask, demand, determine, insist, move, order, pray, prefer, recommend, regret, request, require, suggest,* and *wish*. For example:

    A: I wish it were still in use.

    B: The board recommended that the motion be passed immediately.

    C: I would have helped him out if he hadn't been so lazy.

2. It is the bold, not the meek, who vault higher during hard times. (Para. 12)

This is one type of emphatic structure in English. We use this structure (It is/was…that/who…) to emphasize certain part of a sentence, such as the subject, the object, an adverbial or a prepositional phrase. For example:

    A: It was only after I stepped on stage that I saw him.

    B: It isn't just his sense of humor that I was complaining about.

3. Fear leads nowhere; enthusiasm can lead everywhere. (Para. 12)

A semicolon is used to designate a pause in a sentence, stronger than a comma, but weaker than a period. The two parts of the sentence separated by the semicolon must be closely related. There are three principal uses for a semicolon: 1. to separate items in a list where the items are lengthy or include commas; 2. to fix a run-on sentence by converting it to a sentence with parallel structures; 3. to separate main clauses joined by a conjunctive adverb (conjunctive adverbs include *however, nevertheless, moreover, therefore, consequently, hence, indeed, likewise, furthermore, namely, still* and *then*). For example:

    A: My heroes are Batman, who combines brains and brawn; Captain Picard, who commands respect; and Wiley Coyote, who never gives up.

4. They watch their children grow and steer them toward their strengths with encouragement rather than force. (Para. 14)

I'd rather my children plunge in than hang back. (Para. 20)

Rather than is normally used in parallel structures, for example with two adjectives, adverbs, nouns, infinitives or -ing forms. When the main clause has a to-infinitive, *rather than* is normally followed by an infinitive without *to*.

    A: Rather than sit silent when you don't understand your teacher, always ask for clarification.

    B: You ought to admit your crime rather than defend it.

    C: I would prefer to go in August rather than in July.

Rather than is different from *would rather*. The latter means "would prefer to". It is followed by an infinitive without *to*. For example:

A: *Would* you *rather* stay here or go home? (Would you prefer to stay here or go home?)

We can also use *would rather* to say that one person would prefer others to do something. We use a special structure with a past tense. For example:

A: Don't come today, I would rather you came tomorrow. (I would prefer you to come tomorrow.)

B: I would rather you posted this letter. (I would like you to post this letter.)

C: I would rather you hadn't done that. (I wish you hadn't done that.)

5. With three little boys to raise, I wrote out my grief long into the night until I had a 386-page novel, *The Deep End of the Ocean*, which launched me into the career I had always dreamed of. (Para. 22)

The use of past perfect tense indicates the chronological order of actions in the sentence. Here, the action *had always dreamed of* takes place before another past action *launched me into the career*. Past perfect tense can also show that something happened before a specific time in the past. For example:

A: Suddenly he remembered where he had hidden the money.

B: Had Susan ever studied Thai before she moved to Thailand?

New Words and Expressions

bespectacled /bɪˈspektəkld/ *a.* (*formal*) wearing spectacles 戴眼镜的
e.g. I saw a small, bespectacled man in a suit standing beside the chairman just now.
At the ceremony, a bespectacled professor gave us a wonderful talk.

hit the bull's eye to be exactly right about sth., to achieve the best result possible 命中靶心；达到最佳目标；取得成功
e.g. He hit the bull's eye as he promised.
Do you think John will hit the bull's eye this time?

ponder /ˈpɒndə/ *v.* to think about sth. carefully for a period of time 沉思，考虑，琢磨
e.g. She pondered over the teacher's words after class.
They spent a long time pondering this vexing problem.

on one's account because of what you think sb. wants 为了某人的缘故
e.g. Please don't change your plans on my account.
You should do things on your own account.

fallback /ˈfɔːlbæk/ *n.* a plan or course of action that is ready to be used in an emergency if other things fail 应变计划，退路

e.g. What's our fallback if they don't come up with the money?
We need a fallback if they refuse to do the job.

set sb. up to put sb. in a position in which sth. is likely to happen to them 使陷于某种境地
e.g. This decision set themselves up for attack.

rejection /rɪˈdʒekʃən/ *n.* refusal to accept or consider sth. 拒绝接受，不予考虑
e.g. I understand how you feel when you receive a rejection letter.
His proposal met with unanimous rejection at the meeting.

masses of a large number or amount of 大量
e.g. There were masses of people in town today.
I've got masses of things to do at the weekend.

tricky /ˈtrɪkɪ/ *a.* difficult to do or deal with 难办的，难对付的
e.g. a tricky situation
a tricky business

culinary /ˈkʌlɪnərɪ/ *a.* connected with cooking or food 烹饪的；食物的
e.g. He is famous for his culinary skills in the neighbourhood.

Savor the culinary delights of Mexico food.

flagrantly /ˈfleɪɡrəntlɪ/ *ad.* (of an action) shockingly because it is done in a very obvious and offensive way 骇人听闻地，罪恶昭彰地

e.g. You have flagrantly violated our rights.

He is flagrantly disregarding the law.

impractical /ɪmˈpræktɪkəl/ *a.* not sensible or realistic 不明智的；不现实的

e.g. You should stop making impractical plans.

It was totally impractical for me to complete this task within three days.

next to following in order or importance after sb./sth. 仅次于，紧接着

e.g. I'd say cheese is my favorite food and next to that, chocolate.

I like skating next to playing golf.

haiku /ˈhaɪkuː/ *n.* (from Japanese) a poem with three lines and usually 17 syllables, written in a style that is traditional in Japan 俳句（日本传统诗体，三行为一首，通常有17个音节）

e.g. He has written many beautiful haikus.

I am learning to appreciate the beauty of haiku.

try out for to compete for a position or place in sth., or to be a member of a team 参加……选拔（或试演）

e.g. Jason wanted to try out for the college football team.

This is a position worth trying out for.

shortage /ˈʃɔːtɪdʒ/ *n.* a situation when there is not enough of the people or things that are needed 不足，缺乏，短缺

e.g. There's a shortage of food and shelter in the refugee camps.

The long hot summer has led to a shortage of water.

forklift /ˈfɔːklɪft/ *n.* a vehicle with special equipment on the front for moving and lifting heavy objects 叉车，叉式装卸车

e.g. forklift truck

hold on to one's heart's desire to stick to what one has desired 坚持自己的喜好和梦想

e.g. We should all hold on to our desire no matter how difficult it might be.

He is so determined to hold on to his desire in spite of objections.

sophomore /ˈsɒfəmɔː/ *n.* a student in the second year of a course of study at a college or university（大学）二年级学生

e.g. Their son is a sophomore in college.

What subjects are offered in our sophomore year?

meek /miːk/ *a.* quiet, gentle and always ready to do what other people want without expressing your own opinion 温顺的，谦恭的，驯服的

e.g. She may seem meek and mild but it is all fake.

He is a meek child in the family.

vault /vɔːlt/ *v.* to jump over an object in a single movement, using your hands or a pole to push you（用手支撑或撑杆）跳跃，腾跃

e.g. John vaulted the barrier.

The boy vaulted over the fence very easily.

bind oneself to to stick to 坚持

e.g. He always binds himself to his promises.

choreographer /ˌkɒrɪˈɒɡrəfə/ *n.* a person who designs and arranges the steps and movements for dancers in a ballet or a show 为（芭蕾舞或表演）设计舞蹈动作的人，编舞者

e.g. She wanted to be a choreographer when she grew up.

It takes years of training to become a great choreographer.

steer /stɪə/ *v.* to take control of a situation and influence the way in which it develops 控制；引导

e.g. The main task of the new government will be to steer toward democracy.

He managed to steer the conversation toward the topic.

arena /əˈriːnə/ *n.* an area of activity that concerns the public, especially one where there is a lot of opposition between different groups or countries 斗争场所，竞争舞台

e.g. the political arena

the international arena

self-identify /ˌselfaɪˈdentɪfaɪ/ *v.* to see by oneself 自我发现

e.g. It is important to self-identify our own weaknesses.

Parents should leave children to self-identify what they want to learn.

accordingly /əˈkɔːdɪŋlɪ/ *ad.* in a way that is appropriate to what has been done or said in a particular situation 相应地

e.g. The cost of materials rose sharply last year. Accordingly, we were forced to increase our prices.

We have to discover his plans and act accordingly.

doctrinaire /ˌdɒktrɪˈneə/ *a.* strictly following a theory in all circumstances, even if there are practical problems or disagreement 空谈理论的，脱离实际的；教条主义的
 e.g. doctrinaire attitude
 doctrinaire beliefs
instruct /ɪnˈstrʌkt/ *v.* to tell sb. to do sth., especially in a formal or official way 指示；命令，吩咐
 e.g. The police have been instructed to patrol the building and the surrounding area.
 I instructed him to come to work earlier.
squelch /skweltʃ/ *v.* to stop sth. from growing, increasing or developing 压制，限制
 e.g. squelch a rebellion
 His irritated look squelched all the other objections.
dole out to give out shares of sth. 发放，发给
 e.g. The organization has doled out thousands of dollars in grants.
 The agency doles out food to thousands of needy families each year.
reality check an occasion when you are reminded of how things are in the real world, rather than how you would like things to be 提醒人面对现实而不再想当然的事件
 e.g. Her friends gave her a reality check about her boyfriend.
 He was starting to think he was infallible, so the criticism from his boss served as a reality check.
organically /ɔːˈɡænɪkəli/ *ad.* happening in a slow and natural way, rather than suddenly 逐渐地；自然地
 e.g. The organization should be allowed to develop organically.
 Children's cognitive ability will be improved organically as they grow up.
excess /ɪkˈses/ *n.* an amount of sth. that is more than necessary, reasonable or acceptable 超过；过度，过分
 e.g. The tests found an excess of sodium in his blood.
 He showed an excess of enthusiasm in the project.
plunge in to start doing sth. in an enthusiastic way, especially without thinking carefully about what you are doing 热情投入；贸然行动

 e.g. It was a big project, so we all just had to plunge in and get started.
 She plunged right in the assignment.
hang back to be unwilling to do sth. because of nervousness, fear, etc. （由于紧张或恐惧）不愿做某事
 e.g. When there's work to be done, she doesn't hang back.
 We are not supposed to hang back when difficulty arises.
ear-piercing /ˈɪəˌpɪəsɪŋ/ *n.* the practice of making small holes in sb.'s ears so jewelry can be put in them 穿耳洞，扎耳朵眼儿
 e.g. It is a trend to do ear-piercing.
 Kate thinks ear-piercing will make her more beautiful and fashionable.
boutique /buːˈtiːk/ *n.* a small shop/store that sells fashionable clothes or expensive gifts 精品店；礼品店
 e.g. This boutique shop has become a landmark in the city's downtown area.
chandelier /ˌʃændəˈlɪə/ *n.* a large round frame with branches that hold lights or candles 枝形吊灯
 e.g. high-quality chandeliers
 Chandeliers make an elegant lighting effect in any room.
earring /ˈɪərɪŋ/ *n.* a piece of jewelry that you fasten in or on your ear 耳环，耳饰
 e.g. He wears an earring in his left ear.
visionary /ˈvɪʒənəri/ *n.* a person who has the ability to think about or plan the future in a way that is intelligent or shows imagination 有眼力的人；有远见卓识的人
 e.g. She is known as a visionary.
scribble /ˈskrɪbl/ *n.* a piece of writing or a picture produced carelessly or hurriedly 胡写乱画的东西；潦草的作品
 e.g. I hope you can read my scribble!
waitress /ˈweɪtrɪs/ *v.* to work as a waitress, who serves customers at their tables in a restaurant 做女服务员
 e.g. After waitressing in a coffee bar for three years, she opened a small restaurant with some friends.
hone one's craft to develop or improve a skill over a period of time 磨练；训练技艺
 e.g. She hones her craft with perseverance.
weigh one's options to consider a number of

choices carefully before making a decision 认真考虑，权衡，斟酌（所面临的选择）

e.g. He took time to weigh his options.

Do not rush to a decision — you should weigh your options first!

Language Study

vault

n.

a large room used for storage, especially an underground one 储藏室；库

e.g. a bank vault 银行的金库

a wine vault 酒窖

v. to move suddenly and quickly into a better position 跃升

e.g. The team vaulted into the lead.

She vaulted to fame when her first movie was a hit.

The success of the movie vaulted her to fame.

It's the bold, not the meek, who vault higher during hard times.

It is (was) … that (who)… 强调句型的用法：

当需要强调句中的主语、宾语、状语时，我们常用"It is (was)+被强调部分+that (who)"这种句型。

e.g. He read three books in the library yesterday.

我们可以分别强调主语、宾语、地点状语和时间状语：

It was he who (that) read three books in the library yesterday. (强调主语)

It was three books that he read in the library yesterday. (强调宾语)

It was in the library that he read three books yesterday. (强调地点状语)

It was yesterday that he read three books in the library. (强调时间状语)

使用此句型时，应注意以下几点：

1. 当被强调部分指人时，可用that，也可用who；指物时，只用that。

    e.g. It was Tom who (that) I met last week.

    It is a new bike that his brother wants to buy.

2. 强调状语时，只用that，不用when、where。

    e.g. It is at 5 o'clock that the train will arrive.

3. 被强调的部分是主语时，注意句子的谓语动词和被强调的主语保持一致。在强调结构中，无论被强调的是人还是物，单数还是复数，be动词一律用单数形式is/was。如果原句的谓语动词时态是过去范畴，就用was；如果原句的谓语动词时态是现在范畴，就用is。也可以用"情态动词+be"形式。

    e.g. It is he who is late.

    It is they that were late.

    It was yesterday that he arrived here.

    It might be in the morning that he broke into the house.

4. 强调句的疑问句结构为"Is (Was) it … that…?"或"特殊疑问词+is (was) it that…?"。

    e.g. Was it ten years ago that his father died?

    When is it that you will set off?

5. "not…until…"句型的强调句结构为"It is not until … that …"。应注意把否定词not移到until前面。

    e.g. I didn't go home until the rain stopped.

    强调句为：It was not until the rain stopped that I went home.

    I didn't know the news until yesterday.

    强调句为：It was not until yesterday that I knew the news.

6. 如果我们把It is (was) … that (who) … 从句中删去，所剩的仍是一个完整的句子，只是强调意味已经失去。实际上It is (was) … that (who) … 只是一个框架。

    e.g. It is not only blind men who make such stupid mistakes.

    → Not only blind men make such stupid mistakes.

identify
 vt.
 1. to recognize as being; to establish the identity of sb. or sth. 识别；认明
  e.g. She identified the man on the "wanted" poster.
   The woman identified the stolen watch as hers.
   He was identified by his watch.
 2. to give the name or identifying characteristics of; to refer to by name or some other identifying characteristic property 鉴定；确定
  e.g. The almanac identifies the auspicious months.
   His hoarse voice quickly identified him.
 3. to equate sb. or sth. with 认为……等同于
  e.g. People at that time identified beauty with goodness.
 vi. to think of yourself as having the same problems and feelings as sb. 一致；同情
  e.g. Many readers identify with the characters in her novels.
   He could identify with the problems the athlete was having.
be identified with sb. or sth. / identify oneself with sb. or sth. 与……有密切关联；认为……等同于；支持
 e.g. She identified herself with foreign teachers.
  Wealth cannot be identified with happiness.
  She has always been identified with the civil rights movement.

organic *a.*
 1. grown or made without the use of artificial chemicals 有机生长或种植的
  e.g. organic vegetables
   Is this broccoli certified organic?
 2. of, relating to, or obtained from living things 生物体的；有机物的
  e.g. organic materials
   organic fertilizer
 3. forming an important part of sth. 组成重要部分的
  e.g. He thinks of the city not as a collection of different neighborhoods but as an organic whole.
   This neighborhood is an organic part of the city.

scribble *v.* to write down quickly without much attention to detail; to write hastily or carelessly without regard to legibility or form 潦草地书写或涂画；草率地创作
 e.g. The child loves to scribble with a pencil.
  She scribbled a note to him and then dashed off to her meeting.
  He scribbled down his phone number.

instruct *v.*
 1. to impart skills or knowledge to 教育，教授
  e.g. I instructed them French.
   He instructed me in building a boat.
   The scouts were instructed in signaling.
 2. to make aware of 通知
  e.g. The teacher instructed the class to prepare for a test.

bind *v.*
 1. to tie tightly; to fasten 系；捆
  e.g. They bound the packages with brightly coloured ribbon.
   Bind together the two broken ends.
   The prisoner was bound hand and foot.
 2. to unite people 团结
  e.g. The things which bind them together are greater than their differences.
 3. to tie sth. round a part of the body, especially a part which is wounded 包扎
  e.g. He had already bound the child's arm when I arrived.

4. to make separate pieces of paper into a book 装订
   e.g. There are several different ways to bind a book, for example you can stitch or stick the pages together.

After Reading

READING COMPREHENSION TASKS

1. Complete the following table based on the information in TEXT A.

   What are the author's five children's dreams?

Rob	Design computer games that will be played simultaneously by masses of people around the world
Dan	Become a pastry chef
Marty	Major in musical theatre and retain his concentration on this field
Francie	Work in the FBI
Mia	Be a professional cheerleader and open an ear-piercing boutique for dogs

2. Answer the following questions.

   1) What do parents usually advise their children to do?
      They advise their children to choose a fallback plan and to pursue something they think they can get good at even if they don't love it.

   2) Why does the author encourage her kids to choose a risky path?
      Because she thinks fear leads nowhere and enthusiasm can lead everywhere.

   3) What kind of majors did the sophomore kids in the college chorus choose?
      They chose some seemingly safe majors, such as hotel management, nursing, and pharmacy.

   4) According to the author, what kind of people vault higher during hard times?
      The bold, not the meek, vault higher during hard times.

   5) What do wise parents do to their children?
      They watch their children grow and steer them toward their strengths with encouragement.

   6) What did an athletic coach once tell the author about kids?
      Kids will self-identify and no one has to force a driven kid to achieve.

   7) How does the author differ from the man she met on a train?
      The man squelched the aptitudes and passions to which his boys had devoted their childhoods, while the author thinks the world will dole out its own reality checks to her kids.

   8) What is the author forever grateful for?
      She is grateful that her mother encouraged her Plan A from the very beginning.

   9) What kind of jobs did the author do when she was a teenager?
      She waitressed, and wrote stories for 15 cents a word for a weekly newspaper.

   10) What is the author's best advice to her children when they need to weigh their options?
       Risk everything and grab Plan A.

3. In TEXT A, the author makes several suggestions about how to foster passion in children. Please fill in the blanks accordingly.

   1) The wisest parents I know are honest. They watch their children grow and steer them toward their strengths with encouragement rather than force.
   2) Parents can see which hopes have real promise and help their children make decisions accordingly, but only if they've maintained a supportive relationship with them rather than one that's doctrinaire.
   3) But I believe that learning one's limits organically is better than making choices out of an excess of caution. I'd rather my children plunge in than hang back.
   4) Risk everything, Plans B, C, D, and E will always be there. Grab Plan A.

4. Explain the underlined parts in your own words.

   1) … become a pastry chef — the trickiest of all the culinary arts. (Para. 10)
      the most difficult of all the culinary arts
   2) That was where the money was, he told them … (Para. 16)
      That was where you could make money from
   3) … the man had squelched the aptitudes and passions to which his boys had devoted their childhoods. (Para. 19)
      stopped the aptitudes and passions from growing
   4) I don't know if my children will suffer more for dreaming big. (Para. 20)
      suffer more for having big dreams
   5) And Marty may never cross a Broadway stage except to congratulate someone else. (Para. 20)
      be able to stand on a Broadway stage to perform
   6) … which launched me into the career I had always dreamed of. (Para. 22)
      helped me start off the career

ORAL WORK

Work in groups and discuss why passion matters. Put yourself in the shoes of the author and imagine what you would do if your children chose a risky career path.

The teacher can ask the students to form groups to discuss the topic. The students can either work within groups or individually at this stage of preparation. Once they feel ready, the teacher can ask them to present their opinions first within the group, and then to the whole class.

TRANSLATION OF TEXT A

激情为何重要

杰奎琳·米彻德

1　"我改主意了，"我13岁的女儿弗兰西说，"我不想做律师了，我要去联邦调查局。"我试着想象女儿戴着眼镜从昆迪克的攀爬训练墙上回头看我的那张脸，却怎么也想不出。

2　不过，我依旧答道，"这很酷啊！"

3　"当然，"弗兰西满意地抱着胳膊说道，"那一定很棒。"

4 我也希望如此。我希望她的生活能完全按照梦想展开。哪怕生活之箭未能正中靶心，至少她瞄准了正确的方向。

5 不久前，有人问一名青年歌星的父亲，如果他的儿子不做自写自唱的歌手，会干哪行。这位父亲回答说儿子从没考虑过其他情况。做一名歌手是他的第一理想，从没什么后备方案。恰好我修音乐剧专业的儿子马缇正在考虑修商科或教育学作为第二专业，我便把这事告诉了他。

6 "千万别为了我这么做。"我说。

7 "可我要是不成功怎么办？"他问道。

8 "总有人会这样的。"我答道。

9 朋友们认为我疯了。他们都建议自己的孩子选个保底方案，去从事一些哪怕并不热爱却可能擅长的东西——以防万一嘛。他们总提醒我：时势艰难。我这么做会导致孩子们未来的受挫与失败吗？我理解这种担忧，而我的三个大学生年龄的孩子却无一例外地选择了冒险之路。

10 25岁的罗伯希望能设计出全世界大批人都能同时玩的电子游戏。22岁的丹正学习成为糕点师，这偏偏是烹调艺术中最麻烦的。19岁的马缇的职业理想非常不切实际，也就比写俳句好点。有300个学生报名参加他们学院的音乐剧项目，他是被选出的15人之一。（就像他们教授说的，护士、叉车工可能会缺，演员永远不会缺。）而即使在这选出的15人中，也只有马缇始终坚持着他的梦想。学院合唱团几乎所有的大二学生都纷纷定好了专业——酒店管理、医护、制药或是其他看上去更保险的专业，只有马缇坚守着他对舞台的执着。

11 我当然想保护我的孩子。但是这就意味着他们应该浪费黄金年华去学些几乎不感兴趣的东西吗？这真的是在合理利用时间吗？为什么要教他们无视自己的天分？

12 艰难时势下脱颖而出的不是甘于平庸的人，而是敢于挑战的人。畏惧成不了事，充满热情则百事可成。

13 那些执着于他们所钟爱的事业的人总会在某方面以某种形式获得成功。著名的艾格尼斯·德米尔对舞蹈有着强烈的热爱。即使自己不跳舞了，她仍成了那个时代最具创意的编舞者。大卫·札亚斯为养家在纽约城当了15年警察，并同时学习表演，最终成就了荧幕上最著名的警探形象之一：热门电视剧《双面法医》中的警探安吉儿·巴蒂斯塔。

14 在我看来，最明智的家长是诚实的。他们看着孩子成长，从不强求，而是通过鼓励引导孩子发挥潜能。有时这样的家长也会感到既骄傲又担心。不可否认，当我的儿子马缇进入竞争极其激烈的演艺圈时，我不禁担心这究竟是他的梦想还是我的。

15 然而，我仍旧只是看着他成长。我牢记一名伟大的体育教练对我说过的话：孩子有自我认知的能力。谁都不用强迫一个已有想法的孩子去做什么。7岁时球踢得好是一码事，17岁时踢得好又是另一码事。随着孩子渐渐长大，发挥的空间不断拓展，这时父母便能发现孩子真正的天分在哪，并相应地帮助孩子做出选择。但做到这点需要家长始终只是从旁协助，而非教条训诫。

16 一次，在火车上，我遇到了一位父亲，他跟我谈起了他两个儿子的事。他们都继承了他妻子出众的音乐天赋。他说最近他让两个孩子选择商业科技作为大学专业。毕竟这行最能赚钱，他这么告诉他们，音乐只是爱好而已。

17 "你的孩子们多大了？"我问。

18 "一个11，一个12了。"他答道。

19 孩子小小年纪，父亲便已扼制了他们童年的天性与热情。这不是我这个家长会做的事。真实的世界会让我的孩子面对现实。

20 我不知道我的孩子是否会因为他们的远大梦想而比别人吃更多苦。罗伯或许永远设计不出比《光晕》更成功的电子游戏，丹可能永远无法拥有他梦想中的餐馆"那家餐馆"（这么叫是因为人们总说，"走，我们吃去年去过的那家餐馆吧！"），而马缇也可能只有在祝贺他人时才能站上百老汇的舞台。但我仍然相信，碰了壁而明白自己的局限要好过做决定时就小心翼翼地退而求其次。我更希望我的孩子勇往直前，而不是畏首畏尾。

21 前几天晚上，我10岁大的女儿米娅跑来告诉我说她想做个职业拉拉队员。她还想开家给宠物狗打耳洞的精品店。我没说出我心底的想法，只是回答说，"哦？是嘛？"之后，我还真的纳闷，为什么宠物狗就不兴戴副吊坠耳环呢？兴许，我的女儿还真有点眼光！

22 我始终感激我的母亲从一开始就鼓励我坚持第一理想。她表扬并鼓励我写作，夸我是个小作家，读文学名著给我听。母亲过世时，我只有十几岁。父亲希望我能去打份工。于是我找了份服务生的工作，闲暇时给周报写写故事，一个字十五美分，作为练笔。多年后，我的第一任丈夫英年早逝，我同时做两份兼职（一份做公关，另一份做技术文件撰写员）。要养活三个孩子，我整夜地书写着自己的悲痛，直到完成了《海洋深处》。正是这本386页的小说引领我踏上了梦寐以求的作家道路。我不知道是不是真有天堂，如果有，我的母亲一定会在那里带头为我喝彩。

23 当我的孩子权衡他们的选择时，我会给他们我最好的建议：放手去追吧，一套、两套、多少套备选方案永远都会有。牢牢抓住你的第一选择！

TEXT B Motivation

Before Reading

The purpose of this section is to arouse the students' interest in the theme of the unit, reactivate their relevant background knowledge or elicit their opinions on the related topics, so as to better prepare them for the succeeding tasks.

Before Reading activities can be organized as group work so that the students share with each other their knowledge about self motivation and the techniques to boost it.

Background Information

1 Self Motivation and How to Motivate Yourself

People who are unable to motivate themselves must be content with mediocrity, no matter how impressive their other talents.

— *Andrew Carnegie*

If you want to excel in life, self motivation is essential. You must know how to motivate yourself. You must be able to keep your spirit high no matter how discouraging a situation is. That's the only way to get the power you need to overcome difficulties. Those who are discouraged in difficult times are certain to lose even before the battle is over.

The question is: how do you motivate yourself? Here are several tips I've found to be effective to build self motivation:

Have a cause

I can't think of a more powerful source of motivation than a cause you care about. Such cause can inspire you to give your best even in the face of difficulties. It can make you do the seemingly impossible things. While other causes could inspire you temporarily, a cause that matters to you can inspire you indefinitely. It's a spring of motivation that will never dry. Whenever you think that you run out of motivation, you can always come to your cause to get a fresh dose of motivation.

Have a dream, a big dream

Only as high as I reach can I grow, only as far as I seek can I go, only as deep as I look can I see, only as much as I dream can I be.

— *Karen Ravn*

Your cause is a powerful source of motivation but it's still abstract in nature. You need to make it concrete in the form of a dream. Imagine how the world will be in the future. Imagine how people will live and work. Having a dream is important because it's difficult to be motivated if you don't have anything to shoot for. Just think about people who play basketball. Will they be motivated to play if there is no basket to aim at? I don't think so. They need a goal. You need a goal. That's what your dream is for. But just having a dream is insufficient. Your dream must be big enough to inspire you. It must be realistic but challenging. It must stretch your ability beyond your comfort zone.

Be hungry

Wanting something is not enough. You must hunger for it. Your motivation must be absolutely compelling in order to overcome the obstacles that will invariably come your way.

— *Les Brown*

To be truly motivated, you need to have *hunger* and not just *desire*. Having mere desire won't take you through difficult times since you don't want things badly enough. In many cases, hunger makes the difference between the best performers and the mediocre ones. How can you have hunger? Your cause and your dream play a big role here. If you have a cause you care about and a big dream related to it, you should have the hunger inside of you. If you think that you are losing hunger, all you need to do is to connect again to your cause and dream. Let them inspire you and bring the hunger back.

Run your own race

I do not try to dance better than anyone else. I only try to dance better than myself.

— *Mikhail Baryshnikov*

Comparing yourself with others is an effective way to *demotivate* yourself. Even if you start with enthusiasm, you will soon lose your energy when you compare yourself with others.

Don't let that happen to you. You have your own race, so how other people perform is irrelevant. Comparing yourself with others is like comparing the performance of a swimmer with a runner using the same time standard. They are different, so how can you compare one with the other?

The only competitor you have is yourself. The only one you need to beat is *you*. Have you become the best you can be?

Take one more step

Success is not final, failure is not fatal: it is the courage to continue that counts.

— *Winston Churchill*

When you meet obstacles along the way, there could be the tendency to quit. You may think that it's too difficult to move on. You may think that your dream is impossible to achieve. But this is where you can see the difference between winners and losers. Though both of them face the same difficulties, there is one thing that makes the winners different: *the courage to continue*.

In difficult situations, just focus on taking one more step forward. Don't think about how to complete the race. Don't think about how many more obstacles are waiting for you. Just focus on taking the *next* step.

Let go of the past

Finish each day and be done with it. You have done what you could.

— *Ralph Waldo Emerson*

Believe it or not, one of the best demotivators is your past. Your past can drag you down before you realize it. Your past can give you a heavy burden on your shoulders. The good news is it's a burden you don't have to carry. Take it off your shoulder and leave it. You might have made mistakes in the past. You might have disappointed others with what you did. But it's over. It's already in the past and there's nothing you can do about it. Today is a new day and you have the chance to start again. No matter how bad your past might be, you still have a bright future ahead waiting for you. Just don't let the burden of the past stop you.

Apply these tips and motivate yourself. Don't settle for mediocrity. Let your self motivation take you to excellence.

2 Motivational Techniques

The source of self motivation can come from many different avenues. But first let's define self motivation as the desire or need to achieve something personally significant. It is a very personal emotional thing that tends to drive each of us to accomplish our goals.

Commitment

The spark of self motivation is always personal. One of the primary methods of motivation is to make a commitment to yourself and your personal desire. Try writing down your goal, or sharing it with others — many people find this to be very motivational. Employ your emotions to keep yourself on track — this is a motivating key!

Divide and conquer

Organizing and splitting your personal goals into smaller tasks or parts is useful in curbing your feeling as well as keeping yourself from being overwhelmed.

Use rewards

Perhaps the most important step in any personal journey is rewarding oneself for improvement and progress. Any journey requiring self motivation is difficult — you are working toward change, which is difficult in itself. Any progress is precious and encouraging. Reward yourself at times. This will ensure that the personal self motivation remains high.

Reading

New Words and Expressions

be related to to be connected with sth./sb. in some way 相关联，有关系
e.g. His failure in the exam is related to his laziness and lack of motivation.
These two factors are closely related to each other.

day in and day out every day for a long period of time 日复一日，天天(不间断)
e.g. She does the same thing at her job day in and day out.
It can be difficult to spend all of your time with one person day in and day out.

sleep in to sleep until after the time you usually get up in the morning 睡过头；睡懒觉
e.g. On Sundays, we always sleep in.
Remember not to sleep in tomorrow — we have an important appointment at 9 o'clock sharp!

momentum /məʊˈmentəm/ *n.* the ability to keep increasing or developing 动力；势头
e.g. In an attempt to give new momentum to their plans, the committee set a date for starting detailed discussions.
The company has had a successful year and hopes to maintain its momentum by introducing new products.

ridiculously /rɪˈdɪkjʊləslɪ/ *ad.* unreasonably 荒唐地；难以置信地

e.g. The movie was ridiculously long.
The living expenses nowadays are ridiculously high.

workout /ˈwɜːkaʊt/ *n.* a period of physical exercise that you do to keep fit 锻炼
e.g. Her daily workouts include lifting weights and running on the treadmill.
a light workout

wimpy /ˈwɪmpɪ/ *a.* not strong, brave or confident 懦弱的；软弱的
e.g. wimpy behaviour
I am far too wimpy to go rock climbing.

crunch /krʌntʃ/ *n.* one of the most common abdominal exercises; when performing a crunch, the lower back should not leave the floor 卷腹运动(有别于仰卧起坐)
e.g. I try to do 50 crunches every day.

pushup /ˈpʊʃʌp/ *n.* an exercise in which you lie on your stomach and raise your body off the ground by pressing down on your hands until your arms are straight 俯卧撑
e.g. He is very good at doing pushups.

sap /sæp/ *v.* to make sth./sb. weaker, to destroy sth. gradually 使虚弱，削弱；逐渐破坏
e.g. Moving the couch up the stairs sapped her strength.
Months of rejections after job interviews sapped his confidence.

self-interest /ˌselfˈɪntərɪst/ *n.* one's personal interest or advantage 自身利益，私利
e.g. They acted out of self-interest and fear.
The company's donation was surely motivated by self-interest, as it attracted a lot of media attention.

essentially /ɪˈsenʃəli/ *ad.* used to emphasize the true, important or basic nature of sb./sth. 本质上，根本上；基本上
e.g. It's essentially a dictionary but it differs in one or two respects.
What he's saying is essentially true.

criterion /kraɪˈtɪəriən/ (pl. criteria) *n.* a standard or principle by which sth. is judged, or with the help of which a decision is made（评判或作决定的）标准；准则；原则
e.g. The Health Service should not be judged by financial criteria alone.
What were the criteria used to choose the winner?

marathon /ˈmærəθɒn/ *n.* a long running race of about 42 kilometres or 26 miles 马拉松赛跑（距离约42公里，合26英里）
e.g. He runs a marathon every year.
She did her first marathon in just less than three hours.

back down to withdraw a claim or assertion in the face of opposition 放弃原来的主张；打退堂鼓
e.g. He will never back down from a fight.
The government finally backed down from its position.

hold oneself accountable to take responsibility for one's decisions or actions and be ready to explain them when asked（对自己的决定、行为）负有责任
e.g. I hold myself accountable for the mistakes I have made.
Each child is held accountable for his/her own behavior.

in the meantime in the period of time between two times or two events; at the same time 其间；同时
e.g. He can come back to work when he's feeling better, but in the meantime he should be resting as much as possible.
The project is scheduled for completion in three months, and there's a great deal of work to be done in the meantime.

mantra /ˈmæntrə/ *n.* a word, phrase or sound that is repeated again and again, especially during prayer or meditation（某些宗教的）咒语
e.g. A personal mantra is sometimes repeated as an aid to meditation or prayer.
a Buddist mantra

reminder /rɪˈmaɪndə/ *n.* a thing that makes you think or remember sb./sth. that you have forgotten or would like to forget 引起回忆的事物；提醒人的事物
e.g. The accident was a sobering reminder of the dangers of climbing.
She sent him an e-mail reminder about the meeting.

Language Study

…whether it be related to productivity, waking early…
虚拟语气用在由whether引导的让步状语从句中时，从句谓语用动词原形。
e.g. All engines work on this principle, whether they be large or small.
We must finish the work before we go home, whether it be early or late.
All matter, whether it be gas, liquid or solid, is made up of atoms.
在此句型中，可省去whether，而将be放在从句主语前。
e.g. Be it so, we must continue to do the test.
We must do our best to fulfil the task, be it ever so hard.

relate *v.*
1. to understand and like or have sympathy for sb. or sth. 能够理解并同情，了解，体恤
   e.g. You must be feeling awful. I went through something similar myself last year, so I can relate.
   The audience needs to be able to relate to the characters in the story.
2. to tell (sth., such as a story) 讲述
   e.g. The book relates a tale of jealousy and heartache.
   We listened eagerly as she related the whole exciting story.

relate to to be connected with (sb. or sth.); to be about (sb. or sth.) 与……有联系的
  e.g. The readings relate to the class discussions.
    Their grudge relates back to a misunderstanding that took place years ago.
related *a.*
  1. connected in some way 相关的，有联系的
    e.g. ancient history and other related subjects/areas/fields
      drug-related crimes
  2. in the same family 属同一家族的，有亲属关系的
    e.g. I just found out that my best friend and I are related through distant cousins.
      My stepmother and I are not related by blood.
      My sister-in-law and I are related by marriage.
ridiculous *a.* arousing or deserving ridicule; extremely silly or unreasonable 荒谬的
  e.g. She looks ridiculous in that outfit.
    It was a ridiculous suggestion.
    That's an absolutely ridiculous price for that sweater.
  synonym: absurd
marathon *n.*
  1. sth. (such as an event or activity) that lasts an extremely long time or that requires great effort 需要花费很长时间或精力的活动
    e.g. We watched a marathon of our favourite movies.
      a movie marathon
      a shopping marathon
  2. a contest in which people compete with each other to see who can do sth. for the longest amount of time 能坚持最长时间的比赛
    e.g. a dance marathon
remind *v.* to put in mind of sb.; to cause to remember 提醒（通常与介词of搭配）
  e.g. She'll forget to call the doctor if you don't remind her.
    Remind me to buy some groceries after work.
    I constantly have to be reminded how to pronounce her name.
    I had to remind him that we were supposed to leave early.
    Please remind me of the meeting tomorrow.

After Reading

READING COMPREHENSION TASKS

1. Complete the following table based on the information in TEXT B: use one or two sentences to explain each of the 8 ways to motivate yourself.

Start small	Start with an easy goal and make gradual progress.
One goal	Too many goals may demotivate people. Choose one goal and focus on it completely.
Examine your motivation	Think about your goals and do things for good reasons.
Really, really want it	Your goal has to be something you are really passionate about.

Commit publicly	Hold yourself accountable for your goals and keep your friends and family updated of your progress.
Get excited	Get excited about your goal and carry the energy forward towards realizing it.
Build anticipation	Set a date in the future and make it your Start Date to do a goal. Write out a plan and increase your focus and energy for the goal.
Print it out, post it up	Print out your goal and post it at home and work. It is the reminder of your goal.

2. Answer the following questions.

1) According to Henry Ford, what kind of things are obstacles?
   Obstacles are the things that frighten you when you do not have your goal as a source of courage.

2) What may help you to achieve a goal eventually?
   You need to stick with a goal for long enough and it takes patience and motivation to help you get there eventually.

3) Why does positive motivation work better than negative motivation?
   Because if it is something you really want to do, you will do a much better job than to avoid something you don't want.

4) What can you do to sustain your effort for a much longer time?
   You should find ways to really want to do something.

5) What is the most common mistake that people tend to make when they have several goals to deal with?
   People tend to start with too many goals at once and try to do too much.

6) Why should we examine our motivation?
   Because we should know the reasons for our motivation and we should do the goal for something that we truly want.

7) Why would people go the extra mile to do things said publicly?
   Because nobody likes to look bad in front of others.

8) What can we do to hold ourselves accountable?
   We can commit to giving progress updates to everyone every week or so.

9) What does the author do to keep himself excited about a goal?
   He talks to his wife about his goal and to others as well. He also reads as much about it as possible and visualizes what it would be like to be successful.

10) Why should we delay our start to do a goal?
    Because we can build anticipation and thus increase our focus and energy for our goal.

3. Explain the underlined parts in your own words.

1) One of the biggest challenges in meeting any goal … is finding the motivation to <u>stick with it</u>. (Para. 1)
   continue making efforts towards the goal

2) … <u>not that</u> there's anything wrong with that. (Para. 5)
   not suggesting that

3) … a good start can <u>build momentum</u> that you can sustain for a long time. (Para. 8)
   keep high your energy and motivation

4) Start out with a ridiculously easy goal, and then <u>grow from there</u>. (Para. 9)
   build on it and make gradual progress

5) And it <u>saps energy and motivation</u>. (Para. 10)
   <u>takes away energy and motivation</u>

6) You cannot <u>maintain energy and focus</u>… if you are trying to reach two or more goals at once. (Para. 10)
   <u>keep being energetic and focused all the time</u>

7) … reading as much about it as possible, and <u>visualizing</u> what it would be like to be successful… (Para. 14)
   <u>imagining</u>

8) It helped me quit smoking <u>after many failed attempts</u>. (Para. 15)
   <u>after I failed several times</u>

ORAL WORK

Talk to each other in your group about your New Year resolutions. Make a practical list of the things you wish to achieve next year. Discuss how to motivate yourself from the very beginning.

The teacher can ask the students to form groups to talk about their New Year resolutions. They can make a practical list of the things they wish to achieve next year, and discuss how to motivate themselves from the beginning. Once they feel ready, the teacher can ask them to present their list first within the group, and then to the whole class.

TRANSLATION OF TEXT B

动力

阻碍是当你的注意力游离于目标时才看得到的可怕东西。

——亨利·福特

1   达成目标的最大挑战——不管这个目标是提高效率、早起、改变一个习惯、锻炼，或仅仅是变得开心——是找到坚持的动力。

2   如果你坚持得够久，最后几乎总能达到目的。你需要的仅仅是耐心，还有动力。

3   动力是关键，然而日复一日，要始终找得到动力并不容易。

动力是如何发挥作用的？

4   动力驱使你向目标前进，在境况变得艰难的时候促使你坚持下去，它是你早起锻炼或熬夜完成项目的动因。当然动力有很多种，有积极的也有消极的。老板威胁要炒你鱿鱼是动力——在那样的压力下，你也许会更加努力工作来完成项目。但我发现积极的动力效果更好——如果做一件事是因为你真正想做，而不仅仅是为了避免你不想要的结果（比如被炒），你会做得好得多。

5   所以，动力的最佳形式就是你想做一件事。打个比方，我们有时会不想早起，这个时候你非常想睡懒觉（这并没有什么错）。但如果你有一个想要早起的理由，有一件你真正想去做的事，你就会兴奋地从床上一跃而起。

6   最好的动力就是你真正想要某个东西，你为它而兴奋，对它充满了激情。请记住，虽然我们还有很多其他种类的动力（特别是消极的），但就我的经验而言，这种最有效果。

7   当你尝试激励自己去做不喜欢、不愿意做的事时，你能坚持的时间并不长。但如果你找到办法使你真正想做某件事，你坚持努力的时间要长得多。

从一开始就正确激励自己的8个窍门

8 我发现带着正确的动力开始是很重要的，因为一个好的开始可形成冲劲，让你坚持很长一段时间。如果你有一个正确的开始，你将拥有更多成功机会。以下是一些如何开好头的小技巧：

9 1. 从小处开始。这是激励你自己追求目标最重要的技巧之一。不要一开始就给自己订立太大的目标！从一个小得出奇的目标开始，然后从那里慢慢发展起来。举个例子，假设你想要锻炼，也许会觉得必须每周做5天高强度的锻炼。别这么做——反之，做一些小的、简单的步骤。做个两分钟的练习就行了。这听起来微不足道，但其实很有用。保证每天两分钟的锻炼，坚持一个星期。你也许想做得更多，但坚持这两分钟就好。这太容易了，你不会做不到。每天在固定的时间做这件事。你可以做一些卷腹运动，两个俯卧撑，或者跑跑步。等你在一星期内能够每天坚持做两分钟运动了，把两分钟增加到5分钟，然后再坚持一个星期。一个月内，你就会增加到15至20分钟了。想要早起吗？别一下想起5点起床。在一星期内比原来早10分钟起床，就这样做。一旦你做到了，再早10分钟起床。像婴儿学步一样慢慢来。

10 2. 只树立一个目标。有太多的人一次带着太多的目标开始，想做太多的事情，于是耗完了精力和动力。这大概是人们最常犯的错误了吧。如果你想一次达成两个或者更多目标，你将无法维持和集中精力(这是完成一个目标最重要的两个因素)。你做不到的。你暂时只能选择一个目标，然后全心全意倾注在上面。我知道这很困难，然而这也是经验之谈。完成了这一个目标之后，你仍然可以继续追求其他目标。

11 3. 检查你的动机。对你做事的理由要心中有数。想一想它们，然后把它们写下来。如果你有爱的人，是为了他们而努力，就会比仅仅为了自身利益而努力时更充满力量。为了自己而努力也很好，但你必须是为了真正、确实想要的东西而努力，为了真正好的原因而努力。

12 4. 真正地、打心底地想要它。这一条和上面那条本质上是相同的，但我要强调它：仅仅觉得取得某一项成就很酷是不够的。你必须对它充满激情，你会为了它而极为兴奋，你打心底地想要它。确认你的目标符合这些标准，否则你将无法长久地坚持下去。

13 5. 公开承诺。我们都想在别人面前有个好形象。如果我们公开承诺一件事情，就会格外努力。比如，当我想要开始跑第一次马拉松时，我在当地的日报上开了一个有关它的专栏。整个关岛(16万人口)都知道了我的目标。我不能放弃，即使我的动力时高时低，我依旧坚持并完成了目标。当然，你不用也在日报上公开承诺你的目标，但你可以告诉朋友、家人和同事，或者在博客上把它公之于众，如果你有博客的话。你要对它负责——不要仅仅承诺一次，要承诺你将一周左右更新一次。

14 6. 激发你的热忱。一开始这个目标可能来自于别人激励，但你必须把它化为自己的动力并且坚持下去。以我为例，我发现通过和妻子或其他人谈论一个目标，或尽可能多地阅读与之相关的东西，或描绘目标达成时候的样子(我在脑海中想象它的好处)，我会为它感到兴奋激动。一旦我的热忱被激发了，剩下的就仅仅是推进这股兴奋劲、把它保持下去的问题了。

15 7. 建立期望。这听起来很难，许多人会跳过这个技巧。但它真的很有用。它帮我戒了烟，而之前我试了很多次都没戒成。如果你有完成一个目标的想法，不要马上行动。许多人会感到兴奋，然后想要今天马上开始，这是错误的。设定一个未来的日子——一个星期或两个星期，甚至是一个月后，然后把它定为你开始的日子。在日历上把它标出来。让你自己为了这天的到来兴奋起来。把它当做你人生中最重要的一天。与此同时，着手制订一个计划。通过延迟开始时间，你逐步建立起期望，集中注意力和精力完成目标。

16 8. 打印出来，贴起来。用大号的字体把你的目标打印出来。把你的目标写成一句只有几个字的话，就像一个口号("每天锻炼15分钟")，然后把它贴在墙上或冰箱上。把它贴在家里或办公室。把它放在电脑桌面上。你要有醒目的东西来提醒自己的目标，保持兴奋度。

INTEGRATED EXERCISES

1 PUBLIC SPEECH TRAINING

The following is part of a speech about the origins of U.S. immigrants. Listen and then practice after the recording.

(The speech will be read twice. For the first time, the students just listen and try to understand the meaning. When it is read for the second time, there are pauses in the recording. Ask the students to practice after the speaker during these pauses and pay attention to the speaker's intonation, voice [e.g. loudness, pitch, tempo] etc.)

Script

As you can see from this chart, / which is based on the figures of the U.S. Census Bureau, / 36 percent, more than one third, / of recent U.S. immigrants have come from Asia. / 14 percent have come from Mexico / and 11 percent have originated from Europe and the Caribbean, respectively. / The next three groups consist of almost one quarter of the total: / South America with 10 percent, / Africa with 9 percent, / and Central America with 5 percent. / An additional 4 percent come from other parts of the world.

2 DICTATION

Listen to the following passage and write it down. The passage will be read four times. During the first reading, which will be done at normal speed, listen and try to understand the meaning. For the second and third readings, the passage will be read sentence by sentence, or phrase by phrase, with intervals of 15 seconds. Write down what you hear. The last reading will be done at normal speed again and during this time you should check your work.

Script

Do you ever lie in bed and think about your upcoming workday? / You think, "I'm going to call that new customer after I have my first cup of coffee." / Then you decide the call can wait. / We all want to be more productive and achieve success. / But at times, we find it difficult to motivate ourselves to take action / — especially first thing in the morning. / Some people view motivation as something of a puzzle: / they don't understand how people can always be energized. / Getting started has less to do with whether you have the energy / and more to do with your desire and willingness to accomplish any given task. / As an entrepreneur, you are passionate about your business. / Once you dig in, start a project and see the results of your labour, / you become even more motivated. / Stop delaying your success, and begin your day with enthusiasm by taking action.

3 VOCABULARY STUDY

Task One

Put the proper form of the words in the corresponding blanks.

1) He was chosen as the manager of our company because he was considered a ___visionary___. (vision)

2) She arrived at 10 o'clock as __instructed__. (instructor)
3) Mary wanted to become a __choreographer__ when she grew up. (choreograph)
4) The organization should be allowed to develop __organically__. (organic)
5) It was totally __impractical__ to think that we could finish the job in two months. (practical)
6) They called her Miss Mouse because she was so __meek__ and mild. (meekly)
7) I wish I could improve my __culinary__ skills. (culinarily)
8) He has just received a __rejection__ letter after his interview last week. (reject)
9) They cannot help __pondering__ whether the money could be better used elsewhere. (ponder)
10) The equipment can be very __tricky__ to install. (trick)

Task Two

Replace the underlined words with the correct form of the words in the box. You may need to make other changes.

1) Our flight __eventually__ left five hours later.
2) The dinner was __ridiculously__ expensive.
3) The sun __sapped__ our energy and made us much weaker.
4) I really appreciate how much he has __instructed__ me over the semester.
5) We should give it a second thought when we are faced with several __options__ and have to make a decision.
6) We need __a fallback__ plan if they won't do the job.
7) I know I should be motivated in order to __accomplish__ my purpose.
8) I have __anticipated__ a lot of difficulties in completing this task.
9) Mom has been encouraging me from the __get-go__.
10) She __pondered__ his questions after the meeting.

Task Three

Choose the best answers from the options given.

1) We all think her plan sounds too _____.
   A. imperative   B. immaculate   **C. impractical**   D. imaginable
2) The situation is so _____ that we have to ask for their help.
   A. obvious   B. simple   C. trivial   **D. tricky**
3) I'd always prefer to work with the _____ rather than the bold.
   A. mechanical   **B. meek**   C. courageous   D. daring
4) She _____ a note to her sister before leaving.
   A. scrambled   B. scripted   C. screamed   **D. scribbled**
5) We totally enjoyed his theatric _____ last night at the City Centre.
   A. persecution   **B. performance**   C. perplexity   D. personage
6) Are you suffering from an _____ of stress in your life?
   A. excess   B. exceed   C. extreme   D. exit
7) He struggled to _____ control of the situation.
   A. retrieve   **B. retain**   C. retrace   D. restrain
8) This incident served as a timely _____ of just how dangerous mountaineering can be.
   A. remedy   B. remembrance   C. relief   **D. reminder**

9) Our records are regularly _____.
   A. changed   B. **updated**   C. unexpected   D. tracked
10) Which planets can _____ life?
   A. support   B. suspect   C. surpass   D. **sustain**

Task Four

Fill in the following blanks with appropriate words from the box.

Motivational stories of people who have hit rock bottom, only to turn around and live amazing lives is not only 1) __inspirational__, but astounding. One such 2) __motivational__ story is that of Joe Roberts. He became CEO of Mindware Communications — a 3) __company__ in Canada. To look at Joe, you'd never believe he was a drug-addicted, homeless bum living on the streets of Canada. He 4) __lived__ this way for 10 years before vowing to turn his life 5) __around__. What was Joe's life like back then? Joe explains, "I was a 6) __homeless__ person living in doorways and under bridges in Vancouver's 7) __notorious__ drug-infested East End. My life was a series of disappointments, painful experiences, suffering circumstances, and very bad choices. I finally was 8) __confronted__ with an ultimatum. Face the fear, pain and uncertainty of changing the 9) __course__ of my life or face death." Your rock bottom may be different from Joe's; however, you can use his life 10) __lessons__ to motivate you through your own 11) __adversity__. The first thing you must do is CHOOSE. You have to WANT to make your life 12) __better__. I 13) __share__ Joe's story with you, because it served and continues to serve as 14) __powerful__ motivation whenever I deal with obstacles or 15) __challenges__. Joe challenges, "What if I told you that your 16) __past__ does not define you at 17) __all__? What if I told you that every mistake you have made will have no 18) __bearing__ on what your future holds? What if I told you that you could not fail at anything you believe you can 19) __achieve__? What if your future dreams and 20) __hopes__ are a reality waiting for you to experience? Well, it's true."

4 GRAMMAR FOCUS

Read the following passage, underline the one mistake in each line and write the correction after the bracketed number.

Vince Lombardi <u>is</u> born in Brooklyn, New York, in 1913 and was   1) was
<u>bought</u> up in a very strict Catholic household. He started to school   2) brought
to be a priest at age 15, but soon <u>change</u> his mind. Two short years 3) changed
later, he started <u>play</u> football at Fordham University. He was   4) playing
famous <u>for</u> one of their "Seven Blocks of Granite" players. In 1937, 5) as
he graduated and began going to law school. <u>Instead</u> becoming an   6) Instead of
attorney, though, he <u>was taken</u> on a teaching and coaching job with 7) took
a school in New Jersey. He <u>married to</u> his sweetheart, Marie, in   8) married
1940. They went on to have two children, a boy and a girl. He <u>becomes</u> 9) became
<u>coach</u> for Fordham University in 1947. In 1949, he became   10) a coach

Red Blaik's assistant coach in West Point. In 1954-1958, he served for an assistant coach to the New York Giants. Lombardi was known for being a workaholic and soon receiving an offer to be the assistant coach for the Green Bay Packers. He became an head coach and went on to lead the Packers to 5 winning seasons and championship.

11) at
12) as
13) received
14) a
15) championships

1) 时态错误：出生应该用过去时。
2) 词汇错误：根据上下文，应该用bring的过去时brought，而不是buy的过去时bought。
3) 时态错误：全文叙述过去的事，这里应该保持时态一致。
4) 动词搭配错误：start后面应该用动词-ing形式。
5) 介词搭配错误：此处famous后面应该搭配介词as，意为"作为"，而不是for。
6) 副词搭配错误：instead后面漏掉了of。
7) 语态错误：此处应该用主动态而非被动态。
8) 动词使用错误：此处marry是及物动词，后面不用介词。
9) 时态错误：这里应该保持时态一致，用过去时。
10) 冠词错误：此处漏掉了冠词a。
11) 动词搭配错误：serve后面搭配as，表示"任……职"。
12) 介词错误：此处惯用at，而不是in。
13) 谓语动词错误：根据上下文，此处receive这个动作和前面的was known for平行，而不是与being平行。
14) 冠词错误：head前面用a。
15) 单复数错误：此处应用复数。

5 TRANSLATION

Task One

Translate the following paragraph from English into Chinese.

　　对于那些对任何与学习和课外活动有关的事物都没有兴趣的学生，老师通常都会感到难办，很难使他们行动起来。站在学生的角度，也许人生中会有这么一个阶段，个人或其他方面的问题会影响你的工作学习，你就是觉得很难集中注意力或积极地参与活动。这样的话，你就表现出了缺乏动力（如缺乏兴趣、无精打采）的典型特征，总是感到无聊，一味拖延行动。在这个阶段，你需要灵感或动力来激发热情，让自己行动起来。那么，既然我们都明白自我激励是最好、最有效的方法，为什么还要去寻找外在的动力呢？首先，在开始付出努力之前，设立一个梦想中的目标十分重要，这个目标应该是有一定难度的，但也并非遥不可及。心中有了明确的目标，你才有可能为达到目标而制定计划。其次，一旦设下目标，你就应该把它写下来，或者将其铭记在心，直至实现这个目标。试着制定两个你认为有助于达成目标的计划，但要尽量确保这些计划是切实可行的。第三，你有了梦想，设定了目标，制定了计划，然后就是执行这个计划了。你没有时间可以浪费，不要拖延！

Task Two

Translate the following paragraph from Chinese into English.

　　Encouragement is the best spiritual source for children as well as the best motivator in their learning, so teachers should make efforts to look for the shining qualities in children. Every student has an inclination to stand out and show his abilities and likes to be praised. When his performance receives praise from the teacher, he will feel rejoiced and his confidence will hence be boosted. He will become more proactive and take more initiative in his later performances. Consequently, he will show more interest and confidence in learning. If his performance is fairly good but the teacher fails to offer timely praise, he will feel extremely disappointed and bored, and later on he will probably feel reluctant to speak up in class. Praise and encouragement are the magic weapons in education. Teachers should, without any reservation, offer children smiles and compliments so that they can grow up freely in a relatively free and relaxed environment.

6 CLASSROOM INTERACTION

Activity A   Listening

1) What kind of desire does intrinsic and extrinsic motivation reflect respectively?

   Intrinsic motivation reflects the desire to do something because it is enjoyable, while extrinsic motivation reflects the desire to do something because of external rewards such as awards, money, and praise.

2) What are the examples of intrinsic motivation?

   Writing short stories because you really enjoy writing them, reading a nonfiction book because you are curious about the topic, and playing chess because you enjoy effortful thinking are some examples of intrinsic motivation.

3) What are the examples of extrinsic motivation?

   The examples include the writer who only writes poems to submit to poetry contests and the person who accepts a sales position only to earn a good salary. A third example is selecting a major in college based on prestige or employment outlook, rather than personal interest.

4) Which type of motivation may teachers be interested in fostering, and why?

   Teachers may be very interested in fostering intrinsic motivation, because students who are intrinsically motivated may enjoy challenging work, and may think in greater depth.

Script

Motivation is an important concept in psychology. It provides insight into why we may behave the way we do. Motivation is an internal process that leads to the desire to achieve certain goals. It can be divided into two basic types: intrinsic motivation and extrinsic motivation. Intrinsic motivation reflects the desire to do something because it is enjoyable. If we are intrinsically motivated, we would *not* worry about external rewards such as praise or awards; the enjoyment we experience would be sufficient for us to want to perform the activity. Writing short stories because you really enjoy writing them, reading a nonfiction book because you are curious about the topic, and playing chess because you enjoy effortful thinking are some examples. Extrinsic motivation reflects the desire to do something because of external rewards such as awards, money, and praise. People who are extrinsically motivated may not enjoy certain activities, but only wish to receive the external rewards. There are also many examples, like the writer who only writes poems to submit to poetry contests, or the person who accepts a sales position only to earn a good salary. A third example is selecting a major in college based on prestige or employment outlook, rather than personal interest. Teachers may be very interested in fostering intrinsic motivation. If students are only interested in receiving high grades or praise, and do not enjoy learning, then teaching may be very difficult. In contrast, students who are intrinsically motivated may enjoy challenging work, and may think in greater depth.

Activity B   Debate
The teacher can let the students fill in the following table of opinions before asking them to carry out the debate.

Pro Side	Con Side

Activity C   Mini-speech
The teacher can give the students ten minutes to prepare and then choose a few students to give mini-speeches to the whole class.

WRITING

Writing Skills: Narrative Essays

This unit discusses how to write a narrative essay. The Student's Book starts with clarifying two concepts: narration and essay. The purpose of this discussion is to tell the students that their job in this unit is to learn to write an essay using narrative evidence, not just write a narrative story.

The sample is very simple, but provides a quite interesting story and clear structure. The topic may arouse interest in the students. The four questions after the sample are given to help the students find the key elements in a narrative essay. Possible answers may be like this:

1. The writer tries to give an account of how important marriage proposal is in her life.
2. The essay is made up of three parts. The first paragraph is introduction, the last paragraph is conclusion, and the other paragraphs together constitute the body part, the story. The thesis statement is the first sentence in the second paragraph. It clarifies the point the writer wants to make. The last sentence in the last paragraph can be regarded as a conclusion, i.e., her appreciation to God for sending her John.
3. The whole story is short but complete in structure. The characters are the writer and John. The setting is the afternoon of September 21, 2002, on a small hill on her campus. The plot is that John makes a proposal to the writer. The climax is her speechless state after getting the proposal. The ending is she accepts the proposal.
4. The writer provides not only factual information like time and place, but also details through vivid verbs, dialogues, and descriptions of her feelings.

The next step in the Student's Book is to discuss the features of a successful narrative essay. Among the eight features, the first, second, and the last are about essay writing, and the others are about story writing. The teacher can discuss how to write a story before talking about how to write a narrative essay.

In addition to the suggestions in the Student's Book, the teacher may also give the students these two tips: 1) A story is usually made up of four sections: background — plot development — climax — solution. 2) A story should provide a conflict and solve it.

Writing Assignment

1. What is the purpose of narration? What is the difference between a narration and a narrative essay?

A narration is written to tell readers what has happened. Providing facts is an important task in this kind of writing. Usually a narration focuses on providing the factual information of the happening, although there may also be a hidden point the author wants to make. But in an essay, the point becomes the focus, and the narrative story is only a way to prove or develop the point.

2. Read the following story, think about the possible point the author wants to make, and provide an introduction paragraph to turn it into a narrative essay.

Life is full of paradox. Although people who love you really care about you, they may be those who try to cheat you. Sometimes, truth may come from those who really hate you.

3. Write a narrative essay on one of the following topics.

Answers may vary.

4 KNOWLEDGE AND DEVELOPMENT

TEXT A   The Earth's Learning Curve

Before Reading

The purpose of this section is to arouse the student's interest in the theme of the unit, reactivate their relevant background knowledge or recall their personal experience, so as to better prepare them for the succeeding tasks.

The pictures provided show technological devices that have fundamentally changed people's life. The two pictures on the left are an old desktop and a modern laptop respectively. The picture on the right shows an evolution of mobile phones. Ask the students to focus on the impacts of these devices on human society. The students are encouraged to talk about more changes, both positive and negative, which scientific inventions have brought to humankind.

As the fruits of human knowledge, scientific revolutions continue to change people's life in modern society. The questions provided in this section serve as prompts for the students to do more philosophical thinking on the role that knowledge plays in society and the relationship between knowledge and wisdom. The students can be encouraged to have further discussions in Oral Work.

Background Information

1 Knowledge Economy

Knowledge Economy is a term that refers either to an *economy of knowledge* focused on the production and management of knowledge in the frame of economic constraints, or to a *knowledge-based economy*. In the second meaning, more frequently used, it refers to the use of knowledge technologies (such as knowledge engineering and knowledge management) to produce economic benefits as well as job creation. The phrase was popularized by Peter Drucker as the title of Chapter 12 in his book *The Age of Discontinuity*, and, with a footnote in the text, Drucker attributes the phrase to economist Fritz Machlup.

The essential difference is that in an *economy of knowledge,* knowledge is a product, while in a *knowledge-based economy,* knowledge is a tool. This difference is not yet well distinguished in the subject matter literature. They both are strongly interdisciplinary, involving economists, computer scientists, engineers, mathematicians, geographers, chemists and physicists, as well as cognitivists, psychologists and sociologists.

Various observers describe today's global economy as one in transition to a "knowledge economy", as an extension of an "information society". The transition requires that the rules and practices that determined success in the industrial economy need rewriting in an interconnected, globalized economy where knowledge resources such as know-how and expertise are as critical as other economic resources. According to analysts of the *knowledge economy*, these rules need to be rewritten at the levels of firms and industries in terms of knowledge management and at the level of public policy as knowledge policy or knowledge-related policy.

2 Some Proverbs or Quotes on Knowledge and Wisdom

Knowledge is power. 知识就是力量。 — Francis Bacon

Knowledge comes through practice. 实践出真知。 — a Celtic proverb

Science is organized knowledge. Wisdom is organized life. 科学是整理过的知识，而智慧则是整理过的人生。 — Immanuel Kant

Knowledge is never used up. It increases by diffusion and grows by dispersion. 知识是用不完的，传播使其更丰富。 — Daniel J. Boorstin

Integrity without knowledge is weak and useless, and knowledge without integrity is dangerous and dreadful. 没有知识的正义是羸弱无用的，而缺乏正义感的知识是危险而可怕的。 — Samuel Johnson

It is the province of knowledge to speak. And it is the privilege of wisdom to listen. 口若悬河只是知识所能，但用心倾听却是智慧的特权。 — Oliver Wendell Holmes

Reading

Text Analysis

- ### Text Summary

This text is a *Newsweek* column (《新闻周刊》专栏文章) which explains the author's opinion on knowledge and wisdom. By tracing back the history of social development and citing examples of economic progress, the text demonstrates the changes that knowledge, especially the rise and diffusion of scientific knowledge, has brought about to humankind. However, knowledge is not a cure-all to the problems in human society. To live a better life with peace and quiet, human beings need wisdom.

- ### Text Organization

Paragraph 1: introduction	Human beings have been getting smarter since the late 16th or early 17th century. Before that, economical growth had developed extremely slowly.
Paragraphs 2-8: main body	Knowledge has always been playing a crucial part in the development of the health and wealth of humankind. The rise of science marks the first great trend in the economic development, and the diffusion of knowledge accelerates this trend. Evidence of progress can be seen in countries all over the world. Knowledge, in the author's words, is liberating. Thanks to the knowledge that human beings have been constantly pursuing and spreading, people are getting smarter and the world is getting healthier and richer.
Paragraph 9: conclusion	Knowledge can help humankind to prosper, but it cannot guarantee them a peaceful and harmonious life. We need wisdom to achieve that goal.

● **Text Features**

As an opinion column(说明观点的专栏文章), this text is informal in style and personal in tone, which can help shorten the distance between the author and the reader. These features are characterized by the use of some imperative sentences (those beginning with words like *imagine*, *consider*, etc.), short simple sentences, personal pronouns (*you*, *we*, *I*, *us*, etc.), contractions (*don't*), colloquial terms (*put simply*, *has gotten*, *things*, *of course*, etc.). However, sentences in formal style are interwoven to achieve emphatic effect (e.g. *And most crucially, it does not … and catastrophe.*). Another feature of this text is the author's skillful play of "big" words (*leapfrog*, *exertion*, *caveat*, etc.) as well as simple words in the description.

This text follows a chronological order(时间顺序) in describing the changes that knowledge has brought about to human society by citing concrete examples, dating from the scientific revolution to the present day. It employs several organizational patterns in developing the ideas. First, it makes use of the pattern of cause and effect(因果关系), which is characterized by the use of words like *because*, *because of*. It also makes use of comparison(对比) in describing the situations in "the world of winners" and "the world of losers". Another organizational pattern is problem and solution(问题与办法) as demonstrated in the last paragraph.

It is also worth noticing that the author makes good use of adverbs in the text to modify verbs (e.g. *famously*, *systematically*, *dramatically*), adjectives (e.g. *purely*, *overly*, *equally*), adverbs (e.g. *remarkably*, *extremely*) or to describe the whole sentence (e.g. *most crucially*).

● **Key Sentences**

1. For most of humankind life was as the English philosopher Thomas Hobbes famously described it in 1651 — "solitary, poor, nasty, brutish, and short". (Para. 1)

In this sentence, *as the English philosopher Thomas Hobbes famously described it in 1651* is an adverbial clause of manner(方式状语从句) introduced by the conjunction(连词) *as*. *As* can be used to introduce other types of adverbial clauses as well. For example:

    A: She spilled the milk just as she was getting up. (time)
    B: As the test is difficult, you'd better get some good preparation. (reason)
    C: Ridiculous as it may seem, the story is true. (concession)

2. Others, like Germany, benefited from starting late, leapfrogging the long-drawn-out process that Britain went through. (Para. 3)

In this sentence, *leapfrogging … went through* is used as an adverbial to express a result. Other examples of -ing participle used as adverbial (-ing分词作状语的几个例子):

    A: Working hard, you will pass the exam. (condition)
    B: Putting down my newspaper, I walked over to the window. (time)
    C: Having failed my medical exams, I gave up rock climbing. (reason)
    D: It rained for two weeks on end, completely ruining our holiday. (result)
    E: The children ran out of the room, laughing and talking merrily. (manner)
    F: Whether waking or sleeping, he always has the subject in his mind. (concession)

3. …but let not the worries over who is winning and losing the knowledge race obscure the more powerful underlying dynamic … (Para. 8)

In this sentence, *not* is used directly after the verb *let* to express negation, which is different from its usage in modern English, i.e. *not* usually follows an auxiliary verb like *do* to form negation. In modern English, this sentence should be: *…but **do not** let the worries over who is winning and losing the knowledge race obscure the more powerful underlying dynamic…* This form of negation is archaic and sounds formal. Another good example is the sentence used by John F. Kennedy in his 1961 inaugural address: "Ask not what your country can do for you, ask what you can do for your country."

4. Some will do well on one measure, others on another. (Para. 8)

In this sentence, *others on another* is an elliptical sentence which leaves out the predicate (谓语) *will do well* after the subject (主语) *others*. In English, when there are two sentences with the same pattern and the same verb/predicate, we do not need to repeat the verb/predicate in the second one. However, this kind of omission happens only in rather formal English. For example:

A: The new warehouse contains furniture and the old one electrical goods.

(= … and the old one contains electrical goods.)

B: William has played ten games but Linton only eight.

(= … but Linton only played eight games.)

New Words and Expressions

accelerate /əkˈseləreɪt/ *v.* to happen or go faster than usual (使)加快，加速
e.g. measures to accelerate the rate of economic growth
The search for wealth accelerated later that year.

exponentially /ˌekspəʊˈnenʃəlɪ/ *ad.* more and more rapidly 越来越快地
e.g. As the population size of settlement increases, the land provision declines exponentially.
The Industrial Revolution was imposing new and appalling burdens while increasing exponentially the capacity to create wealth.

prosper /ˈprɒspə/ *v.* to grow and develop in a successful way, especially by becoming rich or making a large profit 兴旺，发达，繁荣
e.g. Businesses across the region are prospering.
Las Vegas continues to boom and prosper in much the same way as it has always done.

endure /ɪnˈdjʊə/ *v.* to remain alive or continue to exist for a long time 持续存在；持久
e.g. a city built to endure
fame that will endure for ever

track /træk/ *v.* to record or study the behaviour or development of sb. or sth. over time 跟踪记录
e.g. The progress of each student is tracked by computer.
A radio and a satellite dish were used to track their position.

trend /trend/ *v.* to show a particular tendency 有……趋势
e.g. house prices trending upward
The rubber market is expected to trend higher this week.

be limited to to exist or happen only in a particular place, group, or area of activity 局限于，限定在……范围
e.g. The damage was limited to the roof.
Our discussion is limited to three aspects of the subject.

elite /eɪˈliːt/ *n.* a group of people who have a lot of power and influence because they have money, knowledge, or special skills 精英；上层人士
e.g. a struggle for power within the ruling elite
the domination of power by a small political elite

priest /priːst/ *n.* sb. who is specially trained to perform religious duties and ceremonies 神职人员
e.g. a parish priest
He was born a priest.

philosopher /fɪˈlɒsəfə/ *n.* sb. who studies and develops ideas about the nature and meaning of existence, truth, good and evil etc. 哲学家
e.g. Plato, Aristotle, and other Greek philosophers

This idea was developed further by Montesquieu, the French philosopher.

solitary /ˈsɒlɪtəri/ *a.* spending a lot of time alone 孤独的，无伴的
e.g. Pandas are solitary creatures.
He led a rather solitary existence.

brutish /ˈbruːtɪʃ/ *a.* uncivilized, coarse, not refined 粗俗的
e.g. brutish manners
The poor people lived in brutish conditions.

put simply to say or explain sth. in a way that is easy for people to understand 简而言之
e.g. Put simply, a transistor is a small, crystal-based component.
Put simply, £100 received today could be invested at 10% per annum and so be worth £110 next year.

fit into to be accepted by others in a group or in harmony with sth. 与……相融合；与……相配合
e.g. She fitted into the team very well.
How does this fit into the company's overall marketing strategy?

divine /dɪˈvaɪn/ *a.* coming from or relating to God or a god 神的；如神的
e.g. divine power
To err is human, to forgive divine.

harness /ˈhɑːnɪs/ *v.* to control and use the natural force or power of sth. 利用
e.g. We can harness the power of the wind to generate electricity.
The scheme was established by Labour in 1975 to harness the creativity of graduates.

ongoing /ˈɒnˌɡəʊɪŋ/ *a.* continuing or continuing to develop 不间断的；不断发展的
e.g. ongoing negotiations
an ongoing search for a new director

diffusion /dɪˈfjuːʒən/ *n.* the spread of ideas or information among a lot of people 传播
e.g. diffusion of values
diffusion of knowledge through books and lectures

phenomenon /fɪˈnɒmɪnən/ *n.* sth. that happens or exists in society, science, or nature, especially sth. that is studied because it is difficult to understand 现象
e.g. the growing phenomenon of telecommuting
Language is a social and cultural phenomenon.

a succession of a number of (people or things of a similar kind following one after the other) 一连串；一系列
e.g. a succession of disasters
A succession of visitors came to the door.

commercial /kəˈmɜːʃəl/ *a.* related to business and the buying and selling of goods and services 商业的；商务的
e.g. a commercial organization
Our top priorities must be profit and commercial growth.

leapfrog /ˈliːpfrɒɡ/ *v.* to achieve sth. more quickly than usual by missing some of the usual stages 跨越；超越
e.g. Michael leapfrogged two ranks and was made a colonel.
The company leapfrogged its rivals into a leading position.

dramatically /drəˈmætɪkəli/ *ad.* considerably 大幅度地
e.g. Her attitude changed dramatically.
The population in that country decreased dramatically.

at the peak of at the height of 在高峰期；在鼎盛期
e.g. She was at the peak of her popularity.
Hotel rooms are difficult to find at the peak of the holiday season.

exertion /ɪɡˈzɜːʃən/ *n.* a lot of physical or mental effort 努力；费力
e.g. mental exertion
The afternoon's exertions had left us feeling exhausted.

dominant /ˈdɒmɪnənt/ *a.* more powerful, important, or noticeable than other people or things 突出的；占优势的
e.g. The dominant male gorilla is the largest in the group.
Japan became dominant in the mass market during the 1980s.

classic /ˈklæsɪk/ *a.* having all the features that are typical or expected of a particular thing or situation 典型的
e.g. a classic example
Too many job hunters make the classic mistake of thinking only about what's in it for them.

basket case a country with many severe economic and social problems that are likely to continue for a long time 有严重经济、社会问题的国家

e.g. This country used to be an economic basket case.
a basket-case economy (used as modifier 作修饰成分)

triple /ˈtrɪpl/ *a.* having three parts or involving three groups, people, events etc. 有三个……的
e.g. a triple alliance
the triple world champion

soar /sɔː/ *v.* to increase quickly to a high level 猛增，骤升
e.g. Her temperature soared.
The price of petrol has soared in recent weeks.

sector /ˈsektə/ *n.* a part of an area or activity, especially of business, trade etc. 部门；行业
e.g. the agricultural sector of the economy

constraint /kənˈstreɪnt/ *n.* sth. that limits the freedom of sb. or sth.; restriction 限制
e.g. the constraints of family life
There have been financial and political constraints on development.

sensibly /ˈsensəblɪ/ *ad.* reasonably; practically 理智地；实际地
e.g. Try to use your time sensibly.
They sensibly invested their prize money rather than spending it.

reluctant /rɪˈlʌktənt/ *a.* slow and unwilling 勉强的，不情愿的
e.g. She gave a reluctant smile.
Maddox was reluctant to talk about it.

unmistakable /ˌʌnmɪˈsteɪkəbl/ *a.* easy to recognize 清楚的；无误的
e.g. the unmistakable sound of gunfire
There was an unmistakable fault in the material.

markedly /ˈmɑːkɪdlɪ/ *ad.* noticeably, strikingly 明显地，显著地
e.g. Sales have slowed down quite markedly.
Johnson and Rivera have markedly different leadership styles.

monetary /ˈmʌnɪtərɪ/ *a.* relating to money, especially all the money in a particular country 货币的；金融的
e.g. objects of little monetary value
the government's tight monetary policy

temper /ˈtempə/ *v.* to make sth. less severe or extreme 缓和
e.g. The heat in this coastal town is tempered by cool sea breezes.
Naturally this judgment has to be tempered by the unrepresentative nature of the sample of reports.

boom /buːm/ *n.* a quick increase of business activity 繁荣，兴旺
e.g. a sudden boom in the housing market
The boom has created job opportunities.

bust /bʌst/ *n.* a time or period of widespread financial depression 萧条
e.g. His only fear is the region could become trapped in a cycle of boom and bust.
Bankers consider the region's diversified economy to be good protection against a possible real estate bust.

mild /maɪld/ *a.* not serious enough to cause much suffering 轻的，不严重的
e.g. a mild setback
The debate between them has been comparatively mild.

recession /rɪˈseʃən/ *n.* an extended decline in general business activity 衰退期
e.g. the economic recession of the early 1980s
There is deep recession in the UK.

penetration /ˌpenɪˈtreɪʃən/ *n.* the act of entering a country or organization so as to establish influence or gain information 渗透
e.g. the penetration of Islam into the region
foreign penetration of the secret service

reinforce /ˌriːɪnˈfɔːs/ *v.* to give support to an opinion, idea, or feeling, and make it stronger 加强，强化
e.g. The news reinforced her hopes.
The film reinforces the idea that women should be pretty and dumb.

inequality /ˌɪnɪˈkwɒlətɪ/ *n.* an unfair situation, in which some groups in society have more money, opportunities, power etc. than others 不平等
e.g. social/gender/racial inequality
inequalities between men and women

marked /mɑːkt/ *a.* very easy to notice 显著的，明显的
e.g. a marked lack of enthusiasm
The patient showed a marked improvement in her condition after changing medication.

vaccine /ˈvæksiːn/ *n.* substance which contains a weak form of the bacteria or virus that causes a disease and is used to protect people from that disease 疫苗
e.g. Doctors worried that there would not be enough vaccine for everyone who needed it.

scrutiny /ˈskruːtɪnɪ/ *n.* careful and thorough examination of sb. or sth. 审查；检查
- **e.g.** Their activities have come under police scrutiny.
  Careful scrutiny of the company's accounts revealed a whole series of errors.

optimistic /ˌɒptɪˈmɪstɪk/ *a.* believing that good things will happen in the future 乐观的
- **e.g.** Andrew took a more optimistic view.
  We are still relatively optimistic that the factory can be saved.

obscure /əbˈskjʊə/ *v.* to make sth. difficult to know or understand 使不显著；使难理解
- **e.g.** Recent successes have obscured the fact that the company is still in trouble.
  In a multicultural society, we must not allow our idolatry of art and literature to obscure issues of immense social and political significance.

underlying /ˌʌndəˈlaɪɪŋ/ *a.* the most important, although not easily noticed 根本的，基本的
- **e.g.** the underlying causes of her depression
  There is an underlying assumption that younger workers are easier to train.

dynamic /daɪˈnæmɪk/ *n.* sth. that causes action or change 动力；活力
- **e.g.** Feminism is seen as a dynamic of social change.
  She regards class conflict as a central dynamic of historical change.

amazing /əˈmeɪzɪŋ/ *a.* very impressive, excellent 极好的
- **e.g.** an amazing tennis player
  We had an amazing meal that night.

living standard   the level of comfort and the amount of money that people have 生活水平
- **e.g.** rising living standards
  Living standards have improved over the last century.

on the whole   generally 总的来说，总而言之
- **e.g.** On the whole, I thought the film was pretty good.
  On the whole, life was much quieter after John left.

caveat /ˈkævɪæt/ *n.* a warning that sth. may not be completely true, effective etc. 警告；提醒
- **e.g.** a final caveat
  She will be offered treatment, with the caveat that it may not work.

paucity /ˈpɔːsətɪ/ *n.* an insufficient quantity or number 缺乏，不足
- **e.g.** a paucity of information
  There is a paucity of green space within the town centre where shoppers can rest a few minutes.

destruction /dɪˈstrʌkʃən/ *n.* the act or process of destroying sth. or being destroyed 摧毁；破坏
- **e.g.** the destruction of the rainforest
  the environmental destruction caused by the road building programme

generosity /ˌdʒenəˈrɒsətɪ/ *n.* the quality of showing a readiness to give more of sth., especially money, than is strictly necessary or expected 慷慨，大方
- **e.g.** his generosity to the poor
  I shall never forget the generosity shown by the local people.

crucially /ˈkruːʃəlɪ/ *ad.* decisively or critically 关键地，重要地
- **e.g.** Most crucially, she chose the job out of interest rather than salary.

farsightedness /ˈfɑːˈsaɪtɪdnɪs/ *n.* seeing ahead; knowing in advance; foreseeing 远见
- **e.g.** No individual or political party would have had the courage and farsightedness.
  Whether the authorities have the will and farsightedness to study the problem in depth is a matter of concern.

chaos /ˈkeɪɒs/ *n.* a situation in which everything is happening in a confused way and nothing is organized or arranged in order 混乱；无序
- **e.g.** The kitchen was in chaos.
  The country was plunged into economic chaos.

catastrophe /kəˈtæstrəfɪ/ *n.* a terrible event in which there is a lot of destruction, suffering, or death 灾难
- **e.g.** The Black Sea is facing ecological catastrophe as a result of pollution.
  This country requires food immediately to avoid a humanitarian catastrophe.

Language Study

endure *v.*
1. to be in a difficult or painful situation for a long time without complaining 忍受，忍耐
   e.g. He can't endure being apart from me.
   It seemed impossible that anyone could endure such pain.
2. (especially in negative sentences) to bear; to tolerate （尤用于否定句）容忍
   e.g. I can't endure that woman.
   I can't endure to see children suffer.

track
v. to search for a person or animal by following the marks they leave behind them on the ground, by their smell etc. 追踪
   e.g. The dogs tracked the wolf to its lair.
   The police have been tracking the four criminals all over Central America.

n.
1. [*usu. pl.*] a line of marks left on the ground by a moving person, animal, or vehicle 踪迹；痕迹
   e.g. We followed the tyre tracks across a muddy field.
   The tracks, which looked like a fox's, led into the woods.
2. a narrow path or road with a rough uneven surface 崎岖的道路或小径
   e.g. a steep mountain track
   The road leading to the farm was little more than a dirt track.
3. a circular course around which runners, cars etc. race, which often has a specially prepared surface 跑道；赛道
   e.g. a cycling track
   To run a mile, you have to run four circuits of the track.

phenomenon *n.* sth. or sb. that is very unusual because of a rare quality or ability that they have 非凡的人（或事物）
   e.g. He's a basketball phenomenon.
   Jackie Chan is an international martial arts phenomenon.

classic *n.* a book, play, or film that is important and has been admired for a long time 名著，经典
   e.g. *La Grande Illusion* is one of the classics of French cinema.
   The play has become an American classic.

unmistakable
Usage of the prefix *un-* 前缀 un- 的用法：
The prefix *un-* can be added to adjectives or adverbs to mean "not or the opposite of". Other examples are: *unhappy*（不高兴的），*unfortunate*（不幸的），*unintentionally*（无意地），*unofficially*（非正式地）。
Also *un-* can be added to a verb to express the reversal of some action or state, or removal, deprivation, release, etc. For example *uncover*（揭露，发掘）; *unfasten*（解开）; *unfold*（展开），*unlock*（开锁）.

temper *n.*
1. a tendency to become angry suddenly or easily 易怒
   e.g. That temper of hers will get her into trouble one of these days.
   Be careful, he's got a pretty violent temper.
2. [U] the way you are feeling at a particular time, especially when you are feeling angry for a short time 生气，发怒
   e.g. Peter hit his brother in a fit of temper.
   It's no use talking to him when he's in a temper.

   to keep one's temper to stay calm when it would be easy to get angry 捺住性子
   e.g. I was finding it increasingly difficult to keep my temper.
   Edward kept his temper extremely well.

   -tempered (forming compound adjectives 构成复合形容词) having or showing the specified type of temper 脾气……的，性情……的
   e.g. a hot-tempered man
   Minnie was always good-tempered and agreeable.

dynamic *a.*
1. full of energy and new ideas, and determined to succeed 精力充沛的
   e.g. dynamic and ambitious people
   Such dynamic and far-sighted traders did not operate in a context which was generally favourable to the development of wage-paid labour.
2. continuously moving or changing 动态的
   e.g. a dynamic schedule
   a dynamic and unstable process
3. relating to a force or power that causes movement 动力的
   e.g. dynamic systems
   dynamic meteorology

After Reading

READING COMPREHENSION TASKS

1. Complete the following statements according to the information in TEXT A.

1) Humans sought for knowledge just to harmonize with nature or religions before __the scientific revolution__.
2) The building of machines to harness energy drove __the Industrial Revolution__.
3) Visitors to Britain reported to their countries on the innovations in __technology and commerce__.
4) Examples given as the classic basket case are countries like __Turkey and Brazil__.
5) The careful __monetary policy__ has made milder the economic ups and downs of the industrial world.
6) Studies are made to compare nations in everything from __Internet penetration__ to inflation.
7) In the world there are still __billions of people__ living a terrible life.
8) Knowledge cannot create __the farsightedness__ that will allow people to live together peacefully.

2. Answer the following questions.

1) Why is the learning curve long and flat before the late 16th or early 17th century?
   Because before then the fruits of productive labour were limited to a few elites — princes, merchants and priests.
2) What were the results of the rise of machines that could harness energy?
   The rise of these machines drove the Industrial Revolution, and created a whole new system of life.
3) According to Thomas Hobbes, what was life like for most of humankind?
   Life was "solitary, poor, nasty, brutish, and short" for most of humankind.
4) What factors contributed to the rapid development of countries like Singapore?
   The factors include: their energies and exertions, reasonably free markets, open trade, a focus on science and technology, etc.
5) According to the writer, what were Turkey and Brazil like 20 years ago?
   They were classic basket-case, Third World economies, with triple-digit inflation, soaring debt burdens, a weak private sector and snail's-pace growth.
6) What are the examples given in the text to illustrate the statement "this learning is forcing action"?
   The examples are:
   a. There is more money being spent on vaccines and cures for diseases in Africa and Asia today than ever before in history.

b. Foreign-aid programmes face constant scrutiny and analysis.

7) Why do we need wisdom?
Because wisdom can produce good sense, courage, generosity, tolerance, and the farsightedness that will allow people to live together peacefully.

3. Explain the underlined parts in your own words.

1) The scientific revolution … marked a fundamental shift. (Para. 2)
was a sign of a most important change

2) Today the search for knowledge continues to produce an ongoing revolution in the health and wealth of humankind. (Para. 2)
make fundamental changes constantly in the area of human health and wealth

3) Others … leapfrogging the long-drawn-out process that Britain went through. (Para. 3)
catching up quickly without experiencing the extremely slow development process that Britain had

4) The diffusion of knowledge is the dominant trend of our time and goes well beyond the purely scientific. (Para. 5)
the main tendency of our age and its influence is not confined to the pure science

5) … make it difficult to push far-reaching reforms… (Para. 5)
carry out more in-depth reforms

6) But even here, there is change. (Para. 7)
But even in the world of the people who are still not living a decent life, changes are taking place.

7) … and this learning is forcing action. (Para. 7)
this recognition of global inequalities is pushing organizations or governments to take some actions

8) …knowledge is liberating. (Para. 8)
knowledge can make life easier and better

ORAL WORK

It is mentioned in TEXT A that knowledge "does not produce the farsightedness that will allow us all to live together — and grow together — on this world without causing war, chaos and catastrophe". Do you agree with this idea? Discuss with your classmates and give specific examples to support your argument.

This task is to invite further discussion on the role of knowledge in the development of humankind. The students are encouraged to make full use of the information in TEXT A as well as that in the Before Reading discussion. They may add more ideas or examples if they have any. They may either share their viewpoints in small groups or make a presentation to the whole class.

TRANSLATION OF TEXT A

人类的学习曲线

法里德·扎卡利亚

始于300年前的科学革命呈几何级数加速。其快速发展使知识的传播成为我们时代的特点。学习速度较快的国家将繁荣昌盛，但要长期保持这种局面，还需要另外一种东西——智慧。

1　设想一下，如果画一条曲线，起点为人类在地球上出现，然后记录此后人类社会的经济发展轨迹，那么这条线在16世纪晚期或17世纪初期之前是绵长而无起伏的。但自那以后，这条线开始了上升趋势。在此之前，生产劳动的成果仅属于少数精英：王公贵族、商人和神职人员等。对多数人来说，人生正如英国哲学家托马斯·霍布斯1651年那句著名的描述一样："孤独、贫穷、肮脏、粗俗和短暂。"但是就在霍布斯写下这些的时候，他周围的世界正在发生改变。简而言之，人类当时正变得越来越聪明。

2　当然，人们一直都在探索新知识，但是在当时的西欧，像伽利略、牛顿和笛卡尔这样的伟人，已开始系统地研究如何去理解和支配周围环境。科学革命以及其后出现的启蒙运动标志着一次根本性的转变。人类不再仅仅寻求各种顺应自然或神灵的方式，而是设法改变这一切。人类一旦找到驾驭能源的方式——使用蒸汽机，他们就能制造出机器，这些机器产生的动力远比任何人或马所产生的动力都要大。这样，人们工作起来就不会觉得累了。这些机器的出现推动了工业革命，从而创造了一种全新的生活方式。在当今人类的健康和财富领域，对知识的探索仍继续带来不断的革命。

3　如果科学的兴起是这一历程中的第一个伟大趋势，那么第二个伟大趋势就是科学的传播。工业革命期间英国发生的一切并不是孤立的现象。人们接连不断地去英国访问，回去后都会向自己的国家报告他们在那里所见到的科技和商业上的创新。有时，有的社会能够以极快的速度学习，如美国。而另外一些社会——如德国——则因起步晚而受益，因为它们跨越了英国所经历的漫长过程。

4　近几十年来，知识的传播速度大大加快。最近30年，我们目睹了日本、新加坡、韩国以及当今中国的飞速发展，速度是英国或美国在工业革命巅峰时期发展速度的三倍。诚然，它们能够迅速发展源于它们投入的精力与努力，但同时也是由于它们明智地，或者说是幸运地，采纳了一些在西方行之有效的发展理念——其中包括相当自由的市场、开放的贸易和对科技的关注。

5　知识的传播是我们这个时代的主流，而且远远超出了单纯的科技领域。试想一下土耳其和巴西的情况。如果你在20年前问一名经济学家对这两个国家的看法，他会说它们是典型的不可救药的国家，是第三世界经济体，通货膨胀率达到三位数，债务负担疾速增加，私营经济薄弱，增长速度极为缓慢。但如今，它们全都管理有方，通货膨胀率是一位数，经济增长率则达到了5%以上。而且全世界都在发生着这种改变。从泰国、南非、斯洛伐克到墨西哥，各国的经济管理远比过去任何时候要好。即使是在像巴西、墨西哥以及印度这样的国家，虽然政治上的束缚使改革的深入推行有难度，但政府仍然能够合理地管理各项事务。

6　我们有时不愿相信进步论，但是证据确凿，事实的确如此。在过去几年里，一些主要经济体的管理水平显著提高。谨慎的货币政策缓和了工业世界经济繁荣与萧条循环交替的局面，经济衰退较温和，造成较少的冲击。每天，人们都会读到对比各国状况的新研究结果，内容涉及从因特网普及到通货膨胀等各个方面。这些研究和所列举的事例标志着一种不断加速的学习过程，它们强调了成功的经验和失败的教训。因此我们说这是一个寻求最佳实践方法的世界。

7　我知道我所描述的是属于胜利者的世界。现在仍有数十亿人被挡在全球市场的大门外，他们的生活仍然可以用霍布斯那些无情的词语来准确描述。但即使是在这样的地方也有了变化。现在，人们对全球不平等状况的认识比过去更加清楚，而且这种认识正在促使人们采取行动。现在，用在非洲和亚洲的疫苗以及疾病治疗上的钱比以往任何时候都要多，外国援助计划经常要接受仔细审查与分析。如果事情不能按计划进展，我们也会知道。这使人们去关注援助计划或地方政府，促使它们不断改进。

8　这可能听起来过于乐观了。每场竞赛都有输赢，但是不要让对这场知识竞赛输赢方的担忧妨碍我们理解其背后更强大的动力：知识具有解放力。知识让变革和完善在方方面面都成为可能。它可以创造出神奇的设备和技术、拯救生命、提高生活水平以及传播信息。有的知识会在这个方面起作用，而另外一些则会在其他方面起作用。但总体来说，知识型的世界会是一个更为兴旺和富足的世界。

9　我要告诫大家的并不是某个国家缺少工程师或计算机，这些问题都能够解决。但是知识与智慧不是一回事。知识也可以有意或无意地创造出毁灭人类的强大手段。它能产生仇恨，设法毁灭。知识本身并不能回答"什么是好的生活？"这一古希腊问题。它并不能让人明智、勇敢、慷慨和宽容。最重要的是，它不能使人们具有一种远见，这一远见能够让我们在这个世界上共同生活——而且共同发展——同时避免战争、混乱和灾难。为此，我们需要智慧。

TEXT B Thinking Patterns

Before Reading

The purpose of this section is to arouse the student's interest in the theme of the text, reactivate their relevant background knowledge or recall their personal experience, so as to better prepare them for the succeeding tasks.

The picture on the left is an illustration of the typical thinking pattern of the Western people, which is linear in nature. The picture on the right is the typical thinking pattern of the Chinese people, which favours a roundabout way or "beating about the bush". Encourage the students to use their imagination and give as many specific examples as possible about the two typical ways of thinking. Please note that these generalizations on thinking patterns are not necessarily true to everyone in the culture.

Other questions in the Before Reading part can be used for group discussion so that the students can further understand the importance of realizing the difference of thinking patterns.

Background Information

1 the Shroud of Turin

a linen cloth bearing the image of a man who appears to have suffered physical trauma in a manner consistent with crucifixion. It is kept in the royal chapel of the Cathedral of Saint John the Baptist in Turin, northern Italy. The origins of the shroud and its image are the subject of intense debate among scientists, theologians, historians and researchers. Some contend that the shroud is the actual cloth placed on the body of Jesus Christ at the time of his burial, and that the face image is the Holy Face of Jesus, while others contend that the artifact was created in the Middle Ages.

2 the Star of Bethlehem

(also called the Christmas Star) a star in Christian tradition that revealed the birth of Jesus to the Magi, or "wise men", and later led them to Bethlehem. According to the Gospel of Matthew, the Magi were men "from the east" who were inspired by the appearance of the star to travel to Jerusalem. There they met King Herod of Judea, and asked where the king of the Jews had been born. Herod then asked his advisers where a messiah could be born. They replied Bethlehem, a nearby village, and quoted a prophecy by Micah. While the Magi were on their way to Bethlehem, the star appeared again. Following the star, which stopped above the place where Jesus was born, the Magi found Jesus with his mother, paid him homage, worshipped him and gave gifts.

3 Roderick McLeod

the first foreign accountant to set up shop in China and later became the founder and CEO of two Chinese-American joint ventures. He learned about doing business in China by profiting from his own mistakes as well as those of other Westerners who had come to China with high hopes but no cultural sensitivity. The real value of his book, *China Inc: How to Do Business with the Chinese* (New York, 1988), lies in the ten "Businessmen's Horror Stories" he tells about the cultural errors made by foreigners in China and in his discussions of typical business problems — some Chinese in origin, some Western in origin, some common to both sides. The book has a breezy style that makes for easy reading.

Reading

New Words and Expressions

personnel /ˌpɜːsəˈnel/ *n.* the people who work in a company, organization, or military force 员工；人员
e.g. senior military personnel
All personnel are to receive security badges.

workforce /ˈwɜːkfɔːs/ *n.* all the people who work in a particular industry or company, or are available to work in a particular country or area 全体从业人员；劳动力
e.g. Women now represent almost 50% of the workforce.
The company is in great need of skilled workforce.

engage in to be doing or to become involved in an activity 参加，参与
e.g. Only 10% of American adults engage in regular exercise.
The two parties engaged in an escalating political struggle.

Christian /ˈkrɪstjən/ *a.* related to Christianity 基督教的；信奉基督教的
e.g. the Christian church
the Christian religion

sacred /ˈseɪkrɪd/ *a.* relating to a god or religion 神的；宗教的
e.g. the miraculous powers of sacred relics
Certain animals were considered sacred.

secular /ˈsekjʊlə/ *a.* not connected with or controlled by a church or other religious authority 与教会无关的；世俗的
e.g. secular education
our modern secular society

inquiry /ɪnˈkwaɪərɪ/ *n.* an official investigation 探索；调查
e.g. On further inquiry, it emerged that Malcolm had not been involved in the incident.
The local council set up a committee of inquiry to look into policing arrangements.

intersect /ˌɪntəˈsekt/ *v.* to meet or go across each other 和……相交
e.g. The line AB intersects the line CD at X.
The road intersects the highway a mile from here.

the faithful the people who believe in a religion 教徒；信众

e.g. read the Sacred Scriptures to the faithful
church bells calling the faithful to evening prayer

bear /beə/ *v.* to have or show a sign, mark, or particular appearance, especially when this shows that sth. has happened or is true 带有
e.g. The letter bore no signature.
The town still bears the scars of the bombings during the war.

Christ /kraɪst/ *n.* Jesus Christ, the man who is worshipped by Christians as the son of God 基督
e.g. a follower of Christ
The Portuguese came to Brazil to win souls for Christ and to win gold for the king.

unbelief /ˌʌnbɪˈliːf/ *n.* a lack of religious belief, or a refusal to believe in a religious faith 无信仰；不信宗教
e.g. The distinction between doubt and unbelief is valid and useful.
He suggests that there is no difference between belief and unbelief and that each is more tempted by the other.

Biblical /ˈbɪblɪkəl/ *a.* written in or relating to the Bible 《圣经》的；有关《圣经》的

account /əˈkaʊnt/ *n.* a written or spoken description that says what happens in an event or process 描写；叙述
e.g. This gives a first-hand account of the war.
Eye-witness accounts told of the unprovoked shooting of civilians.

astronomical /ˌæstrəˈnɒmɪkəl/ *a.* relating to the scientific study of the stars 天文的；天体的
e.g. an astronomical device
Its existence casts doubt on the current astronomical theory of the distribution of galaxies and the large-scale structure of the universe.

knowing /ˈnəʊɪŋ/ *n.* the process or act of getting to know 认知，认识
e.g. Awareness is the first order of knowing.
If he didn't keep his promise, there was no knowing what Lee would do.

schizophrenic /ˌskɪdzəʊˈfrenɪk/ *a.* inconsistent, contradictory 分裂的；自相矛盾的

e.g. schizophrenic attitude
The film was an example of schizophrenic movie-making at its worst.

Hindu /ˈhɪnduː/ *n.* sb. whose religion is Hinduism 印度教徒
e.g. The cow is a sacred animal to Hindus.
Many Hindus believe that they must visit Varanasi and bathe in the Ganges at least once in their lifetimes.

undertaking /ˌʌndəˈteɪkɪŋ/ *n.* an important job, piece of work, or activity that you are responsible for 所承担的任务；事业
e.g. Getting married is a serious undertaking.
Starting a new business can be a risky undertaking.

episode /ˈepɪsəʊd/ *n.* an event or a short period of time during which sth. happens 片段
e.g. That's an episode in my life I'd rather forget!
one of the most interesting episodes in his career

occupy /ˈɒkjʊpaɪ/ *v.* to live or stay in a place 居住；占用
e.g. He occupies the house without paying any rent.
The building was purchased and occupied by its new owners last year.

seamlessly /ˈsiːmlɪslɪ/ *ad.* consistently; perfectly 自然地；完美地
e.g. Software is integrated seamlessly from site to site.
Fairfax could fit into any of those photographs seamlessly.

unseen /ˌʌnˈsiːn/ *a.* not noticed or seen 看不见的；潜在的
e.g. unseen dangers
Rachel crept out of the house unseen.

ineffable /ɪnˈefəbl/ *a.* too great to be described in words 难以表达的，难以名状的
e.g. an ineffable sadness
Mr. Sparks sat behind his desk with a smile of ineffable self-satisfaction.

inexpressible /ˌɪnɪkˈspresəbl/ *a.* too strong to be described in words 无法表达的
e.g. inexpressible gratitude
After silence, that which comes nearest to expressing the inexpressible is music.

by any means in any way possible; to any extent 不管怎样；无论如何
e.g. He insisted that all of us should be there on time by any means.
By any means, we should tell him frankly what we think of his proposal.

delineate /dɪˈlɪnɪeɪt/ *v.* to show by drawing or describing; to portray 描绘；描写
e.g. delineate her features
He delineated his plans to the audience.

to a greater extent to a greater degree; more 更大程度上，更加
e.g. Its success will depend to a greater extent on local attitudes.
It will affect farmers in France and to a greater extent in Spain.

shaman /ˈʃæmən/ *n.* sb. in some tribes who is a religious leader and is believed to be able to talk to spirits and cure illnesses 萨满
e.g. a Siberian shaman
a native American shaman

vary /ˈveərɪ/ *v.* to be different from each other 不同
e.g. flowers that vary in colour and size
Test scores vary from school to school.

verify /ˈverɪfaɪ/ *v.* to make sure that sth. is correct or true 证实；核实
e.g. verify the figures
A computer programme verifies that the system is working.

frame /freɪm/ *v.* to carefully plan the way to ask a question, make a statement etc. 表达；设计
e.g. frame a question
She wondered how she was going to frame the reply.

be capable of to have the qualities or ability needed to do sth. 能做……
e.g. I don't think he's capable of murder.
The company isn't capable of handling an order that large.

socialization /ˌsəʊʃəlaɪˈzeɪʃən/ *n.* the process by which people, especially children, are made to behave in a way that is acceptable in their society 适应社会
e.g. individual socialization
Schools play an important part in the socialization of our children.

monocultural /ˌmɒnəʊˈkʌltʃərəl/ *a.* involving or including people or ideas of one country, race, or religion 单一文化的
e.g. a monocultural society
In a monocultural classroom, students and teacher are from one culture.

counterpart /ˈkaʊntəpɑːt/ *n.* sb. or sth. that has

the same job or purpose as sb. or sth. else in a different place 对应的人或物
e.g. Belgian officials are discussing this with their French counterparts.
The Danish government has lodged a protest with its Norwegian counterpart.

invoke /ɪnˈvəʊk/ *v.* to make a particular idea, image, or feeling appear in people's minds 引起；唤起
e.g. a painting that invokes images of the Rocky Mountains
During his speech, he invoked the memory of Harry Truman.

shrink /ʃrɪŋk/ *v.* to become or to make sth. smaller in amount, size, or value 减少；缩小
e.g. We want to expand the business, not shrink it.
The firm's staff had shrunk to only four people.

widget /ˈwɪdʒɪt/ *n.* a gadget or mechanical device 小装置；小机械
e.g. Company A produces 200 widgets a day at a unit price of $3.
Annotations can be added to any widget to clarify functionality.

productivity /ˌprɒdʌkˈtɪvəti/ *n.* the rate at which goods are produced, and the amount produced, especially in relation to the work, time, and money needed to produce them 生产率；生产力
e.g. high productivity levels in manufacturing
It cost the country $4 million in lost productivity.

accountant /əˈkaʊntənt/ *n.* sb. whose job is to keep and check financial accounts, calculate taxes etc. 会计
e.g. My accountant has advised me to stop claiming.
The man described himself as a self-employed accountant.

campaign /kæmˈpeɪn/ *n.* a series of actions intended to achieve a particular result relating to politics or business, or a social improvement 活动；运动
e.g. launch a campaign for equal rights
Florida was a key state in his campaign for re-election.

linear /ˈlɪniə/ *a.* involving a series of connected events, ideas etc. that move or progress from one stage to the next 直线型的
e.g. linear thinking
Students do not always progress in a linear fashion.

arrowhead /ˈærəʊhed/ *n.* sth. that resembles the head of an arrow in shape 箭头（形状）
e.g. They were going to put the dots in the shape of an arrowhead.
A great arrowhead, outlined with coloured markers, had split the British Front wide open.

descriptor /dɪˈskrɪptə/ *n.* a word or expression used to describe or identify sth. 描述词
e.g. The descriptor is not specific to any language.
Each descriptor has to be updated.

Aristotelian /ˌærɪstɒˈtiːliən/ *a.* of or relating to Aristotle or to his philosophy 亚里士多德的；亚里士多德学派的
e.g. Aristotelian logic
Aristotelian physics was to some extent quite successful.

syllogism /ˈsɪlədʒɪzəm/ *n.* a statement with three parts, the first two of which prove that the third part is true 三段论；演绎推理
e.g. It was on the basis of that syllogism that the connection between schools and parents developed for another decade or more.
"All men will die, Socrates is a man, therefore Socrates will die" is an example of syllogism.

embed /ɪmˈbed/ *v.* to implant a certain idea, attitude or feeling so that people believe or feel it very strongly 深信；强烈感受
e.g. deeply embedded feelings of shame
Feelings of guilt are deeply embedded in her personality.

intercultural /ˌɪntəˈkʌltʃərəl/ *a.* between different cultures 不同文化间的
e.g. an intercultural marriage
intercultural exchange in the arts

syllogistic /ˌsɪləˈdʒɪstɪk/ *a.* of, relating to, resembling, or consisting of a syllogism or syllogisms 三段论的；演绎推理的
e.g. Finally, Gassendi attacks the idea that proofs must be syllogistic in form.
The logical theory of syllogistic arguments was developed in great detail by Aristotle.

and so forth　and so on; et cetera 等等
e.g. In our hometown, people grow wheat, rice, cotton, and so forth.
She started telling me about her bad back, her migraines, and so forth.

parallelism /ˈpærəlelɪzəm/ *n.* the state of occurring or existing at the same time or in a similar way 对应；一致
e.g. There is a parallelism between fatigue and the ability to sleep.

sequence /ˈsiːkwəns/ *n.* a series of related events, actions etc. that happen or are done in a particular order 一连串
e.g. the sequence of events leading up to the war
He's had a sequence of business failures.

antithesis /ænˈtɪθɪsɪs/ *n.* the complete opposite of sth. 对立，相反
e.g. This is not democratic. It is the antithesis of democracy.
Theorists have constantly and explicitly used antitheses such as active/passive, reason/emotion.

nevertheless /ˌnevəðəˈles/ *ad.* in spite of a fact that has been mentioned 仍然；不过
e.g. It does indicate, nevertheless, a step in the right direction.
What you said was true. It was, nevertheless, a little unkind.

exclusive /ɪkˈskluːsɪv/ *a.* not admitting sth. else; rejecting other considerations 排他的
e.g. The list is not exclusive.
Lesbianism and motherhood are not mutually exclusive.

linkage /ˈlɪŋkɪdʒ/ *n.* a connection or relation; an association 关联，联系
e.g. the linkage between wages and prices
The present work aims to investigate the linkage between "organizational culture" and effectiveness with regard to consumer representation.

wholeness /ˈhəʊlnɪs/ *n.* the state of being complete and entire 整体性；整体
e.g. a vision of wholeness
Emotions are part of our wholeness.

liken /ˈlaɪkən/ *v.* to show the resemblance between one thing and another 类比
e.g. Life has been likened to a journey.
Critics have likened the new theatre to a supermarket.

momentous /məʊˈmentəs/ *a.* very important because of its great influence on the future 重要的
e.g. a momentous decision
His colleagues all recognized that this was a momentous occasion.

encounter /ɪnˈkaʊntə/ *n.* an occasion when people meet 见面，会面
e.g. His first encounter with Wilson was back in 1989.
Bernstein began training the young musician after a chance encounter at a concert.

figure /ˈfɪɡə/ *v.* to appear or be mentioned, especially prominently 出现；被谈及
e.g. Social issues figured prominently in the talks.
My wishes didn't figure among his considerations.

specifically /spɪˈsɪfɪkəli/ *ad.* in a specific manner 特别是
e.g. Specifically, the department wanted answers to the following question.
More specifically, they hold very similar views on the issues of authority and law.

substantive /ˈsʌbstəntɪv/ *a.* having a firm basis in reality and so important, meaningful, or considerable 实在的；实质性的
e.g. a guarantee of substantive progress
The Government reported that substantive discussions had taken place between the two parties.

at hand needing to be dealt with now 目前需要做的
e.g. Peter turned his attention to the task at hand.

philosophical /ˌfɪləˈsɒfɪkəl/ *a.* of, relating to, or based on the study of the fundamental nature of knowledge, reality, and existence 哲学的
e.g. lots of people will welcome your philosophical position.
Colleagues are impressed by her willingness to link large philosophical issues with day-to-day matters.

daunting /ˈdɔːntɪŋ/ *a.* frightening in a way that makes people feel less confident 令人生畏的
e.g. The trip seemed rather daunting for a young girl.
We must not be complacent because the challenges ahead are indeed very daunting.

complexity /kəmˈpleksəti/ *n.* the state of being complicated 复杂性
e.g. a design of great complexity
There is increasing recognition of the complexity of the causes of poverty.

quantum /ˈkwɒntəm/ *n.* a unit of energy in

nuclear physics 量子
e.g. quantum mechanics
quantum leap   a very large and important development or improvement 大突破，突飞猛进
e.g. The treatment of breast cancer has taken a quantum leap forward.
There has been a quantum leap in the range of the wines sold in the UK.
categorize /ˈkætɪɡəraɪz/ v. to put people or things into groups according to the type of person or thing they are 分类，归类
e.g. Keene doesn't like to be categorized as an economist.
The population is categorized according to age, sex, and social group.

contradiction /ˌkɒntrəˈdɪkʃən/ n. a difference between two statements, beliefs, or ideas about sth. that means they cannot both be true 矛盾，不一致
e.g. apparent contradictions in the defendant's testimony
a contradiction between the government's ideas and its actual policies
reconcile /ˈrekənsaɪl/ v. to make (aims, statements, ideas, etc.) agree when they seem to conflict 调和；使……和谐
e.g. The possibility remains that the two theories may be reconciled.
He tried to reconcile the evidence with the facts.

Language Study

print v.
1. to produce words, numbers, or pictures on paper, using a machine which puts ink onto the surface 留印记；打印
   e.g. I need to make a few changes before I print the document.
2. to produce many printed copies of a book, newspaper etc. 出版；印刷
   e.g. Over five million copies of the paper are printed every day.
3. to write words by hand without joining the letters 用印刷体手写
   e.g. Please print your name clearly in the top right hand corner of the page.

account
   n. an arrangement in which a bank keeps your money safe so that you can pay more in or take money out 银行账户
   take sth. into account   to consider or include particular facts or details when making a decision or judgment about sth. 考虑；包括
   e.g. These figures do not take account of changes in the rate of inflation.
   on account of sth.   because of sth., especially a problem or difficulty 由于
   e.g. She was told to wear flat shoes, on account of her back problem.
   v. to think of (sb. or sth.) in a specified way 考虑，认为
   e.g. Their first project was accounted (= considered) a success.

venture v.
1. to go somewhere that could be dangerous 冒险
   e.g. When darkness fell, he would venture out.
   She paused before venturing up the steps to the door.
2. to say or do sth. in an uncertain way 冒昧地问；大着胆做
   e.g. "You're on holiday here?" he ventured.
   I ventured to ask him what he was writing.

occupy v.
1. to fill a period of time 占用（时间）
   e.g. Football occupies most of my leisure time.
   Only six percent of police time is occupied with criminal incidents.
2. to enter a place in a large group and keep control of it, especially by military force 占领；占据
   e.g. an occupying army

Students occupied Sofia University on Monday.

3. to fill a particular amount of space 占用（空间）

    e.g. A bed occupies the corner of the room.

    Family photos occupied almost the entire wall.

4. to use sth. such as a seat or bed 占用（座位、床位等）

    e.g. Many patients who are occupying hospital beds could be transferred to other places.

monocultural

Usage of the prefix *mono-* 前缀mono-的用法：

The prefix mono- means "one". Other examples include: *monoplane* 单翼机；*monolingual* 只用一种语言的；*monologue* 独白；*monogamy* 一夫一妻制.

exclusive *a.*

1. available or belonging only to particular people, and not shared 独有的，专享的

    e.g. This offer is exclusive to readers of *China Daily*.

    Our figure skating club has exclusive use of the rink on Mondays.

2. of (places, organizations, clothes etc.) very expensive so that not many people can afford to use or buy 高级的；专供富人的

    e.g. an exclusive girls' school

    Bel Air is an exclusive suburb of Los Angeles.

3. deliberately not allowing sb. to do sth. or be part of a group 排外的

    e.g. a racially exclusive hiring policy

    He is part of an exclusive social circle and belongs to an exclusive club.

4. excluding all but the thing specified 唯一的

    e.g. Painting has not been her exclusive occupation.

    The committee's exclusive focus will be to improve public transportation.

5. not including sth. 不算在内，不包括

    e.g. Our prices are exclusive of sales tax.

    The ship has a crew of 57 exclusive of officers.

After Reading

READING COMPREHENSION TASKS

1. Read the following statements and decide whether they are true (T) or false (F).

1) Most organizations have training programmes for employees because they engage in global activities. (F)
2) In Christian cultures, faith is supposed to help people know spiritual truths. (T)
3) For the Hindus in India, material life and spiritual life cannot be separated. (T)
4) People's life experiences are closely related to their patterns of thinking. (T)
5) Cause-and-effect thinking is the only pattern for members of Western cultures. (F)
6) Aristotelian syllogism is a natural phenomenon of the human mind. (F)
7) Chinese patterns of thinking are always seeking links to show contrasts. (F)
8) Roderick McLeod promises that patterns of thinking will help cross-cultural understanding. (F)

2. Answer the following questions.

1) What are the examples given to support the statement "science's findings have little effect on the beliefs of the faithful"?

    a. Scientific analyses of the Shroud of Turin have had little effect on belief or unbelief.

b. Similarly, attempts to explain the Star of Bethlehem by astronomical computer programmes run backward in time have had little effect on belief.

2) What is the Hindus' view of *knowing*?
   There is no separation between sacred and secular. No separation is made between material life and spiritual life. All of life is sacred.

3) Why do people like priests, shamans, wise women enjoy a high status?
   Because they are in the position to explain the ineffable and inexpressible in their culture.

4) What does a "reasonable person" mean in Western culture?
   A "reasonable person" is one who sees relationships of cause and effect between things.

5) Is the cause-and-effect pattern a universal phenomenon? Why?
   No. Actually, it is an invention of the human mind. It has been deeply embedded in the Anglo-European tradition for such a long time that speakers of English tend to assume that it is a natural phenomenon of the human mind.

6) What is the fundamental philosophical basis for the thinking patterns found in Chinese business communication?
   The unity of human experience with the whole of life is the fundamental philosophical basis for the thinking patterns in Chinese business communication.

7) What is Russians' attitude towards extremes and contradictions?
   Russians like extremes and contradictions. They do not seek to reconcile them but to see them exist together in a pattern.

3. Explain the underlined parts in your own words.

1) The need to learn is unavoidable when an organization engages … (Para. 1)
   There is inevitably a need to learn about cultural differences

2) In Western Christian cultures …spiritual truths are generally held to be knowable through faith … (Para. 2)
   it is generally believed that spiritual truths can be made known through faith

3) … science's findings have little effect on the beliefs of the faithful. (Para. 2)
   do not change the beliefs of the Christians

4) …all life is seamlessly part of the real, unseen but felt realm of the divine. (Para. 3)
   all life is naturally part of the spiritual world which is real but invisible, and can be felt by people

5) …these people enjoy a high status. (Para. 4)
   people like priests, shamans and wise women receive much respect in society and they are on the upper part of the social ladder

6) … but babies learn to pattern thinking after the patterns their world shows them. (Para. 6)
   babies learn to think in the way that their world shows them

7) … and to discern the difference in an individual's patterns of thought that the cultural change brings. (Para. 6)
   to find out the difference in one's way of thinking when one moves from one culture to another

8) So deeply embedded is this notion that it is assumed to be universal. (Para. 9)
   This concept of Aristotelian syllogism is so deeply rooted in Western culture that many Westerners would believe that it is common to all other cultures.

9) But that is itself a pattern generated by culture. (Para. 15)
   to identify opposites and categorize is actually a pattern of thinking determined by culture

10) <u>In Russia, thinking patterns embrace contradictions rather than oppose them.</u> (Para. 15)
    <u>Russians are happy to accept the existence of contradictions and extremes.</u>

ORAL WORK

Conduct a research on the differences of thinking patterns between Chinese people and Western people and prepare a mini report to your group. Give specific examples to support your points of view.

This task is to encourage the students to make full use of the different resources at hand (library, Internet, etc.) to search for reliable information. The teacher may, if necessary, give guidance to the students on how to do research on a specific topic and make a mini report to a group of people.

TRANSLATION OF TEXT B

思维方式

琳达·比默

1　文化决定了认知和学习的含义。对于任何打算或者已经雇用了具有多元文化背景的员工的组织机构来说，这一基本事实很重要。大部分组织机构为员工提供培训，期望他们能随着技术和机构需求的变化继续学习新知识。而如果一个组织的员工具有多元文化背景或者该组织第一次开展跨国业务，学习是必不可少的。

2　什么是可知的？是否有些东西是不可知的呢？在西方基督教文化中，自从千百年前宗教与世俗社会分离后，一般认为宗教的真谛只有通过信仰才可以知晓：如果你相信，那么它就是可知的。即使在科学调查和信仰相交叉时，科学发现对于信仰者的信念也基本没有影响。对都灵裹尸布——有些基督徒坚信上面印有耶稣的身体轮廓——进行的科学分析，目前并没有对信教或不信教产生多少影响。对于《圣经》里记载的耶稣降生时出现的伯利恒之星，天文科学家们用电脑程序将时间倒退以模拟当时的星空，尝试作出解释，但这同样对精神信仰没有产生什么影响。对于这一文化传统中的基督徒来说，精神世界与物质世界中的认知途径是不同的。

3　其他文化的人们则认为这种认知途径很奇怪，而且很分裂。对他们来说，宗教与世俗是无法分离的。比如，对于印度教徒来说，人类所有的行为以及大自然的一切——实际上是所有东西——都与精神密不可分。教徒每天都会进庙膜拜，有时候一天去三四次。商人投资时会祈求神的保佑，新的工作场所投入使用前也会进行祈福活动。物质生活和精神生活不可分；生活的一切都是真实无形但可感知的神的王国密不可分的一部分。生活的一切都是神圣的。任何希望在印度开展业务的外国公司必须接受这一认知观。

4　有些东西太难以言传——太神圣，难以用言语表达——因而也无法被认知。描绘和界定这些东西的更可能是那些专司此职的人——牧师、萨满和智女们——而不是一般的商人。在这些不可认知的东西受重视的文化中，这些人的社会地位就很高。

5　人们的认知方式和思维方式是紧密相关的。思维方式也因文化的不同而不同。它反映出一个人的生活经历（反之亦然：生活经历可以验证思维方式）。思维方式影响着人们怎样组织生活中的交往。

6　思维方式是人出生后就开始习得的，具有文化决定性。我们认为正常的婴儿能用人类历史上所有使用过的思维方式去思考，但是他们会学着仿照所接触到的思维方式来塑造自己的方式。如果他们足够幸运，能够在社会化的过程中接触到不止一种文化，那么他们将会学到比单一文化中的同龄人更多的思维方式。观察一个人从一种文化进入另一种文化，辨识出他的思维方式由此所产生的变化，是一件非常有趣的事。

7　或许西方文化中最典型的思维方式就是因果式。英语中的讲"道理"就是讲理由、讲为什么。事实上，一个人"讲道理"就是指这个人明辨事物之间的因果关系。西方文化中的"为什么"问题必然引起对原因的解释：为什么在马来西亚某小产品的市场份额减少了？为什么三月份的生产率数据提高了？为什么总会计师今天没有上班?(因为我们的竞争对手"某有限公司[Widgets Inc.]"上月发起了营销活动。因为三月份新设备运行顺畅。因为她丈夫做手术了。)

8 因果思维方式是直线性的,在"因"与"果"之间可以画一条直线,箭头指向"果"。英语中的很多句子都运用了这一模式。就以上一句话为例:主语是"句子",带有描述词("很多"、"英语中的");"运用"是"句子"发出的动作;"这一模式"是结果,或者说是动词的动作所引起的结果。

9 西方人认为因果思维是符合逻辑的,"逻辑"意即因果,这是西方人所说的亚里士多德三段论。三段论在西方思想中根深蒂固,被认为具有普遍性。但正如一些跨文化专家所提醒人们的,事实并非如此:

10 亚里士多德的三段论……不是一个普遍现象;它在盎格鲁-欧洲文化传统中历史悠久,以致讲英语的人往往认为这不是大脑的一种创造,而是人类思维的自然现象。

11 当西方商人发现逻辑对于西方世界以外的人们意味着迥然不同的东西时,他们多么震惊啊!例如,中国人经常使用含有性质对比的逻辑:有A必有B,有热必然有冷等等。这种思维方式所带来的逻辑形式就是平行对立,或者说是一系列并不相互排斥的对立。

12 中国式思维方式的关键是联系。人们总是在寻求联系来说明人生的整体性,即使这一整体里包含各种对立也没关系。现在的事情会与过去发生的大事相类比。中国商人在谈判中也使用这一联系的思维模式。比如,谈判双方的见面会被比作很久以前历史上发生的国家间的重大交流。这种对历史事件的重提通常会发生在谈判开始时期的非正式场合,尤其是在中方向外方客人致祝酒词时。而西方商人通常不能理解这种做法,因为他们从这些历史中看不出任何与当前商业谈判之间的联系。这种人类经验与人生整体的统一性,是中国商人在商业交往中思维方式的哲学基础。

13 罗德里克·麦克劳德在《中国公司:如何和中国人做生意》中描述了中国式思维方式:

14 我认为如果能对思维方式的深刻内涵及其复杂性进行充分研究的话,跨文化沟通与交流有望取得"量子跃迁"式的重大突破。

15 欧洲人倾向于分类的思维方式。这次对于思维方式的探讨就涉及了两个极端,一个是因果,另一个是联系。也就是说,确立了对立的双方。然而这本身就是一种由文化产生出的思维模式。在俄罗斯,人们的思维方式是接受矛盾,而不是排斥矛盾。俄罗斯人愿意看到极端和对立,他们不会寻求两者的调和,而是很乐于见到它们在一种模式中共存。

INTEGRATED EXERCISES

1 PUBLIC SPEECH TRAINING

The following is part of a speech to persuade people to become regular blood donors. Listen and then practice after the recording.

(The speech will be read twice. For the first time, the students just listen and try to understand the meaning. When it is read for the second time, there are pauses in the recording. Ask the students to practice after the speaker during these pauses and pay attention to the speaker's intonation, voice [e.g. loudness, pitch, tempo] etc.)

Script

Are you at least 17 years old? / Do you weigh more than 110 pounds? / Do you consider yourself fairly healthy? / If you answered yes to all these questions, / you should be donating blood every two months. / In my survey of the class, / I found that only 50 percent of you have ever donated blood before / and that only 1 out 13 of you donate on a regular basis. / The lack of participation of eligible donors / is a serious problem that requires immediate action. / Through extensive research and two years of faithfully donating blood, / I've come to realize the magnitude of this problem / and just how easy the solution can be. / Today I would like to show why blood donors are in such desperate need / and encourage you to take action to meet this need. / Let's first take a look at the overwhelming need for blood donors.

2 DICTATION

Listen to the following passage and write it down. The passage will be read four times. During the first reading, which will be done at normal speed, listen and try to understand the meaning. For the second and third readings, the passage will be read sentence by sentence, or phrase by phrase, with intervals of 15 seconds. Write down what you hear. The last reading will be done at normal speed again and during this time you should check your work.

Script

According to a survey published recently by a Japanese think-tank, / there are greater differences between the career ambitions / of Chinese female teenagers and their Japanese counterparts. / The top five desired careers among Chinese female teens / included president or chief executive of a company, senior manager, or teacher. / The top five list for Japanese girls included housewife, flight attendant and childcare worker. / The survey said that Japanese youths have a strong desire for stability. / In contrast, young Chinese want to move up in the world. / Some economists have noted that women are Japan's most under-utilized resource. / It was recently reported that if Japanese female participation rates rose to levels currently seen in the US, / this would add 2.6 million people to the workforce. / This would raise Japan's trend GDP growth rate / from 1.2 per cent to 1.5 per cent over the next two decades.

3 VOCABULARY STUDY

Task One
Put the proper form of the words in the corresponding blanks.

1) There are __inequalities__ in wealth distribution. (equal)
2) The film was a huge __commercial__ success. (commerce)
3) They were doing some type of statistical __analysis__. (analyze)
4) Medical treatment __varies__ greatly from state to state. (various)
5) I was reluctant to trust my senses but the sign was __unmistakable__. (mistake)
6) __Constraints__ on spending have forced the company to rethink its plans. (constrain)
7) Bankers are cautiously __optimistic__ about the country's economic future. (optimism)
8) Scientists have many theories about how the universe first came into __existence__. (exist)
9) There is now clear __evidence__ that these chemicals are damaging the environment. (evident)
10) Much of our debate focused on the __philosophical__ problem of whether there is free will. (philosophy)

Task Two
Fill in the blanks with the correct form of the words or expressions in the box. You may need to make other changes.

1) Love and hate are __extremes__ of passion.
2) The economy went __from boom to bust__ very quickly.
3) How is the extra work going to __fit into__ the schedule?
4) Though very intelligent, she is __nevertheless__ rather modest.
5) The British Empire was __at its peak__ in the mid 19th century.
6) She decided she would try to forget the __episode__ by the lake.
7) There's been a decline in the __living standards__ of old people.
8) All these __attempts__ aimed to pull the country out of recession.
9) He was too shocked to give an __account__ of what had happened.
10) This advertisement is a __typical__ example of their marketing strategy.

Task Three
Choose the right word and use its proper form to complete each sentence.

1) limit   limitation   constraint
   - It's a good little car, but it has its __limitations__.
   - The cheque must not exceed the __limit__ set by the banker's card.
   - There have been financial and political __constraints__ on development.

2) amazing   amazed
   - You'd be __amazed__ how much money you can save.
   - The __amazing__ picture was taken by a *Mirror* reader seconds before the plane crashed.

3) compare   contrast
   - The snow was icy and white, __contrasting__ with the brilliant blue sky.
   - The report __compares__ the different types of home computer available.
   - Miller's organized desk stood in marked __contrast__ to the rest of the office.

4) destruction   damage
- The closure of the factory will cause severe __damage__ to the local economy.
- They decided to close the plant in order to compensate for the __destruction__ of the local economy.

Task Four
Fill in the following blanks with appropriate words from the box.

The significance of toasts to North Americans is not deep; it is a friendly invitation to others to join the toaster in a drink. This 1) __pleasant__ but shallow meaning is the one Chinese advisers 2) __identify__ for Chinese businessmen who may find themselves at North American banquet 3) __tables__. One writer reports that banquet toasts in the US are very simple, usually just to the 4) __health__ of the guest of honor, to the prosperity of the US or sometimes is just a simple "Cheers!" 5) __Occasionally__, he declares, the toast is to the "new dish". He 6) __assures__ his readers that Westerners do not emphasize toasts. They do, 7) __however__, emphasize conversation during meals, says this writer. Therefore, Chinese must be 8) __cautious__ and conduct themselves as if on a battleground with victory at stake. 9) __Clearly__, the significance attached to this 10) __toasting__ business is greater in Chinese culture than in the 11) __West__. Not are Western business travelers 12) __reluctant__ to understand; there are simply no guides to 13) __explain__ what is going on. This article will show that toasts are 14) __nothing__ less than the opening statement by the Chinese of their negotiating position, and Western business guests who dismiss them risk 15) __losing__ a key opportunity to understand their Chinese 16) __hosts__. To appreciate the meaning behind toasts, we will first look at the historical use of toasts, then at the present-day use, with a modern example.

4 GRAMMAR FOCUS

Read the following passage, underline the one mistake in each line and write the correction after the bracketed number.

Third Culture Kids (TCKs) are children who spent a significant part of his or her developmental years out the parents' culture. They grow up in a genuine cross-cultural world and incorporate different culture on the deepest level, so as to have several cultures incorporated with their thought processes. This not only meant that TCKs have deep cultural access to at least two cultures; that also means that their thought processes are truly multicultural. That, in return, influences how TCKs relate with the world around them, and make TCKs' thought processes different even from members of the cultures they have deep-level access to, a phenomena know as cultural jet lag. TCKs also have certain personal characteristics as common. Growing up in the third culture reward certain behaviors and personality traits in different ways than growing up in a single culture does, that results in common characteristics.

1) have spent
2) outside
3) genuinely
4) cultures
5) into
6) means
7) this
8) turn
9) to
10) makes
11) phenomenon
12) known
13) in
14) rewards
15) which

1) 时态错误：描述已完成并对现在造成影响的动作，应该用现在完成时have spent。
2) 介词使用错误：表示"在……之外"，应该用outside。
3) 副词搭配错误：修饰形容词cross-cultural应该用副词genuinely。
4) 名词单复数错误：这里culture用作可数名词，应该是cultures。
5) 介词搭配错误：incorporate应该和into搭配。
6) 时态错误：从上下文看这里应该用一般现在时means。
7) 指代错误：这里是并列结构，前文用this，这里也应该用this。
8) 固定搭配错误：根据上下文逻辑关系，这里应该是in turn（转而，反过来）。
9) 介词搭配错误：relate应该和to搭配。
10) 主谓一致错误：这句话的主语是that，所以make应改为makes。
11) 名词单复数错误：phenomena是phenomenon的复数形式。
12) 非谓语动词错误：应该用过去分词known（表示被动态）来修饰前面的名词。
13) 固定搭配错误：这里应该是in common（共有的）。
14) 主谓一致错误：这句话的主语是动名词词组Growing up，所以reward应改为rewards。
15) 引导词错误：非限定性定语从句不能由that引导，应改为which。

5 TRANSLATION

Task One
Translate the following paragraph from English into Chinese.

BBC四台正在播出一部系列纪录片，阐述了统计学并非枯燥的催眠曲，而是世界上最令人兴奋的话题之一。纪录片《统计的乐趣》既属于公共数据领域的插科打诨，也清醒地洞察到我们对周遭社会认识的不足。BBC找到了最合适的主持人——汉斯·罗斯林来带领观众领略数字的魅力。罗斯林是瑞典国际卫生教授，长期致力于探索这个变化的世界的事实和数据。在接下来的BBC系列片节选中，罗斯林用一种新方式做了他最著名的一个演讲，让我们了解了过去200年的世界历史，以及全球财富和卫生状况的不均衡发展。没有人能像罗斯林那样使统计听起来如此令人敬畏。

虽然这不是罗斯林第一次做这个讲座，但这是他第一次在演讲中应用增强现实技术。他一直不断努力寻求既能传递信息又能吸引听众的数据呈现方法。长期以来，罗斯林一直用精彩的演讲向世人表明，了解世界变化的历史对规划美好未来意义重大。

Task Two
Translate the following paragraph from Chinese into English.

People are now enjoying one of the greatest technological boom times in human history. While the invention of automobiles was a landmark in the technological evolution of humankind, the widespread use of computers and telecommunications technology has dramatically reshaped the nature of the society. One might have benefited a lot from one's improved ability to move rapidly from one place to another because of the availability of automobiles, yet one can benefit even more with the advent of the Internet. With Internet access, the world has become accessible to people and one can perform many tasks at home and let their fingers do the walking. Lifestyles are changed by modern technologies in equal measure. Computers and the Internet have liberated people from busy work or other chores and consequently allowed people to enjoy more leisure time.

6 CLASSROOM INTERACTION

Activity A   Listening

Issues of communicating with people from another culture

I. Use of Silence

   Silence may be regarded as:
   - a sign of 1) __thoughtfulness__ and deference to the original speaker;
   - a sign of 2) __hostility__ .

   3) __Twenty__ seconds of silence during a meeting can make Westerners feel uncomfortable.

II. Use of 4) __Humor__

   It is important to know 5) __humor__ is not universally appropriate in all contexts.

   Use of 6) __laughter__ can be experienced as a sign of disrespect.

III. Sequencing elements during conversation

   It is important to know the right time to touch upon more 7) __sensitive__ issues.

   The subsequent 8) __behavior__ of the listener can be greatly influenced by the timing of questions.

   Sequencing and 9) __timing__ do matter.

Script

Good morning everybody! Today I'd like to touch upon some issues regarding communicating with people of a different culture. The first point is about the use of silence. In some forms of communication, silence is to be expected before a response, as a sign of thoughtfulness and deference to the original speaker, yet at other times, silence may be experienced as a sign of hostility. In the West, twenty seconds of silence during a meeting is an extraordinarily long time, and people will feel uncomfortable with that. Someone invariably will break in to end the uncomfortable silence. However, the same customs around silence are not universal. Secondly, there is the issue of the use of humour. In the West, we often try to build immediate rapport through humor, but of course, this is not universally seen to be appropriate in all contexts. The use of laughter can be experienced as a sign of disrespect by some, and so it is important to understand that this is another area where misunderstandings can be very likely to occur. Next, I'd like to mention the sequencing of elements during conversation. At what point during a conversation is it appropriate to touch upon more sensitive issues? Since all cultures develop customs through which sensitive issues can be addressed in a way that connotes respect to all people involved, and since those systems all can differ, it is important to understand the influence that sequence has on effectiveness. The right question, asked in the right way, but asked too soon or too late, according to custom, can connote very different things to the listener, and highly influence subsequent behaviour. So, sequencing and timing do matter.

Activity B   Discussion

This exercise is to encourage the students to think about the positive as well as the negative sides of modern science and technology. The teacher is advised to encourage the students to discuss the topic in small groups, and then make a presentation to the whole class. After that, the teacher can summarize their opinions.

Activity C   Picture Description

Reference for teachers

This picture shows an abuse of the Internet. A boy has got some homework to do, on which he does not want to make any efforts. Therefore, he finds a "clever" way out. He gets access to the Internet to search for the key to his homework. To his great joy, there is the key right on the Internet! "What a fabulous thing!" thinks the boy, delighted with the result and his brilliant idea. So he sits merrily in front of the desktop using the distant help on the Internet to finish his homework.

This picture reveals the problem that the Internet sometimes does not help in a proper way. Instead, it makes people lazier and less creative, which is extremely harmful to children and young people.

We can learn from this cartoon that although technological improvements have brought great benefits to humankind, they have drawbacks as well. Advances in science and technology themselves are neutral; it is human beings who make them a blessing or disaster.

During the discussion the teacher can also refer to the proverbs or quotes on knowledge and wisdom provided in Background Information in TEXT A.

WRITING

Writing Skills: Descriptive Essays

Unit Four discusses how to write descriptive essays. This topic may seem intimidating to students because most of them find description hard to manage. Another difficulty may come from confusion between a description and a descriptive essay. So the first part in the Student's Book tries to clarify these points. Telling the students the real purpose of description (creating a feeling or drawing a mental picture) can lessen their anxiety, and emphasizing the purpose of a descriptive essay can help them see the difference more clearly.

The Student's Book also provides a brief discussion of the key elements in an effective descriptive essay. The teacher may ask the students to study these key elements, and divide them into different categories. Generally speaking, the first (purpose) and the last (structure) are about essay writing in general, and the second (details) mainly concerns the quality of description. For this element, the teacher can highlight two points. One, the telling vs. showing distinction; two, the inclusion of the five senses in description. Following is another example of telling and showing, which the teacher may find useful:

- I grew tired after dinner. (telling)
- As I leaned back and rested my head against the top of the chair, my eyelids began to feel heavy, and the edges of the empty plate in front of me blurred with the white tablecloth. (showing)

The sample in the Student's Book describes a teacher in Harvard University. It is a good description, but not a complete descriptive essay. The teacher may use it to explain how to describe effectively, and how it can be turned into an essay. Answers to the questions are listed below for reference.

1. This sample describes a teacher in Harvard University. The writer wants to show that he is a teacher of much personal charm and influence among students.
2. The writer provides information on his movement (the way he walks, smokes and looks) and his dressing. Students' reaction is also provided to strengthen the central point.
3. Although it has already created a vivid picture in readers' mind, this sample does not have a conclusion part as an essay. It could be a good essay if an ending were added. A possible reference may be: "Even years later, I still remember how Prof. Kittredge walked, talked and looked. He seemed to have absorbed all my mind, and filled it with his energy, knowledge and wisdom."

The checklist reminds the students once again of both description and essay writing. The teacher can advise the students to use them in the revision stage.

Writing Assignment

1. What is the major purpose of description? What is the difference between a description and a descriptive essay?

These two questions try to remind the students of the definition of descriptive essay, and may be answered together. Description aims at creating a feeling for readers by providing effective details. The key to a successful description is the choice of details. Description itself means choosing and presenting detailed information to create a scene, while a descriptive essay tries to make a point with the help of description. In such an essay, the point is the real purpose, rather than the details.

2. Study the following sample carefully, and add a beginning to clarify the point of description.

This essay is taken from a student assignment. It is successful in presenting descriptive details, and the purpose is also clear, though not directly stated. Chinese writers may find it satisfactory, but to conform to conventions of English essay writing, the writer still need to specify and express the point. A possible answer may be: "University is not only a place to study, but also a place to meet different people. Some become your friends, some enemies. I usually count myself fortunate because I met a good friend on the first day on campus."

3. Write a descriptive essay about a person, object, place or scene that has impressed you very much.

Answers may vary.

5 BUSINESS COMMUNICATION

TEXT A Nonverbal Business Conventions in Face-to-Face Encounters

Before Reading

The purpose of this section is to arouse the students' interest in the theme of the unit, reactivate their relevant background knowledge or elicit their opinions on the related topics, so as to better prepare them for the succeeding tasks.

Before Reading activities can be organized as group work so that the students share with each other their knowledge about business communication, cross-cultural communication as well as nonverbal communication.

Background Information

1 Cross-Cultural Communication Strategies

The key to effective cross-cultural communication is knowledge. First, it is essential that people understand the potential problems of cross-cultural communication, and make a conscious effort to overcome these problems. Second, it is important to realize that one's efforts will not always be successful, and to adjust one's behavior appropriately.

For example, one should always be aware of a significant possibility that cultural differences are causing communication problems, and be willing to be patient and forgiving, rather than hostile and aggressive, if problems develop. One should respond slowly and carefully in cross-cultural exchanges, not jumping to the conclusion that he or she knows what is being thought and said.

William Ury's suggestion for heated conflicts is to stop, listen, and think, or as he puts it, "go to the balcony" when the situation gets tense. By this he means to withdraw from the situation, step back, and reflect on what is going on before you act. This helps in cross-cultural communication as well. When things seem to be going badly, stop or slow down and think. What could be going on here? Is it possible I misinterpreted what they said, or they misinterpreted me? Often misinterpretation is the source of the problem.

Active listening can sometimes be used to check this out — by repeating what one thinks he or she heard, one can confirm that he or she understands the communication accurately. If words are used differently between languages or cultural groups, however, even active listening can overlook misunderstandings.

2 Nonverbal Language in Intercultural Communication

How often have we listened to someone speak and wondered what the speaker really was saying? We may agree intuitively with the words, but in the back of our minds we feel that there is more to the message than the words. We may even come to the conclusion that the speaker means the opposite of what he or she says. We may base our judgment on an evaluation of tone, intonation, emphasis, facial expressions, gestures, hand movements, distance, and eye contact — in short, nonverbal signals or the silent language.

Although nonverbal signals tend to enhance and support language, they can minimize or even contradict the verbal message. For example, the phrase, "I would love to meet with you and discuss this issue in more detail," can take on different meanings depending on the nonverbal signals accompanying the words:

- A smile while pulling out a calendar will support the words.
- Going on without pausing to the next topic after the statement may very well indicate that the speaker is not serious and not interested in meeting, at least not now.
- A frown and a search for something on the desk while uttering the words may contradict the message altogether.

Some researchers maintain that in face-to-face communication up to 93 percent of an oral message is communicated nonverbally and that the nonverbal elements are a much better indicator of the true meaning than the actual words.

Yet, the true meaning and the interpretation will depend on a variety of factors. People from different cultures attach different meanings to nonverbal signals. As one example: In Western cultures eye contact can signify honesty, whereas in Asian cultures it may indicate rudeness.

The interpretation of nonverbal signals is further complicated by the fact that within a culture not all people use the same signals. Men and women often use different nonverbal language. Men in Western cultures tend to be more outspoken than women; however, with women asserting their rights more, women's communication is changing. People from different social classes within one culture also may use nonverbal signals differently. People from the upper classes or people in leading positions may be more assertive and outspoken in many cultures when communicating with people from lower classes and lower positions.

Nonverbal communication is influenced by a number of factors, including:

- Cultural background
- Socioeconomic background
- Education
- Gender
- Age
- Personal preference and idiosyncrasies

All these factors complicate the interpretation of the nonverbal aspects of communication.

Needless to say, valid generalizations are difficult and always must be reevaluated and seen in the context of the situation. For example, in a Western cultural setting, crossing one's arms may be interpreted as being defensive, rejecting the other person, or being closed-minded. However, it is also possible that the nonverbal signal simply means that the speaker is cold. The isolated symbol may not carry any deeper meaning.

Other nonverbal symbols are interesting but not that important. For example, when Europeans use their fingers counting to five, they start with the thumb and go in sequence of the fingers to the little finger. Americans, on the other hand, start with the index finger, go on to the little finger, and count the thumb last.

While this difference is interesting, it does not influence the meaning of what is being said.

You may wonder why we are concerned at all with nonverbal communication if the interpretation is so difficult. The point is that nonverbal communication, because it varies so much and because it carries so much of the meaning, needs our close attention so that we can decode and get our message across more effectively. While we examine nonverbal language of some cultures, keep in mind that these are generalizations, and while the descriptions are true generally for a culture, there are many variations within a culture. As you learn more about a culture and as you meet more people from a culture, you may adapt and adjust your interpretation of the nonverbal language signals.

Reading

Text Analysis

- ### Text Summary

This expository essay deals with nonverbal business conventions in face-to-face encounters. The author starts with clarifying some key concepts concerning the nonverbal communication, and then moves on to elaborate on two major types of nonverbal signals — eye contact and facial expressions, focusing on their diverse implications under different cultural settings. With detailed and extensive illustrations, the author demonstrates how varied the interpretations of nonverbal signals could be depending on the different social and cultural backgrounds that people come from.

- ### Text Organization

Paragraphs 1-2: introduction	Nonverbal messages can be broken down into subcategories, and either consciously or unconsciously, speakers use many of them at the same time. Some signals reflect our true feelings and reactions.
Paragraphs 3-8: body part 1	Regarding eye contact, people from different social positions, gender groups and cultural backgrounds are subject to different social conventions. In addition, people in different cultures associate eye contact with different moral qualities, which leads to different codes of conduct.
Paragraphs 9-18: body part 2	Smiling and anger showing are two important facial expressions. Depending on the culture, smiling varies in intensity, frequency and association with hospitality. Similarly, the expression of anger also varies from culture to culture both in terms of intensity and type of expression.

- ### Text Features

This piece of exposition introduces nonverbal messages and their implications and interpretations in different cultures, with clarity and intelligibility. To hammer the point home that nonverbal signals, depending on the culture, indicate different attitudes and feelings, the author employs various means. Firstly, the author adopts classification. As a common type of essay development, classification enables readers to follow the author's main points more easily. This article is developed on the basis of the main categorial division of the nonverbal signals — eye contact and facial expressions. The former is further divided into "eye contact as a sign of honesty" and "eye contact as a sign of invasion of privacy", and the latter into "smiling" and "showing anger". Subtitles in bold-type letters are used to highlight the major divisions and subdivisions of the text. Secondly, the author relies on a heavy use of exemplification to illustrate the various reactions to the same nonverbal cues among people from different cultural backgrounds, including Americans, Japanese, Arabs, Germans and Russians. Thirdly, the author employs comparison and contrast to demonstrate the wide spectrum of cultural diversities with regard to the same nonverbal messages. Here is one instance: *In these cultures eye contact is related to honesty. In other cultures eye contact is seen as an invasion of privacy.* (Para. 4)

This article is taken from a textbook on intercultural communications, with a heavy use of formal words and expressions (c.f. *manipulate*, *subordinates*, *shifty*) and a flexible use of simple, compound and complex sentences. Striving for clarity in exposition, the author sticks to the present tense throughout the article. It should also be noted that the author demonstrates a skillful use of cohesive devices to achieve unity of the text, among which are logical connectors (逻辑连接词) (c.f. *however*, *but*, *as a result*) and parallel structures (并列结构). Here is one instance of parallelism: *In many cultures, when people are surprised, they may open their eyes wide and open their mouths. When they like something, their eyes may beam, and they may smile. When they are angry, they may frown and narrow their eyes.* (Para. 9)

- **Key Sentences**

1. The nonverbal messages that give listeners the most trouble are those that accompany words. (Para. 1)

This sentence contains two *that*-clauses, both of which are restrictive relative clauses (限制性关系分句). The first *that*-clause modifies the subject and the second *that*-clause modifies the subject complement (主语补足语). A restrictive relative clause is closely attached to the head. Unlike a non-restrictive relative clause, a restrictive relative clause is not separated from the head by a break in intonation, or by a comma in writing. Here are two more instances:

    A: Some birds are birds that sing.

    B: My typewriter is not the machine that it was.

It should be noted that relative pronoun (关系代词) *that* is normally used as subject complement in an SVC (Subject-Verb-Complement) construction or as notional subject (实义主语) of an existential clause (存在句) for both personal and non-personal reference. In addition, when the antecedent is an indefinite pronoun such as *all*, *anything*, *something*, or *nothing*, the following relative clause usually requires a relative *that* as subject, and *that*/zero as object. For example:

    A: All that live must die.

    B: All (that) I want is peace and quiet.

Moreover, when the antecedent is composed of a personal head with such determiners as *only*, *all*, *any*, the subject of the following relative clause is more frequently expressed with *that*. For example:

    A: Any boy that wants to succeed must work hard.

    B: He was the only person that knew all the answers.

2. Since several cultures consider the eye to be "the window of the soul", eye contact or lack thereof is interpreted to have special meaning. (Para. 4)

This sentence contains a metaphor (暗喻), in which *the eye* is compared to *the window of the soul*. Different from simile (明喻), metaphor does not state a comparison explicitly. Rather, it implies the comparison, omitting such words as *like* or *as*. For example:

Simile

A: When we grow, we tend to feel it, *as* a young seed must feel the weight and inertia of the earth when it seeks to break out of its shell on its way to becoming a plant.

B: To hold America in one's thoughts is *like* holding a love letter in one's hand — it has so special a meaning.

Metaphor

A: I cannot and will not cut my conscience to fit this year's fashions.

B: A school is a hopper into which children are heaved while they are young and tender; therein they are pressed into certain standard shapes and covered from head to heels with official rubber stamps.

3. Why, for example, should a waitress smile? (Para. 11)

This rhetorical question (反问句) expresses the doubt held by people living outside America as to why Americans smile so often. A rhetorical question is a question that one asks as a way of making a statement, without an answer. The purpose of using a rhetorical question is mainly to emphasize ideas and enhance variety. Here is one more instance:

A: Another word that has ceased to have meaning due to overdue is *attractive*. *Attractive* has become verbal chaff. Who, by some stretch of language and imagination, cannot be described as attractive?

New Words and Expressions

nonverbal /ˌnɒnˈvɜːbəl/ *a.* not using words 不用言辞表达的
e.g. Body language is a powerful form of nonverbal communication.
Nonverbal signals form an important part of communication.

convention /kənˈvenʃən/ *n.* (an example of) a usual or accepted way of behaving, especially in social situations, often following an old way of thinking or a custom in one particular society 行为规则；惯例
e.g. Convention dictates that it is the man who asks the woman to marry him and not the reverse.
In many countries, it is the/a convention to wear black at funerals.

subcategory /ˌsʌbˈkætɪɡəri/ *n.* a secondary or subordinate category 亚类；子种类；子范畴
e.g. There are really two major ways in which we can divide up verbs into subcategories.

isolation /ˌaɪsəˈleɪʃən/ *n.* a situation when one group, person, or thing is separate from others 隔离；孤立
e.g. I can't think about it in isolation (= separately) — I need some examples of the problem.
The prisoner had been kept in isolation (= alone without other people) for three days.

accompany /əˈkʌmpəni/ *v.* to go with sb. or sth.; to be provided or exist at the same time as sth. 伴随；与……一起发生
e.g. The course books are accompanied by four cassettes.
Depression is almost always accompanied by insomnia.

manipulate /məˈnɪpjʊleɪt/ *v.* to control sth. or sb. to your advantage, often unfairly or dishonestly 操纵；控制（人或局势）
e.g. Throughout her career she has very successfully manipulated the media.
The opposition leader accused government ministers of manipulating the statistics to suit themselves.

subordinate /səˈbɔːdɪnət/ *n.* a person who has a less important position than another in an organization 下属
e.g. He left the routine checks to one of his subordinates.

ogle /ˈəʊɡl/ *v.* to look at sb. with obvious sexual interest (挑逗地)注视；抛媚眼

e.g. The boys spent most of their time at the beach ogling girls in bikinis.

I saw you ogling the woman in the red dress!

harassment /ˈhærəsmənt/ *n.* behaviour that annoys or upsets sb. 骚扰；侵扰；困扰的事

e.g. Monroe complains too about her early adolescent experiences of sexual harassment.

So great was his harassment that he wanted to destroy his tormentors.

flirt /flɜːt/ *v.* to behave as if sexually attracted to sb., although not seriously 调情

e.g. Christina was flirting with just about every man in the room.

She accused him of flirting with other women.

innocent /ˈɪnəsənt/ *a.* (of a person) not guilty of a particular crime; (of a thing) harmlessly intended 清白的；无罪的

e.g. He firmly believes that she is innocent of the crime.

It was an innocent remark; I didn't mean to hurt his feelings.

offensive /əˈfensɪv/ *a.* causing sb. to feel upset or annoyed 冒犯的；无礼的；使人愤怒的

e.g. This programme contains language that some viewers might find offensive.

He told some really offensive sexist jokes.

thereof /ˌðeərˈɒv/ *ad.* (formal) of or about the thing just mentioned（正式用法）在其中，其

e.g. Please refer to the Regulations and in particular Articles 99 and 100 thereof.

Money, or the lack thereof, played a major role in their marital problems.

trustworthiness /ˈtrʌstˌwɜːðɪnɪs/ *n.* the quality of being able to be relied on as honest or truthful 值得信赖

e.g. He is a man of trustworthiness and honesty.

integrity /ɪnˈtegrəti/ *n.* the quality of being honest and having strong moral principles 正直

e.g. No one doubted that the president was a man of the highest integrity.

Rooney brought dignity and integrity to the profession.

shifty /ˈʃɪfti/ *a.* looking dishonest 诡诈的；躲躲闪闪的

e.g. He's got shifty eyes.

You're looking very shifty. What have you been up to?

There's a couple of shifty-looking people standing on the street corner.

suspicious /səˈspɪʃəs/ *a.* thinking that sb. might be guilty of doing sth. wrong or dishonest 表示怀疑的

e.g. They were suspicious about his past.

boundary /ˈbaʊndəri/ *n.* a real or imagined line that marks the edge or limit of sth. 边界

e.g. The Ural Mountains mark the boundary between Europe and Asia.

Residents are opposed to the prison being built within the city boundary.

concentrate /ˈkɒnsəntreɪt/ *v.* to direct mental powers or efforts towards a particular activity, subject or problem 全神贯注；聚精会神

e.g. I can't concentrate on my work with all that noise.

I find running concentrates the mind (= helps me to think).

proximity /prɒkˈsɪməti/ *n.* nearness in space, time, or relationship（时间、空间、关系的）靠近；亲近

e.g. Do not operate microphones in close proximity to television sets.

The best thing about the location of the house is its proximity to the town centre.

samurai /ˈsæmjʊraɪ/ *n.* a member of a military class of high social rank in the 11th to 19th century in Japan（旧时日本的）武士

e.g. A samurai was publicly marked out from the rest of society by his appearance and his bearing of two swords.

code /kəʊd/ *n.* a set of rules, laws, or principles that tell people how to behave 准则；规范

e.g. Historians are interested in the stern code of that ancient dynasty.

Each entry in this dictionary has a grammar code.

a system of words, letters or signs which is used to represent a message in secret form, or a system of numbers, letters or signals which is used to represent sth. in a shorter or more convenient form 密码；代码

e.g. The message was written in code.

She managed to decipher/break/crack (= succeed in understanding) the code.

enforce /ɪnˈfɔːs/ *v.* to make people obey a law; to make a particular situation happen or be accepted 实施（法律或规章）；强制履行（义务）

e.g. It isn't always easy for the police to enforce speed limits.

The new teacher had failed to enforce any sort of discipline.

regarding /rɪˈɡɑːdɪŋ/ *prep.* about 关于

e.g. The company is being questioned regarding its employment policy.

Regarding the punishment, what would you advise?

peril /ˈperɪl/ *n.* great danger, or sth. that is very dangerous（严重且迫在眉睫的）危险；威胁

e.g. I never felt that my life was in peril.

The journey through the mountains was fraught with perils (= full of dangers).

carry (sth.) over to continue to exist in a new situation 使继续下去；继续存在

e.g. I try not to let my problems at work carry over into my private life.

bubble /ˈbʌbl/ *n.* a transparent domed cover or enclosure 透明的穹顶；透明圆罩

e.g. The piglets were born into a sterile bubble.

preservation /ˌprezəˈveɪʃən/ *n.* the act of keeping sth. unchanged or preventing it from being damaged 维护；保全

e.g. There is great public concern about some of the chemicals used in food preservation.

The cathedral is in a poor state of preservation (= has not been kept in a good condition).

beam /biːm/ *v.* to smile with obvious pleasure 面露喜色；满脸堆笑

e.g. She beamed with delight/pleasure at his remarks.

The child beamed at his teacher as he received the award.

frown /fraʊn/ *v.* to bring your eyebrows together so that there are lines on your face above your eyes to show that you are annoyed or worried 皱眉

e.g. She frowned at me, clearly annoyed.

He frowned as he read the instructions, as if puzzled.

intensity /ɪnˈtensətɪ/ *n.* the quality of being felt very strongly or having a strong effect 强烈，剧烈

e.g. The explosion was of such intensity that it was heard five miles away.

The intensity of the hurricane was frightening.

subdued /səbˈdjuːd/ *a.* (of a person or their manner) quiet and rather reflective or depressed（人或举止）克制的；低沉的

e.g. I felt strangely subdued as I drove home.

"Oh," she said in a subdued voice.

guarantee /ˌɡærənˈtiː/ *v.* to promise that sth. will happen or exist 确保

e.g. European Airlines guarantees its customers top-quality service.

The label on this bread says it is guaranteed free of/from preservatives (= it contains no preservatives).

bluntly /ˈblʌntlɪ/ *ad.* (of a person or remark) uncompromisingly forthright（人、话语）直率地；生硬地；耿直地

e.g. She told me bluntly that I should lose weight.

To put it bluntly, I can't afford it.

reserved /rɪˈzɜːvd/ *a.* slow to reveal emotion or opinions 矜持的；拘谨的

e.g. She is a quiet, reserved woman.

The English have a reputation for being reserved.

intrude /ɪnˈtruːd/ *v.* to go into a place or situation in which you are not wanted or not expected 侵入；闯入；侵扰

e.g. I didn't realize your husband was here, Dr Jones — I hope I'm not intruding.

Newspaper editors are being urged not to intrude on/into the grief of the families of victims.

necessarily /ˈnesəsərəlɪ/ *ad.* used in negatives to mean "in every case" or "therefore" 必定；无可避免地

e.g. The fact that something is cheap doesn't necessarily mean it's of low quality.

You may love someone without necessarily wanting to marry him/her.

dictate /dɪkˈteɪt/ *v.* to give orders or state sth. with total authority 命令；规定

e.g. The UN will dictate the terms of troop withdrawal from the region.

He disagrees with the government dictating what children are taught in schools.

The tennis club rules dictate that suitable footwear should be worn on the courts.

readily /ˈredɪlɪ/ *ad.* without any problem 无困难地；容易地

e.g. Larger sizes are readily available.

suck /sʌk/ *v.* to pull in liquid or air through your mouth without using your teeth, or to move the tongue and muscles of the mouth around sth. inside your mouth, often in order to dissolve it 吸

e.g. She was sitting on the grass sucking lemonade through a straw.
I sucked my thumb until I was seven.

let (sth.) out to cause sth. to come out 放出来

e.g. He let the air out of the balloon.
She let out a scream (= She made this noise).

opponent /əˈpəʊnənt/ *n.* a person who disagrees with sth. and speaks against it or tries to change it 对手

e.g. He is the senator's chief political opponent.
Leading opponents of the proposed cuts in defense spending will meet later today.

epithet /ˈepɪθet/ *n.* a word or short phrase used to describe sb., usually to criticize or praise them(表述人或事物性质、特征的)表述词语

e.g. The opera-singer's 104-kilo frame has earned him the epithet of "Man Mountain" in the press.
He hardly deserves the epithet "fascist".

expressive /ɪkˈspresɪv/ *a.* showing what sb. thinks or feels 富于表情的；富于表现力的

e.g. He would use his expressive face to bring the stories to life.
She has large, expressive eyes.

tirade /taɪˈreɪd/ *n.* a long angry speech expressing strong disapproval 激愤的长篇演说；长篇的指责性发言

e.g. She launched into an angry/furious tirade about how she had been unfairly treated.
In a furious tirade of abuse, the opposition spokesperson demanded the minister's resignation.

outrage /ˈaʊtreɪdʒ/ *n.* a feeling of great anger and shock 盛怒；极度的震惊；极大的愤慨

e.g. These murders have provoked outrage across the country.
Many politicians and members of the public expressed outrage at the verdict.

illustrate /ˈɪləstreɪt/ *v.* to show the meaning or truth of sth. more clearly, especially by giving examples, charts, pictures etc.(用例子、图表、图片等)表明，阐明

e.g. The lecturer illustrated his point with a diagram on the blackboard.
This latest conflict further illustrates the weakness of the government.
The exhibition will illustrate how life evolved from water.

decipher /dɪˈsaɪfə/ *v.* to discover the meaning of sth. written in a difficult or hidden way 破译（密码）

e.g. Can you decipher the writing on this envelope?
Visual signals help us decipher what is being communicated.

overstate /ˌəʊvəˈsteɪt/ *v.* to describe or explain sth. in a way that makes it seem more important or serious than it really is 把……讲得过分；夸大

e.g. The impact of the new legislation has been greatly overstated.
The shareholders seem to think that the executive board is overstating the case for a merger.

Language Study

convention *n.*

1. a large formal meeting of people who do a particular job or have a similar interest, or a large meeting for a political party（尤指政党或专业人士举行的）大会；会议

    e.g. the national Democratic convention
    Where are they holding their party convention?

2. a formal agreement between country leaders, politicians and states on a matter which involves them all 国际协议；公约

    e.g. the Geneva Convention
    a convention on human rights

counter

n.

1. a person or machine that counts 计算者；计算器

    e.g. The counter tells you how many pictures you have taken.

2. a long flat narrow surface or table in a shop, bank, restaurant, etc. at which people are served 柜台
   e.g. There was nobody behind/on the counter when I went into the bank, and I had to wait to be served.
   You will find sausages on the meat counter/rolls on the bread counter.

over the counter (drugs, medicines, etc.) that you can buy in a shop without a prescription from a doctor（不要处方或许可）直接购买
   e.g. over-the-counter medicines

under the counter that you can only buy secretly and usually illegally（一般指非法的买卖）偷偷地；私下地
   e.g. It's risky, but you can get alcohol under the counter.

v. to react to sth. with an opposing opinion or action; to defend yourself against sth. 反对；对抗
   e.g. When criticisms were made of the school's performance, the parents' group countered with details of its examination results.
   Extra police have been moved into the area to counter the risk of violence.

dictate *v.*
1. to influence sth. or make it necessary 施加影响或使有必要
   e.g. The party's change of policy has been dictated by its need to win back the support of voters.
   I wanted to take a year off, but my financial situation dictated that I got a job.
2. say or read aloud words to be typed, written down, or recorded on tape 口授
   e.g. I have four letters to dictate.

After Reading

READING COMPREHENSION TASKS

1. Complete the following table based on the information in TEXT A.

Nonverbal signals	Interpretations in different cultures
Eye contact	In **the United States**, "ogling", looking at the other sex, may be interpreted as a form of **sexual harassment** and even have **legal consequences**.
	European women regard the innocent game of looking and establishing eye contact as a means of **flirting**.
	In **North American** and **northern European** cultures, eye contact shows openness, **trustworthiness**, and **integrity**.
	Arabs, in addition to making close eye contact and standing very close to the listener, also **touch the listener**.
	In **Japan**, to look someone in the eye is invading someone's space. It's **rude**.
	Latin and Arab cultures use more intense facial expressions, whereas **East Asian** cultures use more subdued facial expressions.
	In an attempt to appear open and friendly, people in **the United States** smile a lot.
	In **Japan** people don't smile the way people from the United States do, because they don't want to intrude.

Facial expressions	_Germans_ smile, but not nearly as much as people in the United States, because they recognize that the world is not necessarily a pleasant place.
	One of the milder forms of showing anger in Western cultures is _frowning_.
	Another way of showing anger is _shouting_ and _gesturing_.
	People from _the Middle East_ use intense and expressive gesturing to show anger.
	Asian cultures tend to restrict the range of facial expressions by Western standards. As a result, anger is not openly expressed in their work environments.

2. Read the following statements and decide whether they are true (T) or false (F).

1) In the process of communication, speakers use nonverbal signals in isolation, rather than at the same time. (F)
2) To successfully deliver a message, a person must solely rely on the verbal language to get his meaning across. (F)
3) The Japanese, who prefer not to make direct eye contact, may seem shifty and suspicious in the eyes of Americans and Europeans. (T)
4) People in all cultures smile, though the meaning of a smile may vary. (T)
5) When Germans are angry, they may address the opponent in a rude and informal way. (F)

3. Explain the underlined parts in your own words.

1) Nonverbal messages can be broken down into subcategories. (Para. 1)
   be divided into
2) …that speakers use nonverbal signals in isolation. (Para. 1)
   separately
3) …although we may not feel like smiling. (Para. 2)
   want to smile
4) …a strict code of behaviour was enforced… (Para. 7)
   set of rules telling people how to behave
5) …had a hard time teaching waitresses… (Para. 11)
   had great difficulty in
6) …do not really smile by US standards. (Para. 12)
   according to US standards
7) …whereas the subordinate is well advised not to react in kind. (Para. 14)
   should be sensible enough not to respond in the same angry manner

ORAL WORK

In TEXT A, the author discusses how the Japanese, Americans, Europeans and Arabs typically behave in terms of eye contact and facial expressions in business contexts. Now discuss with you group members and find out how Chinese people would act in similar situations. Make a list of points and support them with arguments. Then report your group opinions to the whole class.

The teacher can ask the students to work in groups first and then choose a few groups to present their opinions to the whole class.

TRANSLATION OF TEXT A

面对面商务交流中的非言语交流惯例

1　非言语信息可以分为几个子类别。虽然如此分类使讨论更加容易，但我们却必须得小心，不要想当然地认为说话人会孤立地使用这些非言语信号。多数情况下，说话人同时使用几种不同信号来达意。我们可能会同时既做手势、点头、微笑，又保持密切的眼神接触。伴随言语的非言语信号最让听话人头疼。正是别人说话的音调、面部的表情，或者眼神交流的缺乏使你怀疑自己是否听懂了。

2　在某种程度上，我们可以有意识地操纵信号，例如我们可能因为别人希望我们微笑而微笑，尽管未必愿意。然而在很多情况下，我们在无意识的状况下传达非言语信号。专家们都认为这些信号是我们真实情感和反应的体现。跨文化交际的一个目的就是解释所有的非言语信号。

眼神接触

3　在多数文化中，地位高的人可以更加自由地目视地位低的人，反之则不然。传统上讲，相比女人看男人，男人可以更多地看女人。比如说，在美国，"抛媚眼"，即挑逗性地注视异性，可能被视为一种性骚扰，甚至产生法律后果。因此在这种文化下，眼神接触就变得颇为复杂。欧洲女人有时评论美国男人冷漠，不知如何调情——展开一场无伤大雅的注视游戏并建立起相应的眼神接触。而美国女人在到了南欧国家，在男人的注视下经常会觉得颇为不自在，她们认为这是一种无礼的凝视。

4　有好些文化都将眼睛视为"心灵的窗户"，因此眼神接触或缺乏眼神接触会被诠释为带有某种含义。在一些文化中，眼神接触与诚实品质密切相关；而在其他一些文化中，眼神接触却被视作一种对隐私的侵犯。

5　**眼神接触作为一种诚实的标志**　"他甚至不能直视我的眼睛"在西方文化中是一句常见的表达，表明此人有所隐瞒。在北美和北欧的文化中，眼神接触表示坦诚、值得信赖和诚实正直。某人无所隐瞒。如果一个美国女人直视某人，她就允许对方也同样直视她的眼睛，并依此判断她是否值得信任。没有直接眼神接触的人被认为是狡猾不可靠的，会引起听话人的怀疑。人们会根据各自的文化背景来看待眼神接触，而同绝大多数非言语行为一样，眼神接触不易跨越文化边界。

6　阿拉伯文化也利用密切的眼神接触，通过关注眼睛移动来读懂对方的真正意图，比西方文化尤甚。他们感觉眼睛是不会骗人的。为了更加清楚地观察眼睛，阿拉伯人会靠近对方，这使得非阿拉伯人颇不习惯。以日本人为例，他会因对方热切的眼神和过近的身体距离而感到非常不适。如果阿拉伯人除了密切注视和有过近的身体距离外，还触碰他，日本人就更不舒服了。在这种情形下，阿拉伯人传递了三个非常强烈的非言语信号，而所有这些都和日本文化所接受的非言语行为背道而驰。

7　**眼神接触作为一种侵犯隐私的行为**　在日本，直视某人的眼睛是一种侵犯私人空间的行为，非常粗鲁。在武士当权的时代，关于谁可以看谁，可以看多久，都有严格的行为准则，违背这些行为准则则会招来麻烦。这一传统延续到了现代社会。日本人可以在一个办公室里坐得很近，但他们很少直视对方的眼睛。

8　日本人对于直接的眼神接触感到颇为不适，从而力图避免。此外，不直接看某人的眼睛可以保护对方的私人领地不受侵犯。在一个拥挤的国家，采用一切手段来保护隐私被认为是非常必要的。表达问候时，他们鞠躬，不看对方。美国人那种眼神接触的尺度被视为凝视，是粗鲁的。即使在拥挤的地铁和火车上也没有眼神接触。每个人都不看对方。

面部表情

9　说话时常常伴有特定的面部表情。在很多文化中，人们惊奇时会睁大眼睛、张开嘴巴。喜欢什么的时候，眼睛就会流露喜色，面带微笑。生气时他们会皱起眉头，眯起眼睛。虽然很多面部表情在不同文化里表达类似的含义，但这些表情的使用频率和强度通常有差别。拉丁文化和阿拉伯文化使用较为强烈的面部表情，而东亚文化则使用比较含蓄的表情。

10　**微笑**　任何文化中的人都常常微笑，但是微笑的含义却可能有差别。不同的文化中，微笑可以表达开心和有趣，但也可以表示尴尬。

11　为了表现出坦率和友好，美国人笑得很多。每个人都向每个人微笑。而在其他文化看来，美国人的微笑常常显得不真诚。比如，为什么侍者一定要微笑？美国的餐馆努力培训所有的员工展现出恰当的微笑。世界上其他地方似乎并不像美国人那样重视微笑，美国人对此颇感诧异和不解。例如，麦当劳费了好大力气来培训莫斯科的员工，让他们认识到微笑的重要性，并让他们笑得恰到好处。

12　在日本，人们不像美国人那样微笑。一个人不会随心所欲地表达情感，并将自己的感情强加于人。男人在公开场合不微笑，女人更要笑不露齿。为了保证牙齿不露出来，日本女人通常在大笑的时候用一只手掩住嘴巴。那些在银行和商店里向顾客深深鞠躬的女人并不作美国式的微笑。她们看上去和蔼可亲，但不会像美国人那样对顾客微笑。

13　德国人也微笑，但是绝不像美国人那么多。他们会直白地说："生活不易，没什么值得笑的。"德国人更加保守，但出于和日本人不同的原因。日本人是不想打扰别人，而德国人是因为认识到了世界不是什么愉快的地方。生命是履行责任，而责任本身不适合以笑颜相对。

14　**表达愤怒**　不同的文化在表达愤怒的强度和表情类型上也通常有所不同。此外，文化价值观也决定了哪些人可以公开表达愤怒。年长的人、男人、有权力的人相比年轻人、女人、下属更容易表达愤怒。老板可以对下属发脾气，但下属最好不要予以反击。因此对愤怒的诠释和表达受文化的影响。

15　比如在西方文化中，一种比较温和的表达愤怒的方式是皱眉。不同场合下，皱眉可以表示愤怒、怀疑、对权威的质疑、猜忌或持有不同意见。在不鼓励公开表现情绪的文化中，皱眉可能会被更大程度地克制。例如，日本人通过移开视线的方式来隐藏愤怒；在商务场合，即使皱皱眉来公开表达愤怒都被视为不妥。

16　另一种表达愤怒的方式是大吼和比划。德国人、加拿大人、阿拉伯人和拉丁人在生气时经常提高嗓门。日本人却很少如此。相反，他们表达愤怒时更多的是深吸气，而不是大声喊叫。德国人生气时脸会变红，也会大吼，但是通常他们在称呼对方时仍然颇为得体。很多人仍然会称对手为"Sie"（"您"的正式用法），即使他们的话已经颇为不敬。

17　有一些文化使用大幅度的和颇具表现力的动作来表达愤怒。来自中东的人在激愤指责对方时，会伴有夸张的动作。整个身体都充分参与到表达愤怒的过程之中，似乎是为了体现整个人都受到了影响。表达愤怒不仅意味着一场言辞的战斗，还是一场整个存在体的战争。

18　按照西方的标准，亚洲文化在面部表情方面相对克制。因此在很多亚洲文化中，人们并不在工作场合公开表达愤怒。来自亚洲文化的人能够读懂非言语交流下微妙的面部表情所传达的愤怒讯息，但是来自西方文化的人对此却常常一头雾水。另一方面，与日本文化相比，阿拉伯文化中的面部表情会过度表达感情，例如愤怒。从面部表情上，外人可能很难判断某个中东人到底生气到何种程度。关键是来自同一个文化的人不难读懂相关的讯息，而当人们跨越文化边界，进入一个表情和姿势传达不同含义的交际系统时，问题就来了。

TEXT B Dumb Things We Do

Before Reading

The purpose of this section is to arouse the students' interest in the theme of the unit, reactivate their relevant background knowledge or elicit their opinions on the related topics, so as to better prepare them for the succeeding tasks.

Before Reading activities can be organized as group work so that the students share with each other their opinions on making mistakes in life.

Experience is the name everyone gives to their mistakes. — Oscar Wilde (1854 - 1900) Irish poet, playwright and wit	
To err is human; to forgive, divine. — Alexander Pope (1688 - 1744) English poet	
A man who has committed a mistake and doesn't correct it, is committing another mistake. — Confucius (551 - 479 BC) Chinese philosopher	

Reading

New Words and Expressions

err /ɜː/ *v.* to make a mistake or do sth. wrong（正式用法）出错；犯错误
e.g. He erred in agreeing to her appointment.
    The judge had erred in ruling that the evidence was inadmissible.
overwhelmingly /ˌəʊvəˈhwelmɪŋlɪ/ *ad.* very great in amount 压倒多数地

e.g. The officials are overwhelmingly male.
attributable /əˈtrɪbjʊtəbl/ *a.* likely to have been caused by sth. 可归因于……的
e.g. Do you think that these higher-than-average temperatures are attributable to global warming?
crash /kræʃ/ *n.* an accident involving a vehicle

in collision with another or with an object (车辆等)猛撞；(飞机等)坠毁

e.g. The newspaper reported a car crash in the morning.
Very few people survived the plane crash last month.

eliminate /ɪˈlɪmɪneɪt/ *v.* to remove or take away 消除；清除；根除

e.g. A move towards healthy eating could help eliminate heart disease.
We eliminated the possibility that it could have been an accident.

bias /ˈbaɪəs/ *n.* a tendency to support or oppose a particular person or thing in an unfair way by allowing personal opinions to influence your judgment 偏袒；偏见

e.g. The government has accused the media of bias.
Reporters must be impartial and not show political bias.

perceive /pəˈsiːv/ *v.* to come to an opinion about sth., or have a belief about sth. 感知，感觉；认为

e.g. How do the French perceive the British?
Women's magazines are often perceived to be superficial.

prone /prəʊn/ *a.* tending to suffer from an illness or show a particular negative characteristic 易于发生……(不幸或不受欢迎之事)的，有发生……(讨厌的事)倾向的

e.g. I've always been prone to headaches.
He was prone to depression even as a teenager.

identify /aɪˈdentɪfaɪ/ *v.* to recognize a problem, need, fact, etc. (especially sth. considered worthy of attention) 认出；辨别出(尤指值得注意的事物)

e.g. The research will be used to identify training needs.
You need to identify your priorities.

afflict /əˈflɪkt/ *v.* to cause pain or trouble to (问题、疾病)使痛苦，折磨；影响；困扰

e.g. It is an illness which afflicts women more than men.
This country is afflicted by civil war.

commit /kəˈmɪt/ *v.* to do sth. illegal or sth. that is considered wrong 犯(错，罪)；干(坏事)

e.g. He was sent to prison for a crime that he didn't commit.
Brady committed a series of brutal murders.

gaffe /gæf/ *n.* a remark or action that is a social mistake and not considered polite 失礼；失言；失态

e.g. I made a real gaffe — I called his new wife "Judy", which is the name of his ex-wife.
Was that a bit of a gaffe then, starting to eat before everyone else had been served?

recall /rɪˈkɔːl/ *v.* to bring the memory of a past event into your mind, and often to give a description of what you remember 回忆

e.g. The old man recalled the city as it had been before the war.
He recalled (that) he had sent the letter over a month ago.

riddle /ˈrɪdl/ *n.* a person or thing that is difficult to understand or explain 谜

e.g. Doctors have found a new clue to the riddle of cot death.
How do we solve the riddle of the disappearing marriage?

distort /dɪˈstɔːt/ *v.* to change sth. from its usual, original, natural or intended meaning, condition or shape 扭曲；使变形

e.g. My original statement has been completely distorted by the media.
His face was distorted with rage.

transcript /ˈtrænskrɪpt/ *n.* an official record of a student's work, showing courses taken and grades achieved 学生成绩报告单

e.g. You need to submit your high school transcript before applying for this job.

inflate /ɪnˈfleɪt/ *v.* to make sth. larger or more important 夸张，夸大

e.g. They inflated their part in the rescue operation every time they told the story.
You have a very inflated opinion of your worth.

self-flattering /ˌselfˈflætərɪŋ/ *a.* holding an unjustifiable high opinion of oneself or one's actions 自我夸耀的

e.g. His self-flattering manner is really annoying.

parenting /ˈpeərəntɪŋ/ *n.* the raising of children and all the responsibilities and activities that are involved in it 养育；抚养；教养

e.g. The programme aims to teach young men parenting skills.
What, in general, is the effect of such rigid parenting?

prescribe /prɪˈskraɪb/ *v.* to recommend (a substance or action) as sth. beneficial 推荐，推举

e.g. Marriage is often prescribed as a universal remedy.

gambler /ˈgæmblə/ *n.* sb. who often bets money, for example in a game or on a horse race 赌徒

e.g. They set up a self-help group for compulsive gamblers.
The gambler turned a deaf ear to all advice.

keenly /ˈkiːnlɪ/ *ad.* strongly or extremely 强烈地；激烈地

e.g. They are keenly aware that this will be their last chance to succeed.

inclination /ˌɪnklɪˈneɪʃən/ *n.* a preference or tendency, or a feeling that makes a person want to do sth. （人的）自然倾向

e.g. My own inclination would be to look for another job.
We should be basing our decisions on solid facts, not inclinations and hunches.

multitask /ˈmʌltɪˌtɑːsk/ *v.* to perform several tasks at the same time 同时进行多项工作

e.g. Women are often very good at multitasking.
The machine allows multitasking without the need to buy extra hardware.

juggle /ˈdʒʌgl/ *v.* to succeed in arranging your life so that you have time to involve yourself in two or more different activities or groups of people 力图使平衡；尽力应付

e.g. Many parents find it hard to juggle children and a career.
I don't think any man can ever understand the difficulties of juggling motherhood and politics.

geometric /ˌdʒɪəʊˈmetrɪk/ *a.* (of a pattern or arrangement) made up of shapes such as squares, triangles or rectangles 几何图形的

e.g. He tries to identify a geometric design of overlapping circles.

evaporate /ɪˈvæpəreɪt/ *v.* to disappear 消失

e.g. Halfway through the film reality evaporates and we enter a world of pure fantasy.
Hopes of achieving peace are beginning to evaporate.

distraction /dɪˈstrækʃən/ *n.* a thing that prevents sb. from giving their full attention to sth. else 分散注意力的事

e.g. The firm found passenger travel a distraction from the main business of moving freight.
I can turn the television off if you find it a distraction.

square (sth.) with (sth.) to match or agree with sth., or think that one thing is acceptable together with another thing 符合

e.g. Her story doesn't quite square with the evidence.
I don't think I could spend that much money on a jacket — I couldn't square it with my conscience (= I would feel guilty).

incoming /ˈɪnkʌmɪŋ/ *a.* being received; arriving at or coming towards a place 正在移入的；进来的；到来的

e.g. incoming mail/telephone calls
an incoming flight

stray /streɪ/ *v.* to start thinking or talking about a different subject from the one you should be giving attention to 分散注意力；离题

e.g. I think we've strayed too far from our original plan.
Sorry — I've strayed from the subject.

demonstration /ˌdemənˈstreɪʃən/ *n.* an act of showing that sth. exists or is true by giving proof or evidence 证明，证实

e.g. This disaster is a clear demonstration of the need for tighter controls.
Let me give you a demonstration of the need for more workers.

charter /ˈtʃɑːtə/ *n.* the hiring of an aircraft, ship, or motor vehicle for a special purpose （飞机、船只、机动车的）租用，包租

e.g. a plane on charter to a multinational company
The airline is now primarily a charter service.

entourage /ˌɒntʊˈrɑːʒ/ *n.* the group of people who travel with and work for an important or famous person 随行人员；随员

e.g. The rock-star arrived in London with her usual entourage of dancers and backing singers.
The Monach was followed by an entourage of his courtiers.

vent /vent/ *v.* to express a negative emotion in a forceful and often unfair way （强烈情绪或能量的）发泄；表达

e.g. Please don't shout — there's no need to

vent your frustration/anger/rage on me.

memorial /mɪˈmɔːrɪəl/ *n.* an object, often large and made of stone, which has been built to honour a famous person or event 纪念建筑；纪念碑；纪念馆

e.g. a war memorial

The statue was erected as a memorial to those who died in the war.

parkway /ˈpɑːkweɪ/ *n.* a wide road, usually divided, with an area of grass and trees on both sides and in the middle (北美)风景区干道

e.g. This region is separated by a parkway.

There is a parkway running through the middle of the town.

rolling /ˈrəʊlɪŋ/ *a.* (of hills) gently rising and falling (山峦)起伏的

e.g. The train journey took us through a valley past rolling hills.

arched /ɑːtʃt/ *a.* (of a structure) with a curved top and straight sides that supports the weight of a bridge or building 拱形的

e.g. The entrance to the cathedral is through an arched door (= a door with a curved structure over it).

overpass /ˈəʊvəpɑːs/ *n.* a bridge that carries a road or railway over another road 立交桥，天桥，跨线桥

e.g. An overpass is called a flyover or a flypast in England.

clearance /ˈklɪərəns/ *n.* the amount of space around one object that is needed for it to avoid touching another object 净空；余地

e.g. There was less than a foot's clearance between the ship's sides and the wharf.

Always give cyclists plenty of clearance.

slam /slæm/ *v.* to (cause to) move against a hard surface with force and usually a loud noise 碰撞；猛烈撞击

e.g. The wind made the window slam.

Close the door carefully, don't slam it.

collision /kəˈlɪʒən/ *n.* an instance of one moving object or person striking violently against another 相撞或碰撞(事故)

e.g. There has been a collision on the southbound stretch of the motorway.

Two drivers were killed in a head-on (= direct) collision between a car and a taxi last night.

The cyclist was in collision with a bus.

shear off to break apart because of a sideway or twisting force 切断；扭转

e.g. The old screws holding the engine casing had sheared off.

The left wing had been almost completely sheared off.

gaping /ˈgeɪpɪŋ/ *a.* becoming wide open 张口的；敞口的

e.g. The bomb had left gaping holes in the wall.

inattentional /ˌɪnəˈtenʃənəl/ *a.* not paying enough attention 漫不经心的

e.g. I was disappointed by the food and the inattentional service.

investigator /ɪnˈvestɪgeɪtə/ *n.* a person who carries out a systematic or formal inquiry to discover and examine the facts of (an incident, allegation, etc.) so as to establish the truth 调查者

e.g. Investigators have studied the possible effects of contamination.

A team of special investigators have gone to the scene of the explosion.

Language Study

overwhelm *v.*

1. to defeat sb. or sth. by using a lot of force 彻底击败；征服

    e.g. Government troops have overwhelmed the rebels and seized control of the capital.

2. to cause sb. to feel sudden strong emotion 使感情上受不了；使不知所措

    e.g. They were overwhelmed with/by grief when their baby died.

    I was quite overwhelmed by all the flowers and letters of support I received.

3. (water etc.) to cover a place suddenly and completely （水等）埋没或淹没

    e.g. The embankment was overwhelmed and water surrounded the mosque.

overwhelming *a.*

1. difficult to fight against 难以抵挡的

    e.g. She felt an overwhelming urge/desire/need to tell someone about what had happened.
  2. very great or very large 强烈的
    e.g. She said how much she appreciated the overwhelming generosity of the public in responding to the appeal.
      An overwhelming majority have voted in favour of the proposal.

flatter *v.* to speak sth. good about sb. although it might not be true 吹捧
  e.g. Clive flatters himself that he's excellent.
    They were flattering him in order to get that sum of money.

square
 n.
  1. a shape with four straight equal sides with 90° angles at the corners 正方形
    e.g. First of all, draw a square.
  2. a large open area in the centre of a town or city, usually in the shape of a square, or the buildings surrounding it 广场；广场周围的建筑
    e.g. main/market/town square
      The hotel is just off the main square of Sorrento.
  3. the result of multiplying a number by itself 平方
    e.g. The square of 4 is 16.
 v.
  1. (BrE) to win the same number of points or games as the other team or player （英国英语）使（比赛或比分）打平
    e.g. India won the second match to square the series at one each.
  2. to settle or pay (a bill or debt) 结付（账单）；付清（欠款）
    e.g. Would you square up the bill?

square one's shoulders   to stand straight and push one's shoulders back, usually to show determination 挺直（肩膀）
 a.
  1. forming a 90° angle, or being close to or similar to a 90° angle 直角的
    e.g. square corners
  2. (not before noun) parallel with a straight line （不用于名词前）水平的
    e.g. I don't think the shelf is square with the floor.
  3. broad and strong 宽阔结实的
    e.g. a square jaw

square meal   (AmE, informal) a good satisfying meal （美式英语，非正式用法）美餐；饱餐
  e.g. Children should have three square meals a day.

(all) square   (informal) not owing each other any money 两清的，两不相欠的
  e.g. Here's your £10 back, so that makes us square.

square deal   honest and fair treatment from sb., especially in business 诚实的交易
  e.g. I'm not getting a square deal here.

a square peg in a round hole   (informal) sb. who is in a job or situation that is not suitable for them 方枘圆凿，处于与自己能力或性格不合的处境中的人

We see, but we don't see.
 Paradox as a rhetorical device   反论作为一种修辞手段：
 "反论"又称"逆论"或者"似是而非的隽语"，即乍听起来似乎荒唐而实际上却有一番道理的某种说法。TextB中的"We see, but we don't see"就是一个例子。这种看似矛盾、实则入情入理的矛盾修饰方法，汉英语言里都有，例如：
  1. 年年难过年年过，
    处处无家处处家。
   Hard up, we manage to get over it each year;
   Homeless, we try to make home everywhere.

2. 祸兮福所倚，福兮祸所伏。
   From disaster fortune comes, in fortune lurks disaster.

同样，英语中这样的例子也很多，例如：

3. More haste, less speed.
   欲速则不达。

4. What is improbable is extremely probable. (Aristotle)
   不可能的事恰恰最有可能发生。（亚里士多德）

5. A friend to everybody is a friend to nobody.
   人人友，非真友。

6. Everybody's business is nobody's business.
   一个和尚挑水吃，两个和尚抬水吃，三个和尚没水吃。

反论往往包含着有趣的哲学思辨，是构成俗语的重要手段。《圣经》中就有许多内涵丰富的反论，例如：

7. Behold, I send you forth as sheep in the midst of wolves: be you therefore wise as serpents, and harmless as doves. (Matthew 10: 16)
   我差你们去，如同羊进入狼群；所以你们要灵巧像蛇，驯良如鸽。（马太福音10: 16）

在翻译这一修辞格时往往要加词或改词，怎么加，怎么改，要看具体的上下文而决定。

clearance *n.*

1. the removal of waste or things you do not want from a place 清除
   e.g. house/slum clearance

2. the offer of goods for sale cheaply so that people will be encouraged to buy them and there will be space for new goods 清货
   e.g. We bought our new carpet at a clearance sale.

After Reading

READING COMPREHENSION TASKS

1. Complete the following table based on the information in TEXT B.

Descriptions	Four common mistakes that afflict us all
1) The brain slows down when it has to juggle tasks.	A. When we multitask, we get stupid.
2) Sometimes a person can look directly at something and still not see it.	B. We see, but we don't see.
3) We fail to come up with the name of a person we know or, even more embarrassing, we call the person by the wrong name.	C. We make slips of tongue.
4) Without intentionally trying to distort the record, we're all prone to recalling our own words and deeds in a more favourable light than others may recall.	D. We wear rose-coloured glasses.

2. Answer the following questions.

1) How does the author illustrate the point "To err is human" in the first paragraph?
   The author provides examples and statistics to illustrate his point. For example, most airplane crashes (70 percent), car wrecks (90 percent), workplace accidents (90 percent) are attributable to human error.

2) How is the term "slips of the tongue" defined?

   We fail to come up with the name of a person we know or, even more embarrassing, we call the person by the wrong name. Researchers call these gaffes slip-of-the-tongue or tip-of-the-tongue errors, or TOTs, for short.

3) What causes the difficulty for a person to recall the right name?

   Our recall of the right name is often blocked by a wrong name which typically has the same meaning as the right one.

4) In what way do people reconstruct their memories?

   People tend to reconstruct their memories in positive, self-flattering ways.

5) Why do we get stupid when we multitask?

   Our brain slows down when it has to juggle tasks. And the contents of our working memory can disappear when we are distracted.

6) How many details does the author use to support the idea "When we multitask, we get stupid"? What are they?

   Two.

   a. In one experiment, researchers asked participants to identify two images. If the two images appeared at the same time, the reaction time was a full second. But if the participants were asked to identify the images one at a time, the process went almost twice as quickly.

   b. A group of Microsoft employees took on average 15 minutes to get back to serious mental tasks after they responded to incoming e-mails.

7) How does the author account for the paradox "We see, but we don't see"?

   The author provides a lengthy example to illustrate this paradox.

3. Choose the best answer(s) to each of the following questions.

   1) Which method best describes the introduction in Text B?
      A. Quotation.   B. Idea that is the opposite of the one to be developed.
      C. Anecdote.   D. Broad, general statement narrowing to thesis.

   2) How many examples are given to support the idea "We wear rose-coloured glasses"?
      A. One.   B. Two.   C. Three.   **D. Four.**

   3) What strategy or strategies does the author employ to make the writing more effective?
      A. Exemplification.   B. Parallelism.   **C. Definition.**   D. Classification.

   4) Decide which of the following best describes the tone of the text.
      A. Satirical.   B. Humorous.   **C. Matter-of-fact.**   D. Critical.

4. Explain the underlined parts in your own words.

   1) …the cause is overwhelmingly attributable to human error… (Para. 1)
      can be largely contributed to

   2) …and these biases make us prone to commit certain types of errors. (Para. 2)
      make us more likely to

   3) …tip-of-the-tongue errors, or TOTs, for short. (Para. 3)
      in abbreviation

   4) No less than 29 percent of the recalled grades were wrong. (Para. 8)
      as many as

5) Overall, 79 percent of students <u>inflated their grades</u>. (Para. 9)
   exaggerated their test scores

6) …and it <u>keeps track of</u> all the short-term stuff… (Para. 14)
   keeps fully aware of

7) …where the clearance is <u>well over</u> 13 feet. (Para. 20)
   considerably above

ORAL WORK

In TEXT B the author lists four common mistakes that afflict us all. Have you ever committed any of these mistakes? Discuss with your group members and share your experiences.

The teacher can ask the students to work in groups first and then choose a few groups to present their stories to the whole class.

TRANSLATION OF TEXT B

我们都做过的蠢事

约瑟夫·T·哈利南

1　我们都听说过"人孰无过"，这句话颇具真理。出事情时——70%的飞机失事、90%的车祸以及90%的工作场所事故——很大程度上还真得归因于人祸。一旦某个人被定罪，调查就到此结束。但事情并不该如此——如果我们想要彻底根除此类错误的话。

2　我们在看待、回忆、观察世界的方式上有某些倾向，并深受其影响，这些倾向使我们更容易犯某些类型的错误。作为一名多年研究人类错误的记者，我发现了一些人人会犯的常见错误。

1. 我们都发生口误

3　有一种错误，不分年龄和文化背景，人人都会犯：我们想不起某个认识的人叫什么名字，或者更加难为情的是，叫错名字。研究者称这些失礼举动为口误，或者简称TOT。对大多数人来说，这种情况一星期左右就发生一回。

4　研究者发现大多数口误涉及特定的人名或地名。如果你在寻找一个普通名词——如显示文字的计算机部件名称——你可以叫它显示器或者屏幕。但对于专有名词，只有那个词才行得通。

5　当某个名字就在嘴边，却怎么也说不出来时，我们通常倒是能够记起一些所需要的信息。例如，人们经常可以正确猜出该名字中的音节数量，甚至第一个字母。在一项研究中，一个参与者试着辨识女演员Liza Minnelli的照片，这个人虽然说不出她的名字，却能够写出一些相似的词：Monetti, Mona, Magetti, Spaghetti, Bogette。

6　另一条揭开口误谜团的线索是，对一个正确名字的回忆通常会被一个错误名字所妨碍。但是这个错误名字不是任意的，而通常与正确名字有相同的意义。比如说，如果你心中想的是一个聪明人的名字，像阿尔伯特·爱因斯坦，错误的名字就有可能是另一个你认为非常聪明的人。

2. 我们都戴着有色眼镜

7　对于曾说过的话和做过的事，我们比旁人更倾向于以有利于自己的方式来回忆，虽然绝非有意歪曲事实。为了证明这一点，请客观地回答如下问题(不过你得保留所有的成绩册以便核对)：你高中时成绩如何？

8 答案是：可能并不像你记得的那么好——至少俄亥俄威斯理大学的学生记得不那么对。在一项研究中，他们被要求回忆高中时的成绩。研究者将他们的回答和成绩单上的实际成绩作了核对，多达29%的回忆是错的。他们并不是在回忆久远的事；这些是大一和大二的学生，他们回忆的不过是几年前的成绩。

9 此外，这些错误还有倾向性，记得偏高的成绩远多于偏低的（成绩是B却记成了A）。学生们对好成绩比差成绩记得更牢。对A的回忆准确率为89%，而对于D仅为29%。总体而言，79%的学生夸大了自己的成绩。

10 一再有发现表明人们以一种积极的、自我褒扬的方式来重建回忆。父母们对于他们教养方式的回忆比真实情况更贴近专家的建议，而赌徒们关于赢的记忆比输的记忆更加鲜明。

11 这种倾向如此强大，以至于芝加哥大学以及弗吉尼亚大学的研究者发现，我们心目中自己的面容都要比旁人感觉中的更迷人。

3. 当我们一心多用，就会变蠢

12 大脑穷于应付多项任务时，就会变慢。

13 在一次试验中，研究者要求年龄在18岁到32岁之间的成人识别两个图像：有颜色的十字形和几何图案，如三角形。看起来很简单对吗？但是当被测试者同时看到有颜色的十字形和几何图案时，他们需要整整一秒的反应时间来摁按钮。尽管那样，他们还会经常犯错。如果参与者被要求一次识别一个图像——十字形先来，然后识别几何图案——这个过程会快一倍。

14 不断变换任务还会产生其他问题。我们可能会忘记正在做或者打算做的事情。我们脑中要做的任务清单被称为工作记忆，它负责保存所有需要短期记住的事物，如某人刚刚给我们的电子邮件地址。

15 但是我们的工作记忆可能会如同沙漠中的水一样蒸发，仅两秒之后，记忆便开始消失。考虑一个新问题15秒后，旧的问题就被遗忘。在一些情况下，遗忘率可以达到40%。针对办公人员的研究发现，当注意力被分散后，人们需要15分钟的时间来重新达到深层次的精力集中。

16 这一结果与研究者关于微软公司员工工作习惯的研究发现相吻合。接受观察的一组员工在回复了临时接收到的电子邮件后，平均要花15分钟才能重新回到严肃的脑力工作中，比如写汇报或电脑编程。为何需要这么长时间呢？通常这些员工因回复其他信件或浏览网页而分了心。

4. 我们视而不见

17 有时一个人可能盯着某件东西，却没看见它。在20世纪90年代早期的实验中，研究者们发现，惊人数量的参与者在视觉测试中都没有意识到某些物体正呈现在他们眼前。不仅在被呈现物品为小件时有这个倾向，即使呈现的是大件而且相当明显时，也同样如此。

18 一个真实反映"视而不见"的例证发生在2004年，靠近华盛顿哥伦比亚特区的地方。11月14日，一名44岁的包车巴士司机在巴尔的摩/华盛顿机场接了一群学生，送他们到弗农山，乔治·华盛顿的故居。据称，该司机当天情绪很不好。主要是因为随行人员中的另一个司机对他的态度使他很不开心。所以他打电话发泄了一通。

19 当天早晨学生们的出行路线是沿着乔治·华盛顿纪念馆风景区干道开，该干道途经起伏的小山，穿越立交桥的拱形桥洞，包括一座石桥。距离石桥大约四分之一英里处，有一个大的黄色标志警示前方拱形桥洞下右车道的净空刚过10英尺。

20 对于小汽车，这不成问题，但包车大巴有12英尺高。该司机需要换到中间车道，在拱峰下方，那里的净空超过了13英尺。前方领路大巴就是这样做的。

21 但是这第二辆大巴并没有改换车道。司机还打着电话。汽车一头撞到了桥上，这次猛烈的撞击整整削去了大巴右侧的顶部，露出一个大大的裂口。一名学生严重受伤。

22 事后，司机被国家运输安全委员会调查审问。他的陈述表明心不在焉导致的视而不见有多严重。他告诉调查人员，他不仅没有看见那个黄色警示标志，他连桥都没看见。

INTEGRATED EXERCISES

1 PUBLIC SPEECH TRAINING

Regardless of the purpose of your speech, it usually has three main parts — an introduction, a body, and a conclusion. The following speech is about the Great Wall of China. Now listen to the beginning and concluding parts of the speech, and pay attention to how it begins and ends. Practice after the recording.

(The speech will be read twice. For the first time, the students just listen and try to understand the meaning. When it is read for the second time, there are pauses in the recording. Ask the students to practice after the speaker during these pauses and pay attention to the speaker's intonation, voice [e.g. loudness, pitch, tempo] etc.)

Answer for reference

The speech begins with a famous Chinese saying and the speaker's personal travel experience, in order to arouse attention from the audience and establish credibility.

The speech ends with a brief summary of the Great Wall's significance in Chinese culture and identity.

Script

In China there's a saying, / "You won't be considered a great person / until you've been to the Great Wall." / I visited the wall last year while I was in China. / I don't know if it made me a great person, / but I do know that the wall is indeed great. /

…

In conclusion, the Great Wall of China enjoys a rich history. / Built over the course of more than 2,500 years / during the Qin, Han, and Ming Dynasties, / it is a magnificent feat of human engineering. / While the wall no longer serves as a defence against invaders, / it does continue to play a central role in Chinese culture and identity. / Now that you know a little more about the wall, / I hope you have a fuller understanding of why it's regarded as great, / not just in China, but throughout the world.

2 DICTATION

Listen to the following passage and write it down. The passage will be read four times. During the first reading, which will be done at normal speed, listen and try to understand the meaning. For the second and third readings, the passage will be read sentence by sentence, or phrase by phrase, with intervals of 15 seconds. Write down what you hear. The last reading will be done at normal speed again and during this time you should check your work.

Script

Two types of interpersonal communication exist. / The first is impersonal in nature. / When people react to each other according to the role they are playing, / the context is impersonal. / For example, in the relationship between a customer and a clerk, / the customer may say "I'd like this item," / and the clerk may say "That will be 79 cents." / The most important type of interpersonal context, however, / is personal in nature. / When people react to one another as unique human beings with special needs and interests, / a personal context exists and close relationships may develop. / Such things as attraction, self-disclosure, and trust seem to play important roles / in establishing and maintaining long-term social relationships.

3 VOCABULARY STUDY

Task One

Choose the right word and use its proper form to complete each sentence. Note the difference of meaning between the words.

1) **mistake   error   slip**
   - There must be some __mistake__ — I definitely paid the bill last week.
   - Over 50 people were denied a vote through a computer __error__.
   - Sampras was playing badly, making a lot of __mistakes__.
   - Don't worry — we all make __slips__ from time to time.

   Explanation: *Mistake* refers to something incorrect that you do, say, or write without intending to. *Error* refers to a mistake in calculating or in using a language, system, computer etc. *Slip* refers to a small unimportant mistake that is easy to make.

2) **subdued   subtle**
   - There is a __subtle__ difference between these two plans.
   - I felt strangely __subdued__ as I drove home.
   - I think we need a more __subtle__ approach.
   - Far below, the tiniest candle-flame sending out the smallest light, flickering, __subdued__.

   Explanation: *Subdued* means (of a person or their manner) being quiet and rather reflective or depressed, or (of colour or lighting) being soft and restrained. *Subtle* means not being loud, bright, noticeable or obvious in any way, or being small but important.

3) **peril   hazard**
   - They put their own lives in __peril__ to rescue their friends.
   - The rubbish needs to be removed before it becomes a health __hazard__.
   - For international traders, changes in the exchange rate are an unavoidable __hazard__.
   - Politicians ignore this issue at their __peril__.

   Explanation: *Peril* refers to something that can cause danger, especially during a journey, and is used especially in literature. *Hazard* refers to something that may be dangerous, cause accident etc.

4) **avert   avoid   prevent**
   - A special valve __prevents__ the waste gases from escaping.
   - Talks will be held today in a final attempt to __avert__ strike action.
   - Many people now believe that a good diet can help to __prevent__ cancer.
   - I try to __avoid__ supermarkets on Saturdays — they're always so busy.

   Explanation: *Avert* is to do something to prevent something bad that will happen very soon if one does not do it. *Avoid* is to stay away from someone or something or prevent something from happening, or not allow oneself to do something. *Prevent* is to stop something from happening or stop someone from doing something.

Task Two
Put the proper form of the words in the corresponding blanks.

1) It is very hard to realize to what degree __isolationism__ has been a basic feature of the United States. (isolate)
2) When a child learns to picture and __verbalize__ his feelings, he has the opportunity to reason and make intelligent choices. (verbal)
3) The feeling of inferiority is defensively turned into a feeling of __superiority__. (superior)
4) His manner was mildly __flirtatious__ and he had a tendency to glance in my direction, showing off, I suspect. (flirt)
5) Before moving to Paris, Michael went on an __intensive__ course to improve his French. (intense)
6) It was without precedent in the United States, which explains the difficulties encountered by the __preservationists__. (preserve)
7) Refugees cross the rugged San Ysidro Mountains, and it is always a __perilous__ trip. (peril)
8) The committee hopes to __standardize__ the school curriculum and teaching techniques. (standard)
9) Chris had a fine __appreciation__ of drawing. (appreciate)
10) Bagehot's work continued to be regarded as an __authoritative__ work long after the Constitution underwent fundamental change. (authority)

Task Three
Fill in each blank with an appropriate preposition or adverb.

1) The fall in the number of deaths from heart disease is generally attributed __to__ improvements in diet.
2) Though these figures are shocking, they need to be put __into__ perspective.
3) What is her name? It's __on__ the tip of my tongue. Joan. Joan Simpson. That's it!
4) The hat gives a clue __to__ the identity of the killer.
5) __In__ the light of this tragic event, we have canceled the 4th of July celebration.
6) Do those announcements really square __with__ the facts?
7) The ship calls at each port on this coast to pick __up__ passengers and mail.
8) Don't lend yourself __to__ such dishonest schemes.
9) He threw a fierce look __at__ me, so I wondered what I had done wrong.
10) The Tennessee and Red rivers were prone __to__ destructive floods, as were many rivers throughout the US.

Task Four
Fill in the following blanks with appropriate words from the box.

It is important to understand communication as a process — a series of ongoing events that include sending, receiving, and interpreting a message. It is a 1) __mistake__ to think of communication as a thing. Books, encyclopedias, CDs and phonograph records, DVDs, and magazines are indeed 2) __things__. But each of these things is, by 3) __itself__, not communication. Each represents, rather, a message that is 4) __but__ one part of the whole communication process. This 5) __process__ begins when a person feels a need to communicate. For 6) __example__, a student may feel that his or her hair looks messy after gym class. To check it 7) __out__, the student encodes, or places into sound patterns, a message: "Does my hair look 8) __messy__?" Person two hears the sounds and 9) __decodes__, or assigns meanings to, the message: "Chris is worrying about messy hair again." The friend then encodes a 10) __response__ into sound patterns: "Your hair looks 11) __great__, Chris. Stop worrying." Chris hears the 12) __sounds__ and decodes their meaning: "Oh, great. Pat thinks my hair doesn't look messy." This 13) __illustration__ shows how the communication process works for one person-to-person exchange involving a 14) __single__ idea or feeling. In ordinary conversation the communication process is 15) __unlikely__ to stop with a single exchange.

4 GRAMMAR FOCUS

Read the following passage, underline the one mistake in each line and write the correction after the bracketed number.

We use language primarily as a means of communication with other human beings. Each of us shares with the community in which we live a store of words and meanings as well as <u>agreeing</u> conventions as to the way in which <u>words</u> should be arranged to convey a particular message. The English speaker has <u>in</u> his disposal a vocabulary and a set of grammatical rules which <u>enables</u> him to communicate his thoughts and feelings, in a variety of styles, to <u>the other</u> English speakers. His vocabulary, in particular, both that which he uses actively and that which he recognizes, <u>increase</u> in size as he grows <u>old</u>, as a result of education and experience.	1) agreed 2) these/those words 3) at 4) enable 5) other 6) increases 7) older
But, whether the language store is <u>relative</u> small or large, the system remains <u>not</u> more than a psychological reality for the individual, unless he has a means of expressing it <u>on</u> terms able to be <u>seen</u> by another member of his linguistic community; he has to give	8) relatively 9) no 10) in 11) perceived/understood/comprehended
the system a concrete transmission form. We <u>take it</u> for granted the two most common forms of transmission — <u>through</u> means of sounds produced by our vocal organs (speech) or by visual signs (writing). <u>And</u> these are among <u>most</u> striking of human achievements.	12) take 13) by 14) Yet/But/Nevertheless 15) the most

1) 分词错误：此处应为被动态，用过去分词。
2) 限定词错误：应该用限定词these/those来特指前述的words。
3) 介词搭配错误：at one's disposal为固定词组，意为"供……使用，供……自由支配"。
4) 主谓一致错误：动词enable应该与前面的先行词a vocabulary and a set of grammatical rules在单复数形式上保持一致。
5) 冠词错误：不需要使用定冠词表特指关系。
6) 主谓一致错误：主语vocabulary为单数，要求后面动词在数上保持一致。
7) 比较级错误：应该是比较级形式older，意为"年岁渐长"，而非"变老"。
8) 副词错误：应该使用副词relatively来修饰后面的形容词small or large。
9) 语义搭配错误：no more than表示"仅仅，只是"，not more than表示"至多，不超过，不比……更……"。
10) 介词搭配错误：in terms表示"用某种措辞"。
11) 动词语义错误：应该表示"被理解"，而非"被看见"。

12) 动词短语错误：take sth. for granted意为"把……视为理所当然"，take的宾语后置，放到了granted后面。
13) 介词搭配错误：by means of为固定词组，意为"通过，依靠"。
14) 语义衔接错误：上下文语义关系为转折而非递进。
15) 最高级错误：形容词最高级要求使用定冠词the。

5 TRANSLATION

Task One
Translate the following paragraph from English into Chinese.

近年来，许多专职主持人都谈论过演讲中身体语言的重要性。他们阐明了理由：观众不仅仅听你说话的内容，也同时看着你，因此你需要配合适当的姿势来强调所说的观点。以下是一些通常的准则：首先站直了，将身体重量平均分布于两脚上，这一姿势显示出自信和稳重。第二，要与观众眼神交流，如果你不能看着人们的眼睛，大家就会认为你有什么东西在隐瞒着他们。从演讲一开始就该建立眼神交流，因为一旦有了好的开端，就很容易保持下去，而如果你在讲演的头三分钟就没能这么做的话，到后来也不会有勇气做了。最后，从演讲一开始就要保持放松，如果你紧张又不自在，这种感觉会传染给观众。正确的姿势会给观众留下良好的第一印象。

Task Two
Translate the following paragraph from Chinese into English.

Twenty years ago, the mobile phone and the World Wide Web did not yet exist; nor did many people have access to fax machine and personal computers. Today, almost all of us here have a mobile phone with which we can reach another person in another part of the world instantly. People all over the world may watch on the Internet the minute-by-minute returns of the presidential election of a certain country. In this sense, the world has become one. The adage from *The Book of Change* that "The celestial bodies are regular in their motion, so should the superior man labor unceasingly to strengthen his own character" is still very applicable and useful today. To live and succeed in an ever changing world, you must seek to have a firm knowledge of the fundamental nature of the world and never cease to improve yourself.

6 CLASSROOM INTERACTION

Activity A   Listening

1) Five

   1) Make a game plan and rehearse it; 2) Be firm; 3) Be courteous; 4) Be complete;
   5) Allow the individual to keep his dignity.

2) Answers may vary.
3) Answers may vary.

Script

It happens all the time. A valued employee pleads for a salary increase. Your assistant asks for a new piece of office equipment. A customer asks for a refund. And you must decline the request. Limited time, energy and resources are a hard fact of business life, and if you hope to adhere to your priorities, you'll have to say "no" — time and time again.

If you want to learn how to say "no" more effectively, study these simple principles — and use them

when you must turn down a request:
1. Make a game plan and rehearse it

   When you must decline a request, determine in advance exactly what you will say. Rehearse the hypothetical conversation that ensues. You'll feel more confident as a result.

2. Be firm

   Don't try to soften the blow by leaving some vague hope that things might change in future. Indefinite suggestions like "maybe we can talk about this issue again in the future" or "I'd like to see if we can pull this together someday" will lessen your capability. Be up-front.

3. Be courteous

   Whatever you do and whatever the individual says, keep your tone calm. Don't hesitate to smile reassuringly during your conversation, and be sure to use the same level of professional decorum you'd use in any other important business meeting.

4. Be complete

   Explain your decisions as thoroughly as you can. To the extent that you're capable of, discuss the reasons behind your decision. While the individual may not be entitled to an explanation, she will appreciate getting one. If your explanation does nothing else, it will position you as a knowledgeable and concerned individual.

5. Allow the individual to keep his dignity

   In simple terms, when your employee, customer or associate leaves your office or gets off the phone with you, he should feel that you have given him something of worth. It might be sincere thanks for the efforts he made. Or an honest expression of your confidence in him.

When you manage relationships effectively, they will be able to bear the strain of even the strongest "no".

Activity B   Group Discussion

The teacher can ask the students to work in groups first and then choose a few groups to present their suggestions to the whole class.

Activity C   Picture Description
Reference for the teacher

Primitive Means of Communication

In earliest times people came together in groups to avoid loneliness, to help each other hunt and gather food, and to protect themselves from ever-present dangers. In order to live and work cooperatively, they needed to find ways to communicate with each other. They were largely limited to things that could be heard, seen, or felt. They used sounds, gestures, and touch as symbols. A grunting sound might have indicated that a rock was too heavy to lift alone, or a gesture might have stood for "come here" or "get back". Over time a language developed that stood for the objects and actions needed for survival in a hunting society.

Primitive people also expressed their feelings through art and dance. Some of the earliest surviving examples of art are the cave paintings in Lascaux, France, which were drawn some 27,000 years ago and depict animals of the time. It is not known whether these pictures were created for the purpose of religious ceremony, dramatic storytelling, or even the simple tallying of hunters' conquests, but they show that primitive people had both a need and a talent for self-expression.

Primitive people were limited in their ability to communicate across distances. Smoke signals, drums, and fires were used to stretch the boundaries of human sight and sound. Nighttime bonfires were used in early societies as beacons to guide ships at sea. Later, lighthouses were built to extend the range of fire signals. The marble Pharos at Alexandria, Egypt, one of the Seven Wonders of the World, was an early attempt to reach out to those at sea. On land, communication at distances greater than the limits of sight or sound was no faster than the speed of the swiftest runner.

Modern Means of Communication

Instantaneous communication of text, audio, and video information became a reality when digital technology made it possible to compress, store, and transmit large volumes of data efficiently. This development increased the speed and reduced the cost of distance communication for offices and homes. Business teleconferences with people in faraway cities became affordable and routine. Friends increasingly keep in touch with instant messaging or send each other pictures through their telephones. Computers link offices, families, and friends through e-mail, websites, and intranets. Electronic fund transfers give banks and businesses great flexibility in managing money.

WRITING

Writing Skills: Illustrative Essays

This unit discusses how to write an illustrative essay. Some people distinguish *illustration* from *example*, but in this textbook, they are regarded as the same. An illustrative essay here refers to an essay that uses examples to prove the point the writer wants to make.

The teacher is advised to discuss with the students the definition of *example*, because when an essay relies heavily on examples to explain or persuade, the examples need to satisfy certain expectations. They should be self-contained stories rather than a brief mention of some incidents. Readers need to get quite complete information about the five Ws of an event. But on the other hand, these examples should also be different from stories in narrative essays, which means that they are shorter, simpler, and less detailed than those in narrative essays.

The teacher also needs to highlight the criteria for effective examples. In the Student's Book, we have summarized them as being relevant, typical, concrete and sufficient. Efforts need to be made to warn the students against including an example mainly because it is interesting. And the teacher needs to remind the students that, like other types of essays, an illustrative essay should still focus on the central point, and that examples are included because they can explain the point, not because they are interesting or moving.

The sample in the Student's Book is intended to give the students some idea of what an illustrative essay looks like. The topic is familiar with the students.

Here is the reference answers to the questions after the sample:

1. This essay attempts to prove that doing temporary jobs is beneficial to college students.
2. The writer has used three supporting points: doing temporary jobs can improve students' social skills, academic studies, and self-independence. The first two points are supported with examples, while the third point is not. The third point may be regarded as illustrated with logic reasoning, where the evidence is too abstract to be an example.
3. The second paragraph works together with the third paragraph to present the first supporting point. The second paragraph gives the problem and briefly mentions the solution, which is explored in the third paragraph. The second paragraph is not supported with examples.

Writing Assignment

1. Decide which of the following examples can be used to support the point.

Among these examples, 1, 2 and 5 can be used. Examples 3 and 4 are not suitable because they are not closely related to the central point: bloggers are a force to safeguard social justice.

2. Read the following sample carefully, and answer the questions that follow.

1) This essay is mainly about disadvantages of being short. The writer lists awkward situations in medical examination, military training, volleyball match and friends' behaviour as examples. These examples are vivid and typical, and therefore help to prove the point.
2) There is a problem with the structure of this essay. The writer tries to put forward four examples to illustrate the disadvantages of being short, but fails to order them properly. He could follow the ascending

order (from the smallest to the greatest disadvantage) or the descending order (from the greatest to the smallest disadvantage). But he puts the greatest one, "Being short is a handicap and this is something that I hate most", in the middle. This may harm the coherence of the essay.

3. Write an essay on the topic "The advantage/disadvantage of owning a car", and try to illustrate your point with examples.

Answers may vary.

6 MASS MEDIA

TEXT A   Who Killed the Newspaper?

Before Reading

The purpose of this section is to arouse the students' interest in the theme of the unit, reactivate their relevant background knowledge or recall their personal experience, so as to better prepare them for the succeeding tasks.

The first picture describes a person reading from an electronic reader. The second picture shows a traditional newsstand at which newspapers and magazines are sold. Ask the students to focus on the different channels through which news or information is obtained in the pictures. The students are also encouraged to talk about their own experiences of getting news and look ahead for the future of newspapers.

Newspapers have been providing news and other information to people all over the world for years. But with the advent of the Internet, the newspaper industry is confronted with many difficulties, which has made the survival of the industry a hot issue. The questions provided in this section serve as prompts for the students to think about the future of newspapers. The students can be encouraged to do further discussion in Oral Work.

Background Information

1 Mass Media

Mass media refers collectively to all media technologies, including the Internet, television, newspapers, film and radio, which are used for mass communications, and to the organizations which control these technologies.

Mass media can be used for various purposes:

- Advocacy, both for business and social concerns. This can include advertising, marketing, propaganda, public relations, and political communication.
- Entertainment, traditionally through performances of acting, music, and sports, along with light reading; since the late 20th century also through video and computer games.
- Public service announcements.

Mass media plays a significant role in shaping public perceptions on a variety of important issues, both through the information that is dispensed through them, and through the interpretations they place upon this information. They also play a large role in shaping modern culture, by selecting and portraying a particular set of beliefs, values, and traditions (an entire way of life), as reality. That is, by portraying a certain interpretation of reality, they shape reality to be more in line with that interpretation.

2 A Very Brief History of Early Newspapers

The phrase "the media" began to be used in the 1920s, but referred to something that had its origins much further in the past. The invention of the printing press in the late 15th century gave rise to some of the first forms of mass communication, by enabling the publication of books and newspapers on a scale much larger than was previously possible.

On 7 November 1665, *The London Gazette* (at first called *The Oxford Gazette*) began publication. It was published twice a week. Other English papers started to publish three times a week, and later the first daily papers emerged. This was partly due to the postal system between Dover and London.

Newspapers in general included short articles, ephemeral topics, some illustrations and service articles (classifieds). They were often written by multiple authors, although the authors' identities were often obscured. They began to contain some advertisements, and they did not yet include sections. Mass market papers emerged, including Sunday papers for workers to read in their leisure time. *The Times* adopted new technologies and set the standards for other newspapers. This newspaper covered major wars, among other major events.

In Boston in 1690, Benjamin Harris published *Publick Occurrences Both Forreign and Domestick*. This is considered the first newspaper in the American colonies even though only one edition was published before the paper was suppressed by the colonial officials, possibly due to censorship and control issues. It followed the two-column format and was a single sheet, printed on both sides.

In 1704, the governor allowed *The Boston News-Letter*, a weekly, to be published, and it became the first continuously published newspaper in the colonies. Soon after, weekly papers began publishing in New York and Philadelphia. The second English-language newspaper in the Americas was the *Weekly Jamaica Courant*. These early newspapers followed the British format and were usually four pages long. They mostly carried news from Britain and content depended on the editor's interests. In 1783, the *Pennsylvania Evening Post* became the first American daily.

By the early 19th century, many cities in Europe, as well as in North and South America, published newspaper-type publications though not all of them developed in the same way; content was vastly shaped by regional and cultural preferences. Advances in printing technology related to the Industrial Revolution enabled newspapers to become an even more widely circulated means of communication. In 1814, *The Times* (London) acquired a printing press capable of making 1,100 impressions per minute.

3 Electronic Media and Print Media

- Broadcasting, in the narrow sense, for radio and television
- Many instances of various types of recorded discs or tapes. In the 20th century, these were mainly used for music. Video and computer uses followed.
- Film, most often used for entertainment, but also for documentaries
- The Internet — examples include blogs and podcasts (such as news, music, pre-recorded speech, and video)
- Mobile phones, which can be used for rapid breaking news and short clips of entertainment like jokes, horoscopes, alerts, games, music, and advertising
- Publishing, including electronic publishing
- Video games, which have developed into a mass form of media

Reading

Text Analysis

- ### Text Summary

The article discusses the future of newspapers in the context of the rising web journalism. Newspapers are faced with a very difficult situation in their business since they are losing both readers and advertising to the Internet. Although newspapers have taken actions to try to change the situation, the prospect is bleak. However, this is only a cause for concern, not for panic. In the future, some high-quality journalism will definitely survive and newspapers can play even bigger roles together with net journalism.

- ### Text Organization

Paragraph 1: introduction	Newspapers in rich countries are now facing a decline and their business is falling apart.
Paragraphs 2-11: main body	Newspapers are losing both readers and advertising to the Internet, which has already forced some newspapers to shut down. Although newspapers have taken some actions to try to change the situation, some of them are unlikely to survive. However, the future of newspapers is not doomed. High-quality newspapers will continue to play their role as long as they can adjust themselves.
Paragraph 12: conclusion	In the future, high-quality journalism will get more support from various sources and, therefore, may play a greater role together with net journalism. No panic!

- ### Text Features

Originally appearing in *The Economist* as a newsmagazine article, this text bears a very shocking title "Who Killed the Newspaper?" It is written in a formal style with a polite and impersonal tone, which is demonstrated by some distinctive features: the frequent use of more advanced vocabulary (e.g. *endangered species*, *demise*, *chastened*, etc.), technical terms (e.g. *listed*, *shareholders*, *Fourth Estate*, etc.), quotations and statistics, and lengthy complex sentences with grammatical rules strictly observed. The formal style is also indicated in the absence of contractions, colloquial expressions and the first and second person pronouns (*I*, *you*, etc.) in the text.

The text takes a deductive approach in the discussion, which follows the pattern of raising an issue, analyzing the issue and offering a solution. In the analysis, the text quotes important people (e.g. Rupert Murdoch) or refers to other sources (e.g. the Newspaper Association of America) in the field, cites statistics (数据), and gives specific examples to support and develop the ideas. Another feature worth noticing in the organization of the paragraphs is the use of linking devices, some examples are: *(largely/partly) because*, *but*, *even (if)*, *thus*, *therefore*, *according to*, *neither…nor*, *in addition*, etc.

It should also be noted that the frequent use of formal words and many lengthy and syntactically complex sentences in the text may slow the students' reading pace and make the text difficult to understand.

- ### Key Sentences

1. **The business of selling words to readers and selling readers to advertisers, which has sustained their role in society, is falling apart. (Para. 1)**

The subject of the sentence is *The business*, which is the precedent of the non-restrictive relative clause(非限制性关系从句) introduced by the relative(关系代词) *which*. A non-restrictive relative clause does not aid in the identification of the precedent, but only provides additional information about it. Other relatives that can be used to introduce a non-restrictive relative clause include *who, whom, whose, when, where*. For example:

A: Bob's father-in-law, who worked on the project, spent four years in the US.

B: We will put off the picnic until next weekend, when we won't be so busy.

C: The girl, whom we met in New York, is a Yale graduate.

2. Publications like *The New York Times* and *The Wall Street Journal* should be able to put up the price of their journalism to compensate for advertising revenues lost to the Internet — especially as they cater to a more global readership. (Para. 8)

In this sentence, *like The New York Times and The Wall Street Journal* is a prepositional phrase(介词短语) acting as an attributive(定语) to modify *publications*. The past participial phrase (过去分词短语) *lost to the Internet* also functions as an attributive to modify *advertising revenues*. Other examples:

A: Movies *like Shrek* are very popular with kids. (prepositional phrase)

B: I borrowed a novel *written by Mark Twain* from the library. (past participial phrase)

3. Of course, the Internet panders to closed minds; but so has much of the press. (Para. 10)

In the sentence, *so*, as an adverb, is used to mean "in the same way" as indicated by the predicate (谓语) in the previous sentence. For example:

A: — I'm going to the concert.　— So am I. (I am going to the concert, too.)

B: I have finished my assignment. So has John. (John has finished his assignment, too.)

Conjunction *neither* is used to take the place of *so* when expressing a negative meaning. For example:

A: — I don't like travelling by bus.　— Neither do I. (I don't like travelling by bus either.)

New Words and Expressions

muse /mjuːz/ *v.* to say sth. in a thoughtful way 若有所思地说
e.g. It was an odd thing, mused Doctor Lovell.
"I wonder why she was killed," mused Poirot.

a series of a group of (events or actions that are planned to happen one after the other) 一连串；一系列
e.g. The staff will hold a series of meetings over the next few weeks.
This autumn the BBC will be showing a series of French films.

bring down to force a government or ruler to lose power 推翻
e.g. a crisis that could bring down the government
The scandal may bring down the president.

journalism /'dʒɜːnəlɪzəm/ *n.* the job or activity of writing news reports for newspapers, magazines, television, or radio 新闻业；新闻工作
e.g. a career in journalism
The hospital has been the target of investigative journalism.

at one's best in the best state or form 在最好的状态下
e.g. At her best, she's a really stylish player.
He was never at his best early in the morning.

agenda /ə'dʒendə/ *n.* a list of problems or subjects that a government, organization etc. is planning to deal with 议程；议题
e.g. Measures to combat terrorism will be high

on the agenda.

Our Centre has limited its research agenda to four areas.

endanger /ɪnˈdeɪndʒə/ *v.* to put sb. or sth. in danger of being hurt, damaged, or destroyed 危害；使处于危险之中

e.g. Smoking during pregnancy endangers the baby's life.

The lizards are classed as an endangered species (= one that soon may no longer exist).

species /ˈspiːʃiːz/ *n.* a group of animals or plants whose members are similar and can breed together to produce young animals or plants 物种；种群

e.g. Seven species of birds of prey have been observed.

Do you know the author of *On the Origin of Species*?

sustain /səˈsteɪn/ *v.* to make sth. continue to exist or happen for a period of time 维持；支持

e.g. the policies necessary to sustain economic growth

She found it difficult to sustain the children's interest.

fall apart to come to pieces 崩溃；瓦解

e.g. My car is falling apart.

Their marriage finally fell apart.

circulation /ˌsɜːkjʊˈleɪʃən/ *n.* the average number of copies of a newspaper or magazine that are usually sold each day, week, month etc. 发行量

e.g. circulation figures

The newspaper has a daily circulation of 55,000 copies.

hasten /ˈheɪsən/ *v.* to make sth. happen faster or sooner 加速，促进

e.g. Artificial heating hastens the growth of plants.

Their departure was hastened by an abnormally cold winter.

cynical /ˈsɪnɪkəl/ *a.* doubtful as to whether sth. will happen or whether it is worthwhile 怀疑的

e.g. a cynical view of human nature

The public is cynical about election promises.

baron /ˈbærən/ *n.* a businessman with a lot of power or influence 巨头，大王

e.g. drug barons

conservative press barons like Beaverbrook

Briton /ˈbrɪtən/ *n.* (formal) sb. from Britain（正式用法）英国人

e.g. the ancient Britons

the first Briton to win a medal

unseemly /ˌʌnˈsiːmlɪ/ *a.* not polite or not suitable for a particular occasion 不体面的；不合礼节的

e.g. His language is most unseemly, i.e. abusive.

Ann thought it unseemly to kiss her husband in public.

seductive /sɪˈdʌktɪv/ *a.* interesting or attractive 诱惑人的；有吸引力的

e.g. the seductive power of advertising

This offer of a high salary and a free house is very seductive.

supposedly /səˈpəʊzɪdlɪ/ *ad.* according to what is generally assumed or believed (but not known for certain) 据称，据说

e.g. Anne is coming for a visit in March supposedly.

How could a supposedly intelligent person be so stupid?

classified ad a small advertisement put in a newspaper to buy or sell sth. 分类广告

e.g. online classified ads service

A classified ad is called "small ad" in British English and " want ad" in American English.

dry up to become completely dry 干涸

e.g. Taking too much water for household use is drying up the river.

Across central and west Texas, waterholes and wells have dried up.

shut down to stop operating either permanently or for a short time 关闭；停业

e.g. Our local hardware shop has shut down.

We have shut down our factory.

fold /fəʊld/ *v.* to close for lack of financial resources 停业；倒闭

e.g. The company folded (up) last week.

There are many reasons why a business may fold.

listed /ˈlɪstɪd/ *a.* offering its shares for sale on the stock exchange（在股市）上市的

e.g. A company whose shares can be traded on a country's main stock market is called a listed company.

The company claimed that they are listed in the stock exchange of Singapore.

prompt /prɒmpt/ *v.* to make people say or do

sth. as a reaction 激起，引起
e.g. What prompted that remark?
The decision prompted an outcry among prominent US campaigners.

shareholder /'ʃeə,həʊldə/ *n.* sb. who owns shares in a company or business 股东
e.g. Shareholders will be voting on the merger of the companies.
Shareholders have been told to expect an even lower result next year.

relevant /'reləvənt/ *a.* directly relating to the subject or problem being discussed or considered 相关的
e.g. Relevant documents were presented in court.
What experience do you have that is relevant to this position?

meager /'mi:gə/ *a.* small in quantity and poor in quality 贫乏的；不足的
e.g. a school with meager resources
He supplements his meager income by working on Saturdays.

editorial /ˌedɪ'tɔ:rɪəl/ *a.* relating to the preparation of a newspaper, book, television programme etc. for printing or broadcasting 编辑的
e.g. the editorial office
an editorial assistant

uncover /ˌʌn'kʌvə/ *v.* to find out about sth. that has been kept secret 揭露
e.g. Secret agents have uncovered a plot against the President.
Customs officials uncovered a plot to smuggle weapons into the country.

corruption /kə'rʌpʃən/ *n.* dishonest, illegal, or immoral behaviour, especially from sb. with power 腐败；贪污
e.g. officials charged with bribery and corruption
The investigation uncovered widespread corruption within the police force.

fraud /frɔ:d/ *n.* the crime of deceiving people in order to gain sth. such as money or goods 欺诈；诈骗
e.g. tax/insurance/credit card fraud
She was found guilty of fraud.

fit /fɪt/ *n.* a sudden period of vigorous activity 一阵
e.g. a fit of energy/letter writing
The girls collapsed into a fit of the giggles.

bode /bəʊd/ *v.* to be a sign of sth. coming 预示，预兆
e.g. This bodes us no good.
This could bode disaster for the local people.

bode ill for to be a bad sign for the future 预示……不乐观
e.g. Aid failure bodes ill for Haiti.
The opinion polls bode ill for the Democrats.

burgle /'bɜ:gl/ *v.* to go into a building and steal things (非法闯入)盗窃
e.g. We've been burgled three times.
To commit a burglary is to burgle (in British English) or burglarize (in American English).

impunity /ɪm'pju:nɪtɪ/ *n.* exemption from punishment, penalty, or harm 不受惩罚或伤害
e.g. a successful career marked by impunity from early mistakes
The corrupt officials enjoyed complete impunity.
You cannot break the law with impunity.

villain /'vɪlən/ *n.* a bad person or criminal 歹徒，坏人
e.g. The villains were arrested by the police.
Some villains robbed the widow of the savings.

whoop /hu:p/ *v.* to shout loudly and happily 欢呼
e.g. The children whooped with joy at the sight of all the presents.
She whooped with laughter, so infectious that the others had to join in.

trample /'træmpl/ *v.* to step heavily on sth. in order to crush it 践踏；踩碎
e.g. The workmen trampled on my flower bed.
Many people were trampled to death trying to escape the burning building.

victim /'vɪktɪm/ *n.* sb. who has been harmed, injured, or killed as a result of a crime, accident or other event or action 受害者；牺牲者
e.g. the victims of a hoax
He was the victim of an error.

up to clever, good, or well enough for a particular purpose or in order to do sth. 能做，胜任
e.g. I am afraid Tim just isn't up to the job.
Emma isn't really up to long walks at the moment.

citizenry /'sɪtɪzənrɪ/ *n.* all the citizens in a

particular town, country, or state 全体公民

e.g. I am sure the local citizenry remember what was happening on this very spot.

The thrust of the pamphlet is the urgent requirement for both state and citizenry to rebuild a healthy sense of social citizenship.

democracy /dɪˈmɒkrəsɪ/ *n.* a form of government in which people choose leaders by voting 民主政体；民主

e.g. the principles of democracy

The nation has chosen democracy over monarchy.

demise /dɪˈmaɪz/ *n.* the end of sth. that used to exist 结束；消亡

e.g. Losing this game will mean the team's demise.

We have not had truly local news coverage since the town newspaper's demise three years ago.

shun /ʃʌn/ *v.* to keep away from, to avoid 避开

e.g. He shuns parties and social events.

After his divorce he found himself being shunned by many of his former friends.

stuffy /ˈstʌfɪ/ *a.* very formal, serious, or old-fashioned 严肃的；保守的

e.g. a stuffy old judge

the stuffiest members of that exclusive club

investigative /ɪnˈvestɪɡeɪtɪv/ *a.* inquiring intensively into and trying to find out the truth about or the causes of sth. 调查研究的；好查究的

e.g. an investigative report

I like investigative TV programmes like *Panorama*, which has occasionally angered the Government.

as long as if 只要

e.g. I'll go with you as long as you drive.

As long as she's allowed to go first, she's happy.

competent /ˈkɒmpɪtənt/ *a.* acceptable and satisfactory 合适的；足够的

e.g. a competent understanding of law

He speaks quite competent English.

adjust /əˈdʒʌst/ *v.* to gradually become familiar with a new situation 适应；使适合

e.g. It took time to adjust myself to motherhood.

It took a few seconds for her eyes to adjust to the darkness.

publication /ˌpʌblɪˈkeɪʃən/ *n.* a book, magazine, etc., that has been printed and made available to the public 出版物

e.g. a scholarly/scientific publication

She has a very impressive list of publications.

put up to increase the cost or value of sth. 提高

e.g. Our landlord keeps threatening to put the rent up.

Most big stores admit they daren't put prices up for fear of losing their customers.

compensate /ˈkɒmpenseɪt/ *v.* to replace or balance the effect of sth. bad 补偿；抵消

e.g. He took part-time jobs to compensate for the expense on the car.

Her intelligence compensates for her lack of experience.

revenue /ˈrevənjuː/ *n.* money that a business or organization receives over a period of time, especially from selling goods or services 收益，收入

e.g. advertising revenue

Strikes have cost £20 million in lost revenues.

cater /ˈkeɪtə/ *v.* to provide food and drinks at a party, meeting, etc., usually as a business 提供饮食服务

e.g. This is the biggest event we've ever catered for.

Joan has catered functions for up to 200 people.

cater to to provide a particular group of people with the things they need or want 满足；迎合

e.g. an LA bank catering to Asian businesses

Some perfume ads cater to male fantasies.

readership /ˈriːdəʃɪp/ *n.* all the people who read a particular newspaper or magazine regularly (报纸等的)全体读者

e.g. a magazine with a readership of 60,000

They are hoping that the paper will have quite a wide readership.

as with like, the same as 与……一样

e.g. As with so many books, social studies texts are often more reactionary and stereotyped than life itself.

As with most things in this 24-hour-a-day town, the bar never closes.

highbrow /ˈhaɪbraʊ/ *a.* (book, film, etc.) very serious and may be difficult to understand (书、电影等)趣味很高级的；高雅的

e.g. We took the *People* and the *Sunday Post*, neither of them a highbrow paper.

Overall, readers of highbrow papers were

less likely to allege bias in their own paper than readers of middlebrow or lowbrow papers.

entertainingly /ˌentəˈteɪnɪŋli/ *ad.* in an amusing or interesting way 娱乐性地；有趣地

e.g. She wrote an entertainingly honest account of her childhood.

The complexities of economics are clearly and entertainingly explained.

populist /ˈpɒpjʊlɪst/ *a.* of or relating to ordinary people, rather than rich or very highly educated people 平民主义的

e.g. populist leaders

the monarchy which has tried to make itself populist

wayside /ˈweɪsaɪd/ *n.* the land next to a road or path 路旁，路边

e.g. Flowers grew along the wayside.

fall by the wayside to fail, or to stop being done, used or made 半途而废，中途退出

e.g. traditions that are falling by the wayside

With so many domestic problems, foreign policy issues tended to fall by the wayside.

the press newspapers or journalists viewed collectively 报界；新闻界

e.g. freedom of the press

The murder trial has drawn a lot of interest from the press.

investigate /ɪnˈvestɪɡeɪt/ *v.* to try to find out the facts about sth., such as a crime or an accident, in order to learn how it happened, who did it, etc. 调查

e.g. The accident was thoroughly investigated.

The manager promised to investigate when we pointed out an error on our bill.

abuse /əˈbjuːz/ *n.* unjust or corrupt practice 弊病；劣迹

e.g. the buying of votes and other election abuses

lie in to exist or can be found in 存在于；在于

e.g. The future lies in multimedia.

The key to future economic growth in Africa lies in the markets which are being created as towns and cities expand.

equip /ɪˈkwɪp/ *v.* to prepare (sb.) for a particular activity or problem 使有准备；使能够做（某事）

e.g. She is well-equipped to deal with emergencies.

Her training has equipped her for the job.

a handful of a small amount or number of 少数；几个

e.g. Only a handful of countries have implemented these regulations.

A handful of people die each year from mistakenly eating poisonous fungi.

aggregation /ˌæɡrɪˈɡeɪʃən/ *n.* the act of joining or combining things together 收集；聚集

e.g. the aggregation of vast sums of capital from numerous small investors

The administration became the channel of political communication and interest aggregation in the absence of parties and politicians.

blogger /ˈblɒɡə/ *n.* sb. who writes about personal opinions, activities, and experiences on a blog 博客作者

e.g. the best bloggers around the world

Bloggers can be journalists.

itch /ɪtʃ/ *v.* to have a strong desire to do sth. 急切地想做某事

e.g. She was itching for a fight.

He seemed to be itching for an excuse to say something rude.

chasten /ˈtʃeɪsən/ *v.* to cause (sb.) to feel sad or embarrassed about sth. that has happened 惩戒，责罚

e.g. He was chastened by his team's defeat.

Party workers have returned to their home towns, chastened by their overwhelming defeat.

posting /ˈpəʊstɪŋ/ *n.* a public announcement of sth. 公告

e.g. the company's latest posting of profits

a job posting (= an announcement telling people that a position is open)

laptop /ˈlæptɒp/ *n.* a small computer that is designed to be easily carried 手提电脑

e.g. executives with laptops

He uses a laptop for business when he travels.

cable TV (cable television) a system in which television signals are sent through cables rather than through the air 有线电视

e.g. Does our hotel room have cable TV?

The game will be shown on cable TV.

slander /ˈslɑːndə/ *n.* the act of making a false statement that causes people to have a bad opinion of sb. 诽谤，诋毁

e.g. He was a target of slander.
She is being sued for slander.

boundless /ˈbaʊndlɪs/ *a.* not limited in any way 无尽的，无穷的

e.g. the boundless (= limitless, endless) sky
We were filled with boundless joy.

chew over to think about (sth.) carefully 仔细考虑，深思

e.g. He chewed the problem over in his mind.
Chew it over for a while before you decide.

pander /ˈpændə/ *v.* to do or provide what sb. wants or demands even though it is not proper, good, or reasonable 迎合（不良需求）

e.g. newspapers that pander to people's interest in pornography
The film panders to the popular taste for violence in entertainment.

as opposed to unlike, rather than 与……不同，而非

e.g. They use fresh fish, as opposed to fish that has been frozen.
The car gets 30 miles per gallon, as opposed to last year's model, which got only 25.

admittedly /ədˈmɪtɪdli/ *ad.* without denying, truly 不可否认地，诚然

e.g. The movie was a success. Admittedly, it cost much more than expected.
The technique is painful, admittedly, but it benefits the patient greatly.

the front line the most important and active position in a job or field of activity 第一线，前方

e.g. She has been working on the front line to educate the poor.
These researchers are on/at the front line of defense against cancer.

stick to to keep using or doing one particular thing and not change to anything else 只做……

e.g. She would stick to a peanut sandwich for lunch.
They stick to the main roads.

spring up to grow or appear suddenly 突然出现

e.g. The weeds sprang up overnight.
New housing developments are springing up all over the city.

retreat /rɪˈtriːt/ *v.* to move back to get away from danger, attack, etc. 后退；撤退

e.g. They retreated behind trees for safety.
When the enemy attacked, our troops were forced to retreat.

Language Study

bring down

1. to reduce sth. to a lower level 降低

    e.g. Will anything ever bring house prices down?
    The government hopes these measures will help to bring down inflation.

2. to fly a plane down to the ground 使飞机降落

    e.g. The pilot managed to bring the plane down safely.
    He brought the Cessna (塞斯纳小型飞机) down in a hay-meadow by the river.

3. to make a plane, bird, or animal fall to the ground by shooting at it 击落，打下；撂倒

    e.g. The deer was brought down by a single shot.
    A bomber had been brought down by anti-aircraft fire.

hasten

Usage of the suffix *-en*　后缀-en的用法：

The suffix *-en* can be added to a noun or adjective to form a verb meaning "to become or cause to have/be". Other examples are: *lengthen* 延长, *strengthen* 加强, *broaden* 拓/加宽, *shorten* 缩短.

The suffix *-en* can also be added to a noun to form an adjective signifying "made of or consisting of". For example: *woolen* 羊毛的, *earthen* 土制的.

Note that the prefix *en-* can only be used as a verb prefix meaning "to make sb. or sth. be in a particular state or have a particular quality". For example: *enlarge* 扩大, *endanger* 危及, *enrich* 使丰富；使富有.

it is only a matter of time

This expression is often used to say that sth. will definitely happen in the future. Other examples are:

e.g. I fear it is only a matter of time.

It can only be a matter of time before someone is seriously injured.

put up

1. to build sth. such as a wall, fence, building, etc. 建造

   e.g. put up a fence

   They're putting up several new office blocks in the centre of town.

2. to put a picture, notice, etc. on a wall so that people can see it 张贴

   e.g. Can I put up some posters?

   The shops have started to put up Christmas decorations.

3. to raise sth. to a higher position 举起

   e.g. I put up my hand and asked to leave the room.

   Philip put his hood up because it was raining.

4. to let sb. stay in your house and give them meals 为某人提供食宿

   e.g. I was hoping Kenny could put me up for a few days.

   They agreed to put two foreign students up over the summer.

5. to give an amount of money for a particular purpose 拿出……来作奖金；捐款

   e.g. The paper put up a reward for information on the murder.

   An anonymous donor put up 50,000 dollars for the new science lab.

6. to explain a suggestion or idea so that other people can think about it or discuss it 提出（建议、理由等）

   e.g. She put up a good/solid argument in his defense.

   If you can put up a good enough case, the board will provide the finance.

readership

Usage of the suffix *-ship* 后缀-ship的用法：

The suffix *-ship* means "all the people in a particular group". Another example is *membership* 会员.

The suffix *-ship* can also mean:

1. the state or condition of being sth.: *friendship* 友谊, *apprenticeship* 学徒期；见习期
2. the position, status, or duties of sth.: *professorship* 教授（职位）, *ownership* 拥有（权）
3. a particular art or skill: *scholarship* 学问, *craftsmanship* 手艺

handful

Usage of the suffix *-ful* 后缀-ful的用法：

The suffix *-ful* can mean "the number or amount that fills or would fill sth.". Other examples are: *armful* 一抱（之量）, *roomful* 满屋, *mouthful* 一口（之量）, *spoonful* 一匙（之量）.

After Reading

READING COMPREHENSION TASKS

1. Read the following statements and decide whether they are true (T) or false (F).

1) The most cynical news baron denied the fact that more young people are reading news online. (F)
2) Internet has proved to readers that their money is well spent. (F)
3) Half of the classified ads on the Internet are from newspapers. (F)
4) News organizations are supposed to keep the citizens well-informed. (T)
5) Newspapers that invest in investigative stories most beneficial to society are able to survive. (F)
6) *The Guardian* has attracted nearly half as many American readers as the British ones. (F)
7) Bloggers can provide people who are looking for truth with a wide choice of material. (T)

2. Answer the following questions.

1) Why are newspapers now an endangered species in some part of the world?
   Because the business of selling words to readers and selling readers to advertisers, which has sustained their role in society, is falling apart.

2) Why have newspapers lost their classified advertising to the Internet?
   Because the Internet is a seductive medium that supposedly matches buyers with sellers and proves to advertisers that their money is well spent.

3) What happened to Knight Ridder in 2005?
   A group of shareholders got the firm to sell its papers and thus end a 114-year history.

4) What measures have newspapers taken to change the situation?
   Measures taken are:
   a) spending less on journalism to cut costs;
   b) trying to attract younger readers by shifting the mix of their stories towards entertainment, lifestyle and subjects more relevant to people's daily lives;
   c) trying to create new businesses on- and offline;
   d) investing in free daily papers which do not focus on political corruption or corporate fraud.

5) What are the examples of the usefulness of the press?
   The examples are:
   a) investigating abuses;
   b) spreading general news;
   c) holding governments to account — trying them in the court of public opinion.

6) How has the Internet expanded the court of public opinion?
   People looking for information have never been better equipped. They no longer have to trust some national papers or their local city paper. They can log on to news-aggregation sites or the website of the newspaper for information.

7) Why have the results of net journalism been limited in terms of hard-news reporting?
   Because most bloggers operate from their armchairs, not the frontline, and citizen journalists tend to stick to local matters.

8) What do *The Guardian*, *The Christian Science Monitor* and National Public Radio have in common?
   They are backed by non-profit organizations.

3. Explain the underlined parts in your own words.

1) They usually <u>set the news agenda for the rest of the media</u>. (Para. 1)
   take the lead in news reporting, and the rest of the media like TV and radio just follow

2) <u>Of all the "old" media, newspapers have the most to lose from the Internet.</u> (Para. 2)
   Newspapers suffer greater loss because of the Internet than any other form of the traditional media.

3) But in the past few years <u>the Web has hastened the decline</u>. (Para. 2)
   the Internet has made the drop in circulation faster

4) <u>Advertising is following readers out of the door.</u> (Para. 3)
   As readers choose to read online, advertisers are attracted to put their advertisement on the Internet.

5) <u>Tumbling shares of listed newspaper firms have prompted fury from investors.</u> (Para. 4)
   Stock market prices of listed newspaper firms have been falling sharply and this has made their investors extremely angry.

6) Anyone looking for information has never been better equipped. (Para. 9)
   People in search of information are now better than ever provided with various kinds of news sources.

7) …but so has much of the press. (Para. 10)
   much of the press has done the same thing

8) …thousands of fired-up bloggers and well-informed citizen journalists…(Para. 12)
   enthusiastic writers of blogs and amateur journalists who know quite well about various subjects or issues

ORAL WORK

Look at the following chart with some questions on different forms of media and interview at least three people around you for information.

This task is to encourage the students to look for information about different forms of media. The students may conduct interviews after class and prepare a report about their findings. They may add more questions if necessary. In class, they can either share their findings in small groups or make a presentation to the whole class.

TRANSLATION OF TEXT A

谁扼杀了报纸？

1　"我想，好的报纸应该是国家之声。"阿瑟·米勒1961年作出了这样的思索。10年后，《华盛顿邮报》的两个记者写了一系列报道，最后导致尼克松总统下台，报纸地位高涨。在其发展鼎盛期，报纸的影响很大，可以监督政府和企业为其不良行为负责。它们总是引领其他媒体的新闻话题。但在富裕国家，报纸现在已经是濒危物种了。以前报纸在社会中立足的模式就是向读者销售文字，再把读者推销给广告商，但现在这一模式正在解体。

2　在所有"旧"媒体中，报纸由于互联网的兴起而失去得最多。美国、西欧、拉美、澳大利亚以及新西兰的报纸销量数十年来一直在下降（其他地方的销量却在上升），但在过去几年中，网络的发展加速了这种下降。就连最持怀疑态度的新闻大亨都不得不承认越来越多的年轻人主要从网上获取新闻。英国15岁到24岁的年轻人坦言，开始上网以后，他们花在阅读全国性报纸上的时间减少了近30%。

3　广告也跟着读者抛弃了报纸，匆匆忙忙，几乎顾不上体面，主要是因为网络媒体诱惑性强，据说能够将买卖双方撮合在一起，而且能向广告商证明他们的广告费花对了地方。分类广告尤其卖力，正在迅速向网络媒体转移。报业大亨默多克曾经把它们描述为"报界的金河"，但是他去年说："有时河也会干的。"在瑞士和荷兰，报纸的分类广告业务有一半已被网络抢走。

4　现在报纸还没开始大规模倒闭，但那只是时间问题。在未来的几十年里，发达国家中一半的普通报纸都可能会关门。相关的职位一直在减少。根据美国报业协会的统计，1990年到2004年间，报业从业人员的人数下降了18%。上市报业公司的股票急剧下跌，让投资者大为光火。2005年，拥有多家美国日报的奈特里德公司的股东促使公司卖掉报纸，结束了其114年的历史。

5　经过多年无视现实的蹉跎后，报界终于行动了。为了减少开支，他们已经减少了在新闻报道上的开支。许多报纸也正努力吸引年轻读者，把报纸内容转向娱乐、生活方式以及与国际事务及政治相比更关系到人们日常生活的各种话题。他们也在尝试开展网上或者网下的一些新业务。他们还投资免费日报，这些日报不再把他们那点少得可怜的编辑资源用于揭露政治腐败和公司造假。但到目前为止，这些措施不大可能挽救多少报纸。即使能够挽救，报纸等平面媒体作为第四权力体的公共地位也很不乐观。

6　将来，随着报纸的逐渐消失和改变，政客们是否就可以肆无忌惮地闯入对手的办公室盗窃而不受惩罚呢？公司流氓是否就可以欢呼着践踏受害者呢？新闻学院和智库——尤其是在美国——正担心逐渐消失的报纸所带来的负面影响。现在的新闻机构还能"担负起保持民众的知情权这一民主赖以存在的重任"吗？

7　谁都不该对曾经伟大的报纸的消亡感到高兴。但是报纸的衰落并不会像有些人担心的那样对社会造成巨大的危害。不要忘了,虽然20世纪50年代电视的出现造成报纸销量大幅度下滑,但民主制度延续下来了。这是因为当时虽然读者抛弃了报纸,但报纸也作出了改变,在内容上抛弃了那些在更保守的时代被认为是严肃新闻的东西。民主肯定也能承受住未来报纸的衰落。

8　之所以能这样,部分是因为只要少数大报的拥有者能与时俱进,它们就会继续在一些对社会最有利的深入报道方面进行投入,因而很有希望生存下来。《纽约时报》和《华尔街日报》这样的出版物应该能够提高新闻报道的价格,以此来弥补流向网络的广告收入损失——尤其是因为它们的读者遍及世界各地。像许多行业一样,最有可能被淘汰的是那些处于中间地位的报纸,因为它们既没有很高的文化品位,又不走娱乐性的大众路线。

9　新闻界的作用不仅仅限于调查各种社会弊端,甚至不在于传播消息,而在于它能监督政府为其行为承担责任,即由公众舆论法庭来审判政府行为。网络其实扩大了这个舆论法庭。需要信息的人从来没像现在这样拥有这么多渠道。人们不必再去相信几家全国性的大报,或者更糟糕的是,去相信当地的城市报纸。像"谷歌新闻"这样的新闻综合网站聚集了世界各地的新闻来源。英国《卫报》网站的美国读者人数几乎达到了其英国本土读者人数的一半。

10　另外,"网民"记者和博客撰写者们这一股新生力量也跃跃欲试,想去监督政治人物。对于任何有键盘和网络连接的人来说,网络为他们打开了由专业编辑和记者组成的封闭圈。有些公司已经受到了业余发帖者的谴责——"戴尔手提电脑起火","有线电视(公司)维修员在沙发上睡着了"等等。每位博客作者都可能有偏见或言辞不当,但是作为整体,他们提供了海量的材料供寻找真相的人斟酌。当然,网络会迎合一些思想顽固的读者,但是许多报纸也是如此呀。

11　网络新闻对于严肃新闻的报道与评论相比就很有限了。多数博客不是诞生在新闻前线,而是由作者在自己家里写出来的,而且网民记者倾向于只关注本地事件。但它蓄势待发。随着报纸的退却,新的在线模式将迅速涌现。一个叫做"新闻实验网"的非营利团体计划把业余记者和专业记者联合起来,在网络上推出调查性新闻报道。

12　将来一些高质量的新闻工作也会得到非营利机构的支持。几家有影响的新闻机构已经在靠此方式生存了,其中包括《卫报》、《基督教科学箴言报》和美国国家公共电台。现在,一些严肃的精英报纸都有网络版,世界各地都可以阅读;独立的新闻报道得到慈善机构、成千上万热心博客作者和消息灵通的网民记者的支持:这一切都表明:阿瑟·米勒所说的"国家之声"将会比以往任何时候都响亮。

TEXT B Web Journalism

Before Reading

The purpose of this section is to arouse the students' interest in the theme of the text, reactivate their relevant background knowledge or recall their personal experience, so as to better prepare them for the succeeding tasks.

The two pictures show the screens of a computer and a mobile phone respectively on which some pieces of news are shown. On the left is a web page of *The Washington Post*, one of the largest newspapers in the United States. The page provides various contents, including a section of advertisement on the right. The picture on the right presents, on the screen of a mobile phone, a page of *Time* with some news headlines and relevant pictures. Encourage the students to tell each other their own experiences of reading online news and discuss its advantages and disadvantages.

Other questions in this Before Reading part can be used for group discussion so that the students can further understand web journalism.

Background Information

What Is Web Journalism?

With the decline of newspapers, there's been a lot of talk about web journalism being the future of the news business. But what exactly do we mean by web journalism?

Web journalism actually encompasses a whole range of different kinds of sites, including:

Newspaper websites

Websites run by newspapers are basically extensions of the papers themselves. As such they can provide a wide range of articles in a variety of areas — news, sports, business, the arts, etc. — written by their staff of professional reporters.

Example: *The New York Times*

In some cases, newspapers shut down their printing presses but continue to operate their websites (the *Seattle Post-Intelligencer* is one example). Often, however, when the presses stop running the news staff is gutted, leaving only a bare-bones newsroom behind.

Independent news websites

These sites, often found in larger cities, tend to specialize in hard-news coverage of municipal government, city agencies, law enforcement and schools. Some of them are known for their hard-hitting investigative reporting. Their content is typically produced by small staffs of full-time reporters and freelancers.

Many of these independent news sites are nonprofits funded by a mix of ad revenue and contributions from donors and foundations.

Examples: *Voice of San Diego*
          MinnPost

Hyper-local news sites

These sites specialize in coverage of small, specific communities, right down to the individual neighbourhood. As the name implies, the coverage tends to focus on extremely localized events: the police blotter, the agenda of the town board meeting, the performance of a school play.

Hyper-local sites can be independent or run by newspapers as extensions of their websites. Their content is typically produced by local freelance writers and bloggers.

Examples: *The New York Times Local*
The Bakersfield Voice

Citizen journalism sites

Citizen journalism sites run a wide gamut. Some are basically just online platforms where people can post video reports or pictures on virtually any subject. Others focus on a specific geographic area and provide more targeted, specific coverage.

Content for citizen journalism sites is usually provided by a loose affiliation of writers, bloggers and video reporters with varying degrees of journalism experience. Some citizen journalism sites are edited; others are not.

Examples: *CNN's iReport*
The Cournalist

Blogs

Blogs are known primarily for being platforms for delivering opinions and commentaries, but many actually do real reporting as well. Bloggers have varying degrees of journalism experience.

Reading

New Words and Expressions

instant message a message that is sent quickly over the Internet from one computer to another 即时消息
e.g. We sent each other instant messages all night.
I use QQ to exchange instant messages with my friends.
headline /ˈhedlaɪn/ *n.* the title written in large letters over a story in a newspaper （报纸的）标题
e.g. The story of his arrest appeared beneath the headline "Caught!".
She only had time to scan the headlines before she had to rush out the door.
hyperlink /ˈhaɪpəlɪŋk/ *n.* a highlighted word or picture in a website or computer document that will lead to another page or document when clicked 超链接
e.g. We should encourage hyperlinks to each other's web pages.
This tutorial explains how easy it is to create a hyperlink in Flash.
methodically /mɪˈθɒdɪkəlɪ/ *ad.* in good order 有条不紊地
e.g. They are methodically reviewing the evidence.
Bragg extracted the papers from the pigeon-holes, and began to read them methodically.
update /ˈʌpdeɪt/ *n.* the most recent information about sth. 最新消息；更新
e.g. I haven't heard the latest weather update.
We receive daily updates on homes for sale in the area.
headquarters /ˌhedˈkwɔːtəz/ *n.* a place from which sth. (such as a business or a military action) is controlled or directed 总部

e.g. the headquarters of the United Nations
The company's headquarters is/are in Atlanta.

home page the part of a website that is seen first and that usually contains links to other parts of the site 主页
e.g. home page news and features
They have designed a simpler home page that is easier to use.

press /pres/ *n.* a machine that prints books, magazines, newspapers, etc., usually in large numbers 印刷机
e.g. Stop the presses!
The pages rolled off the presses.

countdown /ˈkaʊntdaʊn/ *n.* the period of time before an important or special event（重要或特殊事件发生前的）倒计时阶段
e.g. the steady countdown to war
the countdown to summer vacation

railroad crossing a place where a railway crosses a road, usually protected by gates 铁路和公路的相交道口
e.g. A "railroad crossing" in American English is called a "level crossing" in British English. Many railroad crossings have a gate with flashing lights that close when a train is coming.

upstate /ˌʌpˈsteɪt/ *a.* (AmE) in the northern part of a particular state（美语）（州）北部的
e.g. We come from a tiny, tiny little town in upstate New York.

owe /əʊ/ *v.* to need to pay or repay money to a person, bank, business, etc. 欠钱，负债
e.g. He owes me $5.
We owe no income tax.

while /waɪl/ *n.* a period of time, especially a short one 一段时间
e.g. At last, he could relax for a while.
Mr. Thomas will be with you in a while.

joint /dʒɔɪnt/ *a.* involving two or more people or groups, or owned or shared by them 联合的
e.g. The two ministers have issued a joint statement.
Both companies are involved in the joint development of a new medium-sized car.

affiliate /əˈfɪlieɪt/ *n.* an organization (such as a television station) that is a member of a larger organization (such as a national network) 子公司；分社；附属机构

e.g. the network's local affiliates
Two of the company's regional affiliates lost money in the past year.

primarily /ˈpraɪmərəlɪ/ *ad.* mainly, mostly 主要地
e.g. They seemed primarily interested in getting rich.
The game is designed primarily for younger children.

outlet /ˈaʊtlet/ *n.* a television, radio, or publishing company 电视、广播或出版公司
e.g. a cable TV outlet
media/news outlets

homegrown /ˈhəʊmˈɡrəʊn/ *a.* raised in or coming from the local area 本地产的；来自本地的
e.g. homegrown entertainment
The music festival will feature some homegrown talents this year.

viewer /ˈvjuːə/ *n.* a person who watches TV or reads on a website（电视等的）观众；（网络）读者
e.g. The programme attracts millions of viewers every week.
She is a regular viewer of the entertainment news on this website.

inviting /ɪnˈvaɪtɪŋ/ *a.* attractive in a way that makes people want to do sth., go somewhere, be near sb., etc. 诱人的，吸引人的
e.g. He has an inviting smile.
The room is very inviting.

ride the tide of to go along with circumstances 顺势而为，顺应潮流
e.g. She didn't have any money but they wanted her to go with them so she decided to ride the tide of their generosity.
Young couples can ride the tide of the First Time Homeowners programme if they can meet the August deadline.

involved /ɪnˈvɒlvd/ *a.* actively participating in sth. 参与……的
e.g. You need to get involved in making things better.
Students who stay involved get more out of the programme.

journalistic /ˌdʒɜːnəˈlɪstɪk/ *a.* of or related to journalism 新闻的；新闻业的
e.g. her journalistic career/experience
journalistic styles/standards/techniques

geekiness /ɡiːkɪnɪs/ *n.* the state of being knowledgeable in a certain kind of activity and addicted to it (科技领域的)爱好或纯熟
e.g. I liked her because of her geekiness.
Geekiness is not welcome all the time.

availability /əˌveɪləˈbɪlətɪ/ *n.* the state of being easy or possible to get or use 可用；可得到
e.g. The drug's lack of availability presents a serious problem for them.
She's the perfect candidate for the job, but I need to confirm her availability.

immediacy /ɪˈmiːdɪəsɪ/ *n.* the quality of bringing one into direct and instant involvement with sth., giving rise to a sense of urgency or excitement 即时性
e.g. Television coverage gave the war greater immediacy than it had ever before had.
There is an immediacy in watching a live performance that you cannot get from hearing a recording.

concise /kənˈsaɪs/ *a.* short, with no unnecessary words 简洁的
e.g. a clear and concise account of the accident
Your summary should be as clear and concise as possible.

content /ˈkɒntent/ *n.* the ideas, facts, or images that are in a book, article, speech, movie, etc. 内容
e.g. In terms of content, the article is good, but it is written poorly.
The children aren't allowed to watch movies with violent content.

front page the first page of a newspaper which usually contains very important or exciting content 报纸头版
e.g. She has her picture on the front page of most national newspapers.
The *Daily Telegraph*'s front page carried John Major's warning that the UK faces breakup.

prominence /ˈprɒmɪnəns/ *n.* the state of being important, well-known, or noticeable 著名；显著
e.g. The company rose to prominence in the 1990s.
He quickly gained prominence in medical circles.

point guard a basketball player who is one of the two guards on a team and is the one most responsible for leading the team when it has the ball and is trying to score 篮球控球后卫
e.g. A point guard's primary job is to facilitate scoring opportunities for his team, or sometimes for himself.

tournament /ˈtʊənəmənt/ *n.* a sports competition or series of contests that involves many players or teams and that usually continues for at least several days 锦标赛
e.g. a basketball/golf tournament
She's an excellent tennis player who has won many tournaments.

prominent /ˈprɒmɪnənt/ *a.* easily noticed or seen 突出的，显眼的
e.g. He has a prominent nose/chin.
He placed the award in a prominent position on his desk.

interactivity /ˌɪntəræk'tɪvətɪ/ *n.* the quality of responding to the actions, commands, etc., of a user 互动
e.g. The interactivity lies in the computer's capacity to respond to what the user does.
In other words, interactivity brings a vital element of added value to all electronic information, whether multimedia or not.

database /ˈdeɪtəbeɪs/ *n.* a collection of pieces of information that is organized and used on a computer 数据库
e.g. an online database
All of our customers' information was kept in/on a database.

statistic /stəˈtɪstɪk/ *n.* a fact or piece of data obtained from a study of a large quantity of numerical data 统计数据
e.g. One statistic that stuck out is that 40 percent of those surveyed did not have college degrees.
The statistics show that teenagers are involved in a high percentage of traffic accidents.

on one's mind in one's thoughts 放在心上；担心
e.g. He looked as though he had something on his mind.
Sorry I forgot. I've got a lot on my mind at the moment.

log /lɒɡ/ *n.* a record of performance, events, or activities 记录；日志
e.g. a computer log

The mechanic kept a log showing when repairs were done on the truck.

accuracy /ˈækjʊrəsɪ/ *n.* the quality of being correct or true 准确(性)

e.g. The police questioned the accuracy of his statement.
He could not say with any accuracy what he had seen.

nonlinear /ˌnɒnˈlɪnɪə/ *a.* not arranged in a straight line; not sequential 非线性的

e.g. nonlinear narrative

package /ˈpækɪdʒ/ *n.* a group of related things that go together 一套，一揽子

e.g. My new job offers a great benefits package.
The financial aid packages we'll be awarding this year are smaller than we had hoped they would be.

chunk /tʃʌŋk/ *n.* a large amount or part of sth. 大部分；大块

e.g. She spends a good chunk of her day on the phone.
A huge chunk of the audience got up and left before the end of the show.

span /spæn/ *v.* to cover or include (a wide area, a large number of things, etc.) 跨越；包括

e.g. Their empire once spanned several continents.
Her academic interests span a wide variety of topics.

timeline /ˈtaɪmlaɪn/ *n.* a line that includes marks showing when particular events happened in the past 年表

e.g. the illustrated timeline of art history
The timeline shows the important events in American history.

poll /pəʊl/ *n.* an activity in which several or many people are asked a question or a series of questions in order to get information about what most people think about sth. 民意调查，民意测验

e.g. A recent poll shows a decrease in the number of teenagers who smoke.
The magazine conducted a poll to find out the favorite 100 movies of all time.

Language Study

hyperlink

    Usage of the prefix *hyper-* 前缀hyper-的用法：

    The prefix *hyper-* means "beyond the usual size or limit; excessive, too much".

    Other examples are: *hypersensitive* 高度敏感的, *hyperinflation* 超级通胀, *hypertension* 高血压.

update *v.*

1. to change (sth.) by including the most recent information 更新

    e.g. update all the population figures
    I need to update my address book.

2. to make (sth.) more modern 使现代化

    e.g. an updated version of a classic story

3. to give (sb.) the most recent information about sth. 为……提供最新信息

    e.g. He updated us on his mother's health.
    Can you update me on what's been happening?

outlet *n.*

1. sth. that people use to express their emotions or talents （感情、才能的）发泄或发挥途径

    e.g. They needed a healthy outlet for their anger.
    She used poetry as an outlet for her sadness.

2. a store that sells products made usually by one company and often at reduced prices 批发店，经销公司

    e.g. designer clothing outlets
    a discount furniture outlet

3. a place or opening through which sth. can go out 出口；出路

    e.g. the river's outlet to the sea
    an outlet for the air to escape

content /kən'tent/
- *n.* a feeling of being pleased and satisfied 满意；满足
  - **e.g.** a look of perfect content
- *a.* happy and satisfied 满意的，满足的
  - **e.g.** He seemed quite content to let Steve do the supervising.
- *v.* to make (sb.) pleased and satisfied 使满意
  - **e.g.** The toys contented the children, at least for a little while.

blog

The word *blog* is formed by combining *b* in *web* and *log*. In linguistics, this type of word formation is called "blending". It is different from compounding in that the formation is not based on morpheme structure but on sound structure. The resulting words are called "blends".

Others examples of blending:

smoke and fog → smog

spoon and fork → spork

motor and hotel → motel

breakfast and lunch → brunch

car and hijacking → carjacking

stagnation and inflation → stagflation

cheese and hamburger → cheeseburger

simultaneous and broadcast → simulcast

mock and cocktail → mocktail (cocktail with no alcohol)

spam and blog → splog (fake blog designed to attract hits and raise Google-ranking)

package
- *n.* sth. wrapped in paper, packed in a box and then sent by mail or delivered 包裹
  - **e.g.** A package was left on the front steps.
- *v.* to put (sth.) in a package in order to sell it or send it somewhere 包装
  - **e.g.** Package the books carefully.

After Reading

READING COMPREHENSION TASKS

1. Complete the following statements based on the information in TEXT B.

1) Walker uses __instant messages__ to communicate with his senior editor.
2) Walker's team has to make their websites __inviting__ to attract regular viewers.
3) Walker says __availability__ and __immediacy__ are the major contributing factors in the growth of Syracuse.com.
4) A discussion question at the end of a story is an example of __interactivity__ of the Web.
5) Some __local events__ that ordinarily wouldn't be covered in the paper will be posted by blogs.
6) Walker believes people's faith in the __accuracy__ of websites bodes well for the future of the business.
7) The Web can offer viewers __nonlinear__ choices of accessing information although they may be written in linear order.

2. Answer the following questions.

1) Why do Walker and Clewis move methodically through the web pages of Syracuse.com?
   Because they want to make sure that everything looks right for the update at 9 a.m.

2) What are the news sources for Syracuse.com?
   The Syracuse Post-Standard, WTVH-TV, and several radio stations.
3) What does Walker think of their success in attracting an increasing number of viewers?
   He thinks that they are riding the tide of people moving to the Internet to get their news.
4) What are the journalistic skills mentioned by Walker?
   They are news judgment, writing sharp headlines and knowing AP style.
5) How are the front page of the newspaper and the home page of the website different from each other?
   They give different prominence to the same stories.
6) How can viewers interact with the website?
   They can actively search, read and click on links that include news, entertainment, business, sports, discussion forums and blogs.
7) What is "Yada, Yada, Yada"?
   It's a discussion board where people can post on just about everything that's on their minds.
8) What might be found in a web package created in nonlinear order?
   It might include smaller chunks spanning several pages or links to timelines, related stories, polls and other elements.

3. Explain the underlined parts in your own words.

1) Clewis <u>responds with an instant message that he's fixed the headline</u>… (Para. 1)
   sends an instant message in response saying that he's changed the headline
2) …he tells Clewis <u>to put up the new home (opening) page</u>. (Para. 1)
   to make active the new home page
3) It isn't <u>exactly the equivalent of watching the presses roll at a daily newspaper</u>… (Para. 2)
   the same as standing by and watching the printing machines print one page of a daily newspaper after another
4) But <u>we clearly are riding the tide of people moving to the Internet</u> to get their news. (Para. 6)
   obviously, our success lies in the fact that we have met the needs of the times when people are using the Internet
5) … because <u>he saw it as a growing part of providing information to people</u>. (Para. 7)
   he thought that the Internet would become increasingly popular as a source of information
6) For example, <u>the story on dangerous railroad crossings makes the home page of the website with less prominence than the newspaper</u>. (Para. 10)
   the story on dangerous railroad crossings will be given less importance on the home page of the website than in the newspaper
7) <u>Interactivity, also, sets the Web apart from other media.</u> (Para. 11)
   Interactivity is another quality that makes the Web distinct from other media.
8) … including <u>local events that ordinarily wouldn't be covered in the paper</u>. (Para. 13)
   regional or community events that usually wouldn't be reported in the newspaper
9) … that <u>places much more control in the hands of the user</u>. (Para. 15)
   gives the user much more freedom
10) … meaning that users can <u>access information</u> in any order they choose. (Para. 15)
    get information

ORAL WORK

Suppose you are a journalist from your university website and you are going to interview Mike Walker about his job and career. Design a list of interview questions and then interview one of your classmates who acts as Mike Walker.

This task is to encourage the students to make full use of the information in TEXT B and conduct interviews. The teacher is advised to give guidance to the students on their interview questions and to comment on their interview skills.

TRANSLATION OF TEXT B

网络新闻

卡罗尔·里奇

1　麦克·沃克给他的高级编辑杰米·克鲁易斯发了一条即时信息，要他改动一个标题。克鲁易斯同样用即时信息回复说他已经把标题改好了，但需要沃克修改一个无效的超链接。沃克和克鲁易斯有条不紊地检查了雪城网（Syracuse.com）的网页，确保上午九点的更新都正确无误。沃克是这个网站的主编，他必须等待位于新泽西的总部给他发一个图形指令，然后才可以激活网页。他一接到指令，就会让克鲁易斯更新主页。

2　这跟看着印刷机印刷日报和电视台栏目开播前的倒计时不完全一样，但是沃克和他的七人小组也有时间限制——他们要赶在早上完成更新，在网站上发布各类有趣的新闻。

3　今天纽约州雪城的天气很冷。雪城大学篮球队"橘子人队"的运气也有些僵，他们最近输了四场比赛。比较严肃的新闻是几篇重大犯罪报道，其中包括青少年酒后驾车系列三。在雪城这个位于纽约州北部、拥有15万居民的城市，一些地方的铁路道口依然未得到维修。一个房地产开发商欠税额达到数千美元。

4　"这是我们这阵新闻最好做的日子之一，所以很顺利。"沃克说。自1994年从波士顿大学毕业以来，他在宾夕法尼亚、新泽西和纽约州的数家网络公司和报社工作过。

5　雪城网是一个由《雪城标准邮报》、CBS附属电台WTBH-TV以及几个广播电台联合组成的网站。雪城网主要通过这些报社和电台获取新闻，但是它也有涉猎广泛的各种讨论组和本地博客群，他们的共同努力使得雪城网一个月的浏览量接近50万人次，单个网页浏览量达到2500万次。这比上一年增加了30%。

6　沃克说："现在更多的人上网就是为了看新闻，我们努力使我们的网站更具吸引力，这样人们下次还会看。但是很明显，我们这也正好赶上了人们涌向互联网读新闻的浪潮。"

7　20世纪90年代初，当沃克还在波士顿大学读书时，互联网在人们的日常生活中并不重要。他说他当时之所以和互联网打交道，是因为他看到互联网在向人们提供信息方面发挥着越来越重要的作用。沃克说做网络新闻不一定非要懂得操作电脑软件的所有技能，当然这些知识会挺有用。他更注重好的新闻技能。他说："我希望我们的人具有新闻判断能力，能够写出吸引人的醒目标题，懂得新闻写作手法。如果他们使用互联网就更好，最好还有点高手的味道"。

8　沃克认为，可获得性和即时性是雪城网发展的核心要素。他说："网络新闻的读者不如报纸读者耐心。网上的东西需要更短、更直接、更简洁。"

9　沃克给网站的定位是以最简单的方式提供新闻，重要的更新上午一次，下午两次，主要针对的群体是上班族。"我们大部分的读者说他们主要对体育感兴趣，所以我们将尽力让他们更容易找到体育新闻。"

10　沃克说新闻机构认为网站仅仅是传递新闻内容的另一种方式，而报纸则是这些内容的主要来源。这位网站编辑则看到了《雪城标准邮报》和雪城网之间的异同。报纸头版和网站首页报道的内容基本一样：天气、犯罪报道和一些体育新闻。但是它们给予这些报道的突出程度往往不一样。比如说，关于危险的铁路道口的报道网站首页没有报纸重视。而雪城大学篮球队的控球后卫是否会出现在NCAA联赛上则会被雪城网重点报道。

11 互动性也是网站与其他媒体不同的地方。雪城网的读者可以主动地搜索、阅读、点击各种链接，包括新闻、娱乐、商业、体育、论坛以及博客等。这里的互动可以像报道结束后给出的一个讨论问题那么简单，也可以像建立一些包含学校考试分数或犯罪统计资料的可检索数据库那么复杂。

12 雪城网已经设置了一系列讨论版，许多是关于大学和中学体育活动的。其中最受欢迎的一个名叫"Yada, Yada, Yada"（随便说说），人们可以随意发表任何想说的东西。沃克说："这里感觉就像是个小社会"。

13 雪城网还增添了关于娱乐和当地旅行的博客，也有几个关于体育的博客。"这真是太棒了，它给我们提供了极好的素材。"沃克说，"我们可以在每天晚些时候从某一博客中挑一些内容贴出来，让大家进一步讨论。"有些博主会贴出一些关于郊区的新闻，包括一些报纸一般不会报道的地方事件。

14 现在美国有超过1亿5千万人使用互联网，包括很多上网读新闻的人。尽管许多人依然主要从报纸和电视上获取新闻，但网络作为新闻来源已经取得了迅速发展。更重要的是，人们已经开始相信网络报道的准确性。

15 网络在很多方面都和其他媒体不同。它是其他媒体——印刷、广播、电视和图片——的结合体，让网络读者有更多的控制权。简单来说，网络使读者能够去任何想去的站点，或者进行非线性阅读，就是说读者能以自己选择的顺序来获得信息。而印刷媒体和广播报道一般都是线性的，从头讲到尾，像一条直线那样。这使人们除了读、听和不读不听以外，别无他选。

16 尽管很多报道的叙述可能是线性的，但网络为读者提供了非线性选择，便于他们获取与该报道或该网站相链接的信息。以非线性顺序制作出的网络新闻包可能被分成几个小版块，每个版块含几页内容；也可能包括导向年表、相关报道、网上调查以及其他内容的链接。

INTEGRATED EXERCISES

1 PUBLIC SPEECH TRAINING

In Unit Five you hear the beginning and the end of a speech. In this unit, you will hear the body of the speech. While listening, pay attention to how the speaker organizes his content. Practice the part after the recording.

(The speech will be read once. The Students listen and try to understand the meaning and organization. They may listen again and practice after the speaker.)

Organization of the speech

Introduction: Paragraph 1

Body: Paragraphs 2-8
- The physical distance of the Great Wall
- The history of construction (the Qin Dynasty, the Han Dynasty, the Ming Dynasty)
- Its architectural features

Conclusion: Paragraph 9

(The script of Paragraphs 1 and 9 are in Unit Five.)

Script

As you can see from this photograph, the wall is great in beauty, with its long arms nesting on rolling hills and its towers peering across the valleys. The wall stretches across more than half of China, from the sea in the east, past Beijing, to Gansu Province in the west. At a total length of 4,000 miles, it is the longest human-made construction in the world. If the Great Wall were transported to the United States and stretched out in a straight line, it would run from New York City completely across the Atlantic Ocean — past Spain, England, and France, all the way to Berlin, Germany.

Today I would like to share with you some of the wonders of the Great Wall. I will focus on the three major stages of its construction, moving from the first phase during the Qin Dynasty, to the second phase during the Han Dynasty, and concluding with the third phase during the Ming Dynasty. Let's start more than 2,000 years ago, when the first parts of the wall were built.

The beginning of the Great Wall as we know it dates back to 221 B.C., when Emperor Qin Shi Huang ordered his top general to lead 30,000 soldiers in rebuilding and connecting separate old walls that had been built by princes of warring states. In just 12 years, Qin had a 3,000-mile wall using primarily wood frames filled with stones and compacted earth.

While the wall proved effective in keeping out the tribes who threatened to invade China from the north, it created dissent within China. According to Arthur Waldron's *The Great Wall of China: From History to Myth*, "ditches on the roadside were filled with corpses of men who had been forced into construction of the Great Wall". Compelled into hard labour and burdened by heavy taxes to finance the project, the people grew unhappy, and a year after Qin's death, the peasants revolted. While the wall stood, the empire collapsed.

The second major period of construction for the Great Wall occurred during the Han Dynasty, which lasted from 206 B.C. to 220 A.D. Emperor Wu Di ordered expansion of the existing wall to protect land won when his armies defeated the northern tribes. Workers added 300 miles to the existing wall. They built wooden frames, which they filled with willow reeds and a mixture of fine gravel and water. As you can see from this picture of ruins of the Han wall, it was very different in construction and appearance from the Great Wall as it exists today.

The third major building period of the Great Wall occurred 1,100 years later during the Ming Dynasty. In 1368, during the first year of the Ming Dynasty, Emperor Zhu Yuanzhang ordered more expansion of the wall. Subsequent Ming emperors strengthened and extended the wall further until it reached its current length. Builders of the Ming wall made three important architectural advancements which resulted in the distinctive features of the wall as it exists today.

You can see those features especially well in this photograph. First, rather than using earth and stone, they used kiln-fired bricks to create a stronger wall. Second, they erected more than 3,000 beacon towers to watch the mountain passes for potential invaders. These towers rise from the wall like mighty outposts and are one of the most striking aspects of the wall when you see them in person. Third, the Ming builders made the wall so large that it would be almost impossible to break through. In fact, the wall is so wide that soldiers could ride several horses abreast along the top of the wall.

2 DICTATION

Listen to the following passage and write it down. The passage will be read four times. During the first reading, which will be done at normal speed, listen and try to understand the meaning. For the second and third readings, the passage will be read sentence by sentence, or phrase by phrase, with intervals of 15 seconds. Write down what you hear. The last reading will be done at normal speed again and during this time you should check your work.

Script

The AP Stylebook

The AP Stylebook was first produced in 1953 as a stapled collection of rules totaling 60 pages, / and has grown to a publication of more than 450 pages today. / The book's creation was prompted in part by a technical change in the way the AP transmitted news / as well as a need for consistency among a worldwide editorial staff / that produced stories for newspapers with a variety of style preferences. / There have been major periodic revisions over the past few decades, / the last in 2008, and the print edition is now updated annually. / The new print edition and online subscriptions can be ordered by credit card online at a secure website. / The order form also allows customers to create an invoice to pay by check or money order, / and member news organizations can request direct assessment.

3 VOCABULARY STUDY

Task One
Put the proper form of the words in the corresponding blanks.

1) Her love for her family was __boundless__. (bound)
2) The police are still __investigating__ the murder. (investigative)
3) The advertisement is aimed __primarily__ at children. (primary)
4) Have you noticed a __similarity__ between these movies? (similar)

5) If you want to make things better, you need to get __involved__. (involve)
6) The detective went through the papers __methodically__, one by one. (method)
7) The __availability__ of affordable housing attracted us to this town. (available)
8) The publicity has given him a __prominence__ he doesn't deserve. (prominent)
9) Several managers have tried to increase the speed and __accuracy__ of the workers. (accurate)
10) He began his career originally as a __journalist__, working for the BBC. (journalism)

Task Two

Fill in the blanks with the correct form of the words or expressions in the box. You may need to make other changes.

1) He's __at his best__ in front of a live audience.
2) This movie __caters to__ the worst side of human nature.
3) Fast-food restaurants are __springing up__ all over the town.
4) They are likely to __put up__ interest rates again this year.
5) I'd say she is a good player, __as opposed to__ a great one.
6) My parents had trouble __adjusting__ to living in an apartment.
7) She's the type of person who just says what's __on her mind__.
8) The answer must __lie in__ finding alternative sources of power.
9) Many new cell phones __are capable of__ connecting to the Internet.
10) He is the only party leader __competent__ enough to govern this country.

Task Three

Choose the right phrase to complete each sentence.

1) as with   as regards   as to   as for
   - The eggs are graded __as to/as regards__ size and colour.
   - His position __as regards__ the report had been misunderstood.
   - Frank was very uncertain __as to__ whether it was the right job for him.
   - He was a nice enough person, but __as for/as to__ his suggestions, I found them unhelpful.
   - __As with__ any creative work there can be no prescription that will guarantee a large supply of good teaching ideas.

2) as long as   as far as   as well as   as good as   as well
   - He is loyal, and brave __as well__.
   - She is good at softball __as well as__ basketball.
   - They can do anything they want, __as long as__ they follow the rules.
   - The investigation isn't making much progress, __as far as__ I can see.
   - Those people __as good as__ ruined the school with their foolish ideas!

Task Four

Fill in the following blanks with appropriate words from the box.

How can the newspaper industry survive the Internet? On the one hand, newspapers are expected to 1) __supply__ their content free on the Web. On the other hand, their most 2) __profitable__ advertising — classified ads — is being lost to sites 3) __like__ Craigslist. And display advertising is close behind. 4) __Meanwhile__, there is the blog terror: people are getting their 5) __understanding__ of the world from random lunatics riffing(发表即兴谈话) in their underwear, rather than professional 6) __journalists__ with standards and passports.

Ten years ago, it was a 7) __challenge__ for websites to get people to spend time for pleasure in front of a computer screen. "Your problem will be 8) __solved__ perfectly in the near future," a professor of computer sciences assured a group of 9) __Web__ pioneers, and sure enough, it was. Now the 10) __problem__ is to get people under 50 or so to pick up a newspaper. Damp or encased in plastic bags, or 11) __both__, and planted in the bushes outside where it's cold, full of news that is cold too because it has been sitting around 12) __for__ hours, the home-delivered newspaper is an archaic object. Who needs it? You can sit down at your 13) __laptop__ and enjoy that same newspaper or any other 14) __newspaper__ in the world. Or you can skip the newspapers and go to some 15) __site__ that makes the news more entertaining. And where do these wannabes get most of their information? From newspapers, of course. But that is mere irony. It doesn't pay the cost of a Baghdad bureau.

4 GRAMMAR FOCUS

Read the following passage, underline the one mistake in each line and write the correction after the bracketed number.

Social media <u>has</u> gained greater recognition in the new edition	1) have
of *The Associated Press Stylebook* with a <u>separated</u> section for	2) separate
the first time <u>what</u> also makes "website" one word.	3) that
The new Social Media Guidelines section <u>including</u> information	4) includes
on using tools like Facebook and Twitter, how <u>can journalists</u>	5) journalists can
apply them to their work. Also <u>including</u> are 42 separate entries	6) included
on such terms <u>like</u> blogs, metadata, and wiki.	7) as
The AP said the change <u>with</u> "Web site" to "website" was	8) from
based on <u>increasing</u> common usage both in print and online.	9) increasingly
"Web" remains a capitalized proper noun when <u>use</u> as a	10) used
shortened form of World Wide Web; and e-mail, <u>include</u> the	11) including/with
hyphen, remains unchanged <u>as</u> electronic mail. The new edition	12) for
changes some cities that have appeared <u>lonely</u> in stories, without	13) alone
country identification. *The Stylebook* also <u>takes</u> the distinction	14) makes
<u>of</u> Wal-Mart Stores Inc. and Walmart.	15) between

1) 主谓一致错误：media是medium一词的复数形式，因此助动词也要用复数形式have。
2) 形容词使用错误：separate可以作形容词，表示"独立的，单独的"；而separated意为"分离的，分居的。"
3) 引导词错误：该分句为定语从句，修饰a separate section，应该用that来引导，that在分句中作主语。
4) 谓语动词使用错误：including是现在分词，不能充当谓语，应改为includes。
5) 句子语序错误：由how引导的从句作介词on的宾语，从句中应使用陈述句语序。
6) 语态错误：此句为倒装句式，are和过去分词included构成被动态。
7) 固定搭配错误：such...as是固定搭配。
8) 介词搭配错误："从……变成……"应该是change from...to...。
9) 副词搭配错误：应该用副词increasingly来修饰形容词common。
10) 动词错误：此句的结构是when it is used...的省略形式，应该用use的过去分词形式表被动。

11) 动词使用错误：这个分句的谓语是remains，前面的短句充当状语，应该改为介词including，或用介词with。
12) 介词使用错误：应该用for，意思是用e-mail来表示electronic mail。
13) 副词使用错误：应该用alone，意思是"单独地"；lonely意为"孤独地"。
14) 动词搭配错误：与distinction搭配的动词通常是make，而不是take。
15) 固定搭配错误：distinction后面通常跟between，而不和for搭配。

5 TRANSLATION

Task One

Translate the following paragraph from English into Chinese.

仅在15年以前，要回答"世界上有什么新闻？"这一问题，最好的选择就是去读报。当时，人们的选择有限，只有报刊、广播和电视。而报刊传递新闻的形式令另外两种媒体望尘莫及——这就是文字超越视/听的力量。

首先，读报刊时，信息获取和信息发布完全不用同时，而且报刊非常便于携带。人们收看一个电视节目时会错过其他700家的节目，即使有数字录像机也不行。但是读《泰晤士报》的头版新闻并不妨碍你再读第六版的时尚栏目，抑或其他版面。而且人们除了开车时不能看报，其他任何时候都可以看。

读报也几乎不会给别人带来任何干扰，也不会让读报者听不到周围的谈话。人们可以安静地读新闻和其他信息，而不必迫使房间里的其他人受电视或广播的"噪音"干扰。同样，读报者可以继续参与周围的谈话，不必"到另外一间房间去看电视"或使用随身听（还记得这种东西吗？）。

Task Two

Translate the following paragraph from Chinese into English.

As newspapers will gradually go totally digital, there is something nostalgic about turning the pages of a newspaper. The noise it makes when you shake it out to read the inside articles are admittedly more personal than the droning sound of a double clicking mouse. As we move further and further along the digital path, conventional newspapers just cannot keep up with the Internet in terms of providing up-to-the-minute news that we crave. Many of the headline news stories one reads in newspapers had already been read the day before from an online news source. In today's world, no one has time to read things twice (though we would be much better off if we did and would hopefully understand a lot more of the issues). With advertisers recognizing this digital shift and dumping newspapers, almost all newspapers are left high on the economic endangered species list.

6 CLASSROOM INTERACTION

Activity A   Listening

NPR, or National Public Radio, is a privately and publicly funded non-profit membership media organization in the USA. Listen to a NPR representative talking to journalism students at a university about NPR and complete the notes.

The Development of NPR

1990s

The results of the growing interest in news:

- the expanded 1) __distribution__ of NPR programming
- growth in 2) __audience__
3) __Talk of the Nation__ is NPR's first talk program.
4) __NPR Worldwide__ was launched in 1993, providing programming outside the US.

The year 1994 saw the greatest burst in contributions from 5) __listeners__ and support from the public.

2000s

6) __September 11, 2001__ was a turning point for NPR.

Events that led to sharp increase in the number of audience:
- 9/11
- 7) __Election 2004__
- the Iraq War
- the primaries and Election 2008

Digital platforms such as 8) __NPR.org__ and mobile sites and apps offer more choices to people.

Today

NPR is experiencing another 9) __era of innovation__.

NPR is actively taking advantage of 10) __digital media__ to serve its mission.

Script

Good morning, ladies and gentlemen, today I am going to give you some rough idea on the recent development of NPR in the last two decades. In the 1990s, a growing interest in news led to expanded distribution of NPR programming and growth in audience. The Gulf War in 1990 led to NPR's first talk program, *Talk of the Nation,* and ultimately, the emergence of the public radio news-talk format. NPR launched *NPR Worldwide* in 1993, providing programming beyond the boundaries of the US, and throughout the decade NPR stations expanded their services. The effort in 1994 to eliminate federal funding for public broadcasting led to an unprecedented burst in contributions from listeners, and a groundswell of non-partisan political support from the public. Federal support for public broadcasting was maintained.

September 11, 2001, was a turning point for NPR, which pushed us to shift our orientation even more fully to high-quality, contextual, timely news — both domestic and foreign. 9/11, Election 2004, the Iraq War, the primaries and Election 2008 led to sharp increase in audience, and most of these new listeners stayed with us. Over the last few years, we've extended our focus to building an equally compelling service on NPR.org, as well as mobile sites and apps. These digital platforms offer more ways to listen, learn and experience NPR and stations, and new people are discovering us every day.

Today we are experiencing another era of innovation, not unlike the earliest days of radio, though much faster, and more chaotic and dynamic. Our radio service is a strong foundation upon which to build, as NPR and its stations are actively embracing the power and potential of digital media to serve our mission.

Activity B   Discussion

This exercise is to encourage the students to think about the future of the Internet and mass media by fully employing their prior knowledge as well as what is learned in this unit. The teacher is advised to encourage the students to discuss the topic in small groups, summarize what they have found, and then make a presentation to the whole class.

Activity C Picture Description
Reference for the teacher

This cartoon tells a story about a lady who is confused by the information from the media. One day, the lady hears on the radio that "Studies show cranberry juice can cure infections". She quickly puts "cranberry juice" on her shopping list and rushes to a store. After a while, she checks out with a huge bottle of cranberry juice and drives home merrily. Unfortunately, just as she is putting things down at home, she hears on the radio that "New studies show cranberry juice causes warts". "My goodness, what should I do with it now?" wonders the lady, with the bottle of cranberry juice in her hands. This cartoon reveals the problem that sometimes people may be muddled by the information on the radio, or from any other media.

We can learn from this cartoon that we should think twice before we believe in anything from the media. Sometimes information from the media is not trustworthy. They may just report what they get, but there is no guarantee of truth in their reports.

Some quotes on the mass media

Advertising is legalized lying. 广告是合法地说谎。
— H. G. Wells (1866 -1946)
British-born American author

I keep reading between the lies. 我一直从字里谎间阅读。
— Goodman Ace (1899 -1982)
American humorist

Hastiness and superficiality are the psychic diseases of the twentieth century, and more than anywhere else this disease is reflected in the press. 急躁与肤浅是20世纪的心理疾病，这在媒体中反映最集中。
— Alexander Solzhenitsyn (1918-2008)
Russian novelist, dramatist and historian

The real news is bad news. 坏消息才是真正的消息。
— Marshall McLuhan (1911-1980)
Canadian communications theorist and educator

Advertising is the greatest art form of the twentieth century. 广告是20世纪最伟大的艺术形式。
— Marshall McLuhan

The advertisements are the most truthful part of a newspaper. 广告是报纸最真实的部分。
— Thomas Jefferson (1743-1826)
3rd president of the United States

In the real world, nothing happens at the right place at the right time. It is the job of journalists and historians to correct that. 在现实世界中，没有任何事情会在恰当的时间和恰当的地点发生，新闻工作者和历史学家的工作就是把它们纠正过来。
— Mark Twain (1835-1910)
American humorist and writer

If a person is not talented enough to be a novelist, not smart enough to be a lawyer, and his hands are too shaky to perform operations, he becomes a journalist. 如果一个人不具有小说家的天赋和律师的精明，去做手术的话双手又会抖，他就当记者了。
— Norman Mailer (1923-2007)
American writer

Television is a medium of entertainment which permits millions of people to listen to the same joke at the same time, and yet remain lonesome. 电视这种娱乐媒体能让数以百万计的人们同时听同一个笑话,但仍然都很寂寞。

— T. S. Eliot (1888-1965)
American-English poet and playwright

I find television very educational. Every time someone switches it on I go into another room and read a good book. 我觉得电视对教育很有好处。每次别人打开电视,我都到另一个房间去看一本好书。

— Groucho Marx (1890-1977)
American comedian

TV is chewing gum for the eyes. 电视是眼睛的口香糖。

— Frank Lloyd Wright (1867-1959)
American architect

WRITING

Writing Skills: Development by Comparison and Contrast

This unit discusses how to write comparison and contrast essays. The teacher is advised to clarify the two concepts at the beginning, and make sure that the students realize that comparison focuses on similarity, and contrast on differences. Then the teacher can lead the students to explore the possible content of this kind of essays: writing about similarity (essays of comparison), about differences (essays of contrast), and about both (essays of comparison and contrast).

Structure is another important point to teach. The teacher can have the students brainstorm on any pair of topics, come up with several aspects for comparison or contrast, and arrange all their ideas in a logical order. After that, the teacher introduces the two concepts: *block comparison* and *alternating comparison*. If possible, mention two other terms to them: *whole-by-whole comparison* and *point-by-point comparison*. These two terms are more straightforward, and can help the students to better understand the difference.

The sample in the Student's Book is a good example of combination of comparison and contrast. The four questions after it try to check the students' understanding of the basic concepts, and highlight the importance of cohesive devices in this type of essays. Among the questions, the second one may be a little confusing for the students: some of them may regard it as a block comparison because it seems to be divided into two parts, but actually, in each part, alternating comparison is used. Following are the reference answers to the questions:

1. This essay discusses the similarities and differences between the T-Bird and the Rabbit. It is therefore an essay of comparison and contrast.
2. In this essay, the second paragraph deals with the similarities, and the third paragraph deals with the differences. In both paragraphs, the writer organizes the discussion into different aspects. Therefore, this essay is a sample of alternating comparison.
3. The writer has used many cohesive devices, such as *both*, *so*, *as well as*, *the first difference is …*, *another difference concerns …*, *a major difference is…*, and *in conclusion*.
4. The last part is a suggestion based on the comparison and contrast. This has shown the purpose of comparison and contrast in this essay: making a choice after the comparison and contrast.

The Student's Book also provides some guidelines for writing comparison and contrast essays.

Writing Assignment

1. List some words that can be used to indicate comparison and contrast.

like, similar to, also, in like manner, similarly, in the same way, likewise, again, compared to, in contrast, unlike, contrasted with, on the contrary, however, although, yet, even though, still, but, nevertheless, conversely, at the same time, regardless, despite, while, on the one hand … on the other hand…

2. Study the following essay carefully and produce an outline of it.

  I. Purpose: Contrasting mountain vacation and beach vacation
  II. Differences between the two types of vacation
    A. Mountain vacation
      1) Climate: cold

- 2) Activities: related with cold climate (snowboarding, mountain climbing, mountain biking, hiking, and skiing)
- 3) Location: Canada
- B. Beach vacation
  - 1) Climate: warm
  - 2) Activities: related with warm climate and the sea (swim, play volleyball, play soccer, ride water bikes, dance, and party)
  - 3) Location: Mexico
- III. Conclusion: Both are fun, and the choice may depend on personal interest.

3. Write an essay of comparison and/or contrast on one of the following topics.

Answers may vary.

7 LEARNING

TEXT A Two Kinds

Before Reading

The purpose of this section is to arouse the students' interest in the theme of the unit, reactivate their relevant background knowledge or elicit their opinions on the related topics, so as to better prepare them for the succeeding tasks.

Before Reading activities can be organized as group work so that the students share with each other their opinions on genius and their childhood experiences with parents, especially in terms of the conflict and tension between parental expectations and children's freedom of development.

Background Information

Genius

Genius, in psychology, refers to a person of extraordinary intellectual power.

Definitions of genius in terms of intelligence quotient (IQ) are based on research originating in the early 1900s. In 1916 the American psychologist Lewis M. Terman set the IQ for "potential genius" at 140 and above, a level exhibited by about 1 in every 250 people. Leta Hollingworth, an American psychologist who studied the nature and nurture of genius, proposed an IQ of 180 as the threshold — a level that, at least theoretically, is exhibited by only about one in every two million people. Her work in this area was published posthumously as *Children Above 180 IQ, Stanford-Binet: Origin and Development* (1942).

Psychologists who specialize in the study of gifted children, however, have observed that the genius designation occurs much more frequently than would be expected, leading some to speculate that a "bump" in the normal curve has emerged, with many more geniuses appearing in the general population than would seem statistically probable. There is the possibility, of course, that conventional intelligence tests are ineffective in measuring intellectual ability beyond a certain point. In any event, "genius", as determined by these tests, simply means great intellectual ability and signifies potential rather than attainment. In this sense, the term may be used to characterize children who have not yet had an opportunity to gain eminence by achievement. A growing and probably more practicable usage is to refer to children of this sort as "gifted" and to make a distinction between profoundly gifted children, those in the upper 0.1 percent of the general population, and moderately gifted children, those in the upper 10 percent of the population.

The word *genius* is used in two closely related but somewhat different senses. In the first sense, as popularized by Terman, it refers to great intellectual ability as measured by performance on a standardized intelligence test. In the second and more popular sense, as derived from work of the 19th-century English scientist Sir Francis Galton, it designates creative ability of an exceptionally high order as demonstrated by actual achievement — always provided that such achievement is not merely of transitory value or the result of accident of birth.

Genius is distinguished from talent, both quantitatively and qualitatively. Talent refers to a native aptitude for some special kind of work and implies a relatively quick and easy acquisition of a particular skill within a domain (sphere of activity or knowledge). Genius, on the other hand, involves originality, creativity, and the ability to think and work in areas not previously explored — thus giving the world something of value that would not otherwise exist.

There have been a variety of attempts to explain the nature and source of genius, as well as many investigations of the relationship of genius to madness. Galton, who inaugurated the systematic study of genius, formulated the theory that genius is a very extreme degree of three combined traits — intellect, zeal, and power of working — that are shared by all persons in various "grades". In his *Hereditary Genius* (1869), he put forth the idea that genius, as measured by outstanding accomplishment, tends to run in families. This became a controversial viewpoint, and, since its introduction, scientists have disagreed about the degree to which biological heredity, as distinct from education and opportunity, is responsible for the great differences in achievement between individuals.

New ways of describing genius nearly always incorporate ability, creativity, mastery of a domain, and other personality traits such as autonomy and capacity for endurance. One important contemporary perspective, developed by the American psychologist Howard Gardner, is the theory of multiple intelligences. Gardner identified at least eight particular types of intelligence. Like all human traits, these so-called "multiple intelligences" are thought to be distributed relatively evenly throughout a population. It is likely that the genius, however, is born with extraordinary capacities in at least one of these areas. Gardner's eight key intelligences can be used to illustrate genius in particular fields. For example, great writers possess linguistic intelligence; brilliant scientists have mathematical-logical intelligence; eminent artists display spatial-visual intelligence; great musicians are born with musical intelligence; accomplished dancers have kinesthetic intelligence; great leaders excel in interpersonal intelligence; successful therapists have intrapersonal intelligence; and well-known explorers have naturalistic intelligence. To these categories the American psychologist Robert A. Emmons added spiritual intelligence, as observed in prominent religious leaders. Neuropsychologists have sought the physiological foundation for these intelligences in the human brain, and there has been a race to develop appropriate means of assessing each of these capacities.

Many scholars believe that genius is a function of both heredity and environment. The original potential for exceptional achievement may be inherited, but the fruition of this potential depends also, at least to some extent, on opportunity, training, mastery of a domain, capacity to experience flow, autonomy, endurance, and a combination of hereditary and socially influenced personality traits.

Reading

Text Analysis

• Text Summary

In this poignant remembrance, the narrator recalls the unforgettable, sorrowful experience of her childhood, when she was forced to take a myriad of tests to live up to her mother's hope of becoming a prodigy. The narrator starts with a brief description of her mother — her beliefs and personal background, which paves the way for the subsequent incidents. In a chronological order, the narrator elaborates on three major events — trying to be a Chinese Shirley Temple, taking tests to scout her genius, and gaining a significant insight into herself. Coupling narration with description, the narrator depicts a vivid picture of a typical Chinese mother who goes to great lengths to make her child successful.

• Text Organization

Paragraphs 1-3: the first part	Regarding America as a land of infinite opportunities and possibilities, the narrator's mother, a Chinese immigrant, once firmly believed that her nine-year-old daughter could be a prodigy.
Paragraphs 4-8: the second part	To pick the right kind of prodigy, her mother first tried to make her into a Chinese Shirley Temple, but the result was both disappointing and hilarious.
Paragraphs 9-16: the third part	The prodigy dream was blooming in the hearts of both the mother and the daughter. To realize this dream, her mother presented to her new tests night after night in an unremitting effort to get the prodigy out of her, but the outcome was unproductive.
Paragraphs 17-20: the final part	After having experienced another setback, the narrator finally broke down, but the unexpected gain was that she discovered the prodigy side of herself and set her mind to protect it against her mother's domineering efforts.

• Text Features

In narrating the nine-year-old girl's "bitter" experience of striving for the prodigy dream, the author tries various methods to produce humorous effects. The episodes selected — the dreadful experience of an awful haircut, the ridiculous tests administered by the obsessive mother, the mischievous noncooperation as a way of inner protest — are amusing to readers. Another major source of humor in the article is the extensive use of words or phrases which are most likely to impress readers with vivid pictures. Here are two instances: *I now had hair the length of a boy's, with straight-across bangs that hung at a slant two inches above my eyebrows.* (Para. 8) *I made high-pitched noises like a crazed animal, trying to scratch out the face in the mirror.* (Para. 18) The first sentence provides a vivid depiction of her funny look after the haircut, while the second sentence paints a graphic portrait of her disillusionment and desperation. In her dynamic description of both the outward appearance and the inward feelings of the nine-year-old girl, the author demonstrates a masterful skill of story-telling. In addition, the author makes a good use of dialogue to portray the protagonists' character and mentality.

Here is one instance: *"Of course you can be prodigy, too,"* my mother told me when I was nine. *"You can be best anything. What does Auntie Lindo know? Her daughter, she is only best tricky."* (Para. 2) Between the lines, the readers can perceive a confident and tough-spirited mother who never admits defeat in the face of her peers. Moreover, the author employs figures of speech — such as personification(拟人) and simile(明喻) — to lend more vividness and humor to the narrative description. Here are two instances: *But sometimes the prodigy in me became impatient. "If you don't hurry up and get me out of here, I'm disappearing for good," it warned.* (Para. 11) *I made high-pitched noises like a crazed animal...* (Para. 18) The former features personification, while the latter simile.

The style of the text is characterized by informal and colloquial words and expressions (e.g. *almost, no money down, become rich, instantly*), as well as a flexible use of simple, compound, and complex sentences. In addition, as a retrospective account, this narrative essay is primarily written in the past tense. It should also be noted that the author utilizes parallelism to strengthen emphatic effects and achieve a forceful tone. Here is one instance of parallelism: *You could open a restaurant. You could work for the government and get good retirement. You could buy a house with almost no money down. You could become rich. You could become instantly famous.* (Para. 1)

• Key Sentences

1. Soon after my mother got this idea about Shirley Temple, she took me to a beauty training school in the Mission district and put me in the hands of a student who could barely hold the scissors without shaking. (Para. 6)

This sentence features double negative(双重否定)(*a student who could barely hold the scissors without shaking*). In a double negative, two negative words such as *no, not, none, neither, barely, hardly,* or *scarcely* cancel each other out. Some double negatives are intentional. For example:

A: She was *not unhappy*.

But most double negatives say the opposite of what is intended. For example:

A: Jenny did *not* feel *nothing*.

The above sentence asserts that Jenny felt other than nothing, or something. For the opposite meaning, one of the negatives must be eliminated or changed to a positive. For example:

A: She felt *nothing*.

B: She did *not* feel *anything*.

2. Such a sad, ugly girl! (Para. 18)

This sentence fragment is an emphatic statement, as marked by the exclamation point(感叹号"!"). Apart from an emphatic statement, an exclamation point is also used after an interjection or a command. For example:

A: No! We must not lose the election!

B: Come here immediately!

Exclamation points should be used sparingly. Follow mild interjections and commands with commas or periods. For example:

A: No, the response was not terrific.

B: To prolong your car's life, change its oil regularly.

It should also be noted that exclamation points are never combined with other exclamation points, question marks, periods, or commas. For example:

Faulty

"This will not be endured!," he roared.

Revised

"This will not be endured!" he roared.

3. So now on nights when my mother presented her tests, I performed listlessly, my head propped on one arm. (Para. 20)

This sentence contains an absolute construction(独立结构)(*my head propped on one arm*). What is traditionally called "absolute construction" is essentially a non-finite or verbless clause with an expressed subject of its own. Structurally, "absolute constructions" fall into four types:

Those with an infinitive

A number of officials followed the emperor, some to hold his robe, others to adjust his girdle, and so on.

Those with an -ing participle as verb element

Jim climbed slowly up the creaking steps, his courage slipping away at every step.

Those with an -ed participle as verb element

His voice drowned by the noise, the speaker interrupted his lecture.

Those without any form of verb element

The meal over, prayers were read by Miss Miller.

Like ordinary non-finite and verbless clauses, "absolute constructions" can be used as adverbials of time, cause, condition, manner, as well as accompanying circumstances. It should also be noted that "absolute constructions" are commonly used in formal language as a sort of rhetorical device which helps to achieve concision and vividness.

New Words and Expressions

prodigy /ˈprɒdɪdʒɪ/ *n.* sb. with a very great ability which usually shows itself when that person is a young child 奇才，天才(尤指神童)
e.g. The 16-year-old tennis prodigy is the youngest player ever to reach the Olympic finals.
He read in the paper about a mathematical prodigy who was attending university at the age of 12.

poke /pəʊk/ *v.* to push a finger or other pointed object quickly into sb. or sth. (尤指用手指) 戳，刺
e.g. You'll poke sb. in the eye with that umbrella if you're not careful!
Two kids were poking a stick into the drain.

tap /tæp/ *v.* to make a regular pattern of sounds with one's fingers or feet, especially when listening to music 敲出(节奏)
e.g. a toe-tapping tune
She tapped her feet in time to the music.

purse /pɜːs/ *v.* to bring the lips tightly together so that they form a rounded shape, usually as an expression of disapproval (嘴唇)噘起(多表示不赞成、恼怒)
e.g. "I don't approve of that kind of language," she said, pursing her lips.
Mrs Biddell pursed her lips and shook her head.

scissors /ˈsɪzəz/ *n.* [pl.] a device used for cutting materials such as paper, cloth and hair, consisting of two sharp blades which are joined in the middle, and two handles with holes to put your fingers through [复]剪刀

e.g. a pair of scissors

Could you pass me those scissors, please?

emerge /ɪˈmɜːdʒ/ *v.* to appear by coming out of sth. or out from behind sth. 出现

e.g. She emerged from the sea, blue with cold.

He emerged unhurt from the ruins.

uneven /ˌʌnˈiːvən/ *a.* not level, equal, flat or continuous 不平坦的；参差不齐的

e.g. Take care when you walk on that path — the paving stones are rather uneven.

There is an uneven distribution of wealth across the country from the north to the south.

crinkly /ˈkrɪŋklɪ/ *a.* stiff and curly（毛发等）卷曲的

e.g. His crinkly hair was a glossy brown colour still unmarked by grey; his moustache was neat and trim.

fuzz /fʌz/ *n.* thin soft hair or a substance like hair that covers sth. 蓬松（或卷曲）的毛发，茸毛

e.g. He's got that bit of adolescent fuzz on his upper lip.

the fuzz on a peach

Negro /ˈniːgrəʊ/ *n.* word for a black person, which is now usually considered offensive 黑人；具有黑人血统的人（含歧视义）

lament /ləˈment/ *v.* to express feelings of great sadness about sth. 悔恨；惋惜

e.g. The nation lamented the death of its great war leader.

He lamented that people had expected too much of him too soon.

lop off to cut off in one quick movement 砍掉；剪去；削去（树枝等）

e.g. I'll need to lop off the lower branches of the tree.

soggy /ˈsɒgɪ/ *a.* extremely wet and soft 极度湿软的

e.g. soggy ground

I hate it when cereal goes soggy.

clump /klʌmp/ *n.* a group of trees, bushes, or other plants growing very close together 丛，簇

e.g. a clump of grass/daffodils

The roses were planted in clumps across the park.

assure /əˈʃʊə/ *v.* to tell sb. that sth. will definitely happen or is definitely true so that they are less worried 肯定地对……说；向……保证（以消除疑虑）

e.g. The unions assured the new owners of the workers' loyalty to the company.

"Don't worry, your car will be ready tomorrow," the mechanic assured him.

bangs /bæŋz/ *n.* [pl.] hair cut straight across the forehead [复]刘海儿

e.g. a tall girl with straight brown hair and bangs

slant /slɑːnt/ *n.* a sloping position 倾斜；斜面

e.g. The house is built on/at a slant.

eyebrow /ˈaɪbraʊ/ *n.* the line of short hairs above each eye in humans 眉毛

e.g. "Really?" she said, raising her eyebrows.

This decision caused a few raised eyebrows (= surprised some people).

dainty /ˈdeɪntɪ/ *a.* (of a person) delicate and graceful in build or movement（人）秀丽玲珑的；优雅的

e.g. She was a small, dainty child, unlike her sister who was large and had big feet.

ballerina /ˌbæləˈriːnə/ *n.* a female ballet dancer 芭蕾舞女演员

e.g. When she was a little girl, she dreamed of becoming a ballerina.

All the moves of the ballerina were graceful.

on tiptoe(s) on one's toes with the heels lifted off the ground 踮起脚尖

e.g. The children stood on tiptoe in order to pick the apples from the tree.

They walked across the room on tiptoe so as not to waken the baby.

straw /strɔː/ *n.* the dried stems of wheat or similar plants that animals sleep on, and that are used for making things such as baskets, hats etc. 稻草；麦秆

e.g. a straw basket/hat

A piece of straw drifted to the ground.

manger /ˈmeɪndʒə/ *n.* a long open container that horses, cattle etc. eat from 食槽

e.g. The horses were crunching their straw at their manger.

When I examined the manger where the feed had been put, I found oats and bran.

indignity /ɪnˈdɪgnətɪ/ *n.* a situation that makes one feel very ashamed and not respected

侮辱；耻辱

e.g. They were subjected to various indignities and discomforts, including having to get dressed and undressed in public.
Clint suffered the indignity of being called "Puppy" in front of his girlfriend.

pumpkin /ˈpʌmpkɪn/ *n.* a large round vegetable with hard yellow or orange flesh 南瓜

e.g. I like white gourds, but not pumpkins.

sparkly /ˈspɑːklɪ/ *a.* full of life and energy 活泼的；生机勃勃的

e.g. The radiant smile and the sparkly eyes were the clear signs of a woman still deeply in love.

imaginings /ɪˈmædʒɪnɪŋz/ *n.* [pl.] situations or ideas that you imagine, but which are not true or real [复]想象，幻象

e.g. He indulged himself in the imaginings of becoming a general.

reproach /rɪˈprəʊtʃ/ *n.* the expression of disapproval or disappointment 责备，责怪

e.g. The look of reproach on his face made her feel guilty.
Your reproaches are useless — what's done is done.

sulk /sʌlk/ *v.* to be silent and childishly refuse to smile or be pleasant to people because you are angry about sth. that they have done（因生气、失望而）不说话，愠怒，郁闷

e.g. Nicola sulked all morning.
Cindy always sulks when I won't buy her any candy.

Chinatown /ˈtʃaɪnətaʊn/ *n.* an area of a city outside China where many Chinese people live 中国城，唐人街

e.g. The alleyways are a quaint remnant of the old Chinatown.

multiply /ˈmʌltɪplaɪ/ *v.* to do a calculation in which one adds a number to itself a specified number of times 乘；使相乘

e.g. Children will learn to multiply in the second grade.
If you multiply 7 by 15, you get 105.

deck /dek/ *n.* a pack of cards 一副纸牌

e.g. Irene shuffled the deck.

predict /prɪˈdɪkt/ *v.* to say that sth. will happen, before it happens 预测

e.g. Newspapers predicted that Davis would be re-elected.
It is difficult to predict what the long-term effects of the accident will be.

abundance /əˈbʌndəns/ *n.* a large quantity of sth. 大量

e.g. One quality the team possessed in abundance was fighting spirit.
There was an abundance of wine at the wedding.

sink /sɪŋk/ *n.* a bowl that is fixed to the wall in a kitchen or bathroom for washing dishes or hands etc. in 水槽

e.g. Dirty plates were piled high in the sink.
The kitchen was like a big utility room with a huge sink, a stone floor, and a large wooden table.

high-pitched /ˈhaɪˈpɪtʃt/ *a.* (of a sound) very high 尖声的

e.g. a high-pitched scream
Above the music on the radio was an annoying, high-pitched whistle.

scratch /skrætʃ/ *v.* to cut or damage a surface with or on sth. sharp or rough 抓

e.g. We scratched the paintwork trying to get the bed into Martha's room.
Be careful not to scratch yourself on the roses.

reflection /rɪˈflekʃən/ *n.* the image of sth. in a mirror or on any reflective surface（镜子中或光洁面上的）映像

e.g. In Greek mythology, Narcissus fell in love with his own reflection in a pool of water.
He put silver foil around the fire to increase heat reflection.

blink /blɪŋk/ *v.* to close and then open the eyes quickly once or several times 眨眼

e.g. You've got something in your eye — try blinking a few times.
I blinked as I came out into the sunlight.

willful /ˈwɪlfʊl/ *a.* (of sth. bad) done intentionally or (of a person) determined to do exactly as one wants, even if one knows it is wrong 任性的；执拗的

e.g. The present crisis is the result of years of willful neglect by the council.
They eat huge quantities of sweet and fried foods, in willful disregard of their health.

present /prɪˈzent/ *v.* to give, provide or make known 给予；赠予

e.g. The letter presented the family with a

problem that would be difficult to solve.
The documentary presented us with a balanced view of the issue.

listlessly /ˈlɪstlɪslɪ/ *ad.* feeling tired and not interested in things 无力地；无精打采地

e.g. He read the book listlessly and in the end dozed off.
They walked listlessly in the sun.

prop /prɒp/ *v.* to support sth. physically, often by leaning it against sth. else or putting sth. under it 用……支撑

e.g. I propped my bike (up) against the wall.
She was sitting at the desk with her chin propped on her hands.

bellow /ˈbeləʊ/ *n.* a loud voice, or a loud, deep sound 吼声；轰鸣声

e.g. The headmaster's bellows were heard in the corridor.

foghorn /ˈfɒɡhɔːn/ *n.* a horn that makes a very loud sound in fog to warn ships that they are close to land or other ships（向雾中船只发出警告的）雾号角，雾喇叭

e.g. He has a voice like a foghorn (= an unpleasantly loud voice).
As a kid I would lie awake listening to the foghorns.

bay /beɪ/ *n.* a part of the coast where the land curves in so that the sea is surrounded by land on three sides 湾

e.g. Dublin Bay
the Bay of Naples
We sailed into a beautiful, secluded bay.

drill /drɪl/ *v.* to practise sth., or to make sb. do this 操练，训练

e.g. She was drilling the class in the forms of the past tense.
I acted instinctively because I had been trained and drilled to do just that.

Language Study

tap *v.*
1. to hit your fingers lightly on sth., for example to get sb.'s attention 轻拍；轻击
    e.g. He turned as someone tapped him on the shoulder.
    I went up and tapped on the window.
    Mark tapped his fingers on the tabletop impatiently.
    She tapped ash from her cigarette.
2. to use or take what is needed from sth. such as an energy supply, an amount of money, or information 从……处获得资源、金钱或信息
    e.g. People are tapping into the power supply illegally.
    We hope that additional sources of funding can be tapped.
    Your adviser's experience is there to be tapped.

emerge *v.*
1. to become apparent, important, or prominent 变得显眼（或重要、突出）
    e.g. United have emerged as the bookies' clear favourite.
    a world of emerging economic giants.
2. (of facts or circumstances) to become known（事实、情况）被知晓，暴露
    e.g. Reports of a deadlock emerged during preliminary discussions.
    It emerged that the Trade Secretary and the Chancellor are still in disagreement.
3. to recover from or survive a difficult or demanding situation 恢复；渡过难关
    e.g. The economy has started to emerge from recession.

reflection *n.*
1. [mass noun] the throwing back by a body or surface of light, heat, or sound without absorbing it（光、热或声音的）反射
    e.g. the reflection of light
2. [count noun] an amount of light, heat, or sound that is thrown back in such a way 反射光；反射热；回声
    e.g. The reflections from the street lamps gave them just enough light.

3. [count noun] a thing that is a consequence of or arises from sth. else 反映
   e.g. A healthy skin is a reflection of good health in general.
4. [in singular] a thing that brings discredit to sb. or sth. 有损(人或事)名誉的事
   e.g. It was a sad reflection on society that because of his affliction he was picked on.
5. [mass noun] serious thought or consideration 深思；反省
   e.g. He doesn't get much time for reflection.
6. [count noun] an idea about sth., especially one that is written down or expressed （尤指见诸语言的）想法；意见；思考
   e.g. reflections on human destiny and art

present
  v.
1. to give (sth. to sb.) formally or ceremonially 郑重赠与；授予；呈献
   e.g. The duke presented certificates to the men.
   My pupils presented me with some flowers.
2. to formally introduce sb. to sb. else 正式引见，介绍
   e.g. May I present my wife?
3. to introduce or announce the various items (of a television or radio show) as a participant （电视或电台节目）介绍；播出；主持
   e.g. *The Late Show* was presented by Cynthia Rose.

present oneself   to come forward into the presence of another or others, especially for a formal occasion; appear （尤指在正式场合）出席；到场
   e.g. He failed to present himself in court.

present itself   (of an opportunity or idea) to occur and be available for use or exploitation （机会、观点）出现；呈现
   e.g. When a favorable opportunity presented itself he would submit his proposition.

  a.
1. (of a person) in a particular place （人）在场的；出席的；在座的
   e.g. A doctor must be present at the ringside.
   The speech caused embarrassment to all those present.
2. (*often* **present in**)(of a thing) existing or occurring in a place or thing （事物）存在的
   e.g. Organic molecules are present in comets.
3. existing or occurring now 现在的，目前的
   e.g. She did not expect to find herself in her present situation.
   The present article cannot answer every question.

  n.
1. (*often* **the present**) the period of time now occurring 现在；当代
   e.g. They are happy and at peace, refusing to think beyond the present.
2. a present tense 现在时(态)
   e.g. The verbs are all in the present.

I made high-pitched noises like a crazed animal, trying to scratch out the face in the mirror.
Simile as a rhetorical device   明喻作为一种修辞手段：
本句使用了明喻的修辞手段。明喻是比喻的一种，是对两种具有共同特征的事物或现象进行对比，表明其相似关系，本体和喻体都在对比中出现，且常带有比喻词，如like, seem, be sth. of, as, resemble, comparable to, similar to, akin to, analogous to等。
英语的明喻例证如下：
   My love is **like** a red, red rose. (Robert Burns)
   You are **like** a hurricane: there's calm in your eye, but I'm getting blown away. (Neil Young)
   The day we passed together for a while **seemed** a bright fire on a winter's night. (Maurice)
明喻在汉语和英语中都很常见，有着共同的特点，即存在显而易见的比喻词。
汉语的明喻例证如下：
   她的脸色苍白而带光泽，**仿佛**大理石**似**的；一双眼睛又黑又大，在黯淡的囚房中，宝石**似**的闪着晶莹的光。（杨沫《青春之歌》）

Her face was pale yet **as** lustrous **as** marble, and her large, black eyes sparkled **like** jewels in that murky cell.

在使用明喻的时候，一定要注意明喻表达的有效性，即诉诸想象的明喻必须使主旨明确，清楚易懂，起到强化效果的作用。人们通常把明喻分为描写型、说明型和启发型三种。

在翻译时，英语里as...as...结构的明喻大多可以直译，如：

  as cold **as** ice 冰冷   **as** hot **as** fire 火热

  as busy **as** a bee 像蜜蜂一样忙碌   **as** blind **as** a bat 瞎得像蝙蝠

当然也有例外，如：

  as cool **as** a cucumber 非常冷静   **as** tight **as** a drum 非常小气

上述两个例子不能从字面上翻译，我们只要译出其实际意义即可。

After Reading

READING COMPREHENSION TASKS

1. Complete the following table based on the information in TEXT A.

Statements	Examples
My mother believed you could be anything you wanted to be in America.	1) You could **open a restaurant** . 2) You could **work for the government** and get good retirement. 3) You could **buy a house** with almost no money down. 4) You could become **rich** . 5) You could become **instantly famous** .
We didn't immediately pick the right kind of prodigy.	1) At first my mother thought **I could be a Chinese Shirley Temple** . 2) The first night she brought out a story **about a three-year-old boy who knew the capitals of all the states and even most of the European countries** . 3) The tests got harder — multiplying **numbers in my head** , finding **the queen of hearts in a deck of cards** , trying **to stand on my head without using my hands** , predicting **the daily temperatures in Los Angeles, New York, and London** . 4) One night I had to **look at the Bible for three minutes and then report everything I could remember** .
I pictured this prodigy part of me as many different images, trying each one on for size.	1) I was **a dainty ballerina girl standing by the curtains, waiting to hear the right music that would send me floating on my tiptoes** . 2) I was like **the Christ child lifted out of the straw manger, crying with holy indignity** . 3) I was **Cinderella stepping from her pumpkin carriage with sparkly cartoon music filling the air** .

2. Read the following statements and decide whether they are true (T) or false (F).

1) The narrator's mother believes that America is a land of opportunities. (T)
2) The narrator's mother successfully picks her daughter's prodigy at one stroke. (F)
3) After the hairdressing, the instructor of the beauty training school makes her into, so to speak, a Chinese Shirley Temple. (F)
4) The narrator has been resisting her mother's efforts to change her from the very beginning. (F)

5) The narrator's mother presents her prodigy tests routinely, taking examples from stories of amazing children she has read about in various magazines. (T)
6) The narrator is fairly interested in those tests, finding them both enlightening and amusing. (F)
7) The narrator's mother never wavers in the face of her daughter's resistance and non-cooperation. (F)

3. Choose the best answers to the following questions.

1) Initially, the narrator complies with her mother's will of making her into a genius. Which paragraph in this essay signals the turning point at which she recognizes the wrong of transforming her into what she is not?
   A. Paragraph 4.　　B. Paragraph 6.　　C. Paragraph 17.　　**D. Paragraph 19.**

2) Which method of organization does the author use in this essay?
   A. Time and sequence.　　B. Emphasis.　　C. Deduction.　　D. Classification.

3) Which of the following sentences employs simile?
   A. At first my mother thought I could be a Chinese Shirley Temple.
   B. You look like Negro Chinese.
   C. But sometimes the prodigy in me became impatient.
   D. I made high-pitched noises like a crazed animal, trying to scratch out the face in the mirror.

4) Which paragraph does NOT employ parallelism?
   A. Paragraph 1.　　**B. Paragraph 3.**　　C. Paragraph 9.　　D. Paragraph 10.

4. Explain the underlined parts in your own words.

1) You could buy a house with almost no money down. (Para. 1)
   without any down payment

2) … said my mother as Shirley's eyes flooded with tears. (Para. 5)
   tears welled up in Shirley's eyes

3) … and put me in the hands of a student … (Para. 6)
   left me at the mercy of

4) … and tried to wet down my hair. (Para. 6)
   dampen my hair to remove the hairstyle

5) … many different images, trying each one on for size. (Para. 9)
   putting myself in those images to see whether they are suitable for me

6) I would be beyond reproach. (Para. 10)
   free of blames and criticisms

7) … we had a great assortment. (Para. 12)
   a great variety of magazines

8) The first night she brought out a story about a three-year-old boy … (Para. 13)
   presented her test based on a story about

ORAL WORK

TEXT A is written in the first person from the perspective of the daughter. The first person makes the narrator close up and sound personal so that readers can easily identify themselves with her. Now work with your partner — one of you retells the story in the first person *from the perspective of the mother,* and then the other student retells the story in the third person.

The teacher can ask the students to work in pairs first and then choose a few students to retell the story to the whole class. It is a good practice to use indirect speech to retell a story that carries a lot of direct speech.

TRANSLATION OF TEXT A

两类人

谭恩美

1　妈相信，在美国，你的任何梦想都可以实现。开家饭馆；为政府效劳，安享舒适的退休待遇；几乎无需首付款就买栋房子；发家致富；一夜成名。

2　"你当然也可以成为神童，"在我九岁时妈对我说。"你样样事都可以做到最棒。林多伯母知道什么呀？她那女儿，只不过比别人多些小聪明罢了。"

3　美国是妈所有希望的寄托之处。她20世纪40年代后期来到美国，但回顾往事从来不会心怀遗憾。这里有太多方法使日子越过越好。

4　至于我是哪种天才，妈并没有立刻就拍板定案。起初，妈以为我会成为一名中国版的秀兰·邓波儿。我们一起在电视上看秀兰的老电影，好似在看教学片。妈会捅捅我的胳膊，说："你看。"我看到屏幕上的秀兰跳着踢踏舞，或者唱着水手歌，或者将嘴唇噘成圆圆的"O"型，说道："哦，天哪。"

5　"你看，"当屏幕上秀兰的眼中噙满了泪水，妈又说，"这些你早就做得到，哭可不需要天才！"

6　秀兰·邓波儿这一目标确立后，不久妈就把我带到教区的一所美容技校，交给了一个连剪子都拿不稳的学生处置。结果没理成想象中的大波浪，却把我弄得满头都是起伏不平毛茸茸的小黑卷儿。妈把我拖到盥洗室，想把我的发型洗掉。

7　"你看起来像个中国黑人，"她伤心地说道，好像我有意这样做似的。

8　为了把我的头发弄平，美容技校的指导老师只好将我湿淋淋的乱发剪去。"彼得·潘现在挺走红的，"老师安慰着妈。我现在头发的长度和男孩子差不离，前面的刘海儿齐刷刷地斜在眉毛上方两英寸处。事实上我还挺喜欢这个发型，这使我对日后的星途颇感期待。

9　其实，刚开始我和妈一样兴奋，可能还更起劲些。我将自己的天才设想为多个版本，一一试过。我是站在幕布旁美丽纤细的芭蕾舞女孩，等音乐响起，就踮起脚尖翩翩起舞。我是降生在马槽里的圣婴，哭得神圣而无礼。我是从南瓜车里走出来的灰姑娘，灵动的卡通音乐响彻天空。

10　在我所有的想象中，我满心觉得自己很快就会变得完美。妈和爸会就此而宠爱我。我将不再挨骂。我将再不会为任何事情而郁郁寡欢。

11　但有时，我的天才开始耐不住性子了。"如果你还不抓紧把我放出来，我就会永远消失了，"它提醒我说。"那时你就会一事无成。"

12　每天晚饭后，妈和我就坐在福米加塑料贴面的餐桌旁，她给我做些新测试。她从各种神童故事中选出样板，这些故事来自于《信不信由你》、《好管家》、《读者文摘》以及其他十几种堆放在卫生间的杂志。妈给别人打扫房子，顺便要了这些杂志。她每星期要打扫很多家，我们就有了林林总总的杂志。她每本都浏览，从中找出神童的故事。

13　第一个晚上，她搬出一个三岁小男孩知晓各州首府甚至众多欧洲国家首都的故事。这篇报道还引用一位老师的话说，这个小孩对于那些外国城市的名字还可以做到准确发音。

14　"芬兰的首都是哪里？"妈读到这篇杂志故事的时候问我。

15　我只知道加州的首府，因为萨克拉门托是我们在唐人街里所住的街名。"内罗毕！"我信口开河，冒出个我自认为最外国的名字。她核对了一下，确信这并非是"赫尔辛基"的另一种发音方式，然后才告诉了我正确的答案。

16　测试的题目变得越来越难——包括心算乘法，在一叠纸牌中找出红心皇后，不用手支撑而用头倒立，预测洛杉矶、纽约以及伦敦的每日气温。

17　一天晚上，我被要求用三分钟时间读一页《圣经》，然后汇报我所能记住的一切，"现在，约沙王有了充足的财富和荣誉……我就记得这些了，妈，"我说。

18　又一次看到妈失望的表情，我内心中的某些东西开始死去。我憎恨这些测试，以及每次希望之火被燃起，之后又被泯灭的痛苦经历。那晚睡觉前，我盯着浴室洗脸池上方的镜子，只看到同样一张回视我的脸——我也明白这辈子就这张平常的脸了——我开始失声痛哭。多么悲哀、丑陋的女孩！我发出刺耳的尖叫，好似一只疯狂的小兽，拼命地想把镜中那张脸抓出来。

19　就在这一刻，我似乎看到了我天才的那一面——因为我从来都没有看到过这张脸。我看着镜中的自己，眨着眼睛想瞧个清楚。这个瞪着我的女孩是如此愤怒却充满力量。我就是那个女孩。一个新的想法在我心中升起，一个任性的想法，更确切地说，是装满了很多"不服从"的想法。我不会让她改变我，我对自己起誓。我就要保持原本的自我。

20　所以后来，每当妈晚上再让我做什么测试时，我就无精打采地应付，一只胳膊撑着头，装作无聊的样子。事实上，我的确感到无聊，无聊到当妈换个领域测试我的时候，我便开始数海湾里雾角的鸣响次数。这声音令人感到安心，使我想起跳过月亮的那头牛。第二天，我就跟自己玩了个游戏，想看看妈是否会在第八次雾角响起之前就放弃测试。过了一段时间，我仅仅数到一次，至多两次，她就偃旗息鼓了。最后，她开始逐渐放弃了希望。

TEXT B Learning Styles

Before Reading

The purpose of this section is to arouse the students' interest in the theme of the unit, reactivate their relevant background knowledge or elicit their opinions on the related topics, so as to better prepare them for the succeeding tasks.

Before Reading activities can be organized as group work so that the students share with each other their opinions on learning styles.

Background Information

Learning Styles

There are three basic types of learning styles: visual, auditory, and kinesthetic/tactile. To learn, we depend on our senses to process the information around us. Most people tend to use one of their senses more than the others. The following is a chart which will help people determine which of these learning styles they rely on the most.

This chart helps you determine your learning style. Read the word(s) in the first column and then answer the questions in the successive three columns to see how you respond to each situation. Your answers may fall into all three columns, but one column will likely contain the most answers. The dominant column indicates your primary learning style.

When you…	Visual	Auditory	Kinesthetic & Tactile
Spell	Do you try to see the word?	Do you sound out the word or use a phonetic approach?	Do you write the word down to find if it feels right?
Talk	Do you sparingly but dislike listening for too long? Do you favour words such as *see*, *picture*, and *imagine*?	Do you enjoy listening but are impatient to talk? Do you use words such as *hear*, *tune*, and *think*?	Do you gesture and use expressive movements? Do you use words such as *feel*, *touch*, and *hold*?
Concentrate	Do you become distracted by untidiness or movement?	Do you become distracted by sounds or noises?	Do you become distracted by activities around you?
Meet someone again	Do you forget names but remember faces or remember where you met?	Do you forget faces but remember names or remember what you talked about?	Do you remember best what you did together?
Contact people on business	Do you prefer direct, face-to-face, personal meetings?	Do you prefer the telephone?	Do you talk with them while walking or participating in an activity?
Read	Do you like descriptive scenes or pause to imagine the actions?	Do you enjoy dialogue and conversation or hear the characters talk?	Do you prefer action stories or are not a keen reader?

Do something new at work	Do you like to see demonstrations, diagrams, slides, or posters?	Do you prefer verbal instructions or talking about it with someone else?	Do you prefer to jump right in and try it?
Put something together	Do you look at the directions and the picture?		Do you ignore the directions and figure it out as you go along?
Need help with a computer application	Do you seek out pictures or diagrams?	Do you call the help desk, ask a neighbour, or growl at the computer?	Do you keep trying to do it or try it on another computer?

Reading

New Words and Expressions

dominant /ˈdɒmɪnənt/ *a.* more important, strong or noticeable than anything else of the same type (最)重要的；(最)强大的；(最)有影响的
e.g. a dominant military power
Unemployment will be a dominant issue at the next election.

circumstance /ˈsɜːkəmstəns/ *n.* a fact or situation that makes an event the way it is 情况；条件；形势；环境
e.g. We oppose capital punishment in/under any circumstances.
Under no circumstances should you (= You must not) approach the man.

multiple /ˈmʌltɪpl/ *a.* very many of the same type, or of different types 多个的
e.g. The youth died of multiple burns.
We made multiple copies of the report.
These children have multiple (= many different) handicaps.

approach /əˈprəʊtʃ/ *n.* a way of dealing with sth. 处理事情的方法
e.g. He decided to adopt a different approach and teach the Bible through story-telling.
This book takes an unorthodox approach to art criticism.

linguistic /lɪŋˈɡwɪstɪk/ *a.* of or relating to language or linguistics 语言的；语言学的
e.g. Hearing difficulties can slow down a child's linguistic development.

reinforcement /ˌriːɪnˈfɔːsmənt/ *n.* the act of making sth. stronger 强化
e.g. The harbour walls need urgent reinforcement.
We need to give students plenty of positive reinforcement.

label /ˈleɪbəl/ *v.* to use a word or phrase to describe sb. or sth., but often unfairly or incorrectly 把……称为；把……归类为
e.g. If you spend any time in prison, you're labelled as a criminal for the rest of your life.
n. a classifying phrase or name applied to a person or thing, especially one that is inaccurate or restrictive (用以描述人、物的)标签；称号
e.g. She would not accept the label of modernist.

complimentary /ˌkɒmplɪˈmentərɪ/ *a.* praising or approving 赞美的
e.g. The reviews of his latest film have been highly complimentary.
She wasn't very complimentary about your performance, was she?
Our guests said some very complimentary things about the meal I'd cooked.

spiral /ˈspaɪərəl/ *n.* a process, usually a harmful one, in which sth. gradually but continuously gets worse or better 不断的急剧上升或下降
e.g. We must avoid the downward spiral in which unemployment leads to homelessness

and then to crime.

spatial /'speɪʃəl/ *a.* relating to the position, size, shape, etc. of things 空间的

e.g. This task is designed to test the child's spatial awareness (= understanding of where things are in relation to other things).
The result is that their high social mobility does not entail high levels of long distance spatial mobility.

visualize /'vɪʒuəlaɪz/ *v.* to form a picture of sb. or sth. in your mind, in order to imagine or remember them 使形象化；想像

e.g. I was so surprised when he turned up — I'd visualized someone much older.
Somehow I can't visualize myself staying with this company for much longer.

outcome /'aʊtkʌm/ *n.* a result or effect of an action, situation, etc. 结果

e.g. It's too early to predict the outcome of the meeting.
People who had heard the evidence at the trial were surprised at the outcome.

instinctively /ɪn'stɪŋktɪvlɪ/ *ad.* not thought about, planned or developed by training 本能地

e.g. She knew instinctively that he was dangerous.
He loves drawing almost instinctively.

access /'ækses/ *n.* the right or opportunity to use or benefit from sth. 使用机会；使用权

e.g. The tax inspector had/gained complete access to the company files.

scribble /'skrɪbl/ *v.* to write or draw sth. quickly or carelessly 匆忙地写；草率地画；涂鸦

e.g. The baby's just scribbled all over my new dictionary!
I'll just scribble Dad a note/scribble a note to Dad to say we're going out.

doodle /'duːdl/ *v.* to draw pictures or patterns while thinking about sth. else or when you are bored （心不在焉地）乱涂

e.g. She'd doodled all over her textbooks.
Brad was doodling on a sheet of paper.

aural /'ɔːrəl/ *a.* relating to hearing 听觉的

e.g. aural teaching aids, such as tapes
The opera was an aural as well as a visual delight.

auditory /'ɔːdɪtərɪ/ *a.* of or about hearing 听觉的

e.g. It's an artificial device which stimulates the auditory areas of the brain.
Finally he overcame the auditory difficulties by three years' efforts.

rhythm /'rɪðəm/ *n.* a strong pattern of sounds, words or musical notes which is used in music, poetry and dancing 韵律；节奏

e.g. He beat out a jazz rhythm on the drums.
I've got no sense of rhythm, so I'm a terrible dancer.

hum /hʌm/ *v.* to make a continuous low sound, often a song 哼曲子

e.g. She hummed to herself as she walked to school.
I've forgotten how that tune goes — could you hum it for me?

jingle /'dʒɪŋgl/ *n.* a short simple tune, often with words, which is easy to remember 短口号；短诗句；短曲调

e.g. He writes jingles and obscure Broadway tunes.

prompt /prɒmpt/ *v.* to help sb., especially an actor, to remember what they are going to say or do 提示；提词

e.g. I forgot my line and had to be prompted.

twister /'twɪstə/ *n.* a sentence or phrase that is intended to be difficult to say, especially when repeated quickly and often 绕口令

e.g. "She sells seashells on the seashore" is a well-known tongue twister.

limerick /'lɪmərɪk/ *n.* a humorous poem with five lines 五行打油诗

e.g. Five-line limericks, however, add humor, but be sure they are in good taste.
Maybe she will try writing again, nothing too ambitious, a fun poem in the limerick mode.

kinesthetic /ˌkɪnɪs'θetɪk/ *a.* relating to physical activities 动觉的

e.g. Kinesthetic learners learn best by moving their bodies.

gardening /'gɑːdənɪŋ/ *n.* the activity of working in a garden, growing plants, cutting a lawn, etc. 园艺

e.g. Dad is always in a good humor for gardening.
Many people in Britain are fond of gardening (= working in and taking care of their gardens).

woodworking /'wʊd,wɜːkɪŋ/ *n.* the activity of making objects such as furniture from wood 木工活

e.g. woodworking classes/lessons

I used to enjoy woodworking at school.

texture /ˈtekstʃə/ *n.* the quality of sth. that can be decided by touch; the degree to which sth. is rough or smooth, or soft or hard 纹理；质地

e.g. a smooth/rough/coarse texture

This artificial fabric has the texture of silk.

jigsaw /ˈdʒɪgsɔː/ *n.* a picture, map, etc. pasted on cardboard or wood and cut into irregular shapes that have to be fitted together again 拼图玩具；七巧板

e.g. We spent all evening doing a 1000-piece jigsaw.

upset /ʌpˈset/ *v.* to cause (sb.) to feel nauseous or unwell 使不适

e.g. He can't eat grapes — they upset him/upset his stomach.

repulsive /rɪˈpʌlsɪv/ *a.* extremely unpleasant, in a way that almost makes one feel sick 使人厌恶的，令人反感的

e.g. What a repulsive old man!

I think rats and snakes are repulsive.

fidget /ˈfɪdʒɪt/ *v.* to make continuous small movements because of nervousness or impatience 坐立不安；手足无措

e.g. Children can't sit still for long without fidgeting.

Stop fidgeting about!

reasoning /ˈriːzənɪŋ/ *n.* the process of thinking about sth. in order to make a decision 推理

e.g. Your clear reasoning is quite correct.

The reasoning seems rational.

classify /ˈklæsɪfaɪ/ *v.* to divide things into groups according to their type 分类

e.g. The books in the library are classified by/according to subject.

Biologists classify animals and plants into different groups.

calculation /ˌkælkjʊˈleɪʃən/ *n.* the use of numbers in order to find out an amount, price, or value 计算

e.g. The calculations that you did/made contained a few inaccuracies.

Dee looked at the bill and made some rapid calculations.

trigonometry /ˌtrɪgəˈnɒmɪtrɪ/ *n.* a type of mathematics that deals with the relationship between the angles and sides of triangles, used in measuring the height of buildings, mountains, etc. 三角学

e.g. She is good at trigonometry.

algebra /ˈældʒɪbrə/ *n.* a type of mathematics in which signs and letters represent numbers 代数

e.g. I shuddered at the memory of algebra.

He was not good at algebra in middle school.

numerical /njuːˈmerɪkəl/ *a.* involving or expressed in numbers 数字的；用数字表示的

e.g. Keep your files in numerical order.

The UN forces have a numerical superiority over the rebels (= There are more of the UN forces).

itinerary /aɪˈtɪnərərɪ/ *n.* a detailed plan or route of a journey 旅程；行程

e.g. The tour operator will arrange transport and plan your itinerary.

His itinerary would take him from Bordeaux to Budapest.

strategy /ˈstrætɪdʒɪ/ *n.* a detailed plan for achieving success in situations such as war, politics, business, industry or sport 战略

e.g. The president held an emergency meeting to discuss military strategy with his defense commanders yesterday.

Their marketing strategy for the product involves obtaining as much free publicity as possible.

simulation /ˌsɪmjʊˈleɪʃən/ *n.* the activity of producing conditions which are similar to real ones, especially in order to test sth., or the conditions that are produced 模拟

e.g. The manager prepared a computer simulation (= a model of a problem or course of events) of likely sales performance for the rest of the year.

brainteaser /ˈbreɪnˌtiːzə/ *n.* a problem for which it is hard to find the answer, especially one which people enjoy trying to solve as a game 难题，谜

e.g. The paper publishes two brainteasers every Saturday.

backgammon /ˈbækˌgæmən/ *n.* a game for two people in which the players throw dice and move circular pieces around a special board with narrow triangular shaped patterns on it 巴加门棋戏

e.g. For the rest of the evening they concentrated on backgammon, pushing dimes back and forth across the kitchen table.

If it rained, they stayed in the library, playing cards and backgammon.

interpersonal /ˌɪntəˈpɜːsənəl/ *a.* connected with relationships between people 人际的
 e.g. The successful applicant will have excellent interpersonal skills.
counsel /ˈkaʊnsəl/ *v.* to give advice, especially on social or personal problems 劝告；建议
 e.g. The police have provided experts to counsel local people affected by the tragedy.
  My job involves counselling unemployed people on/about how to find work.
heighten /ˈhaɪtən/ *v.* to increase or make sth. increase, especially an emotion or effect 加高；提高
 e.g. The strong police presence only heightened the tension among the crowd.
  This latest attack has greatly heightened fears of an all-out war.
bounce /baʊns/ *v.* to (cause to) move up or away after hitting a surface 弹起；反弹
 e.g. The ball bounced off the post and into the net.
  Her bag bounced (= moved up and down) against her side as she walked.
click /klɪk/ *v.* to like, understand, and agree with each other 投缘
 e.g. Liz and I really clicked the first time we met.
  The new daytime soap opera has yet to show signs that it's clicking with the television audience.
synergistic /ˌsɪnəˈdʒɪstɪk/ *a.* relating to the combined power of a group of things when they are working together which is greater than the total power achieved by each working separately 增效的；互作用(促进)的
 e.g. This will lead to the synergistic effect.
board game any of many games, for example chess, in which small pieces are moved around on a board with a pattern on it 棋类游戏
intrapersonal /ˌɪntrəˈpɜːsənəl/ *a.* inside a person's mind 个人头脑中的，内心的
introspective /ˌɪntrəʊˈspektɪv/ *a.* tending to think deeply about your own thoughts, feelings, or behaviour 内省的；反省的
 e.g. She is famous for her introspective songs about failed relationships.
  She is a shy and introspective person.
assess /əˈses/ *v.* to judge or decide the amount, value, quality or importance of sth. 估算；估计(性质、能力、质量)
 e.g. The insurers will need to assess the flood damage.
  Examinations are not the only means of assessing a student's ability.
remote /rɪˈməʊt/ *a.* far away in distance, time or relation (地点、时间、关系)远的，遥远的
 e.g. It happened in the remote past, so no one worries about it any more.
  They take little interest in a conflict far from their homes and remote from their everyday problems.
workshop /ˈwɜːkʃɒp/ *n.* a meeting at which a group of people engage in intensive discussion and activity on a particular subject or project 研讨会；讲习班
 e.g. a drama/poetry/training workshop
  The local council runs a stress-management workshop.
self-help /ˌselfˈhelp/ *n.* the activity of providing what you need for yourself and others with similar experiences or difficulties without going to an official organization 自助，自力
 e.g. self-help groups
  It is a group providing self-help for single parents.
brain-imaging /ˈbreɪnˈɪmɪdʒɪŋ/ *n.* a technical process in which pictures of the inside of sb.'s head are produced, especially for medical reasons 大脑成像

Language Study

label *n.*
1. a piece of paper or other material which gives you information about the object it is fixed to 标签，签条
   e.g. Remember to put some address labels on the suitcases.
2. a piece of fabric sewn inside a garment and bearing the brand name, size, or instructions for care（衣服的）标签
   e.g. Labels on clothes should be removed for kids with sensitive skin.
3. the name or trademark of a fashion company 时装公司的名称(或商标)
   e.g. She plans to launch her own designer clothes label.
   Fancy designer labels tend to come with fancy price tags to match.

upset
  v.
1. to make (sb.) unhappy, disappointed, or worried 使心烦意乱；使苦恼
   e.g. The accusation upset her.
   a painful and upsetting divorce
2. to knock (sth.) over 弄翻，打翻
   e.g. He upset a tureen of soup.
   Our dog upset the picnic table, spilling food everywhere.
3. to cause disorder in (sth.); to disrupt 打乱，扰乱
   e.g. The dam will upset the ecological balance.
   The chemicals upset the balance of the environment.

  n.
1. worry and unhappiness caused by an unexpected problem 心烦意乱；苦恼
   e.g. If you are the victim of a burglary, the emotional upset can affect you for a long time.
   How much upset will the new monitoring procedures cause?
2. an illness that affects the stomach and makes one feel sick（肠胃）不适
   e.g. stomach upset

  a.
1. unhappy, disappointed, or worried 心烦的，苦恼的
   e.g. she looked pale and upset.
2. (of a person's stomach) having disturbed digestion, especially because of sth. eaten（肠胃）不适的
   e.g. have an upset stomach

click *v.*
1. to make or cause to make a short sharp sound （使）作咔嗒声
   e.g. The key clicked in the lock and the door opened.
   She clicked off the light.
   Martha clicked her tongue.
2. to move with such a sound 咔嗒着运动
   e.g. Louise turned on her three-inch heels and clicked away.
3. [computing] to press (one of the buttons on a mouse) ［计算机］点击(鼠标键)
   e.g. Click the left mouse button twice.
   Children can click on a sentence to hear it read aloud.
4. [informal] to become suddenly clear or understandable（非正式）变得清楚、明白
   e.g. I wasn't used to such good treatment, and then it clicked: we were wearing suits.
   Suddenly everything clicked and I realized where I'd met him.

approach *v.*
1. to move towards or nearer to sb. or sth. 走近，接近
   e.g. As I approached the house, I noticed a light on upstairs.
   She heard footsteps approaching.
2. to ask sb. for sth., or ask them to do sth., especially when you are asking them for the first time or when you are not sure if they will do it（多指为提建议或有所请求而首次）找……商谈；向……接洽

e.g. Students should be able to approach teachers for advice.
The charity approached several stores about giving food aid.
I have already been approached by several other companies (= offered a job etc.).

3. (an event or a particular time) to come nearer and happen soon （未来时刻）临近
   e.g. She was then approaching the end of her career.
   The time is fast approaching when we will have to make a decision.

After Reading

READING COMPREHENSION TASKS

1. Read the following descriptions in the left column and put in the names of the corresponding learning types in the right column.

You like to work with sound and music. You typically can sing, play a musical instrument.	Aural (auditory-musical)
You like sports and exercise, and other physical activities such as gardening or woodworking.	Physical (kinesthetic)
You find it easy to express yourself, both in writing and verbally. You like playing on the meaning or sound of words.	Verbal (linguistic)
You like using your brain for logical and mathematical reasoning. You like working out strategies and using simulation.	Logical (mathematical)
You prefer using images, pictures, colors, and maps to organize information and communicate with others.	Visual (spatial)
You typically prefer learning in groups or classes, or you like to spend one-on-one time with a teacher or an instructor.	Social (interpersonal)
You like to spend time alone. You prefer to work on problems by retreating to somewhere quiet.	Solitary (intrapersonal)

2. Answer the following questions.

1) What kind of teaching methods does traditional schooling use?
   Traditional schooling used (and continues to use) mainly linguistic and logical teaching methods. It also uses a limited range of learning and teaching techniques. Many schools still rely on classroom and book-based teaching, much repetition, and pressured exams for reinforcement and review.

2) How are people who use less favoured learning styles treated under the traditional teaching methodology?
   Those who use less favoured learning styles often find themselves in lower classes, with various not-so-complimentary labels.

3) How do people of the visual style and the aural style differ from each other?
   People of the visual style prefer using images, pictures, colors and maps to organize information and communicate with others. In contrast, people of the aural style like to work with sound and music.

4) What do people of the verbal style like to do for a pastime?

   They love reading and writing. They like playing on the meaning or sound of words, such as in tongue twisters, rhymes, limericks and the like.

5) How do people of the physical style learn a new skill or topic?

   When they are learning a new skill or topic, they would prefer to "jump in" and play with the physical parts as soon as possible. They would prefer to pull an engine apart and put it back together, rather than reading or looking at diagrams about how it works.

6) Why would some people of the logical style occasionally annoy others?

   They like picking up logic flaws in other people's words, writing or actions, and they may point these out to people.

7) Is a person of the social style popular with people around him? Why?

   Yes. A person of the social style communicates well with other people, verbally and non-verbally. People listen to him or come to him for advice, and he is sensitive to their motivations, feelings or moods. He listens well and understands others' views.

8) How do people of the solitary style tackle problems and find solutions?

   People of the solitary style prefer to work on problems by retreating to somewhere quiet and working through possible solutions.

9) What do researchers use to identify the key areas of the brain responsible for each learning style?

   Researchers use brain-imaging technologies to identify the key areas of the brain responsible for each learning style.

3. Choose the best answer(s) to each of the following questions.

1) Which method of introduction is used in Text B?

   A. Quotation.

   B. Anecdote.

   C. Idea that is the opposite of the one to be developed.

   D. Broad, general statement narrowed to thesis statement.

2) What conclusion technique is used in Text B?

   A. Summary and additional information.

   B. Prediction or recommendation.

   C. Question.

   D. Quotation.

3) What is/are the major writing strategy/strategies that the author employs in Text B?

   A. Division and Classification.

   B. Comparison and Contrast.

   C. Exemplification.

   D. Definition.

4) What is the topic sentence of Paragraph 28?

   A. Your learning styles have more influence than you may realize.

   B. Your preferred styles guide the way you learn.

   C. They also change the way you internally represent experiences, the way you recall information, and even the words you choose.

   D. We explore more of these features in this chapter.

4. Explain the underlined parts in your own words.

1) You can easily visualize objects, plans and outcomes <u>in your mind's eye</u>. (Para. 5)
   in your imagination or mental view

2) … or a theme or jingle <u>pops into</u> your head without prompting. (Para. 7)
   emerges in; comes into

3) You like <u>playing on</u> the meaning or sound of words … (Para. 8)
   making use of

4) … as well as phrases you have <u>picked up</u> recently … (Para. 8)
   learned

5) You would prefer to <u>pull an engine apart</u> and put it back together … (Para. 12)
   separate an engine into pieces

6) You like creating agendas, itineraries, and <u>to-do lists</u> … (Para. 16)
   lists of tasks to perform

7) … and rank them before <u>putting them into action</u>. (Para. 16)
   carrying them out

8) You heighten your learning by <u>bouncing your thoughts off other people</u> … (Para. 20)
   discussing your ideas with other people in order to get their opinions

ORAL WORK

In TEXT B the author explains in details seven common learning styles. Now talk about some people you know, and decide which their main learning styles are.

The teacher can ask the students to work in groups first and then choose a few groups to present their opinions to the whole class.

TRANSLATION OF TEXT B

学习风格

1　很多人认识到，每个人都倾向于不同的学习风格和技巧。学习风格集合了人们学习的常见方式。每个人都是众多学习风格的混合体。一些人可能主要使用某一种学习风格，而很少使用其他类型。另一些人则可能发现他们在不同的场合使用不同的风格。并不存在什么正确的组合，个人风格也不会一成不变，你可能进一步拓展你所擅长的风格，也可能对原先非主要的风格感到越来越顺手。

2　使用多种风格以及"多种智力"来学习是一种相对较新的方法。这个方法是教育家们近来才开始认识到的。传统的学校教育(现在仍被沿袭)主要使用语言和逻辑的教学法，采纳有限的学习和教学技巧。很多学校仍然依赖课堂和书本为基础的教学模式，通过大量的重复、高强度的考试来强化和复习。结果是我们经常给那些采用这些学习风格和技巧的人贴上"聪明"的标签；而采用不受推崇的学习风格的人则会被排到低班，贴上了各种非赞赏性的标签。这会加剧积极和消极的变化，强化某个人是"聪明"或是"愚笨"的信念。

3　通过识别和理解自己的学习风格，你可以使用更适合自己的学习技巧。这会提升你的学习速度和质量。

4　学习风格包括以下几类：

视觉（空间）型

5　如果你使用视觉型风格，你倾向使用影像、图片、颜色和地图来组织信息并与其他人沟通。你轻易就能在头脑中想象出物体、计划、结果。你也有很好的空间感，因而方向感很强。你可以根据地图很容易地确定方位，很少迷路。从电梯里走出来时，你本能地知道朝那一边拐。

6　白板是你最好的朋友(或者一旦拿到，就会是你最好的朋友)。你喜欢素描、乱写、乱画，尤其是和颜色打交道。你善于打扮自己，具备颜色平衡能力(尽管并不总是如此)。

听觉（听觉—音乐）型

7　如果你使用的是听觉型风格，你愿意与声音和音乐打交道。你对音高和节奏有很好的感知力。你通常很会唱歌、弹奏乐器，或者识别不同乐器的声音。某种音乐能够唤起你强烈的情感。你会注意到电影、电视节目以及其他媒体的背景音乐。你经常发现自己会跟着一段音乐或者短曲哼哼或打拍子；或者有时一段主题曲或短曲不需提示就在你的脑子里突然出现。

言语（语言）型

8　言语型风格涉及书面和口头的话语。如果你使用这种风格，你会发现书面和口头表达都很容易。你喜欢阅读和写作，喜欢利用词语的意义或声音玩文字游戏，例如绕口令、押韵小诗、打油诗。你知道很多词语的意义，并时不时花些力气来寻找新词的意义。和其他人交流的时候，你会用上这些新近掌握的词汇及短语。

身体（运动）型

9　如果你更像身体型风格，你通常使用身体和触感来了解周围世界。你很可能喜欢体育和锻炼，以及其他的体力活动，如园艺和木匠活。你喜欢在运动时考虑议题、想法和问题。如果有什么烦心事，你宁愿去跑步或走路，而不是待在家里。

10　你对外面的物质世界更加敏感。你注意并欣赏各种质地，例如衣服料子和家具材质。你喜欢"把手弄脏"，制造模型或玩拼图。

11　你通常使用夸张的手势和其他身体语言来交流。你可能不介意站起来跳个舞，至少时机合适时不会拒绝。你喜欢主题公园里各种乘坐装置带来的动作体验，有时玩得太过火，身体受不了，只好干脆彻底放弃。

12　学习一个新技术或新题目时，你更喜欢"立即投入"，尽快实干起来。你更喜欢将引擎拆开，再组装起来，而不是阅读或者参考产品图解。

13　你一想到参加讲座，坐着听其他人讲话，就觉得讨厌。在这种情况下，你会躁动不安，或者坐不长久。你很想站起来走动走动。

逻辑（数学）型

14　如果你使用逻辑型风格，你喜欢用大脑来进行逻辑和数学推理。你可以轻易识别图案，看到似乎毫无意义的内容之间的关联。这也会促使你对信息进行分类和分组，加深学习或者理解。

15　你善于和数字打交道，能做复杂的运算。你牢记三角学和代数基础，可以做有一定难度的心算。

16　你通常系统地分析问题，喜欢创建流程为日后所用。你爱设立数字化的目标和预算，并跟踪进度。你喜欢创立日程、行程、任务单，通常在行动之前将它们编号并排序。

17　科学的思维方式意味着你经常利用逻辑例证或数据来支撑自己的观点。你总能挑出其他人说话、写作以及行动中存在的逻辑错误，并有可能当面指出(当然不总是令对方感到愉快)。

18　你喜欢制定策略，使用模型。你可能会喜欢脑筋急转弯、巴加门棋、国际象棋之类的游戏。你还可能喜欢沙丘魔堡II、星际争霸、帝国时代以及西德梅尔系列等电脑游戏。

社会（人际）型

19　如果你有很强的社会型风格，你同其他人的语言或非语言沟通都非常顺畅。人们听从你，或者从你那里获取建议。你对他们的动机、情感和情绪也有很好的感知。你善于倾听并理解他人观点。你享受指导他人、提供建议的过程。

20　你通常喜欢在课堂或小组的氛围下学习，或者喜欢以一对一的方式花时间和老师或导师沟通。你通过和别人讨论自己的想法并聆听他人的反馈来加强学习。你愿意和团队共同解决议题、想法和问题。你非常享受与和自己"投缘"或志同道合的一组人共事。

21　你愿意下课后逗留一会儿，和别人聊聊天。你喜欢社会活动甚于独处。你通常喜欢多人参与的游戏，例如打牌或棋类；当然还包括团体运动，如橄榄球、足球、篮球、棒球、排球和曲棍球。

独立（个体）型

22　如果你是独立型风格，你更私密、内省和独立。你专注力好，将思想和情感集中于手头的事。你对自己的想法非常清楚，会分析自己的多种所思所感。

23　你花时间自我分析，经常回忆过去的事件和曾采取的处理方式。你花时间思考和评价自己的成就和挑战，坚持写日志、日记或个人记录，以此来记录想法和事件。

24　你喜欢独处，有个人的爱好。你更喜欢到偏远的地方去旅游或度假，远离喧嚣。

25　你觉得了解自己；你独立思考，了解自己的思想。你可能参加过有关自我成长的研讨会，阅读自助书籍，或用其他方法来加深对自己的认知。

26　你喜欢躲到一个安静的地方处理问题和思考解决方案。有时你可能会花太多时间尝试独立解决问题，而如果和他人讨论，事情会更容易解决。

27　你喜欢制定计划，设立目标。你知道工作和人生的方向。你喜欢为自己工作，或者对此念念不忘。如果不知道目前的人生方向，你会感到很不满意。

28　你的学习风格深刻地影响着你，比你想象的更甚。你所喜欢的风格引导了你学习的方式。它们也改变着你内在表征经历的方式、回忆信息的方式，甚至所选择的词语。我们将在这一章更深入地探讨这些特性。

29　研究表明，每种学习风格使用不同的大脑部位。在学习过程中，更多的大脑参与会使我们对所学的知识记住更多。研究者利用人脑成像技术，已经能够发现负责每种学习风格的大脑关键区域所在。

INTEGRATED EXERCISES

1 PUBLIC SPEECH TRAINING

This is a radio address made on 15th September, 2001 by George W. Bush, his first radio speech after the 9/11 attacks. Listen to the speech and practice after the recording.

(The speech will be read once. The students listen and try to understand the meaning. They may listen again and practice after the speaker.)

Script

Good morning. This weekend I am engaged in extensive sessions with members of my National Security Council, as we plan a comprehensive assault on terrorism. This will be a different kind of conflict against a different kind of enemy.

This is a conflict without battlefields or beachheads, a conflict with opponents who believe they are invisible. Yet, they are mistaken. They will be exposed, and they will discover what others in the past have learned: Those who make war against the United States have chosen their own destruction. Victory against terrorism will not take place in a single battle, but in a series of decisive actions against terrorist organizations and those who harbor and support them.

We are planning a broad and sustained campaign to secure our country and eradicate the evil of terrorism. And we are determined to see this conflict through. Americans of every faith and background are committed to this goal.

Yesterday I visited the site of the destruction in New York City and saw an amazing spirit of sacrifice and patriotism and defiance. I met with rescuers who have worked past exhaustion, who cheered for our country and the great cause we have entered.

In Washington, D.C., the political parties and both Houses of Congress have shown a remarkable unity, and I'm deeply grateful. A terrorist attack designed to tear us apart has instead bound us together as a nation. Over the past few days, we have learned much about American courage — the courage of firefighters and police officers who suffered so great a loss, the courage of passengers aboard United 93 who may well have fought with the hijackers and saved many lives on the ground.

Now we honor those who died, and prepare to respond to these attacks on our nation. I will not settle for a token act. Our response must be sweeping, sustained, and effective. We have much to do, and much to ask of the American people.

You will be asked for your patience — for the conflict will not be short. You will be asked for resolve — for the conflict will not be easy. You will be asked for your strength, because the course to victory may be long.

In the past week, we have seen the American people at their very best everywhere in America. Citizens have come together to pray, to give blood, to fly our country's flag. Americans are coming together to share their grief and gain strength from one another.

Great tragedy has come to us, and we are meeting it with the best that is in our country, with courage and concern for others: because this is America. This is who we are. This is what our enemies hate and have attacked. And this is why we will prevail.

Thank you for listening.

2 DICTATION

Listen to the following passage and write it down. The passage will be read four times. During the first reading, which will be done at normal speed, listen and try to understand the meaning. For the second and third readings, the passage will be read sentence by sentence, or phrase by phrase, with intervals of 15 seconds. Write down what you hear. The last reading will be done at normal speed again and during this time you should check your work.

Script

The lifelong process of acquiring skills, information, and knowledge is called learning. / Many scientists now define learning as the organization of behaviour based on experience. / There are other definitions of learning because there are / many theories about how humans and other animals learn. / But all learning involves an interplay between an individual's brain, / the rest of the nervous system, and the environment — the surrounding world. / An 18th-century philosopher, David Hume, stated that / all knowledge comes through observation and experience. / Other thinkers disagree with him on this understanding of knowledge; / but when his assertion is applied to learning, it certainly seems to be true. / Observation and experience come to a person through perception / — becoming aware of something by means of the senses of seeing, hearing, smelling, touching, and tasting. / Without these senses people would be like inanimate objects, unable to learn.

3 VOCABULARY STUDY

Task One

Replace the underlined words with the correct form of the words in the box. You may need to make other changes.

1) You wouldn't believe all the dust and __fuzz__ that gathers behind the computer.
2) He argued that the __reproaches__ were unfair.
3) She was an authentic __prodigy__, first appearing with an orchestra at age 7.
4) We drank Turkish coffee out of __dainty__ china cups.
5) Bob presses a button, and his bed rises in the back at a __slant__.
6) It is 40 percent more expensive than coal, and there is an __abundance__ of alternative energy sources.
7) I had never met Graham but I __pictured__ him as a pale, thin young man wearing glasses.
8) The referee started to blow his whistle and __bellow__ at me.
9) Billy is a very __willful__ little boy who's constantly being punished for not doing as he's told.
10) Being accused of theft was just one of the __indignities__ I suffered under my last employer.

Task Two

Put the proper form of the words in the corresponding blanks.

1) He fell in love, via a __prodigious__ e-mail correspondence, with another academic whom he had met fleetingly at a conference. (prodigy)
2) Once the best you could hope for was a 50-year-old prima __ballerina__ who sometimes starred at the local opera house. (ballet)

3) It is __lamentable__ that Cassidy will not get to coach his team next season. (lament)
4) Many working women have little time for __reflection__. (reflect)
5) I was supposed to be giving a __presentation__ that morning to some colleagues from the Japanese division. (present)
6) Can you image the sheer __boredom__ of doing the same job day in, day out for fifty years? (bore)
7) The dentist's office sent you a __reminder__ about your appointment next week. (remind)
8) How can viruses induce cells to enter the cycle of rapid __multiplication__ that then leads on to the development of a tumour? (multiply)
9) The situation in the country's poorest region remains volatile and highly __unpredictable__. (predict)
10) The soldier received a parcel containing an __assortment__ of shirts, biscuits, and canned food. (assorted)

Task Three

Fill in the blanks with appropriate prepositions or adverbs.

1) He took the worst jobs he could find __on__ purpose, and then wrote a book about his experiences.
2) The injury may keep him out of football __for__ good.
3) I see developing trees with only two main growth arteries where one has been lopped __off__, leaving an odd-looking lopsided thing.
4) Holding her breath and moving stealthily __on__ tiptoe, she began to ease her way towards the exit.
5) The government introduced measures to prop __up__ the stock market.
6) He kept his disease __at__ bay, changed his diet and actually got bigger and stronger.
7) Can you drag yourself __away from__ the TV for a minute?
8) Some of the kids were poking fun __at__ Judy because of the way she was dressed.
9) A win on Saturday will assure them __of__ promotion to Division One.
10) Recent events have put a new slant __on__ the president's earlier comments.

Task Four

Fill in the following blanks with appropriate words from the box.

Learning affects an individual's behaviour in a number of ways. One of the most obvious ways is the acquiring of a skill. If a person learns to 1) __tie__ shoelaces, ride a bicycle, or swim, that skill will remain with him or her and will be improved by 2) __practice__. Other skills — playing the violin or 3) __programming__ a computer — are more difficult to 4) __acquire__ and will be virtually lost if they are not practiced frequently. Skills like cooking or driving a car may be partially lost through disuse 5) __but__ may be regained fairly 6) __easily__. One form of learning is called conditioning. If a certain signal is 7) __linked__ with a condition, and is repeated a number of times, there will be an automatic learned response 8) __to__ the signal that is just the same as if the condition were present. For 9) __example__, the sudden sound of a nearby car horn will make people automatically jump 10) __for__ safety without stopping to see if a 11) __car__ is actually present. Phobias are also examples of 12) __conditioning__. A person may develop a fear of something quite 13) __harmless__ because it has become associated 14) __with__ a condition that is threatening. Conditioning is sometimes deliberately used in medical 15) __therapy__ as "behavior modification" to break harmful habits or form desirable new ones.

4 GRAMMAR FOCUS

Read the following passage, underline the one mistake in each line and write the correction after the bracketed number.

A number of colleges and universities have announced steep
tuition increases for next year — much steeper than the current
very low rate of inflation. They say the increases are needed
because of a loss in value of university endowments heavily <u>investing</u>   1) invested
in common stock. I am skeptical. A business firm chooses the price
that maximizes its net revenues, <u>irrespective</u> fluctuations in   2) irrespective of
income; and increasingly the outlook of universities in the United
States is indistinguishable from <u>those</u> of business firms. The rise in   3) that
tuitions may reflect the <u>fact</u> economic uncertainty increases the   4) fact that
demand for education. The biggest cost of being in <u>the school</u> is   5) school
foregoing income from a job (this is <u>primary</u> a factor in graduate-   6) primarily
and professional-school tuition): the <u>poor</u> one's job prospects, the   7) poorer
more sense it makes to reallocate time from the job market to
education, in order to make oneself more marketable.
The ways <u>which</u> university make themselves attractive to   8) in which
students include soft majors, student evaluations <u>for</u> teachers, giving   9) of
students a governance role, and <u>eliminate</u> required courses.   10) eliminating
Sky-<u>low</u> tuitions have caused universities to regard their students   11) high
as customers. Just as business firms sometimes collude to <u>shorten</u> the   12) minimize/lessen
rigors of competition, universities collude to minimize the cost to
them of the athletes whom they recruit in order to stimulate alumni
donations, for the best athletes now <u>seldom</u> bypass higher education in 13) often
order to obtain salaries earlier from professional teams. And until
they were stopped by the antitrust authorities, the Ivy League
schools colluded to limit competition for the best students, by
agreeing not to award scholarships <u>at</u> the basis of merit rather than   14) on
purely of need — just like business firms agreeing not to give
discounts <u>on</u> their best customer.   15) to

1) 分词错误：表被动应该用过去分词。
2) 词组搭配错误：形容词irrespective后应该用介词of。
3) 指示代词错误：前文outlook为单数，用于后照应的指示代词应该为单数that。
4) 同位语从句结构错误：同位语从句要求从属连词that不可省略。
5) 定冠词错误：该处表达泛指意义，因此不需要使用表特指关系的定冠词。
6) 副词错误：该处要求用副词，表示mainly，而非形容词。
7) 比较级错误：要符合the more … the more …的比较级结构，该处应该是poorer。
8) 从句结构错误：短语结构是in … way，因此在相应从句中不能省略in。
9) 介词错误：evaluation后面接介词of。

10) 动词形式错误：该处要求动名词结构作宾语成分。
11) 复合名词错误：复合名词应该是sky-high而不是sky-low。
12) 动宾搭配错误：shorten和rigors不匹配，合适的动词应该是minimize或lessen。
13) 副词错误：从上下文看，此处应该用often，而不是seldom。
14) 介词错误：应该是on the basis of，意为"在……的基础上"。
15) 介词错误：应该是give sth. to sb.，意为"给某人某物"。

5 TRANSLATION

Task One
Translate the following paragraph from English into Chinese.

我现在有了一套自己学习外语的方法，该方法建立在对人的思想感情深刻了解基础之上。我想在这里把这种方法介绍给读者，不过稍有保留。第一件要做的事就是到说这种语言的国家的首都去，买一本语法书和两本红封面的小字典，然后再买一张火车票。这张火车票可以让你乘到远离首都的地方，在那里你完全听不到本族语的声音，去个避暑胜地就更好了。这样做是因为你可以玩得很开心，而且你需要伴儿。在火车上，在去避暑胜地的路上，你得做一些艰苦的工作。它是我的学习方法所要求的唯一工作，而且要求你做透。你得学会这门语言中"名词"、"形容词"、"副词"、"动词"、"分词"、"连接词"、"代词"和"介词"分别怎么说。

Task Two
Translate the following paragraphs from Chinese into English.

Are things in the world some difficult and some easy? Given action, difficult things may become easy; otherwise easy things become difficult. Are man's studies some difficult and some easy? Given application, difficult studies may become easy; otherwise easy studies may become difficult.

Being obtuse, I am surpassed by others in intelligence. Being mediocre, I am outstripped by others in ability. But if I work hard on my learning with perseverance till I achieve success, then no one would make much of my obtuseness and mediocrity. Being clear, I have twice as much intelligence as others; being adroit, I have twice as much ability as others. However, if I do not put them to use, they make no difference as compared with obtuseness and mediocrity. So, it was Zeng Shen, an obtuse disciple of Confucius, who succeeded in passing on his teachings to the future. Such being the case, can we say that there is anything immutable concerning the influence of obtuseness and mediocrity on the one hand and cleverness and adroitness on the other?

6 CLASSROOM INTERACTION

Activity A   Listening

1) Scientific studies of language learning show that young children can easily learn multiple languages.
2) Three.
   a. Exposure to language should be systematic and regular.
   b. Making the learning enjoyable will enhance the process of learning.
   c. Repetition stores the language information firmly in children's memory.
3) Answers may vary.

Script

Children are primed to learn. They watch and listen. They imitate and practice — again and again, rolling sounds and words off their tongues repeatedly. Scientific studies of language learning show that young children can easily learn multiple languages. University of California-Los Angeles professor of linguistics Susan Curtis says, "The power to learn language is so great in the young child that it doesn't matter how many languages you throw their way. They can learn as many spoken languages as you can allow them to hear systematically and regularly.

Maybe you can't afford to hire a bilingual nanny or send your infant to a multilingual day-care centre. But you can create an environment in which your child can learn the fundamentals of two or more languages.

First of all, recognize that exposure to language should be systematic and regular, according to Curtis. It's best for each bilingual parent to speak only one language to the child. This creates an inherent need to learn two languages in the home. Nothing motivates better than necessity to learn. Making the learning enjoyable will enhance the process. Fun activities done within the context of hearing the foreign language create pleasant associations in the listener's mind. Finally, repetition stores the language information firmly in their memory. Play the game, sing the song, and recite the poem over and over — until the words and sounds roll off their tongues effortlessly.

The purpose of language, of course, is communication. So the sounds, words and arrangement of words are used as components of communication, and, therefore, are taught to toddlers as functional building blocks of the language.

Activity B   Mini-speech

The teacher can ask the students to work in groups first and then choose a few students to present their mini-speeches to the whole class.

Activity C   Discussion

The teacher can take this opportunity to introduce to the students the proper ways of reading effectively. The teacher can also recommend to the students Francis Bacon's "Of Studies" to emphasize the importance of active reading.

Of Studies

Francis Bacon

Studies serve for delight, for ornament, and for ability. Their chief use for delight, is in privateness and retiring; for ornament, is in discourse; and for ability, is in the judgment, and disposition of business. For expert men can execute, and perhaps judge of particulars, one by one; but the general counsels, and the plots and marshalling of affairs, come best, from those that are learned. To spend too much time in studies is sloth; to use them too much for ornament, is affectation; to make judgment wholly by their rules, is the humor of a scholar. They perfect nature, and are perfected by experience: for natural abilities are like natural plants, that need pruning, by study; and studies themselves, do give forth directions too much at large, except they be bounded in by experience. Crafty men condemn studies, simple men admire them, and wise men use them; for they teach not their own use; but that is a wisdom without them, and above them, won by observation. Read not to contradict and confute; nor to believe and take for granted; nor to find talk and discourse; but to weigh and consider. Some books are to be tasted, others to be swallowed, and some few to be chewed and digested; that is, some books are to be read only in parts; others to be read, but not curiously; and some few to be read wholly, and with diligence and attention. Some books also may be read by deputy, and extracts made of them by others; but that would be only in the less important arguments, and the meaner sort of books, else distilled books are like common distilled waters, flashy things. Reading maketh a full man; conference a ready man; and writing an exact man. And therefore, if a man write little, he had need have a great memory; if he confer little, he had need have a present wit: and if he read little, he had need have much cunning, to seem to know, that he doth not. Histories make men wise; poets witty; the mathematics subtle; natural philosophy deep; moral grave; logic and rhetoric able to contend. *Abeunt studia in mores* [Studies pass into and influence manners]. Nay, there is no stond or impediment in the wit, but may be wrought out by fit studies; like as diseases of the body may have appropriate exercises. Bowling is good for the stone and reins; shooting for the lungs and breast; gentle walking for the stomach; riding for the head; and the like. So if a man's wit be wandering, let him study the mathematics; for in demonstrations, if his wit be called away never so little, he must begin again. If his wit be not apt to distinguish or find differences, let him study the Schoolmen; for they are *cymini sectores* [splitters of hairs]. If he be not apt to beat over matters, and to call up one thing to prove and illustrate another, let him study the lawyers' cases. So every defect of the mind, may have a special receipt.

WRITING

Writing Skills: Development by Classification

This unit discusses classification, which means that the writer tries to put a topic/subject into different classes, or types, and explain their features one by one. The teacher may discuss with the students the difference between classification and comparison and contrast: classification focuses on creating a general picture of the topic to give readers a global understanding, while comparison and contrast mainly deals with the similarities and differences between some, but mainly two, topics.

The students may have had much experience in putting things into different categories, so for a warm-up the teacher may start with a familiar topic and ask the students to divide it. For example, they can try to classify their classmates or teachers. This kind of discussion will prepare the students for their succeeding writing task. The sample on students' purposes of taking sports activities can serve as an example.

Reference answers to the questions after the sample:

1. This essay studies the students taking part in sports. The writer chooses their purpose as the standard of classification.
2. The writer finds three categories. They are "study-oriented sports participants", "fun-oriented sports participants", and "beauty-oriented sports participants", which can be found at the end of paragraphs 2, 3 and 4 respectively.
3. This essay makes use of a typical essay structure. The first paragraph is an introduction, the last paragraph a conclusion, and the other paragraphs the body. The structure is very clear.
4. The writer has put some transitional connections between the body paragraphs, i.e., the first sentences of paragraphs 3 and 4. These sentences make the essay easy to read.

A common problem in the students' writing of classification is the misuse of standard of classification. As in comparison and contrast, choosing a clear and suitable criterion is key to success. Usually, writers need several criteria for comparison and contrast, but only one for classification. The students also need to make sure that the criterion does not cause any overlapping, i.e., there should not be any item that may belong to more than one category. After deciding on the criterion, the students need to be aware that they have to stick to it. The teacher may draw the students' attention to this point if necessary.

The teacher may also emphasize that classification serves as a method of organization; what is important for an essay is its theme. The students need to be told that they should not classify simply for classifying's sake.

Writing Assignment

1. Can you explain the major difference between comparison and contrast essays and classification essays?

An essay of comparison and contrast usually focuses on the similarities or differences of items in a particular topic, while an essay of classification mainly tries to set items in a topic apart by applying a certain standard. Although there will be comparison or contrast to some extent, the central task of classification is to show readers how many groups the items in question can be put into, and what their respective features are. In this way, readers can see a whole picture of the topic.

2. Read the following essay, and answer the questions that follow.

   1) This essay studies unusual shoppers in a supermarket. The title could be "Unusual Shoppers at the Piggly Wiggly". The students are encouraged to suggest other titles so long as they pinpoint the topic under discussion.
   2) The writer classifies the shoppers according to their peculiar behaviour. He finds three categories.
   3) Generally speaking, this essay is a quite good one. It succeeds in focusing on the topic, with no irrelevant ideas. It also indicates the criterion and number of categories clearly, and the description of the three types of shoppers is vivid and detailed. There is, however, one minor problem, i.e., the writer does not provide a clear name for the second type of shoppers. Maybe he could use such a name as "the lonesome elderly shopper" to highlight their feature.

3. Write an essay of classification on one of the following topics.

   Answers may vary.

TEXT A   Do Colleges Have a Future?

Before Reading

The purpose of this section is to arouse the students' interest in the theme of the unit, reactivate their relevant background knowledge or elicit their opinions on the related topics, so as to better prepare them for the succeeding tasks.

Before Reading activities can be organized as group work so that the students share with each other their knowledge about higher education and education in the developing world.

Background Information

1 Higher Education

Education in the largest sense is any act or experience that has a formative effect on the mind, character or physical ability of an individual. In its technical sense, education is the process by which society deliberately transmits its accumulated knowledge, skills and values from one generation to another.

Teachers in educational institutions direct the education of students and might draw on many subjects, including reading, writing, mathematics, science and history. This process is sometimes called schooling when referring to the education of teaching only a certain subject, usually as professors at institutions of higher learning. There is also education in fields for those who want specific vocational skills, such as those required to be a pilot. In addition, there is an array of education possible at the informal level, such as in museums and libraries, with the Internet and in life experience. Many non-traditional education options are now available and continue to evolve.

Higher education, also called tertiary, third stage, or post secondary education, is the non-compulsory educational level that follows the completion of a school providing a secondary education, such as a high school, secondary school. Tertiary education is normally taken to include undergraduate and postgraduate education, as well as vocational education and training. Colleges and universities are the main institutions that provide tertiary education. Collectively, these are sometimes known as tertiary institutions. Tertiary education generally results in the receipt of certificates, diplomas, or academic degrees. Higher education includes teaching, research and social services activities of universities, and within the realm of teaching, it includes both the undergraduate level and the postgraduate level. Higher education generally involves work towards a degree-level or foundation degree qualification. In most developed countries a high proportion of the population now enter higher education at some time in their lives. Higher education is therefore very important to national economies, both as a significant industry in its own right, and as a source of trained and educated personnel for the rest of the economy.

2 Education in the Developing World

In developing countries, the number and seriousness of the problems faced are naturally greater. People in more remote or agrarian areas are sometimes unaware of the importance of education. However, many countries have an active Ministry of Education, and in many subjects, such as foreign language learning, the degree of education is actually much higher than in industrialized countries; for example, it is not at all uncommon for students in many developing countries to be reasonably fluent in multiple foreign languages, whereas this is much more of a rarity in the supposedly "more educated" countries where much of the population is in fact monolingual.

Universal primary education is one of the eight Millennium Development Goals and great improvements have been achieved in the past decade, yet a great deal remains to be done. Researchers at the Overseas Development Institute indicate the main obstacles to greater funding from donors include: donor priorities, aid architecture, and the lack of evidence and advocacy. Additionally, Transparency International has identified corruption in the education sector as a major stumbling block to achieving universal primary education in Africa. Furthermore, demand in the developing world for improved educational access is not as high as one would expect as governments avoid the recurrent costs involved and there is economic pressure on those parents who prefer their children making money in the short term over any long-term benefits of education. Recent studies on child labor and poverty have suggested that when poor families reach a certain economic threshold where families are able to provide for their basic needs, parents return their children to school. This has been found to be true, even if the potential economic value of the children's work has increased since their return to school.

A lack of good universities, and a low acceptance rate for good universities, is evident in countries with a high population density. In some countries, there are uniform, over-structured, inflexible centralized programs from a central agency that regulates all aspects of education. Due to globalization, increased pressure on students in curricular activities, India is now developing technologies that will skip land based phone and Internet lines. Instead, India launched EDUSAT, an education satellite that can reach more of the country at a greatly reduced cost. There is also an initiative started by the OLPC foundation, a group out of MIT Media Lab and supported by several major corporations to develop a $100 laptop to deliver educational software. The laptops are widely available as of 2008. The laptops are sold at cost or given away based on donations. These will enable developing countries to give their children a digital education, and help close the digital divide across the world.

In Africa, NEPAD has launched an "e-school programme" to provide all 600,000 primary and high schools with computer equipment, learning materials and Internet access within 10 years. Private groups, like The Church of Jesus Christ of Latter-day Saints, are working to give more individuals opportunities to receive education in developing countries through such programs as the Perpetual Education Fund. An International Development Agency project called nabuur.com, started with the support of former American President Bill Clinton, uses the Internet to allow co-operation by individuals on issues of social development.

Reading

Text Analysis

- ### Text Summary

This article follows the typical structure of an argumentative essay: first, it presents the background material to contextualize the topic; it then introduces the thesis, discusses the thesis and provides support/examples for the claim; finally, it synthesizes the discussion and draws the conclusion. The title of the article poses a question to readers as to whether colleges have a future. The author sets out the context of the topic by comparing colleges with a knowledge factory, which is breaking down in the 21st century. In response to such a problem, the author claims that colleges need to make a paradigm shift. He then concludes the article by explaining the significance of such a shift.

- ### Text Organization

Paragraphs 1-5: introduction	Many colleges are like a knowledge factory, which is breaking down in the 21st century. Competition has emerged in the process of the transformation to the knowledge society. If colleges do not change, they will not survive.
Paragraphs 6-9: body part 1	Under this circumstance, colleges need to make a paradigm shift and transform from the Instruction Paradigm to the Learning Paradigm. Major changes in the way colleges do business are both desirable and inevitable. There are excellent models of colleges that have been developing the "assessment-as-learning" approach and discussing major restructuring.
Paragraphs 10-11: body part 2	Nonetheless, higher education is in deep crisis. A very important part of our society would be lost if colleges diminish because they hold the place of liberal education and remain the institutional focus of the ideal.
Paragraph 12: conclusion	Changing the paradigm may seem a daunting task but the reason for the survival of the ideal of liberal education is that it addresses the need to nurture the heart and mind of the young people and set them on a course that offers them maturity and wisdom.

- ### Text Features

The text begins with a simile(比喻): many colleges of the postwar period are like a knowledge factory. Simile is a figure of speech in which an expression is used to refer to something else in order to suggest a similarity. In the text, "knowledge factory" is used to suggest the "assembly line" that colleges have, just like that in a factory. Colleges have an assembly line of courses and instructors guide the students along this line of knowledge.

The text uses a number of subordinate clauses(从句) and appositives(同位语) to introduce complex ideas (including the attributive clause, adverbial clause, subject clause and object clause).

- Attributive clause(定语从句)
  (1) … private employers who need skilled employees have found that …
  (2) Hence many providers can compete to serve students who were formerly too distant.
- Adverbial clause(状语从句)
  … if we contrast the glacial rate at which colleges and universities seem inclined to change with the lightning speed with which the society they serve is transforming itself, we must be disturbed by the

contrast.
- Subject clause(主语从句)
    (1) What counts is what students learn.
    (2) That the mission of colleges is to produce learning should be fairly noncontroversial …
- Object clause(宾语从句)

  The shift to the Learning Paradigm would require that colleges begin to take learning seriously, to assess and measure it, and to take responsibility for producing it.
- Appositive(同位语)

  Alverno College in Milwaukee has for decades been developing "assessment-as-learning", an approach that seeks to both monitor and guide students' development towards the mastery …

This article is also characterized by its adroit use of parallel sentences(并列结构) to introduce ideas that are of equal importance. In the parallel construction, the form and the content of language need to be consistent and identical. The purpose is to achieve a reinforced effect. For example:

(1) They hold the place of liberal education, of education for liberty, of the kind of experience through which children grow into citizens, through which men and women learn the exercise of the freedom that is tempered by choosing responsibility.

(2) … it addresses an ongoing need, the need to nurture in the young the development of both heart and mind, the need to set young people on a course that offers not just facility but maturity, not just cleverness but wisdom.

- **Key Sentences**

1. To put that end in its proper place would be to embrace what is called "the Learning Paradigm". (Para. 6)

This sentence uses infinitive both as subject (*to put that end in its proper place*) and predicative (*to embrace what is called "the Learning Paradigm"*). Infinitive can also be used as an attributive, object or adverbial in a sentence. For example:

A: He has a lot of questions to ask. (attributive)
B: He hates to be called by that nickname. (object)
C: She searched the top of the hill and stopped to rest on a big rock by the side of the path. (adverbial)

2. Nevertheless, they will increasingly take on teaching themselves. (Para. 10)

Nevertheless and *nonetheless* are adverbs meaning "despite the fact". These adverbs are used to connect ideas and make them coherent and logic. For example:

A: The book is too long but, *nevertheless*, informative and entertaining.
B: The problems are not serious. *Nevertheless*, we shall need to tackle them soon.

3. Should we, after all, care? What matter if many of our colleges pass away or diminish into support institutions for market-driven forces that can adapt more flexibly to the needs of a changing world? What would be lost? Perhaps not much. Perhaps a great deal. (Para. 11)

The author uses three interrogative sentences that comprise a parallel structure. These three sentences are called rhetorical questions, which is a figure of speech in the form of a question posed for persuasion. It is a question asked to emphasize rather than to obtain information. It is a statement regarding one's opinion of the issue addressed rather than a genuine request to know. It is a device used by the writer to assert or deny an idea. The effectiveness of rhetorical questions in argument comes from their dramatic quality. They suggest a dialogue, especially when the writer both asks and answers the question himself, as if he were playing two parts on the stage.

New Words and Expressions

specialized /ˈspeʃəlaɪzd/ *a.* designed or developed for a particular purpose or area of knowledge 专用的；专门的；专业的
e.g. specialized equipment
specialized skills

bolt /bəʊlt/ *v.* to add an extra part or feature 增加内容
e.g. Other insurers will allow you to bolt on critical illness cover to standard life cover.

fragment /ˈfræɡmənt/ *n.* a small part of sth. that has broken off or comes from sth. larger 碎片；片段
e.g. The police found fragments of glass near the scene.
I overheard a fragment of their conversation.

at a steady pace at a regular tempo 节奏稳定地
e.g. We walked at a steady pace along the shore.
The changes are happening at a steady pace.

chassis /ˈʃæsɪ/ *n.* the frame that a vehicle is built on (车辆的)底盘，底座
e.g. The car's lightweight chassis is made from aluminum sheets.
We need to have the chassis changed as it is broken.

narrowly /ˈnærəʊlɪ/ *ad.* in a limited way 狭窄地；狭隘地
e.g. a narrowly interpreted law
a narrowly defined task

fungible /ˈfʌndʒɪbl/ *a.* interchangeable 可替换的
e.g. Since fruits and vegetables are regarded as fungible in this diet, you are allowed a total of five servings of either or both.
fungible commodities

fracture /ˈfræktʃə/ *v.* break or crack 断裂；折断；破裂
e.g. He suffered a badly fractured arm.
They spoke a sort of fractured German.

dedicate /ˈdedɪkeɪt/ *v.* to set apart for a definite use 专门用于……
e.g. They decided to dedicate the money to their family vacation fund.
The fund is dedicated to the people who suffered from the earthquake.

coherent /kəʊˈhɪərənt/ *a.* (of ideas, thoughts, arguments, etc.) logical and well organized; easy to understand and clear (看法、思想、论点等)合乎逻辑的，有条理的；清楚易懂的
e.g. a coherent explanation
a coherent policy for the transport system

break down to stop working because of a fault 出故障，坏掉
e.g. The telephone system has broken down.
The car broke down on the freeway.

sophisticated /səˈfɪstɪkeɪtɪd/ *a.* (of a machine, system, etc.) clever and complicated in the way that it works or is presented (机器、体系等)复杂巧妙的；先进的；精密的
e.g. highly sophisticated computer system
Medical techniques are becoming more sophisticated all the time.

bring into existence to come into being 使……产生；使……出现
e.g. The advertisements are intended to bring into existence the demand for the product.
The President has announced a plan to bring more new jobs into existence.

corporation /ˌkɔːpəˈreɪʃən/ *n.* a large business company 大公司
e.g. multinational corporations
He has been working for this corporation for many years.

burgeon /ˈbɜːdʒən/ *v.* to begin to grow or develop rapidly 激增；迅速发展
e.g. The market for collectibles has burgeoned in recent years.
Love burgeoned between them.

contemporary /kənˈtempərərɪ/ *a.* belonging to the present time 现代的
e.g. contemporary art
life in contemporary Britain

be bound to to be confined to, be restricted to 局限于
e.g. The discussion about this regulation is

bound to only several schools in this area.
The "No Smoking" ban was said to be bound to only certain venues.

hence /hens/ *ad.* for this reason 因此，由此
e.g. We suspect they are trying to hide something, hence the need for an independent inquiry.
The company lost a great deal of money. Hence the CEO was asked to resign.

formerly /ˈfɔːməlɪ/ *ad.* in earlier times 以前，从前
e.g. I learnt that the house had formerly been an inn.
The European Union was formerly called the European Community.

wither /ˈwɪðə/ *v.* to become less or weaker, especially before disappearing completely 萎缩，渐渐破灭或消失
e.g. All our hopes withered away.
This country is in danger of allowing its industrial base to wither away.

blaze /bleɪz/ *n.* a sudden show of very strong feeling (感情的)迸发；发泄
e.g. a blaze of anger
a blaze of passion

acrimony /ˈækrɪmənɪ/ *n.* angry bitter feelings or words (态度、言辞)尖刻；讥讽
e.g. The dispute was settled without acrimony.
She responded with such acrimony that he never brought the subject up again.

fulminate /ˈfʌlmɪneɪt/ *v.* to criticize sb./sth. angrily 愤怒谴责，怒斥
e.g. I had to listen to Michael fulminating against the government.
The editorial fulminated against the proposed tax increase.

senate /ˈsenɪt/ *n.* the group of people who control a university 大学理事会，大学评议会
e.g. the senate of London University

thrive /θraɪv/ *v.* to become and continue to be successful, strong, healthy, etc. 兴旺发达，繁荣
e.g. New businesses thrive in this area.
These plants thrive with relatively little sunlight.

in some cases in some situations 在某些情况下
e.g. In some cases, people have had to wait several weeks for an appointment.
The company only dismisses its employees in some cases.

implicit /ɪmˈplɪsɪt/ *a.* suggested without being directly expressed 含蓄的，不直接言明的
e.g. Implicit in his speech was the assumption that they were guilty.
implicit criticism

fundamentally /ˌfʌndəˈmentəlɪ/ *ad.* in every way that is important; completely 根本上；完全地
e.g. The two approaches are fundamentally different.
They remained fundamentally opposed to the plan.

mistake…for to think wrongly that sb./sth. is sb./sth. else 把……错当成
e.g. I think you must be mistaking me for someone else.
I mistook him for his father.

confuse…with to think wrongly that sb./sth. is sb./sth. else (将……)混淆，混同
e.g. Be sure not to confuse quantity with quality.

trivial /ˈtrɪvɪəl/ *a.* not important or serious; not worth considering 不重要的；微不足道的
e.g. a trivial detail
I know it sounds trivial but I am worried about it.

noncontroversial /ˌnɒnˌkɒntrəˈvɜːʃəl/ *a.* not causing, or not likely to cause, any disagreement 不会引起争议的；一致的
e.g. This is a noncontroversial issue.
a noncontroversial decision

consistent /kənˈsɪstənt/ *a.* in agreement with sth. 与……一致
e.g. The results are entirely consistent with our earlier research.
What the witness said in court was not consistent with the statement he made to the police.

administrator /ədˈmɪnɪstreɪtə/ *n.* a person whose job is to manage and organize the public or business affairs of a company or an institution (公司、机构的)管理人员，行政人员
e.g. a hospital administrator
She works as a school administrator.

assess /əˈses/ *v.* to make a judgment about the nature or quality of sb./sth. 评估，评定
e.g. It is difficult to assess the effects of these changes.
The young men were assessed as either safe or unsafe drivers.

graduate /ˈɡrædʒʊət/ *n.* a person who has a

university degree 大学毕业生
e.g. a graduate in history
a graduate from this university

transition /træn'zɪʃən/ *n.* the process of a period of changing from one state or condition to another 过渡；变革，变迁
e.g. We need to ensure a smooth transition from the old system to the new one.
the transition from school to full-time work

principal /'prɪnsəpl/ *a.* most important, main 最重要的，主要的
e.g. The principal reason for this omission is lack of time.
New roads will link the principal cities of the area.

certificate /sə'tɪfɪkət/ *n.* an official document that may be used to prove that the facts it states are true 证明；证书
e.g. a birth certificate
a marriage certificate

mastery /'mɑːstərɪ/ *n.* great knowledge about or understanding of a particular thing 精通；熟练掌握
e.g. She has mastery of several languages.
We were impressed by her mastery of the subject.

a set of a group of 一组；一系列
e.g. The doctor said that he hadn't seen a particular set of symptoms before.
We need to establish a new set of priorities.

reward…with to give sth. to sb. because they have done sth. good, worked hard, etc. 奖励，奖赏
e.g. She started singing to the child and was rewarded with a smile.
He rewarded us with a lot of money for helping him.

rigorous /'rɪgərəs/ *a.* demanding that particular rules, processes, etc. be strictly followed 严格的；严厉的
e.g. The work failed to meet their rigorous standards.
rigorous controls

chancellor /'tʃɑːnsələ/ *n.* the head of a university 大学校长
e.g. He has been the chancellor of this university for four years.

restructuring /riː'strʌktʃərɪŋ/ *n.* the organization of a system or a company in a new and different way 调整结构；改组；重建
e.g. The company underwent restructuring and 1500 workers lost their jobs.
We need to talk about the restructuring of the Humanities Department.

glacial /'gleɪsjəl/ *a.* happening or moving extremely slowly 极其缓慢的
e.g. The progress on the bill has been glacial.
The work proceeded at a glacial pace.

inclined /ɪn'klaɪnd/ *a.* tending to do sth., likely to do sth. 有……倾向的，很可能的
e.g. He is inclined to be lazy.
They will be more inclined to listen if you don't shout.

lightning /'laɪtnɪŋ/ *a.* very quick 极快的
e.g. a lightning attack

undergraduate /ˌʌndə'grædʒʊət/ *n.* a university or college student who is studying for their first degree 本科生
e.g. a first-year undergraduate
an undergraduate majoring in physics

foresee /fɔː'siː/ *v.* to think sth. is going to happen in the future, to know about sth. before it happens 预料；预知
e.g. We do not foresee any problems.
The extent of the damage could not have been foreseen.

relic /'relɪk/ *n.* an object or a tradition that has survived from a period of time that no longer exists 遗风；遗迹
e.g. The building stands as the last remaining relic of the town's cotton industry.
During the dig, the archeological team found some relics from the Stone Age.

uncontrollable /ˌʌnkən'trəʊləbl/ *a.* too strong or violent to be controlled 无法控制的
e.g. I was suddenly overcome with an uncontrollable desire to hit him.
a rush of uncontrollable emotions

expenditure /ɪk'spendɪtʃə/ *n.* the use of energy, time, materials, etc. (时间、精力、材料的) 消耗，耗费
e.g. This study represents a major expenditure of time and effort.
the expenditure of funds for the new school

visible /'vɪzəbl/ *a.* obvious enough to be noticed 明显的，能注意到的
e.g. He showed no visible sign of emotion.
She made a visible effort to control her anger.

untenable /ˌʌnˈtenəbl/ *a.* (of a theory, position, etc.) that cannot be defended against attack or criticism (理论、地位等)难以捍卫的；站不住脚的；不堪一击的
  e.g. His position became untenable and he was forced to resign.
  If three people in four no longer support the government, isn't this an untenable situation?
adapt to to change one's behaviour in order to deal more successfully with a new situation 适应(新情况)
  e.g. We have to adapt quickly to the new system.
  A large organization can be slow to adapt to changes.
liberty /ˈlɪbətɪ/ *n.* freedom to live as one chooses without too many restrictions from government or authority 自由(自己选择生活方式而不受政府及权威限制)
  e.g. the fight for justice and liberty
  Hundreds of political prisoners are to be given their liberty.
temper /ˈtempə/ *v.* to improve hardness and tenacity 锻造；锻炼
  e.g. Hardships tempered her will.
ideal /aɪˈdɪəl/ *n.* an idea or standard that seems perfect and worth trying to achieve or obtain 理想
  e.g. political ideals
  She found it hard to live up to his high ideals.
governing /ˈgʌvənɪŋ/ *a.* controlling; with great influence 居支配地位的
  e.g. Their governing motive is money.
nurture /ˈnɜːtʃə/ *v.* to care for and protect sb./sth. while they are growing and developing 养育，养护；培养
  e.g. children nurtured by parents
  As a record company director, his job is to nurture young talents.
  a carefully nurtured garden
facility /fəˈsɪlətɪ/ *n.* proficiency; technique 熟练；技能
  e.g. She has a facility for languages.

Language Study

bolt
  n.
  1. a long narrow piece of metal that can be slided across the inside of a door or window in order to lock it (门窗的)闩，插销
    e.g. I have my bolt fixed today.
  2. a piece of metal like a screw without a point which is used with a circle of metal 螺栓
    e.g. nuts and bolts
bolt of lightning a sudden flash of lightning in the sky, appearing as a line 闪电
  v. to fasten sth. such as a door or window by sliding a bolt across; to be able to be fastened in this way 用插销闩上；可插上插销的
    e.g. Don't forget to bolt the door.
    The gate bolts on the inside.
bolt A to B/bolt A and B together to fasten things together with a bolt 用螺栓把(甲和乙)固定在一起
  e.g. The various parts of the car are bolted together.
dedicate *v.*
  1. to commit to a goal or way of life 致力于
    e.g. He is ready to dedicate his life to public service.
    The new President said she would dedicate herself to protecting the rights of the old, the sick and the homeless.
  2. to inscribe or address by way of compliment 献给
    e.g. dedicate a book to a friend
    A memorial stone was dedicated to those who were killed in the war.
  3. to hold an official ceremony to say that a building or an object has a special purpose or is special to the memory of a particular person 为……举行奉献典礼；为(建筑物等)举行落成典礼

e.g. The chapel was dedicated in 1880.

bound *a.*
1. certain or likely to happen 一定会的；很可能会的
   e.g. There are bound to be changes when the new system is introduced.
   You are bound to be nervous the first time.
2. forced to do sth. by law, duty or a particular situation 受(法律、义务或某种情况)约束(必须做某事)的；有义务(做某事)的
   e.g. We are not bound by the decision.
   You are bound by the contract to pay by the end of this month.

What counts is what students learn.
Usage of subject clauses 主语从句的用法：
When a clause serves as the subject in a sentence, we generally refer to it as a subject clause. The table below shows examples of the major types of subject clauses. 在句中作主语的从句称为主语从句。下表中列举了主语从句的几种形式。

Clause functioning as subject	Example
That-clause	[1] That his theory was flawed soon became obvious.
Nominal clause	[2] What I need is a long holiday.

引导主语从句的关联词有：连词that, whether；连接代词who, whom, whose, what, which；连接副词when, where, why, how；复合词whatever, whoever, whomever, whenever, wherever, whichever, however。为了整个句子的平衡，主语从句经常后置，并用it充当形式主语。

1. that引导的主语从句
   1) that在主语从句中无任何意义，也不充当任何成分，只起连接作用，但不可省略。
      e.g. That he passed the final exam made his mother happy.
      That Taiwan is a part of China is well known.
   2) that引导主语从句时，可用it作形式主语，而将that从句置于句尾。
      e.g. It made his mother happy that he passed the final exam.
      It is well known that Taiwan is a part of China.
   3) 如果以that引导分句的句子是疑问句，就只能用it作形式主语。
      e.g. Is it true that he passed the driving text?
2. whether引导的主语从句
   whether在主语从句中不充当任何句子成分，作"是否"讲，主语从句的语序用陈述句语序。从句位于句首时，只能用whether引导；位于句中时，可用if与whether互换。
   e.g. Whether Tom will come is uncertain.
   It is not known whether/if they will come today.
3. 用哪个wh-词引导主语从句取决于从句里缺少或需要的句子成分
   e.g. What he needs is that book.
   When Jack will come is not known.
4. -ever词引导的主语从句
   whatever, whoever, whomever, whenever, wherever表示"无论什么"、"无论谁"、"无论何时"、"无论哪里"，语气比what, who, when, where等强烈。
   e.g. Whatever I have is yours.
   Whoever is tired may rest.
5. 连接代词、连接副词和复合词引导主语从句时，本身有词义，在从句中往往充当主语、宾语、表语、定语或状语等，从句的语序用陈述句语序。
   e.g. What he needs is that book. (what在主语从句中作need的宾语)
   When Jack will come is not known. (when在主语从句中作时间状语)

market-driven/learning-driven
Usage of *-driven* in compounds 由-driven构成的复合形容词：
influenced or caused by a particular thing 受……影响的；由……造成的

e.g. a market-driven economy
 a character-driven movie

After Reading

READING COMPREHENSION TASKS

1. Complete the following table based on the information in TEXT A.

	Instruction Paradigm	Learning Paradigm
How it regards the mission of colleges	It mistakes a means for an end, confuses offering classes with producing learning.	What counts is what students learn.
How it conducts education and assesses students	Most colleges in the Instruction Paradigm do not assess in any meaningful way what students have learned. They can tell you what classes their students have taken but not what their graduates know or what they can do.	Colleges in the Learning Paradigm begin to take learning seriously, to assess and measure it, and to take responsibility for producing it.

2. Answer the following questions.

   1) How does the assembly line in the knowledge factory work?
      As students pass by, each faculty member affixes a specialized part of knowledge. Then the students move on down the assembly line to the next instructor, who bolts on another fragment of knowledge.
   2) Why do colleges fail?
      Because they are only a fractured system dedicated to the production of parts, which add up to a transcript but not an education.
   3) Why will the demand for higher education increase both in quantity and quality?
      Because more students will require more sophisticated knowledge and skills.
   4) What do private employers find about the graduates of conventional colleges?
      They have found that these graduates are poorly prepared to the work they need to do.
   5) What will happen if conventional colleges hold fast to the Instruction Paradigm?
      They will wither and die.
   6) What is wrong with the Instruction Paradigm?
      The Instruction Paradigm mistakes a means for an end, confuses offering classes with producing learning.
   7) What really counts from the perspective of the Learning Paradigm?
      What counts is what students learn.
   8) What is the problem with most colleges?
      Most colleges do not assess in any meaningful way what students have learned.
   9) When will Western Governors' University reward students with credit?
      Only when the students have established through rigorous assessment that they have mastered the required skills will they be rewarded with credit.

10) Why can the ideal of liberal education survive in our cultural imagination?

   Because it addresses an ongoing need, the need to nurture in the young the development of both heart and mind, the need to set young people on a course that offers not just facility but maturity, not just cleverness but wisdom.

3. Read the following statements and decide whether they are true (T) or false (F).

1) Instructors do different jobs in each semester for the students. (F)
2) In the knowledge factory, the only thing that matters is the grade on the transcript. (T)
3) There will be fewer students who require complicated knowledge and skills. (F)
4) The competition has emerged because the students are all very competent when they graduate from colleges. (F)
5) It is very easy nowadays to have access to educational services. (T)
6) If colleges want to survive, they have to change. (T)
7) There is much controversy about whether the mission of colleges is to produce learning. (F)
8) If colleges make a paradigm shift, they need to take learning seriously. (T)
9) Antioch University has developed the "assessment-as-learning" approach. (F)
10) Some people predict that thirty years from now the big university campuses will disappear. (T)

4. Explain the underlined parts in your own words.

1) No one has the job of quality control for the finished product. (Para. 1)
   ensuring that the products are of required standards
2) They don't add up to a coherent whole. (Para. 2)
   produce
3) … or sought the support of outside vendors to provide educational services. (Para. 4)
   institutions or agencies outside conventional colleges
4) … if conventional colleges hold fast to the Instruction Paradigm … (Para. 5)
   stick to
5) … the Instruction Paradigm mistakes a means for an end … (Para. 6)
   a purpose/goal
6) … major changes in the way colleges do business are both desirable and inevitable. (Para. 8)
   much needed and unavoidable
7) … we must be disturbed by the contrast. (Para. 10)
   annoyed

ORAL WORK

Work in groups and describe the ideal university in your mind. All your group members should participate in the discussion.

The teacher can ask the students to form groups to discuss what an ideal university is in their minds. Once the students are ready, each group can nominate a presenter to report to the whole class their definition of an ideal university.

TRANSLATION OF TEXT A

大学还有未来吗?

约翰·塔格

1　战后的许多大学就如同知识工厂:学生们经过一条课程流水线;当他们经过的时候,每个老师就把某种具体的知识贴到学生身上;然后学生们继续沿着这条流水线走到下一个老师面前,这位老师又装上一部分知识。这条流水线以稳定的速度移动着,每个老师仅有一个学期或一个季度来给每位同学做同样的工作,学生们则被视作同款汽车的底盘,千人一面。这条流水线上的员工们囿于自己分内装配的那部分知识,对教学工作的理解都颇为狭隘。没有人对最后的成品进行质量监测。

2　身处如同知识工厂的大学中,学生们明白,这个系统中唯一被认可的价值,唯一在通往成功的路上可资交换的好东西就是成绩单上的分数。这个支离破碎的系统只生产零件,生产由三个单元组成的课程。大学之所以失败,就是因为各个零件无法拼凑到一起,不能形成一个连贯的整体。他们只拼成了一张成绩单,却不是教育。

3　但在我们进入21世纪后,知识工厂开始瓦解了。向知识社会的转变意味着对高等教育的需求将从质量和数量方面都有提升:更多的学生需要更加复杂的知识和技能。但是这样的转变也同时为高等教育带来了新的东西:竞争。

4　两个原因导致了竞争的出现。首先,需要技术型雇员的用人企业发现传统大学的毕业生对于他们要从事的工作几乎毫无准备。许多公司或创建他们自己的"大学",或寻求外面的教学代理来提供培训服务。竞争激增的第二个原因是,如今信息技术的发展使教育资源变得随处可得。教育不再局限在校园里。因此,许多教育资源的提供者开始争夺那些从前鞭长莫及的生源。

5　面对如此的竞争,如果传统院校还抓住"授课范式"不放,并且继续坚持到校上课才能获得学位的原则,那么许多这样的院校都将萎缩或者关闭。全国各地的大学理事会中,最智慧的人群都在提出谴责,传统大学无疑会在这一片反对声中渐渐式微。如果大学还想振兴,或者在某种程度上说如果他们还想生存,就必须改变。

6　大学需要转变体制,取消那一整套自以为是的固有规章制度,采纳和过去有本质区别的观念。他们必须意识到,授课范式错把手段当作结果,把提供课程和促进学习混为一谈。要解决这个问题,就得采用所谓的"学习范式"。从学习范式的角度讲,知识工厂奉为中心的界定作用是微不足道的。真正重要的是学生学到了什么。毋庸置疑,大学的使命在于促进学习,因为几乎所有大学教员和校长都已经公认了这一点。

7　问题在于绝大多数大学不通过任何有意义的方式去评估学生们的学习成果。他们能够说出学生们都在上什么课,但是却不知道学生毕业时都懂得了什么或者能做什么。要想转变到学习范式,学校需要开始严肃地对待学习,去评估、衡量学习,并对促进学习负责任。

8　越来越多的大学教员和管理者已经认识到这一大学经营中的重大变化是受欢迎的,也是大势所趋。著名的加利福尼亚高等教育政策中心在1996年的报告中敦促"大学开始着手转型,将授予学位或证书的标准由所花学时转变为学生的学习情况"。

9　这类学校的典范是存在的。位于密尔沃基的阿尔弗诺学院早在几十年前就开始了"评估学习"。这种方法旨在监督和指导学生的发展,掌握一系列自由教育所特有的核心能力。在新成立的西部州长大学,学生只有通过了严格的测评,被认定掌握了必备知识,才能获得学分。安迪亚克大学校长阿兰·盖斯金称,全美国有超过两百个学校都在认真地讨论这项改组工作。

10　然而,比较一下大学极为缓慢的改变速度和它们所服务的社会一日千里的变迁,我们会感到非常不安。许多人认为本科院校应付不了知识社会带来的挑战。如一些学者们预测企业依旧会需要传统型大学来进行基础教育和研究,但它们会越来越多地亲自组织培训。另一些人则预测30年后许多大学校园会变为遗迹,大学将会消亡。如此不加控制的支出,教学内容和教学质量却不见进展,都意味着这套制度很快会变得难以维系。高等教育陷入深深危机之中。

11 不过，我们有必要这么在乎吗？如果大多数学院走向没落或者沦为市场动力的附属机构，灵活地服务于变化中的世界，又有什么关系呢？究竟会丧失什么？丧失的或许不多，也或许很多。因为大学在美国社会中占据的地位是其他机构无法代替的。他们代表着大众教育，代表着向往自由的教育，代表着一种从儿童到公民的经历，只有通过它，人们才懂得自由是需要通过承担责任来实现的。我之所以说大学"占据"大众教育的地位是因为我不能说他们真正发挥了作用。但是他们依旧是制度中的理想，依旧作为理想而存在着。

12 对于现在的知识工厂而言，要改变现行的规范而变为以学习为导向的机构，似乎是一个令人畏惧的任务。这就好似要求一个邮局改变为一所教堂。然而，在我们的文化想象中自由教育理想之所以存在，是因为它满足了一种日益增加的需求：年轻人需要心灵和思想的成长，需要获得一种课程，传递的是心智的成熟而不仅仅是才能，是真正的智慧而不是一时的聪明。

TEXT B Turning Study Skills into Life Skills

Before Reading

The purpose of this section is to arouse the students' interest in the theme of the unit, reactivate their relevant background knowledge or elicit their opinions on the related topics, so as to better prepare them for the succeeding tasks.

Before Reading activities can be organized as group work so that the students share with each other their knowledge about secondary education and technology in education.

Background Information

1 Secondary Education

In most contemporary educational systems of the world, secondary education comprises the formal education that occurs during adolescence. It is characterized by transition from the typically compulsory, comprehensive primary education for minors, to the optional, selective tertiary, "post-secondary", or "higher" education. Depending on the system, schools for this period, or a part of it, may be called secondary or high schools, gymnasiums, lyceums, middle schools, colleges, or vocational schools. The exact meaning of any of these terms varies from one system to another. The exact boundary between primary and secondary education also varies from country to country and even within them, but is generally around the seventh to the tenth year of schooling. Secondary education occurs mainly during the teenage years. In the United States and Canada primary and secondary education together are sometimes referred to as K-12 education, and in New Zealand Year 1-13 is used. The purpose of secondary education can be to give common knowledge, to prepare for higher education or to train directly in a profession.

The emergence of secondary education in the United States did not happen until 1910, caused by the rise in big businesses and technological advances in factories that required skilled workers. In order to meet this new job demand, high schools were created and the curriculum focused on practical job skills that would better prepare students for white collar or skilled blue collar work. This proved to be beneficial for both the employer and the employee, because this improvement in human capital caused employees to become more efficient, which lowered costs for the employer, and skilled employees received a higher wage than employees with just primary educational attainment. In Europe, the grammar school or academy existed from as early as the 16th century; public schools or fee paying schools, or charitable educational foundations have an even longer history.

2 Technology in Education

Technology is an increasingly influential factor in education. Computers and mobile phones are used in developed countries both to complement established education practices and to develop new ways of learning such as online education (a type of distance education). This gives students the opportunity to choose what they are interested in learning. The proliferation of computers also means the increase of programming and blogging. Technology offers powerful learning tools that demand new skills and understandings of students, including multimedia, and provides new ways to engage students, such as virtual learning environments. Technology is being used more not only in administrative duties in education but also in the instruction of students. The use of technologies such as PowerPoint and interactive whiteboard is capturing the attention of students in the classroom. Technology is also being used in the assessment of students.

Information and communication technologies are a "diverse set of tools and resources used to communicate, create, disseminate, store, and manage information." These technologies include computers, the Internet, broadcasting technologies (radio and television), and telephony. There is increasing interest in how computers and the Internet can improve education at all levels, in both formal and non-formal settings. Older technologies, such as radio and television, have for over forty years been used for open and distance learning, although print remains the cheapest, most accessible and therefore most dominant delivery mechanism in both developed and developing countries.

The use of computers and the Internet is in its infancy in developing countries, if these are used at all, due to limited infrastructure and the attendant high costs of access. Usually, various technologies are used in combination rather than as the sole delivery mechanism. For example, the Kothmale Community Radio Internet uses both radio broadcasts and computer and Internet technologies to facilitate the sharing of information and provide educational opportunities in a rural community in Sri Lanka. The Open University of the United Kingdom, established in 1969 as the first educational institution in the world wholly dedicated to open and distance learning, still relies heavily on print-based materials supplemented by radio, television and, in recent years, online programming. Similarly, the Indira Gandhi National Open University in India combines the use of print, recorded audio and video, broadcast radio and television, and audio conferencing technologies. The term "computer-assisted learning" has been increasingly used to describe the use of technology in teaching.

Reading

New Words and Expressions

precede /ˌpriːˈsiːd/ *v.* to happen before sth. or come before sth./sb. in order 在……之前发生（或出现），先于
e.g. the years preceding the war
His resignation was preceded by weeks of speculation.
She preceded me in the job.

crucial /ˈkruːʃəl/ *a.* extremely important, because it will affect other things 至关重要的，关键性的
e.g. a crucial factor
Winning this contract is crucial to the success of the company.
The next few weeks are going to be crucial.

correlation /ˌkɒrəˈleɪʃən/ *n.* a connection between two things in which one thing changes as the other does 相互关系；关联
e.g. the correlation between social power and wealth
There is a direct correlation between exposure to sun and skin cancer.

advancement /ədˈvɑːnsmənt/ *n.* progress in a job, social class, etc.(工作、社会等级等的)提升；晋升
e.g. There are good opportunities for advancement if you have the right skills.
All she was interested in was the advancement of her own career.

attain /əˈteɪn/ *v.* to succeed in getting sth., usually after a lot of efforts (经过努力)获得，得到
e.g. Most of our students attained five "A" grades in their exams.
We need to identify the best ways of attaining our goals.

humanities /hjuːˈmænətɪz/ *n.* [pl.] the subject of study that are concerned with the way people think and behave, for example literature, language, history and philosophy [复]人文学科
e.g. I've always been more interested in the humanities than the sciences.
the college of arts and humanities

relatively /ˈrelətɪvlɪ/ *ad.* to a fairly large degree, especially in comparison to sth. else 相当程度上，相当地；相对地
e.g. I found the test relatively easy.
We had relatively few applications for the job.

fraction /ˈfrækʃən/ *n.* a small part or amount of sth. 小部分；少量，一点儿
e.g. Only a small fraction of a bank's total deposits will be withdrawn at any one time.
A tiny fraction of the population never vote.

typically /ˈtɪpɪkəlɪ/ *ad.* usually 通常，一般
e.g. The factory typically produces 500 chairs a week.
A typically priced meal will be around $10.

applied /əˈplaɪd/ *a.* (especially of a subject of study) used in a practical way, not theoretical 应用的，实用的
e.g. applied linguistics
applied science

timescale /ˈtaɪmˌskeɪl/ *n.* the period of time that it takes for sth. to happen or be completed（事情发生或完成所需要的）一段时间；期限
e.g. What's the timescale for the project?
Police officers are trying to construct the timescale of events leading up to the murder.

coursework /ˈkɔːswɜːk/ *n.* work that students do during a course of study, not in exams, that is included in their final mark（计入最终成绩的）课程作业
e.g. Coursework accounts for 40% of the final marks.
You have to complete all the required coursework.

external /ɪkˈstɜːnəl/ *a.* happening or coming from outside a place, an organization, a particular situation, etc. 外界的；外来的
e.g. A combination of internal and external factors caused the company to close down.
Many external influences can affect your state of mind.

individualized /ˌɪndɪˈvɪdjuəlaɪzd/ *a.* prepared or suitable for individual people or things 个性化的
e.g. individualized teaching
The hospital gives individualized care to all its patients.

analyze /ˈænəlaɪz/ *v.* to examine the nature or structure of sth., especially by separating it into parts, in order to understand or explain it 分析
e.g. The job involves gathering and analyzing data.
We need to analyze what went wrong.

commitment /kəˈmɪtmənt/ *n.* the willingness to work hard and give energy and time to a job or an activity（对工作或某活动的）投入；奉献
e.g. A career as an actor requires one hundred percent commitment.
I'd like to thank the staff for having shown such commitment.

course of action a way of acting in or dealing with a particular situation 行动方式；处理方法
e.g. What course of action would you recommend?
The wisest course of action would be to say nothing.

brainstorming /ˈbreɪnˌstɔːmɪŋ/ *n.* a way of making a group of people all think about sth. at the same time, often in order to solve a problem or to create good ideas 集思广益
e.g. We need to do some brainstorming before we get down to detailed planning.
We're having a brainstorming session on Friday.

lateral thinking the way of solving problems by letting the mind consider unusual and apparently illogical approaches to them 横向思维（解决问题的方法，以异乎寻常而表面不合逻辑的方法思考）

capability /ˌkeɪpəˈbɪlətɪ/ *n.* the ability or qualities necessary to do sth. 能力，才能
e.g. beyond the capabilities of current technology
Animals in the zoo have lost the capability to catch food for themselves.
Age affects the range of a person's capabilities.

clarification /ˌklærɪfɪˈkeɪʃən/ *n.* an explanation or more details which make sth. clearer or easier to understand 澄清，阐明
e.g. Some further clarification of your position is needed.
I am seeking the clarification of the regulations.

purely /ˈpjʊəlɪ/ *ad.* entirely; exclusively 完全地
e.g. On a purely practical level, it is difficult to see how such proposals would work.
We made this decision purely for financial

reasons.

textual /ˈtekstʃʊəl/ *a.* connected with or contained in a text 文本的；篇章的

e.g. textual analysis
textual errors

conceptual /kənˈseptʃʊəl/ *a.* related to or based on ideas 概念上的；观念上的

e.g. a conceptual framework within which children's need are addressed
a conceptual model

turn upon   to depend on 取决于

e.g. Whether you can pass the exam turns upon how much effort you make.
Success turns upon many factors.

reconceptualize /ˌriːkənˈseptjʊəlaɪz/ *v.* to form an idea or principle again 再次构思；重新形成观念

e.g. He argued that morality could be reconceptualized as a series of principles based on human reason.
We need to reconceptualize the framework.

customary /ˈkʌstəmərɪ/ *a.* usual, traditional 习惯的；习俗的

e.g. Is it customary to tip hairdressers in this country?
She dressed in her customary fashion.

thought-path /ˈθɔːtˈpɑːθ/ *n.* train of thought 思路

potentially /pəʊˈtenʃəlɪ/ *ad.* possibly 潜在地，可能地

e.g. Hepatitis is a potentially fatal disease.
This crisis is potentially the most serious in the organization's history.

cogitation /ˌkɒdʒɪˈteɪʃən/ *n.* meditation; serious thought; carefully considered reflection 仔细思考，深思熟虑

e.g. His cogitations were dutifully recorded in his daybook.
After much cogitation, he rejected the offer.

interactive /ˌɪntərˈæktɪv/ *a.* acting upon or in close relation with each other; involving people working together and having an influence on each other 相互影响的；互相配合的

e.g. interactive multimedia system
The school believes in interactive teaching methods.

orientate /ˈɔːrɪenteɪt/ *v.* to direct sb./sth. towards sth.; to make or adapt sb./sth. for a particular purpose 确定方向；使适应

e.g. profit-orientated organizations
She needs to orientate herself to her new job.

committee /kəˈmɪtɪ/ *n.* a group of people who are chosen, usually by a larger group, to make decisions or to deal with a particular subject 委员会

e.g. She is on the management committee.
The committee has decided to close the restaurant.

prevalent /ˈprevələnt/ *a.* existing very commonly or happening often 流行的；普遍的

e.g. These diseases are more prevalent among young children.
Trees are dying in areas where acid rain is most prevalent.

private sector   businesses and industries that are not owned or controlled by the government (国家经济的)私营部分

e.g. Thirty percent of graduates are working in the private sector.
private-sector employers

corollary /kəˈrɒlərɪ/ *n.* sth. that naturally results from sth. else 必然的结果(或结论)

e.g. Unfortunately, violence is the inevitable corollary of such a revolutionary change in society.
Blind jealousy is a frequent corollary of passionate love.

professionalization /prəʊˌfeʃənəlaɪˈzeɪʃən/ *n.* the social process of giving (an occupation, activity or group) qualities required by a certain profession 职业化

e.g. the professionalization of American sports
the professionalization of warfare

diversity /daɪˈvɜːsətɪ/ *n.* the state or quality of being different or varied; variety 多样性

e.g. Does television adequately reflect the ethnic and cultural diversity of the country?
There is a wide diversity of opinions on the question of unilateral disarmament.

specialism /ˈspeʃəlɪzəm/ *n.* an area of study or work that sb. specializes in 专业；专长

e.g. a business degree with a specialism in computing
Dr. Crane's specialism is tropical diseases.

authoritative /ɔːˈθɒrɪtətɪv/ *a.* able to be trusted as being accurate or true; reliable 有权威性的

e.g. authoritative information
an authoritative dictionary

participant /pɑː'tɪsɪpənt/ *n.* a person who takes part in or becomes involved in a particular activity 参与者
  e.g. He seems to be a willing participant in the activity.
  The gathering satisfied both the participants and the organizers.
consideration /kənˌsɪdə'reɪʃən/ *n.* a factor to be considered in forming a judgment or decision (作计划或决定时)必须考虑的事(或因素)
  e.g. Safety is the most important consideration in choosing a car.
  commercial considerations
expertise /ˌekspɜː'tiːz/ *n.* expert knowledge or skill in a particular subject, activity or job 专门知识；专门技能
  e.g. They have considerable expertise in dealing with oil leakage.
  We have the expertise to help you run your business.
in question being discussed 讨论(或议论)中的
  e.g. I stayed at home on the night in question.
  On the day in question we were in Cardiff.
preparatory /prɪ'pærətəri/ *a.* done in order to prepare for sth. 预备的；筹备的
  e.g. preparatory meetings
  Security checks had been carried out preparatory to the President's visit.
at stake that can be won or lost, depending on the success of a particular action 成败难料；有风险
  e.g. We cannot afford to take risks when people's lives are at stake.
deliberate /dɪ'lɪbərət/ *a.* intentional or planned 有目的的，有计划的，刻意的
  e.g. a deliberate attack/insult/lie
  We made a deliberate decision to live apart for a while.
seminar /'semɪnɑː/ *n.* a class at a university or college when a small group of students and a teacher discuss or study a particular topic (大学教师带领学生作专题讨论的)研讨课
  e.g. a graduate seminar
  a seminar room
  Teaching is by lectures and seminars.
viewpoint /'vjuːpɔɪnt/ *n.* a way of thinking about a subject 观点，看法
  e.g. Try looking at things from a different viewpoint.
  She will have her own viewpoint on the matter.
show off to try to impress others by talking about your abilities, possessions, etc. 炫耀；卖弄
  e.g. He is just showing off because that girl he likes is here.
  He likes to show off how well he speaks French.
co-operative /kəʊ'ɒpərətɪv/ *a.* involving doing sth. together or working together with others towards a shared aim; helpful by doing what you are asked to do 同心协力的；配合的
  e.g. Co-operative activity is essential to effective community work.
  Employees will generally be more co-operative if their views are taken seriously.
tutorial /tjuː'tɔːrɪəl/ *n.* a period of teaching in a university that involves discussion between an individual student or a small group of students and a tutor 大学导师的辅导课
  e.g. Methods of study include lectures, tutorials and practical work.
  I totally enjoyed today's tutorial.
invaluable /ɪn'væljuəbl/ *a.* extremely useful 宝贵的；有用的
  e.g. The new job will provide you with invaluable experience.
  Such data will prove invaluable to researchers.
dynamics /daɪ'næmɪks/ *n.* the way in which people or things behave and react to each other in a particular situation (人或事物)相互作用的方式，动态
  e.g. the dynamics of political changes
  The dynamics of international trade have influenced our business decisions on this matter.
self-selected /ˌselfsɪ'lektɪd/ *a.* being in a situation in which people decide for themselves to do sth. rather than being chosen to do it 自行决定的，自我选择的
  e.g. a self-selected committee
  a self-selected organization
switch off to stop thinking about sth. or paying attention to sth. 不再注意；失去兴趣
  e.g. The only time he really switches off is when we are on vacation.
  When I hear the word "football", I switch off.

smooth out to make problems or difficulties disappear 消除问题；克服困难
e.g. His main job is to smooth out the friction that so often arises.

friction /ˈfrɪkʃən/ *n.* disagreement or a lack of friendship among people who have different opinions about sth. 分歧；不和
e.g. There's a lot of friction between my wife and my mother.
Border clashes have led to increased friction between the two countries.

secure /sɪˈkjʊə/ *v.* to get sth., sometimes with difficulty (经过努力)获得
e.g. He was disappointed by his failure to secure the top job with the bank.
She secured 500 votes.

acceptance /əkˈseptəns/ *n.* general agreement that sth. is satisfactory or right, or that sb. should be included in a group 同意；接受
e.g. His idea rapidly gained acceptance in political circles.
The party marked his acceptance into the community.

obtrusive /əbˈtruːsɪv/ *a.* tending to push self-assertively forward; brash 强加于人的；莽撞的
e.g. a spoiled child's obtrusive behaviour
Beneath his obtrusive exterior, he is still a little boy inside.

overly /ˈəʊvəlɪ/ *ad.* too, very 很，十分；过于
e.g. I am not overly fond of pasta.
We think you are being overly optimistic.

voluble /ˈvɒljʊbl/ *a.* talking a lot, with enthusiasm about a subject 健谈的，滔滔不绝的
e.g. Evelyn was very voluble on the subject of women's rights.
Many see Parker as the obvious leader, whose voluble style works well on TV.

explicitly /ɪkˈsplɪsɪtlɪ/ *ad.* clearly and exactly 清晰明确地
e.g. I told you quite explicitly to be home by midnight.
The report states explicitly that the system was to blame.

assessment /əˈsesmənt/ *n.* the act of judging or forming an opinion about sb./sth. 评定，评估
e.g. written exams and other forms of assessment
Objective assessment of the severity of the problem was difficult.

to the extent that to the same degree as; as much as 到了……的程度
e.g. The rich will not benefit from the proposed changes to the tax system to the same extent as the lower paid.
The administrative overheads of a business will be low to the extent that everyone working in the business can be trusted to behave in a way that best promotes the interests of the firm.

tutor /ˈtjuːtə/ *n.* a teacher whose job is to pay special attention to the studies or health, etc. of a student or a group of students 指导老师
e.g. his history tutor
He was my personal tutor at university.

participation /pɑːˌtɪsɪˈpeɪʃən/ *n.* the act of taking part in an activity or event 参加，参与
e.g. a show with lots of audience participation
A back injury prevented active participation in any sports for a while.

subsequent /ˈsʌbsɪkwənt/ *a.* happening or coming after sth. else 随后的，之后的
e.g. Subsequent events confirmed our doubts.
Developments on this issue will be dealt with in a subsequent report.

milestone /ˈmaɪlstəʊn/ *n.* a very important state or event in the development of sth. 里程碑；重要阶段
e.g. He felt that moving out from his parents' home was a real milestone in his life.
Her getting the job of supervisor was a milestone in her career.

precisely /prɪˈsaɪslɪ/ *ad.* accurately 准确地；精确地
e.g. She pronounced the word very slowly and precisely.
He works slowly and precisely whereas I tend to rush things and make mistakes.

react /rɪˈækt/ *v.* to change or behave in a particular way as a result of or in response to sth. 对……作出反应；回应
e.g. Local residents have reacted angrily to the news.
You never know how he is going to react.
The market reacted by falling a further two points.

query /ˈkwɪərɪ/ *n.* a question, especially one asking for information or expressing a doubt about sth. 疑问；询问

e.g. Our assistants will be happy to answer your queries.

If you have a query about your insurance policy, contact our helpline.

orally /ˈɔːrəlɪ/ *ad.* spoken rather than written, verbally 口头地

e.g. Answers can be written down or presented orally on tape.

compass /ˈkʌmpəs/ *n.* a range or an extent, especially of what can be achieved in a particular situation 范围；范畴

e.g. The discussion went beyond the compass of my brain.

afford /əˈfɔːd/ *v.* to allow sb. to have sth. pleasant or necessary 提供

e.g. The hut afforded little protection from the elements.

Her seat afforded her an uninterrupted view of the stage.

commonplace /ˈkɒmənpleɪs/ *a.* happening often, or often seen or experienced and so not considered to be special 常见的，普遍的

e.g. a commonplace remark

Home computers are increasingly commonplace.

polytechnic /ˌpɒlɪˈteknɪk/ *n.* a college for higher education, especially in scientific and technical subjects 理工学院

e.g. I considered applying to university, but I eventually decided to go to the local polytechnic.

I have taken a number of courses at a polytechnic nearby.

subheading /ˈsʌbˌhedɪŋ/ *n.* a word, phrase or sentence which is used to introduce part of a text 副标题

e.g. The subheadings are numbered within each chapter.

You can find the chart in the "Financial Matters" chapter under the subheading "Mortgages and Loans".

visual /ˈvɪʒʊəl/ *a.* relating to seeing 视觉的

e.g. visual stimulus

visual impact

representation /ˌreprɪzenˈteɪʃən/ *n.* the act of presenting sth. in a particular way; sth. that shows or describes sth. else 表现；描述；描绘

e.g. the negative representation of single mothers in the media

The snake swallowing its tail is a representation of infinity.

projector /prəʊˈdʒektə/ *n.* a device for showing films or images on a screen or other surface 投影仪

e.g. a slide projector

I need a projector in my presentation.

write-pad /ˈraɪtpæd/ *n.* a pad on which people can write things down 手写板

e.g. I like to use a write-pad when I have to explain ideas to my group members.

Write-pads are very useful at business meetings.

exposition /ˌekspəʊˈzɪʃən/ *n.* a clear and full explanation of an idea or theory 解释；说明；阐述

e.g. It purports to be an exposition of Catholic social teaching.

The students prepared expositions on familiar essay topics.

routinely /ruːˈtiːnlɪ/ *ad.* often, usually 例行地；惯常地

e.g. Health and safety rules are routinely ignored.

Visitors are routinely checked as they enter the building.

premium /ˈpriːmɪəm/ *n.* sth. particularly important or valuable 珍贵；重视

e.g. put a premium on the company's services

Employers set a premium on honesty and hard work.

manageable /ˈmænɪdʒəbl/ *a.* easy or possible to deal with 可控制的；可处理的

e.g. The work has been divided into smaller, more manageable sections.

Government targets for increased productivity are described as "tough but manageable".

comprehensive /ˌkɒmprɪˈhensɪv/ *a.* complete and including everything that is necessary 全面，综合的

e.g. We offer you a comprehensive training in all aspects of the business.

Is this list comprehensive or are there some names missing?

He has written a fully comprehensive guide to Rome.

coverage /ˈkʌvərɪdʒ/ *n.* the extent to which sth.

deals with sth. else 提供的数量；覆盖范围(或方式)
- **e.g.** For more complete coverage of this issue, see Chapter Six.
  The book gives full coverage to the history of the word.

flowery /ˈflaʊərɪ/ *a.* using too many complicated words or phrases in an attempt to sound skilful 过分复杂的；华而不实的
- **e.g.** a flowery description
  a flowery speech

phrasing /ˈfreɪzɪŋ/ *n.* the choice of words used to express sth. 措词
- **e.g.** The phrasing of the contract is rather ambiguous.
  Please make sure the phrasing is easy to understand.

rhetoric /ˈretərɪk/ *n.* speech or writing which is intended to be effective and influence people 华丽的言语
- **e.g.** How far the president will be able to translate his campaign rhetoric into action remains to be seen.
  the rhetoric of political slogans

factual /ˈfæktʃʊəl/ *a.* using or consisting of facts 事实性的
- **e.g.** She gave a clear, factual account of the attack.

analytic /ˌænəˈlɪtɪk/ *a.* examining or liking to examine things very carefully 分析性的
- **e.g.** He has a very analytic mind.
  Some students have a more analytic approach to learning.

resemble /rɪˈzembl/ *v.* to look like or be like sb. or sth. 像，显得像
- **e.g.** You resemble your mother very closely.
  After the earthquake, the city resembled a battlefield.

debug /diːˈbʌg/ *v.* to look for and remove the faults from 排错
- **e.g.** The computer programme ran much faster after it was debugged.
  I need some expert to help me debug the programme.

incremental /ˌɪnkrɪˈmentəl/ *a.* increasing in amount or value gradually and by a regular amount 递增的
- **e.g.** Changes at the newspaper are more incremental than radical.

departure /dɪˈpɑːtʃə/ *n.* a change from what is expected, or from what has happened before 背离；变更
- **e.g.** There can be no departure from the rules.
  It was a radical departure from tradition.

status quo the present situation 现状
- **e.g.** Certain people always want to maintain the status quo.

recommend /ˌrekəˈmend/ *v.* to suggest that sb. or sth. would be good or suitable for a particular job or purpose, or to suggest that a particular action should be done 推荐
- **e.g.** I can recommend the chicken in mushroom sauce — it's delicious.
  She has been recommended for promotion.

robust /rəʊˈbʌst/ *a.* strong and not likely to have problems 稳健的
- **e.g.** It was typically a robust performance by the Foreign Secretary.
  a robust mind

satisfactory /ˌsætɪsˈfæktərɪ/ *a.* good or good enough for a particular need or purpose 令人满意的
- **e.g.** The teachers seem to think his work is satisfactory.
  We hope very much to find a satisfactory solution to the problem.

optimal /ˈɒptɪməl/ *a.* best; most likely to bring success or advantage 最佳的；最适宜的
- **e.g.** the optimal uses of resources
  the optimal conditions for effective learning

outline /ˈaʊtlaɪn/ *v.* to give the main facts about sth. 概述；略述
- **e.g.** At the interview she outlined what she would be doing.
  We outlined our proposals to the committee.

alternative /ɔːlˈtɜːnətɪv/ *a.* available as another possibility 可供选择的
- **e.g.** The opposition parties have so far failed to set out an alternative strategy.
  An alternative venue for the concert is being sought.

mechanics /mɪˈkænɪks/ *n.* the way sth. works or happens 方法；手段
- **e.g.** He knows a lot about the mechanics of running a school.
  The exact mechanics of how payment will be made will be decided later.

assemble /əˈsembl/ *v.* to come together in a

single place or bring parts together in a single group 聚集；收集
e.g. We assembled in the meeting room after lunch.
assemble data
At the staff meeting, the manager told the assembled company that no one would lose their job.

time-span /ˈtaɪmˌspæn/ *n.* a period of time 一段时间；时段
e.g. These changes have occurred over a long time-span.
I bumped into an old friend I haven't seen for a long time-span.

compose /kəmˈpəʊz/ *v.* to produce music, poetry or formal writing 创作；写作
e.g. The music was specially composed for the film.
He composed this poem for his wife.
My lawyer is going to compose a letter of complaint.

correspond /ˌkɒrɪˈspɒnd/ *v.* to match or be similar or equal 一致；符合
e.g. The money I've saved corresponds roughly to the amount I need for my course.
His story of what happened that night didn't correspond with the witness's version.

Language Study

decision-making

n.+v-ing　由名词+动词分词形式构成的复合形容词：
此类形容词修饰动作发出者，用现在分词表示主动。比如课文中出现的decision-making(作决定的)，idea-generating(激发思想的)，point-scoring(得分的)，risk-minimizing(把风险最小化的)。此类复合形容词还有energy-consuming(消耗能量的)，epoch-making(划时代的)，peace-loving(热爱和平的)，breath-taking(惊人的)，body-building(健身的)，labor-saving(省力的)，record-breaking(破纪录的)，paper-cutting(剪纸的)等等。

reconceptualize

Usage of the prefix *re-*　前缀re-的用法：
usually used in verbs and related nouns, adjectives and adverbs, meaning "again"　构成动词及相关的名词、形容词和副词，表示"又，再，重新"
e.g. retell; reconnect; reincarnation; reappraisal; reassuring

large-sized

Usage of the compound with *-sized*　由-sized构成的复合形容词的用法：
having the size mentioned　……大小的；……规模的
e.g. small-sized; medium-sized

After Reading

READING COMPREHENSION TASKS

1. Complete the following table based on the information in TEXT B.

Career skills	Skills developed when studying for a degree
problem-solving	brainstorming, idea-generating, lateral-thinking capabilities in concept clarification and essay writing
working in committees	the ability to encourage shy participants, to stimulate people who have switched off, to smooth out frictions, to make progress in discussion, to secure acceptance of agreed points, and to shut up obtrusive or overly voluble participants

oral presentation	the ability to use subheadings and visual representations to clarify the themes and ideas in a talk, and the personal skills involved in giving a clear, brief oral exposition to accompany a paper
report writing	the ability to write clear and well-organized essays, addressing specific questions, outlining alternative viewpoints and suggesting a conclusion

2. Answer the following questions.

1) According to the author, is academic performance highly correlated with career success?
   There are rather low correlations between academic performance and career success.

2) How are issues involved in career situations different from those involved in higher education?
   Problems are much more applied and immediate, needing to be tackled in a relatively short timescale. In academic coursework, referring to source materials can resolve many questions directly, but career problem-solving rarely involves finding an answer in an external source.

3) How are academic questions different from career problem-solving?
   Academic questions are much more purely textual or conceptual than career problem-solving, where real outcomes turn immediately upon the choice of options.

4) What abilities are important and valuable in management contexts?
   Lateral thinking and the ability to reconceptualize problems outside customary thought-paths are important and valuable in management contexts.

5) In what way do ideas and decisions emerge?
   Ideas and decisions emerge out of the interaction between committee participants, with different policy considerations and areas of expertise focused down on to the particular problem in question.

6) What does the character of your work life depend upon?
   It depends upon being able to actively sell your ideas in committee.

7) Why are seminars and class discussions important to a student?
   Because they provide the student with invaluable opportunities first to observe and understand small-group dynamics, and second to develop essential personal skills through trying to influence or manage the flow of discussion.

8) What skills are explicitly included in some forms of assessment in higher education?
   Effective communication skills are explicitly included.

9) What are you expected to do at meetings?
   Since meetings are fairly short, they require you to express viewpoints precisely and briefly, to react effectively to comments and queries, and to stimulate and guide effective discussion arising from your presentation.

10) What can provide an invaluable training for report writing?
    Clearly written, well-organized essays, addressing specific questions, outlining alternative viewpoints and suggesting a conclusion can provide an invaluable training for report writing.

3. Read the following statements and decide whether they are true (T) or false (F).

1) The period of making career choices precedes studying for a degree. (F)
2) Attending committee meetings is a basic management activity in all walks of life. (F)

3) Academic questions are more textual or conceptual than career problem-solving. (T)
4) Committees have become a prevalent form of organization only in private-sector corporations. (F)
5) The formal structure of classes can be easily altered. (F)
6) Oral presentations are more important in subsequent career activities. (T)
7) Oral skills are not so important as written skills in committee work. (F)
8) Higher education fails to provide enough opportunities to practice oral presentation skills. (F)
9) Professional reports are roughly the same as essays. (F)
10) Business reports usually recommend risk-minimizing courses of action. (T)

4. Explain the underlined parts in your own words.

1) Higher education institutions play a key role in <u>switching people into different career paths</u>… (Para. 1)
   preparing people for taking up different jobs

2) … make the right commitment to one course of action, and <u>live with the consequences</u>. (Para. 2)
   accept whatever results

3) Academic questions are typically much more purely textual or conceptual than career problem-solving, where <u>real outcomes turn immediately upon the choice of options</u>. (Para. 3)
   the actual results depend directly on the choice you have made

4) Problem-solving in career contexts is usually <u>not the product of individual cogitation</u> but of interactive discussions between work colleagues. (Para. 3)
   not the result of personal consideration

5) Committees and meetings bring together a diversity of people, <u>each narrowly informed in one specialism and also authoritative in that area of knowledge</u>. (Para. 4)
   each with his own specialized area of expertise as an authority

6) … at least to the extent that class teachers or tutors <u>grade students on "participation"</u> in group debates. (Para. 7)
   assess students according to how well they participate

7) … you will frequently have to <u>explain ideas orally in a brief compass to rushed superiors</u>… (Para. 8)
   present yourself briefly to superiors who usually have a tight schedule

8) Some of the more expensive equipment of conference presentations are still <u>far from commonplace</u> in universities and polytechnics. (Para. 9)
   not commonly used at all

9) They define options — usually <u>involving incremental departures from the status quo</u>. (Para. 10)
   more or less reflecting the status quo yet still slightly different from it

ORAL WORK

Work in groups and talk about the study skills you have been developing since you entered the university. Imagine which skills might be useful in your future career, and discuss why.

The students can either work within groups or individually at the stage of preparation. Once they feel ready, the teacher can ask them to present their ideas within the group or to the whole class.

TRANSLATION OF TEXT B

变学习技巧为生活技能

帕特里克·邓利维

1 通过学习取得学位后，人们常常会立刻进入选择职业的重要阶段。虽然一个人的学业表现和他的事业成就并没有太大关系(至少在职位和工资两方面是如此)，高等教育学府还是对人们选择不同的职业道路起到了举足轻重的作用。在工作中，人文和社会科学的学生们很少直接用到课堂上的知识，但几乎每个人都会用到一点大学里掌握的学习技巧或工作方法，因为在学习中，一些工作技巧也会得到很大提升。

解决问题

2 在许多行业中，应对问题是一种基本的事务处理活动。通常，在工作中遇到的问题和在学校里的问题很不一样，它们更实际，更紧迫，需要在较短的时间内处理好。做课程作业时，参考原始资料就可以解决大部分问题。但工作中的问题很少能在外部资料中找到答案，它们更加个性化和多样化，你需要针对具体情况直接分析所面临的困难，确定自己的角色，采取适当的行动，并且为之承担责任。

3 学习技巧中，对于解决职场问题最重要的就是厘清概念和写作时所用到的"头脑风暴"、思想激发和横向思维能力了。学术问题通常更纯书本化和概念化，而在职场问题中，往往一作出选择就会有实际后果。但在任何管理中，横向思维能力、不拘泥于常规思维定式对问题作出新理解的能力将会显得难能可贵。工作中，解决问题通常不是靠个人苦思冥想，而是靠与同事们互动与讨论。头脑风暴和思想激发也不再像在学校里那样倾向于用书面材料表达，而多通过口头方式表达。这表明在毕业生就业的道路上，会议或委员会中的决策能力十分重要。

在委员会中工作

4 参加委员会议是大中型组织的一项主要活动。由于在一定程度上管理规划人员专业化程度越来越高，因此委员会已经成为公共机构和私有企业最普遍的组织形式之一。参加委员会和各种会议的人多种多样，他们各有专攻，并且在自己的知识领域享有权威。在讨论问题时，不同的人有各自侧重的决策考量和专业领域，大家通过互动协商集思广益，做出决定。

5 很少有大学生认识到说服同事接受自己观点的能力是十分重要的。不管你供职于公司、政府部门，还是从事专业性较强的工作，能不能把自己的观点推销给委员会，决定了你职业生涯的品质。你的部门或者你个人花了几个月时间准备一个项目，付出了许多心血，意味着在关于这个项目的会议上，你的表现比起做学生时事关重大得多。而大学里，较少有学生会在课堂或者研讨会上刻意花工夫说服别人接受自己的观点。参加课堂讨论的目的(不管是对积极发言的学生还是对保持沉默的学生)在于得分，在于向老师"炫耀"掌握的知识，而不是通过合作的方式推进对某个问题的认识。

6 由于大学中的学生活动常常是个性化的，所以这种情况也不令人奇怪。但学生却错失了很多这类机会。讲座、课堂讨论和小组辅导课在学生生活中占到很大比重，应该利用这样珍贵的机会，一方面观察小组活动的互动情况，再通过尝试影响和主导讨论的过程，发展自身的交际技巧。由于班级成员(这与朋友圈和学生团体不同)是不能选择的，而班级架构也不能轻易改变，班级比其他大多数学生组织更接近委员会的构成。怎样鼓励害羞的人参与讨论，怎样吸引对议题不感兴趣的人，怎样化解干戈，怎样在讨论中取得进展，怎样确保已经达成共识的观点被接受，怎样示意冒失或过于侃侃而谈的人停止发言——这些技巧对于今后的职业生涯都十分重要。

口头报告

7 委员会工作中还有一项重要能力是可以在学业讨论中培养的，那就是阐述问题的能力。大学中一些考核形式明确地将高效的交流技巧列为评分标准之一，至少任课老师或导师在评价学生小组辩论的表现时是这样的。

8　出于多方面原因，口头报告在将来的职业活动中会更加重要。大多数工作都是以小组形式进行的。会议及委员会在大型组织的项目进程和决策中有着极其重要的意义。会议通常很短，你必须简明精确地阐述观点，对各种评价和问题给出适当的应答，有效激发并引导衍生出的讨论。即使不在正式会议上汇报案例，你也常需要向繁忙的上司扼要地陈述观点，而会议上的口头表达技巧在这里也同样适用。同样的，如果你在组织中处于领导位置，也常需要通过简明扼要的报告，向同事们介绍新的工作程序或分析复杂问题。

9　高等教育为我们提供了大量锻炼口头报告技巧的机会。虽然很多大学和理工学院还无法配备较为昂贵的会议报告设施，但是几乎在所有班级，学生都可以将报告的小标题和部分陈述内容通过投影仪投射出来，或书写在白板上，这些基本技巧能够十分有效地帮助学生更清晰地表述主题和观点。同时，学生常要做关于论文的口头陈述，并力求简洁清楚，而这种重要的个人技能可以在任何学习小组讨论中得到经常锻炼。

撰写报告

10　撰写报告也是重要的工作内容。商务报告与职业报告在很多方面不同于学术论文。这些报告常写成摘要形式。它们一般由上级布置，或是应某会议、委员会要求撰写，所以报告的主题并非由撰写人本人决定。报告的审阅者通常时间很紧张——各大公司的高层决策者都会培养员工分秒必争的态度，同时，审阅者也会秉持严格谨慎的态度。因此，一篇报告须尽可能短小精悍，清楚针对某一可解决的问题，但也必须全面提供已取得的相关材料。另外，在撰写的时候，要注意语言精练，避免使用花哨的辞藻，尽量少用华丽的语言，要贯穿一种分析推论和实事求是的基调。一篇报告可以类似于回答论述题那样澄清问题，也可以列举与现状有所不同的几种选择，还可以给出决策意见。大多数商务报告与职业报告倾向于给出一个"稳健"或风险最小化的行动方案，这样一来，可以用一种令人满意的方式解决问题，不必是最优选择，但可以得到人们的一致认同。

11　一篇好的学术论文必须结构清晰，提出明确的问题，列出不同的观点，最后给出结论，所以写论文为写报告提供了宝贵的锻炼机会。甚至论文写作的各个步骤——在有限的时间内收集整理资料，制定写作计划，安排段落顺序——都可能与日后的职业活动紧密相连。

INTEGRATED EXERCISES

1 PUBLIC SPEECH TRAINING

The following is the 2000 Presidential Concession Speech given by Al Gore on 13th December 2000. Listen to the speech and then practice after the recording.

(The speech will be read once. The students listen and try to understand the meaning. They may listen again and practice after the speaker.)

Script

Good evening.

Just moments ago, I spoke with George W. Bush and congratulated him on becoming the 43rd president of the United States. And I promised him that I wouldn't call him back this time. I offered to meet with him as soon as possible so that we can start to heal the divisions of the campaign and the contest through which we've just passed.

Almost a century and a half ago, Senator Stephen Douglas told Abraham Lincoln, who had just defeated him for the presidency, "Partisan feeling must yield to patriotism. I'm with you, Mr. President, and God bless you." Well, in that same spirit, I say to President-elect Bush that what remains of partisan rancor must now be put aside, and may God bless his stewardship of this country. Neither he nor I anticipated this long and difficult road. Certainly neither of us wanted it to happen. Yet it came, and now it has ended, resolved, as it must be resolved, through the honored institutions of our democracy.

Over the library of one of our great law schools is inscribed the motto, "Not under man but under God and law." That's the ruling principle of American freedom, the source of our democratic liberties. I've tried to make it my guide throughout this contest, as it has guided America's deliberations of all the complex issues of the past five weeks.

Now the US Supreme Court has spoken. Let there be no doubt, while I strongly disagree with the court's decision, I accept it. I accept the finality of this outcome which will be ratified next Monday in the Electoral College. And tonight, for the sake of our unity as a people and the strength of our democracy, I offer my concession. I also accept my responsibility, which I will discharge unconditionally, to honor the new President-elect and do everything possible to help him bring Americans together in fulfillment of the great vision that our Declaration of Independence defines and that our Constitution affirms and defends.

Let me say how grateful I am to all those who supported me and supported the cause for which we have fought. Tipper and I feel a deep gratitude to Joe and Hadassah Lieberman, who brought passion and high purpose to our partnership and opened new doors, not just for our campaign but for our country.

This has been an extraordinary election. But in one of God's unforeseen paths, this belatedly broken impasse can point us all to a new common ground, for its very closeness can serve to remind us that we are one people with a shared history and a shared destiny. Indeed, that history gives us many examples of contests as hotly debated, as fiercely fought, with their own challenges to the popular will. Other disputes have dragged on for weeks before reaching resolution. And each time, both the victor and the vanquished have accepted the result peacefully and in a spirit of reconciliation.

So let it be with us.

I know that many of my supporters are disappointed. I am too. But our disappointment must be overcome by our love of country.

And I say to our fellow members of the world community, let no one see this contest as a sign of

American weakness. The strength of American democracy is shown most clearly through the difficulties it can overcome. Some have expressed concern that the unusual nature of this election might hamper the next president in the conduct of his office. I do not believe it need be so.

President-elect Bush inherits a nation whose citizens will be ready to assist him in the conduct of his large responsibilities. I, personally, will be at his disposal, and I call on all Americans — I particularly urge all who stood with us — to unite behind our next president. This is America. Just as we fight hard when the stakes are high, we close ranks and come together when the contest is done. And while there will be time enough to debate our continuing differences, now is the time to recognize that that which unites us is greater than that which divides us. While we yet hold and do not yield our opposing beliefs, there is a higher duty than the one we owe to political party. This is America and we put country before party; we will stand together behind our new president.

As for what I'll do next, I don't know the answer to that one yet. Like many of you, I'm looking forward to spending the holidays with family and old friends. I know I'll spend time in Tennessee and mend some fences, literally and figuratively.

Some have asked whether I have any regrets, and I do have one regret: that I didn't get the chance to stay and fight for the American people over the next four years, especially for those who need burdens lifted and barriers removed, especially for those who feel their voices have not been heard. I heard you. And I will not forget.

I've seen America in this campaign, and I like what I see. It's worth fighting for and that's a fight I'll never stop. As for the battle that ends tonight, I do believe, as my father once said, that "No matter how hard the loss, defeat might serve as well as victory to shape the soul and let the glory out."

So for me this campaign ends as it began: with the love of Tipper and our family; with faith in God and in the country I have been so proud to serve, from Vietnam to the vice presidency; and with gratitude to our truly tireless campaign staff and volunteers, including all those who worked so hard in Florida for the last 36 days.

Now the political struggle is over and we turn again to the unending struggle for the common good of all Americans and for those multitudes around the world who look to us for leadership in the cause of freedom.

In the words of our great hymn, "America, America": "Let us crown thy good with brotherhood, from sea to shining sea."

And now, my friends, in a phrase I once addressed to others: it's time for me to go.

Thank you, and good night, and God bless America.

2 DICTATION

Listen to the following passage and write it down. The passage will be read four times. During the first reading, which will be done at normal speed, listen and try to understand the meaning. For the second and third readings, the passage will be read sentence by sentence, or phrase by phrase, with intervals of 15 seconds. Write down what you hear. The last reading will be done at normal speed again and during this time you should check your work.

Script

Primary education consists of the first five-seven years of formal, structured education. / In general, main education consists of six or eight years of schooling starting at the age of five or six, / although this varies between, and sometimes within, countries. / Globally, around 70% of primary-age children are enrolled in primary education, / and this proportion is rising. / Under the Education for All programmes driven by UNESCO, / most countries have committed to achieving universal enrollment in primary education by 2015. / And in many countries it is compulsory for children to receive primary education. / The division between primary and secondary education is somewhat arbitrary, / but it generally occurs at about eleven or twelve years of age.

3 VOCABULARY STUDY

Task One
Put the proper form of the words in the corresponding blanks.

1) She has hired a lawyer who __specializes__ in divorce cases. (specialize)
2) There is a lot of __competition__ between computer companies. (compete)
3) The book is __dedicated__ to the author's husband. (dedicate)
4) He criticized the novel __implicitly__. (implicit)
5) Would you say that is a fair __assessment__ of the situation? (assess)
6) No one seemed to be __inclined__ to help. (incline)
7) There are __rigorous__ controls governing the sale of shares. (rigor)
8) This is a carefully __nurtured__ garden. (nurture)
9) If three people out of four no longer support the government, isn't this an __untenable__ situation? (tenable)
10) Many software companies have __adapted__ popular programs to the new operating system. (adapt)

Task Two
Replace the underlined words with the correct form of the words in the box. You may need to make other changes.

1) One __corollary__ of the rise of television was the massive makeover of radio programming.
2) Vitamins are __crucial__ for maintaining good health.
3) Teachers should __individualize__ their lessons to address differences in their students.
4) We need to seek __external__ help in order to solve this problem.
5) The job offers many opportunities for professional __advancement__.
6) I am happy to answer any __queries__ from the audience.
7) They gave him the __liberty__ to handle the problem himself.
8) I can well __foresee__ the difficulties ahead.
9) The patient showed no __visible__ symptoms.
10) We share similar __viewpoints__ in most cases.

Task Three
Choose the best answers from the options given.

1) We should make _____ use of resources.
   A. minimal   **B. optimal**   C. huge   D. considerable
2) She _____ a letter to her sister.
   A. controlled   B. considered   **C. composed**   D. compressed
3) Scientists are developing an _____ approach to treating the disease.
   A. alternate   B. another   **C. alternative** D. alien

4) Each number _____ to a location on the map.
   A. corresponds   B. correlates   C. conforms   D. cooperates

5) The book gives full _____ to the history of the word.
   A. account   **B. coverage**   C. summary   D. view

6) This is a _____ list of all the paintings generally attributed to the Dutch artist Rembrandt.
   A. general   B. simple   C. partial   **D. comprehensive**

7) When I told her what happened, she _____ with anger.
   A. repeated   B. remembered   **C. responded**   D. refined

8) They have provided _____ assistance to us.
   A. trivial   **B. invaluable**   C. inevitable   D. voluble

9) The teaching methods are still _____ at some schools.
   A. preventive   B. previous   C. prestigious   **D. prevalent**

10) She refused to let the injury keep her from _____ her goal of being in the Olympics.
    A. attaining   B. attracting   C. assembling   D. acquiring

Task Four
Fill in the following blanks with appropriate words from the box.

There has been work on learning 1) __styles__ over the last two decades. Dunn focused on identifying 2) __relevant__ stimuli that may 3) __influence__ learning and manipulating the school 4) __environment__, at about the same time as Joseph 5) __recommended__ varying teaching strategies. Howard identified individual 6) __talents__ or aptitudes in his Multiple Intelligences theories. Some scientists 7) __focused__ on understanding how people's personality affects the way they 8) __interact__ personally, and how this 9) __affects__ the way individuals respond 10) __to__ each other within the learning environment. It is currently fashionable to 11) __divide__ education into different learning "modes". The learning 12) __modalities__ are probably the most 13) __common__: a. visual: learning based on observation and seeing what is being 14) __learned__; b. auditory: learning based on listening to instructions; c. kinesthetic: learning 15) __based__ on hands-on work and engaging in 16) __activities__. Although it is claimed that, depending on their 17) __preferred__ learning modality, different teaching techniques have different levels of effectiveness, recent research has 18) __argued__ "there is no adequate 19) __evidence__ to justify incorporating learning style assessments 20) __into__ general educational practice."

4 GRAMMAR FOCUS

Read the following passage, underline the one mistake in each line and write the correction after the bracketed number.

It has been argued that high <u>rate</u> of education are essential	1) rates
for countries to be able to achieve high levels of <u>economical</u> growth.	2) economic
Empirical analyses tend to support the theoretical <u>predict</u> that	3) prediction
poor countries should grow <u>fast</u> than rich countries because	4) faster
they can <u>adapt</u> cutting-edge technologies already tried and tested	5) adopt
by rich countries. However, technology transfer requires <u>knowledge</u>	6) knowledgeable
<u>manager</u> and engineers who are able to operate new machines or	7) managers
production practices <u>borrow</u> from the leader in order to close the	8) borrowed
gap <u>about</u> imitation. Therefore, a country's ability to learn from	9) through

<u>a</u> leader is a function of its stock of "human capital". Recent study of the determinants of aggregate economic growth have <u>stress</u> the <u>important</u> of fundamental economic institutions and the role of cognitive skills. <u>Above</u> the individual level, there is a large literature, generally related back <u>with</u> the work of Jacob Mincer, on how earnings are related to the <u>school</u> and other human capital of the individual.

10) the
11) stressed
12) importance
13) At
14) to
15) schooling

1) 单复数错误：此处应该用复数形式，对应谓语动词are，也呼应下文levels。
2) 形容词错误：economical意思是"节约的"，economic意思是"经济的"，根据上下文，此处应该用economic。
3) 词性错误：此处应该用名词形式。
4) 形容词比较级错误：根据上下文，此处应该用比较级。
5) 动词错误：adapt意思是"适应"，adopt意思是"采纳"，此处应该用后者。
6) 词性错误：此处应该用形容词knowledgeable。
7) 单复数错误：此处应该用复数形式。
8) 语态错误：此处应该用borrow的过去分词表示被动语态。
9) 介词错误：根据上下文，此处应该用through，表示"通过……的手段、途径"。
10) 冠词错误：此处应该用定冠词the，与前文一致。
11) 动词形式错误：此处是现在完成时，应该用过去分词stressed。
12) 词性错误：此处应该用名词形式importance。
13) 介词错误：此处应该用at，表示"在……层面上"。
14) 介词错误：此处related应该搭配to。
15) 选词错误：根据上下文，此处应该用schooling，表示"学校教育"。

5 TRANSLATION

Task One
Translate the following paragraph from English into Chinese.

　　教师需要充分了解一门学科才能将其精髓传递给学生。尽管传统做法是教师讲课，但是一些新的教学方法，比如小组学习，将教师的角色转变成了课程设计者，讨论督导者和教练，学生则变成了积极的学习者，并在此过程中逐渐挖掘这门课程的主题。不管在哪种情况下，教学目的都是打好坚实的知识基础，扎实学到技能。这样，日后学生面对不同的生活经历，能在此基础上不断提高。好老师能够将信息、敏锐的判断力、经验和智慧转化成学生可以理解、掌握并传递给他人的相关知识。

Task Two
Translate the following paragraph from Chinese into English.

　　If we take an overview of the top universities in the world, we may find that all of them have the best tradition. Such a tradition has left a deep mark on the history of university development and thus become the spirit and character of the university. The former Vice Chancellor of Cambridge University Professor Alec Broers expounded on the Cambridge spirit as such: dynamic cultural integration and strong academic freedom. When Mr. Stanford first established the Stanford University, he advocated that students should "gear knowledge to practical use". These spirits have been encouraging generations of university students to study hard and strive for innovativeness, which has rendered universities a long-lasting place and a resplendent pearl in the human history.

6 CLASSROOM INTERACTION

Activity A Listening

1) The history of education began either millions of years ago or at the end of 1770.
2) The evolution of culture depended on the practice of transmitting knowledge.
3) Schooling was already in place in Egypt between 3000 and 500 BC.
4) Due to population growth and the proliferation of compulsory education, UNESCO has predicted that in the next 30 years more people will receive formal education than in all of human history thus far.

Script

The history of education, according to Dieter Lenzen, president of the Freie Universität Berlin 1994, "began either millions of years ago or at the end of 1770". Education as a science cannot be separated from the educational traditions that existed before. Adults trained the young of their society in the knowledge and skills they would need to master and eventually pass on. The evolution of culture, and human beings as a species depended on this practice of transmitting knowledge. In pre-literate societies this was achieved orally and through imitation. Story-telling continued from one generation to the next. Oral language developed into written symbols and letters. The depth and breadth of knowledge that could be preserved and passed soon increased exponentially. When cultures began to extend their knowledge beyond the basic skills of communicating, trading, gathering food, religious practices, etc., formal education and schooling eventually followed. Schooling in this sense was already in place in Egypt between 3000 and 500 BC. Nowadays some kind of education is compulsory to all people in most countries. Due to population growth and the proliferation of compulsory education, UNESCO has predicted that in the next 30 years more people will receive formal education than in all of human history thus far.

Activity B Debate

The teacher can let the students fill in the following table of opinions before asking them to carry out the debate.

University degree is the most important factor in job hunting

Pro Side	Con Side

Activity C Mini-speech

The teacher can give the students ten minutes to prepare and then choose a few students to give mini-speeches to the whole class.

WRITING

Writing Skills: Development by Cause and Effect

In this unit we discuss how to write an essay of cause and effect. Despite the name, the teacher needs to make it clear that there are actually three possibilities: an essay of cause, or of effect, or both. In most cases, students at the present level will be expected to deal with only the first two. The teacher can also help deal with some vocabulary tricks. The Chinese word *yuanyin*(原因) can be translated as both *cause* and *reason*, and *jieguo*(结果) can be translated as *effect* or *result*, but in English people use fixed phrases like *cause and effect* or *reason and result* instead of other possible combinations.

The sample in the Student's Book is meant to make the discussion fun with an interesting topic, and the teacher is advised to start with this topic as a warm-up activity. The sample essay can be used to illustrate the type of cause-and-effect essays, proper structure, as well as language devices. Reference answers to the questions are listed below:

1. This essay is written to warn boys not to be absent from their promised date with their girlfriends by listing possible negative consequences of doing so. It is about effect.
2. The thesis statement of the essay is "We will discuss the three main effects of doing so", and the topic sentences are "The first effect of standing up a girl is that she may be driven to a plan to torture you"; "The second effect would be that she may never talk to you again"; and "The most serious effect is that you will be faced with great danger." (Note: they are all the first sentences of the body paragraphs.) The structure of the essay is clear: The first paragraph is an introduction where the writer clearly specifies his intended readers and his central idea; the three paragraphs in the middle are body paragraphs where the writer develops the three negative effects; and the last paragraph is a conclusion where the author warns his readers not to make the mistake.
3. *The first effect; the second effect, the most serious effect* — these three phrases serve as clear indications from one point to another.
4. This essay is written mainly in an informal style, which is suitable in that the topic is in fact a casual one, and the intended readers are young people.

To help the students write effective cause-and-effect essays, the teacher needs to tell the students that they should select from many possible causes or effects to write really meaningful articles, and that they have to learn to avoid logical errors in the reasoning process. The short examples of fallacy provided in the Student's Book serve such a purpose. When dealing with this part, the teacher is advised to adopt a process approach, working with the students through the stages of brainstorming for ideas, selecting and organizing ideas and putting them down on paper. The checklist provided is a reminder of how to write this type of essays.

Writing Assignment

1. How can you write an essay of cause and effect?

In order to write a successful essay of cause and effect, I need to know whether I am going to write about the cause, the effect, or both. I need to place the causes or the effects in proper order, and keep them within reasonable scope. Another very important issue is that the thesis of the essay should be presented directly so that readers can see my purpose clearly.

2. Read the following essay and answer the questions that follow.

1) The topic of this essay is soccer. It is about cause and explains why soccer cannot become popular in the US.

2) This essay follows the expected structure, with the thesis statement and topic sentences placed at the most ideal positions. These sentences can be used to produce an outline shown below:

   I. There are many reasons for this (why soccer is not popular in the United States).

   II. Reasons for the unpopularity of soccer in the USA.

   A. The biggest reason (for soccer's failure as a mass appeal sport) is that it doesn't conform easily to the demands of television.

   B. Second, Americans love their violence, and soccer doesn't deliver on this score the way that American football and hockey do.

   C. Third, it is just too difficult to score in soccer.

   D. Finally, the field in soccer is too enormous.

   III. Conclusion

   It (soccer) will never make it big in the United States the way these other sports have, not until it changes some of its fundamental strategies.

3) Besides cause and effect, this essay also employs comparison and contrast to help with explanation. For example, in the first cause, the author compares soccer with basketball in terms of television adaptability; in the second cause, the author compares soccer with American football and hockey in terms of levels of violence; in the third cause, the author compares soccer with American football and basketball in terms of scoring difficulty, and in the last cause, the author compares soccer with American football and hockey in terms of field size. The comparison and contrast helps to make the differences easier to understand to ordinary readers.

3. Write an essay on one of the following topics.

Answers may vary.